STOP DRESSING YOUR

Six-Year-Old

 LIKE A *Skank*

A Slightly Tarnished Southern Belle's
Words of Wisdom

Celia Rivenbark

 St. Martin's Griffin New York

For my parents,
Howard and Caroline Rivenbark,
with love and gratitude
for never letting me look skanky

www.stmartins.com

Library of Congress Cataloging-in-Publication Data

Rivenbark, Celia.
    Stop dressing your six-year-old like a skank : a slightly tarnished
southern belle's words of wisdom / Celia Rivenbark.
        p. cm.
    ISBN-13: 978-0-312-33994-4
    ISBN-10: 0-312-33994-1
    1. American wit and humor. 2. Southern states—Humor. I. Title

PN6165.R59 2006
814'.6—dc22

                                                    2006043881

            10 9 8 7 6 5 4 3

"In some 32 short essays on the ridiculousness of modern life, Rivenbark (*Bless Your Heart, Tramp; We're Just Like You, Only Prettier*) wanders through Tweenland at the mall thinking a better name would be 'Little Skanks'...This is a hilarious read, perhaps best enjoyed while eating Krispy Kreme doughnuts with a few girlfriends."
—*Publishers Weekly*

"She kills in the 'Kids' and 'Southern-Style Silliness' sections, putting the fear of Mickey into anyone planning a trip to Disney World (character breakfasts must be scheduled 90 days in advance) and extolling the entertainment value of obituaries ('If there's a nickname in quotes, say Red Eye, Tip Top, or simply, Zeke, then my entire day is made')."
—*Entertainment Weekly*

"Celia Rivenbark has a mouth on her, but it's a very funny mouth as you will learn if you read her new book...she certainly strikes at the hilarious heart of what one often feels without being able to express in polite society. In any case, if you need down-to-earth information about celebrity babies, selling a bowl of grits on eBay that looks like Willie Nelson, or Barbie's creepy new Australian boyfriend, then Celia Rivenbark is for you."
—*Daily Herald*

"Rivenbark's collection of essays will have you snorting with laughter (unless you're a deb, of course, who would never dream of snorting). It's obvious where the author stands on fashions for little girls, but she also pokes fun at the necessity of taking children—or not—to Disney World, trying to get phone assistance from people in India, hating the knitting craze, and the Southern obsession with ailments. She encourages moms to not only slow down but slack off. And she's not afraid to poke fun at rednecks."
—*Daily Advertiser*

Also by Celia Rivenbark

We're Just Like You, Only Prettier

Bless Your Heart, Tramp

Contents

Contents

Part II: Celebrities

Part III: Vanity Flares

Contents

Contents

PART I

Kids

1

There's Always Tomorrow(land)

"If You Really Loved Me, You'd Buy Me Pal Mickey"

Studies say that children don't remember all that much, and certainly nothing good, until they are at least six years old. So there was no way we were going to waste hundreds, perhaps millions, of dollars on a family trip to Disney World until Sophie could remember *in minute detail* what wonderful, generous parents we were.

That said, the trip was finally scheduled, and we began to anticipate five days and four nights of fabulous forced family fun, fun, fun! When I told another mom of our plans at a birthday party, she beamed. "Did you get the early seating at Cinderella's Gala Feast?"

"Say who?"

"The Gala Feast! What about your character breakfast? Did you book Pooh at the Crystal Palace or Pluto and Goofy at

Liberty Square or Donald and Mickey at Restaurantosaurus?"

"Huh?"

"Oh, for heaven's sake," she huffed. Turning away from me, she summoned a few of the other moms over. "She's going to Disney and she hasn't booked her character breakfasts yet."

Some of them laughed so hard, they turned inside out.

My friend Lisa whipped out her dog-eared copy of the 475-page Katie Couric—endorsed *Walt Disney World with Kids,* a book that I have since discovered is more valuable than a dime-store poncho for the wacky waterfall rides. (Sure, you could buy the officially sanctioned Disney poncho, for approximately twenty-six dollars, but why not pack the ninety-nine-cent version from Eckerd?)

"You must book these things ninety to a hundred and twenty days in advance," she said. "Do you think that tickets to the Hoop-Dee-Doo Musical Revue just fall out of the sky?"

Hoop-Dee-Do-What?

As it turns out, you must—and I am not making this up—call the Disney dining hotline at exactly 7:00 a.m. exactly ninety days ahead of time. At that moment, mommies across this great land are groggily poised over their phones in hopes of getting these in-demand seats.

"Why can't I just call at nine?" I moaned. "I'm not really a morning person."

"Well, you can," said Lisa, "but you'll end up eating

chicken out of a bucket with Sneezy. *Is that what you want? Is it?*"

I was so ashamed. Who knew?

Thank goodness I'd had this whole conversation in time to right the wrong. I hovered over my phone exactly sixty days before our trip, just as I had been told during an exploratory call to the Disney dining folks.

"Sorry, that event is ninety days out. We have nothing left," said the chirpy Disney rep.

"No, no! You told me sixty days, not ninety!"

"I'm sorry, but these things change according to season and demand. I'm afraid you'll have to eat chicken out of a bucket with Sneezy."

Good thing we've got the ponchos, I thought to myself.

The Disney wars had been raging in my little family for two years, ever since that fateful school holiday when we were the only family that didn't leave town.

When I first learned that my daughter would have a week off of kindergarten because of "spring break," I laughed so hard, I almost choked on my McRib. (Motto: "Back but still alarmingly mediocre!")

"Spring break!" I snorted. "For kindergarten?" Does a five-year-old honestly need a whole week off after a tough four months of learning to share?

Was she going to demand a trip to Daytona Beach with some gal pals, a rented convertible, and a beer bong?

What up? I asked some of the savvier moms.

"This is when you go to Disney World," they chanted in unison. Their arms shot straight out from their bodies, and they toy-soldier-marched away from me, the Clueless Mommy.

Well, Disney World was certainly better than my mental image of tots showing up on MTV's *Spring Break Party and STD Fest* screaming "wooo-woooo!" for no apparent reason.

Having no idea that we were supposed to go to Disney World for spring break, I decided to salvage the situation by devising a week of "fun activities." On Day One, I spent four hours assembling a child-size pottery wheel before hurling the useless gizmo across the kitchen after realizing that a part was missing. Then it was off to the park, where I was overjoyed to see a mommy and daughter we knew playing together.

"Guess we're the only ones in town who didn't go to Disney World," I said brightly.

She hung her head. "We're leaving in the morning. Couldn't get a flight out until then."

Her tone was so serious that I had a flashback to those poor souls clinging to the helicopter skids during the fall of Saigon in 1975.

Sophie happily recited how she'd had a fun morning of watching mommy wrestle with the pottery-wheel-that-wasn't and screaming "Taiwanese piece of shit!" a lot.

It was a Kodak moment, I tell you.

On Day Two of our fun-filled Disney-less holiday, we decided to visit another park, one with a few more slides and swings.

"Wow! Now this is a park!" I said with much more enthusiasm than I felt. I tried not to pay attention to the fact that we were the only people there outside of a few home-schooled kids who, for reasons that I've never understood, insist on wearing long denim skirts everywhere they go.

Whew, I thought to myself. At first I thought the Rapture had come and we'd been overlooked, but I'm sure the homeschoolers would've made the cut.

"Isn't this great, honey?" I said in my best fake gush.

"At Disney World, they have a forty-foot-tall Pongo from *101 Dalmatians* and a swimming pool shaped like a grand piano *and* a waterslide where you spit right out of the sea serpent's mouth!" my daughter said.

"Oh, yeah? Well, over there is a fire ant hill. What do you want? Fantasy or real life?"

"I want the Seven Seas Lagoon and breakfast with Snow White and the Seven Dwarfs," she said.

"Not to worry. That guy sleeping on the bench over there looks a lot like Dopey."

Of course, after a couple of years of this, we realized there was no putting off our trip to Disney any longer.

We'd done rustic, noncommerical kinds of vacations (read: no cable) before, but I was sick of all the nature and lobsters that we found in our visits to a family cabin in Maine. I was craving total escape and plastic happiness, and no one delivers that like Disney.

Besides, I was getting a little burned out on lobster. The last time we'd gone to Maine (state motto: "The Prettiest Place on Earth for Maybe Forty-five to Sixty Days of the Year"), we went during the high season for lobsters.

Here's a typical restaurant experience in Maine.

ME: I'll have the fillet wrapped in bacon, and steamed broccoli for my side dish.

WAITRESS: I'm sorry. We're out of that. How about some delicious Maine lobster?

ME: Well, it is undeniably delicious, but I've eaten steamed lobster now three times a day for five days, and I'm fairly much over it. Do you have anything else?

WAITRESS: Sure we do! We have lobster salad, lobster rolls, and lobster bisque.

ME: No, no, I mean do you have any specials that don't involve lobster?

WAITRESS: This is Maine. Isn't this why you come up here? All the tourists love our lobsters and our delicious Maine syrup that we sell in overpriced bottles shaped just like maple leaves.

ME: Yes, they're charming. Okay, how about a sandwich for my kid? Maybe some peanut butter?

WAITRESS *(excited)*: With lobster jelly?

Suffice it to say, we were all ready for a change, and you

couldn't get further from the scenic beauty of Maine than Disney World, still beautiful in its own way.

So we did it! We bought plane tickets and even opted to stay at a hotel on-site, although Disney World's definition of *on-site* is rather generous. While technically still on Disney property, our, ahem, budget-priced Disney hotel was still a twenty-minute bus ride from everything.

My husband complained that "Next time, we're going to stay at one of the places on the monorail," and I explained that they cost five hundred dollars a night compared to our nifty sixty-eight dollars a night with tub faucets that let you twist Jimmy Neutron's head clean off if you want to. And I have always wanted to.

"Only the codgers stay in this place," I said, trying not to look wistful as we strolled across the shiny marble floors in the Grand Floridian's lobby.

There was no denying that boarding that bus every morning for our fourteen-hour day was getting a little old. Most of the time we managed to get seats, but this meant that the twenty or so left standing stuck their behinds in our faces. I pressed my head to the window and turned sideways, making myself flat as a flounder to avoid the dreaded face full of stranger ass.

On our first night at Disney, we surprised Sophie with late seating for Cinderella's Gala Feast, where you get to spend thirty-seven dollars for chicken fingers and buttered noodles shaped like Ariel the mermaid. It's worth it because Cinderella herself strolls from table to table posing for pictures and smiling demurely.

Thanks to a tip from a smart mommy friend of mine, I knew that Sophie would need to be dressed in full princess regalia: a poufy ice-blue Cinderella gown and coordinating "glass" slippers. Otherwise, we'd have been like the sad Ohio family with the screaming little girl: "Everybody else is dressed up. *I HATE YOU!*"

We spent the next three days getting up at dawn, wolfing microwaved pancakes shaped like Mickey's head at the "food" court, and queuing up for the bus that would take us to whatever magical adventure awaited.

At the end of our fourth fourteen-hour day in a row, I found myself standing under the big metallic golf ball thingy in Epcot, screaming to my husband: "If you don't let us rest, I'm going to kill you and then divorce you!"

"Fine, fine," he muttered absentmindedly while consulting his wrinkled park map. "You can rest while we board Spaceship Earth. By the way, did you know that Epcot stands for Experimental Prototype Community of Tomorrow?"

"We know, Daddy," said Soph.

He looked hurt.

Disney had turned my normally laid-back hubby into a goal-oriented nut job. On Day One, we visited Magic Kingdom and Epcot; Day Two was Animal Kingdom and back to Epcot; Day Three was MGM and, you guessed it, Epcot; Day Four was Magic Kingdom, Epcot, and Downtown Disney;

Day Five was Magic Kingdom until the flight home. Never have so few seen so much in such a short time.

I started to understand why so many people rent electric scooters to get through the park, although I grew to hate their irritated-sounding little horns as drivers tried to part the sea of tourists like Moses on a moped.

Disney inspires this sort of weird competitiveness. My husband took enormous pride in having us first in line every morning at the park of the day. He planned our stops with military precision, at one time warning us that we had "T minus three minutes to pee" or we'd miss Buzz Lightyear's Space Ranger Spin.

As we hurried out of yet another sparkling Disney restroom (these people descend on a gum wrapper like a SWAT team), I heard a little boy crying and watched his father get down on one knee to console him. "You know, son, you better tell me what the shit you're crying about, 'cause *you're the only reason we're here!*"

What can I tell you? Failure to get a Fastpass for Space Mountain can make a parent do crazy things.

As the week wore on, we became a Disney movie unto ourselves. *Honey, I Shrunk the Bank Account* opens with a tight shot of the three of us wolfing four-dollar hot dogs washed down with Cokes in twelve-dollar souvenir cups in Tomorrowland. I tried not to think about how much delicious Maine lobster that would have bought.

Is Disney expensive? Well, yes. Is it worth it? You bet your eleven-dollar fluorescent hot pink spring-loaded mouse ears it is.

Like any place that attracts kids, there were gift kiosks and shops everywhere. I had to admit it was all a lot more cheery than our last family trip, which had included a visit to the traveling *Titanic* exhibit. After a heartrending tour of the ship, you were dumped directly into a themed gift shop that sold glow-in-the-dark "icebergs" and even a foot-long replica of the *Titanic* made of milk chocolate. What kind of lesson was that? "Titanic: The Candy Bar That Hundreds Died For! Bite steerage in the morning and save first class for an afternoon snack!"

I saw plenty of Disney-philes push-pulling huge coolers full of snacks through the parks. I can't imagine going to the trouble, myself. There's sensible, and then there's just stupid-cheap. (Overheard in front of Mickey's PhilharMagic: "Sissie, it's you and Memaw's turn to watch the cooler.") You've already paid $150 for a four-day park pass, and you're quibbling over a sixteen-dollar lunch? Get over yourself.

A friend who always stays at the Disney campground (remember, Disney-style camping isn't exactly roughing it—they have their own *shows* and cabins with cable) told me she can fix dinner right there and save money on meals out. I told her I'd rather have a threesome with Chip 'n' Dale than cook on vacation, but to each her own.

By the end of the trip, Disney's merchandising magic had done its job: Sophie became obsessed with Pal Mickey, a "huggable, lovable interactive Theme Park tour guide." He's stuffed, stands about a foot tall, and costs $56.33. She tearfully begged for Pal Mickey, and we said no. It was silly, we thought, to buy a stuffed animal that yammered endlessly about park hours and attractions when we'd be home soon.

On our last day, as we boarded the very last bus that would take us back to the hotel before grabbing a cab to the airport, Sophie seemed to have moved past Pal Mickey. We had gone exactly one hour and thirty-five minutes without hearing about him. Home free, I thought.

There was only one seat left on the bus. Soph and I took it. And then I saw Pal Mickey grinning at us across the aisle. Soph started talking to his owner, who later became known as "You know, the little girl whose parents really *do* love her."

The little girl's parents, who were wearing matching XXL Donald Duck sweatshirts and fanny packs emblazoned with all seven dwarfs, glared at my husband and me as if we should be reported to Child Protective Services.

I could read their minds: *Cheap jerks. Buy the kid Pal Mickey.* And I hoped they couldn't read mine: *Y'all are really fat.*

The truth is, everybody at Disney World is fat. If you're not fat when you go, you're fat coming out. I walked fourteen miles a day and couldn't zip my jeans by the end of the trip. Go figure.

I think it's something in the hot dogs.

2

Yo Yo Yo! Where Can a Sista Get a Cowgirl Outfit?

Holidays Make This Mama Wanna Get in Your Grille

So, it's practically Valentine's Day, and I've found myself paying special attention to how the kindergarten set deals with affairs of the heart.

"Valentimes," as my kindergartener explained it, is a very big deal. It's truly the sweetest age, the last year when little boys will skip together while holding hands and not think twice about it.

Thankfully, there have been some improvements to the old Valentine system I remember from grade school, when the not-so-popular kids got five or six valentines and everybody else got a whole bunch. It was a hateful little ritual that nobody seemed to notice was slap-your-baby cruel.

Now, because we have Oprah, we're a little more aware of how this sort of dissing can not only damage self-esteem but also lead to a life of crime or sitcom writing. So notes are sent home saying that "Valentines should be given to every child in the class, not just the cute, rich, and smart ones." (Well, that was the gist of it.)

The girls, as you might expect, seem to be ahead of the game on things romantic. They prefer to play house during recess with designated "mommy," "daddy," and "baby" instead of the boys' favorite, some sort of army-man, video-game soldier thing that involves lots of running around for no reason and screaming *"You're my prisoner!"* to the pampas grass.

Not long ago, my daughter confided that one of the little boys in her class had threatened to kiss her on the playground. Apparently a romantic subplot had developed among the soldiers.

Because hubby and I are basically nerds, we considered this a "teachable moment" and launched a loving but firm and very PC lecture about not allowing anyone to do anything to you that you don't like.

But then the truth came out.

"Well," she said, "he didn't really want to that much, but all of us girls chased him and finally caught him and he said he'd kiss us if we didn't let him go."

Ah, well, then. Carry on, soldiers. War does strange things to a man's brain, I guess.

With so much romance in the air, the princess has been thinking about her own marital future. "I don't think I'm going to get married until I'm *fifteen*," she announced at the dinner table one night.

Well, that's a relief. We were afraid she was going to do something crazy.

"Where on earth will you live?" I asked.

"Well, here, of course," she said. And the groom? "Well, he'll have to go live with his mommy and daddy. After he gets a job and buys me some stuff."

Okay, this might work out after all.

While Valentine's Day is a favorite holiday around our house (how can anything dedicated to chocolate be bad?), it's not as much fun as Halloween.

This year, we decided that the princess would be a cowgirl. It was so fabulously retro, I decided. You know. Fringed suede vest, maybe a ruffly denim skirt, red bandanna, hat, boots, and a little six-shooter.

Easy enough, I thought.

Because I am famously incapable of sewing (having sewn the pockets onto the inside of my final-exam apron back in seventh grade home ec class), it was going to have to be store-bought.

Our first stop was a famous toy store that has a backwards *R* in the middle.

"Where are your six-shooters, hon?" I asked the earnest-faced young man standing in the weapons aisle.

"Huh?"

"Toy pistols, hon. You know, maybe a couple of them

with a holster so Missy Poo here can be a proper cowgirl for Halloween."

He looked at me with disdain. "We don't carry guns here."

"No, of course you don't," I said. "I want a *toy* gun. I'm sure y'all have those here at We Be Toys, don't you?"

"No guns!" he kind of shrieked. The princess and I looked at each other, puzzled.

I tried logic. "But you've got machetes, tanks, and missile launchers right here," I said. "What's the big deal?"

"No guns!"

"Okay," I said, using my best hostage-negotiator-calm voice. "I got the whole guns-kill-people thing, but what do you think is on the front of that huge green regulation army tank on the shelf behind you? Are those babies going to fire chocolate frosting onto the enemy? I think not."

For reasons that I don't come close to understanding, I have noticed that, the older I get, the more often I am prone to lapse into a pathetic middle-aged-white-woman attempt at rapper cool when extremely frustrated.

The first time it happened was when my cable went out and, therefore, my Internet connection. I had spent the whole day home alone with an inability to Google myself. Yes, I know it sounds nasty, but it's more fun than a big bowl of meth. Kidding!

Anywho, I heard myself tell the nice cable man, "Listen

bruh, you better MacGyver something quick, cuz I'm jonesin' for my broadband."

So, it was happening again in the toy store. Frustration leads to rap in me. Fo' shizzle.

I eyed the sales boy. "Don't you see, er, home slice, it's the same thing? Except we want a six-shooter."

"Look, it's store policy not to carry them," my vested friend said, hoping that someone, anyone, would page him. And soon.

"I feel ya, my face gator," I said, again lapsing into this curious rapspeak and wondering why, even as I was saying it. "But I just want to make a point here. . . . I mean I'm up in here with my girl. I'm in the house and I got the Benjamins, so whassup?"

Alas, we finally accepted defeat, but only after I'd, I think, flashed some gang signs and announced "It's all good" to no one in particular.

We got back into my ghetto sled and moved on to search for the costume components. Six stores and endless rap frustration later, the closest we'd come was something called Diva Cowgirl! It was a hideous hot pink shiny metallic skirt with a fringy top. Frankly, it looked like it would have been more at home in an Old West brothel, worn by one of those hoochie mamas you always saw hugging the bar at Miss Kitty's saloon on *Gunsmoke*.

Once again, I silently cursed the fact that I was a craft feeb.

Across town, my friend was busily stitching a VW Beetle costume, complete with working windshield wipers for her daughter.

Bitch.

We even stopped at the fabric store, where I thought I could buy some cow-print fabric and cut a little vest out.

"Mommy, what are you *doing?*" asked my daughter, horrified.

"It's a pattern. Mommy can use this to make your Halloween costume. How hard can it be to make a vest?"

"Have you been drinking?"

Whoa. That hurt. Although it was a perfectly reasonable question.

That night, I discovered everything I wanted on eBay, the catch being that it would cost $150 or, with shipping, about $386.

The white sheet with cut-out eyeholes was starting to look really good.

But not good enough for the princess, who ended up borrowing a fabulous real suede cowgirl outfit from my friend Amy, who always comes through in a pinch.

Amy's one of those friends who is relentlessly prepared for everything. So, in less time than it took for me to transform into Gangsta Mama, I had everything we needed, including a tiny little pearl revolver and matching holster.

We loved the cowgirl outfit so much that it became that year's Christmas card.

My friend Mona, whose kid is not allowed to play with guns and therefore spends all day fashioning Uzis from bent pecan tree limbs, was horrified.

"Is that a gun in that holster?" she asked, incredulous.

"Well, hell yeah, Mona. She'd look pretty goofy wearing an empty holster, now, wouldn't she?"

"You shouldn't encourage that sort of thing," she said while I watched her son turn a magnolia seedpod into an amazingly realistic grenade.

"Fire in the hole, y'all!" he hollered.

Once we got past the horrors of Halloween, there was scarcely time to take a breath before it was time for the annual Freeze Your Ass Off Fall Festival Fund-raiser at school.

If you have a kid in elementary school, you know all about the Fall Festival, which is held to celebrate the old-time notion of "harvest." This is a cute idea, I guess, but if you think about it, it's not like any of these kids has brought in a crop or will ever contemplate going to the barn dance with a gal named Millie.

It is, however, an excuse to have fun and raise a little money, usually for the PTA, which I most certainly believe in and would never, ever say anything against on account of these people have more power in their pinkie toenail than I will ever have in my whole pathetic life. So, go PTA!

The Fall Festival, then, isn't about celebrating a bounteous harvest. No, no. It is about finding the one dummy in the planning session who says, "Sure! I'll run the popcorn concession."

Looking back on it, I was actually smug about my assignment. Let the rest of them run the bingo, the salmonella—er, petting zoo—or the thing I did last year: the throw-the-beanbag-through-the clown's-eyes until you either win a prize or burst into tears and scream *"Mean lady!"* and get *two* prizes and all the change in the mean lady's pockets.

The popcorn concession, as it turned out, was a two-foot-tall glass box that said *Hot Popcorn* on it in happy red script. It was stashed on the floor of a broom closet and weighed approximately eighteen hundred pounds.

After a few minutes of huffing and puffing, I found Hans and Franz to help me tote the thing across the playground.

Okay, I said, looking at the empty glass box, *start popping!* After a few wretched moments, I realized this was no microwave but rather some sort of Amish popcorn concession that used—get this—oil and actual popcorn kernels.

All alone at my post and surrounded by freckle-faced accusers who wanted to know when the popcorn would be ready, I decided to read the directions. Turns out you had to heat the thing for eight minutes. Next, you had to measure oil into the basket gizmo. Then (and here's the tricky part) while the blasted thing rotated with tiny blades that stir the kernels, you had to dodge the blades to continually add kernels.

It was then that I realized that the proper name for this

particular corner of Fall Festival hell was Let's Visit the Whirling Popcorn Machine of Death.

Burn, spatter, dodge, weave.

I finally managed to make my first sale, and the kid complained that the popcorn was burned.

"Yeah? Well, so am I. Get used to it."

He looked hurt.

"Oh, all right. And here's all the change in my pockets."

We'd barely had time to take a breath after all the "fun" of the Fall Festival when my daughter announced plans for Thanksgiving.

As she sat in the backseat on the way to school, she solemnly examined her cuter-'n'-hell hot pink velour pantsuit.

"What's wrong, pumpkin?" I said cheerily after seeing a definite frowny face in my rearview window.

"We were *supposed* to wear black dresses so we could be pilgrims today," she said petulantly.

"Huh?" I asked, mildly irritated that the Allman Brothers classic "Blue Sky" had just come on the radio and, instead of listening to it, I must now discover that, through no fault of my own, I was pilgrim-deficient.

"You know, Mommy, for the Thanksgiving feast. You're making the mashed potatoes and it's at nine thirty and all the other mommies are going to be there and one of them's even going to make *gravy!*"

Okay, that hurts. Every kid in the neighborhood knows

that I make the worst gravy in seven states. It is notoriously thin and flavorless and is eventually tossed with great drama and some few tears onto the backs of lingering yard cats every danged Thanksgiving afternoon.

"Whoa," I said, while the Brothers crooned about blue skies and sunny days and Lord knows what they'll do if she takes her love away.

"Okay," I said as calmly as possible. "A costume? You're supposed to wear a costume?"

"Well, just a black dress, kind of pouffy, you know, like the Pilgrims wore to eat with the Native Americans."

"Indians," I growled.

"Mommy!"

Oh, spare me a PC grade-schooler. And why had I picked this morning to give up caffeine? Why hadn't I given up, I dunno, maize instead?

"Honey," I said, "why didn't you tell me about this last week? You know Mommy needs a little more than (looks at watch), hmmm, thirty-six seconds' notice."

"There was a note in my backpack. Didn't you read it?"

Busted. Okay, I admit it. There are so *many* notes that I may have missed a few. Late library books, homework sheets, Picasso-like artwork—I tell you, hons, some days I expect to pull a live squirrel monkey out of that thing.

OKAY, DO NOT PANIC, I thought. I thought it just like that, in capital letters. There was still, after all, twenty-two seconds to return home and throw on the most somber and Pilgrim-like dress she had, and that's what we did.

"Thee looks beautiful," I said as we raced into the school, a ten-pound bag of potatoes slapping against my sweat-pants.

"Thanks, Mommy," she said with a bright smile. "Oh, and Mommy, don't forget, I said you'd make the corny-copia."

Thee is *so* grounded.

3

Stop Dressing Your Six-Year-Old Like a Skank

The princess had just graduated to a size 7 when everything went to shit. We headed for our favorite department store, ready to take that leap into the new world of 7–16. Bye-bye, 4–6X, I thought to myself with a tug of sadness. My baby was growing up.

And apparently into a prostitute.

"Where are the sevens?" I asked the sixty-something clerk who wore her glasses on a chain just like me.

"You're standing in 'em," she said.

Oh, no, I thought, looking around. *Oh no, no, no, no, no, no.*

"There must be some mistake," I said. "These are, well, slutty-looking. I'm talking about clothes for a little girl in first grade."

"That's all we got."

"But these look like things *a hooker would wear!*"

She smiled sadly. "You have no idea how many times I hear that every day."

Okay, breathe. This is just some weird marketing experiment. Right?

I went to my second-favorite department store and was invited to peruse the awfulness that is Tweenland! A better name would be Lil Skanks!

Sequins, fringe, neon glitter tank tops with big red lips on them, fishnet sleeves, scary dragon faces lunging from off-the-shoulder T-shirts. Whither the adorable seersucker? The pastel floral short sets? The soft cotton dresses in little-girl colors like lavender, pale pink, periwinkle blue? This stuff practically screamed SYRINGE SOLD SEPARATELY.

I get it. Now that my kid is practically of childbearing age (is six the new seventeen?) I must choose from ripped-on-purpose jeans and T-shirts that scream things like BABY DOLL and JAIL BAIT, not to mention a rather angry GIRLS *RULE* AND BOYS *DROOL!* where an embroidered flower with buzzing bee should be.

When did this happen? Who decided that my six-year-old should dress like a Vegas showgirl? And one with an abundance of anger issues at that?

And why are parents buying this junk fashioned from cheesy fabrics that surely leave your dryer's lint filter full of glitter and fuzzy sequined balls?

I hope you won't take this the wrong way—you, the mom

on the cell phone flipping your check card to your kid so she can buy the jeans that say SPANK ME on them—but you're going down, bitch.

No, really. I'm taking you out, putting you on notice, slapping some sense into your sorry ass.

Just for old times' sake, I wandered through the 4–6X section. It was just an arm's length away, but it was the difference between a Happy Meal at the playground and bulimia at the bar. So far, these clothes had been left mercifully untouched by the wand of the skank fairy, whom I envision as looking a lot like Tara Reid.

Instead of being able to buy pretty things for my daughter, sweet somethings in ice cream colors, I must now shop at big, boxy unisex stores where you can still buy shorts that don't say DELICIOUS on the bottom or T-shirts that are plain instead of, swear to God, a size 7 belly shirt with MADE YA LOOK on the front. Look at what? There's not supposed to be anything to look at on a seven-year-old. *Because they're children.*

Sweet Jesus, what I'd do for a lousy ladybug collar on a smocked dress. Instead, this season's Easter look consisted of sequined and chiffon body-hugging sheaths.

I know that my daughter and I will fight about clothes in a few years, perhaps horribly, but, for now, there will be none of this Little Ladies of the Night look.

And while moms and daughters have always fought over clothes (let's face it, even Marcia Brady wore some shockingly short dresses, and those baby-doll pj's in front of stepbrother Greg were icky), the clothing wars were usually taking place between mom and teen, not mom and first-grader.

When you see a size 7 shirt that says SEXY! or a mom and her little girl strolling through the mall in matching shorts with JUICY scrawled across the butt, you have to wonder what the hell is going on.

The saddest part about all this is that if you dress like you're a twenty-two-year-old going out to a club after a tough day at work in the city, you don't get to enjoy being a little kid.

Deliver me from an outraged third-grader who thinks she's entitled to the entire line at Abercrombie & Fitch. Put on a normal pair of jeans and go play kickball, you brat! And tell yo mama I said so.

If you examine the offerings in the 7–16 department, you'll quickly discover that it's no different from the stuff in the juniors' department and beyond. There is no distinction between a kid in second grade and one in twelfth grade and a college grad who's started her first real job. Never mind how essentially stupid a little fifty-pound kid looks wearing an off-the-shoulder top with FOOL FOR LOVE in glitter letters. Hell, some of these kids can't even read cursive writing and they're wearing this junk. They adore it because it's what Gwen or Avril or Ashlee is wearing. *But you're not on stage,* I want to scream. *You're on the monkey bars!*

The big difference between my childhood and my daughter's is that these days, the kid gets the final say. What's up with that? I can promise you that if I was eight years old and told my parents I needed eighty-dollars for sparkly jeans to rest on my hip bones and a midriff top that read TOO RICH FOR YOU, they'd have thought I had fallen off my bike and my brain had spilled out my ears.

If you want to get at the heart of the problem, which is the parents, of course, you need look no further than those "nanny to the rescue" shows on TV.

It's the oddest thing: In almost every show, the moms are spilling out of too-tight tank tops and Daisy Dukes. They look like teenagers, and the kids run all over them.

When the sturdy, bespectacled Supernanny shows up at the jam-stained front door, it's clear that a new sheriff is in town. The kids see her as someone they should probably listen to. Hmmm. Wonder if that has anything to do with the fact that she's not wearing a tank that says SWEET THANG. She means business, while Mama's over there cowering in the kitchen corner, all hair extensions and implants talking 'bout "I can't do a thing with these young'uns."

These children should be thanking the TV gods that they didn't dispatch a tough-talking Southern bubba instead of the Supernanny. Bubba doesn't care about any Dr. Phil–ish reasons for misbehavior. He'd just arrange for "a date with Mr. Hickory Stick" and a dessert of Dial soap while saying things like, "I'll learn you some respect, lil tater."

Okay, that's going too far, but you get the idea. I always preferred the count-to-three method of discipline. It was astonishingly effective. You want to take back parental power? Try saying "Onnnne," then "Twooooo." I never made it to "Threeeee," because my preschooler shaped up, for which I am eternally grateful, because, let's face it, if I ever got to three, I had nothing. Nada. Zip.

If you ask me, the Supernanny should put the parents, not the kids, in the naughty room and not let them out until Mom promises to buy some clothes that fit and Dad can stop being such a wimp. ("Brandon calls his Mama names, and I just wanna cry!") Grow a spine, you freak. It's time to "man up"!

They're kids, not short grown-ups. Remember?

4

Flower (Girl) Power

We've Got the Dress—
Just Let Us Know When and Where

While attending the sixth wedding of the summer (doesn't anybody live in sin anymore?), my daughter once again looked longingly at the flower girl floating down the aisle to "Taco Bell's Canon," as she calls it.

The little girl scattered petals from a white wicker basket, her moiré taffeta skirt swishing noisily past us, her tulle hair bow taunting us.

"Why won't anybody ask me to be a flower girl?" Soph wailed.

"Oh, sweetie, being a flower girl isn't a big deal," I said. "It's just a few moments of glory, a gorgeous new outfit, a fancy hairstyle, and listening to a bunch of strangers tell you how beautiful you are when it's over. Rather like an episode of *Queer Eye for the Straight Guy*."

"Huh?"

"Never mind, sugar lump. I'm sure your time will come."

At that moment, her little friend piped up behind us, "I'm going to be a flower girl for the *third time* next month and I'm going to get my hair curled on top of my head and I'm going to look just like Cindy-rella. You've *never* been a flower girl?" She tossed back her head and laughed, then formed the dreaded *L* with her pudgy little nail-bitten fingers, identifying my precious as a "loser."

"That's okay," I said, a trifle too loudly. "She's just acting mean because she knows that her parents don't love her as much as her little sister."

"Waahhh!"

After this unpleasantness, I decided to put the word out that I had a flower girl for hire. We even had a dress. Last spring, when a friend postponed her wedding indefinitely on account of her fiancé lost his life's savings on one of those gambling cruise boats, we found ourselves stuck with a tastefully simple white organza dress with tiny yellow daisies dancing across the empire waist.

I told everyone that Sophie was ready to be a flower girl, and I was past the point of caring if it was for anyone we even knew. I knew she'd be great at it, not melting down like the really young ones. I hate it when people put their toddlers in weddings and end up pushing them down the aisle. It's not like we don't see all this, and it detracts from the sacredness of the moment to see the fat bottom of some woman in a silk shantung suit duck-walking down the aisle going, "Go on now, Misty Rae! You can do it!" Inevitably this is greeted with tears, and the flower basket is tossed until the duck-mama gives up and says loud enough for everyone to hear, "If you want that Dora's Talking Doll House, you'll move your ass down that aisle right now, little missy, you hear me?"

My daughter wouldn't even need to eat your reception food. Unless you were actually planning to serve Rugrats apple sauce and PB&J without the crusts, of course, which she would be powerless to resist.

And I'd make sure she stayed away from that nasty chocolate fountain that everybody's so crazy about now. I went to a wedding reception, and there was a little boy sticking his finger in the fountain, licking it down to his knuckle and then *sticking it back into the fountain*. It's not just kids, of course. Grown-ups act like idiots when they get around a chocolate fountain, oohing and aahing and *double-dipping* their half-eaten wedges of pound cake and strawberries, spreading their germs everywhere. And there's always that one redneck who thinks it's hilarious to stick his head in the fountain and let the chocolate drip down his throat. I swear, we near 'bout got divorced over that one.

The point is, my kid deserved to be a flower girl, and so, amazingly, she finally got her chance when my husband's sister, Linda, got married for the first time at age fifty-one.

We were thrilled for Linda and Todd because they seemed so well-suited for one another but, to be honest, I was even more thrilled that Sophie would finally get to be a flower girl. Unless . . .

What if Linda decided that she wanted a simple ceremony without any attendants whatsoever? I adore my sister-in-law, but she's a threat to go all intellectual-hippie on me at any given time. To be fair, when a woman has waited fifty-one years to marry the man of her dreams, she has every right to have the wedding she wants. Unless I decide otherwise.

I decided to give her a long-distance call.

"Linda, if you don't ask Sophie to be your flower girl, I swear that I will never speak to you again as long as I live."

"What are you talking about?" Linda said, genuinely puzzled. "Of course I want her to be my flower girl. I wouldn't have it any other way."

Oh, thank God! I had lost enough sleep over this. Sophie and I went shopping for the perfect flower girl dress (the one with the daisies was too small by now) and counted down the days to the big event.

Todd and Linda decided to incorporate some rituals from his Native American heritage into their wedding ceremony. Before the service began, they had a friend set some sage on fire and "smudge" the sanctuary of the church to purify it.

This was lovely and quite meaningful to everyone except for the late-arriving Aunt Tiny and Uncle Dink.

While a nephew home from college for the festivities optimistically noted that "Cool, this church smells like pot," Uncle Dink noisily shuffled from corner to corner, sniffing for the source of the "fire."

I suppose it's true that once a volunteer fireman, always a volunteer fireman, because even as Sophie walked into the church in her first-ever flower girl outfit, back straight, hair festooned with tiny white flowers, shy smile in place, Uncle Dink was swatting at the air in front of her. "The whole damn church is going to be on fire and nobody seems to give a damn. It's the damndest thing I've ever seen," he said, finally settling back into his rightful spot beside Aunt Tiny.

All we could think was, *Damn*.

I discreetly pulled Uncle Dink aside and told him that nothing was on fire, that it was just a purification ritual that involved burning sage. He looked relieved, but the nephew looked crestfallen.

"Oh, for God's sake," I hissed at him. "Did you think we were going to hand out big fat doobies like little bubble soap containers?"

He hung his head.

The wedding was beautiful, and the best part was seeing the flower girl proudly posing for pictures beside her beloved aunt after the ceremony.

Sophie had not only been a flower girl at last, but she had done it for someone she genuinely loved, not just some random couple that broke up because the groom-to-be couldn't stay away from the Lucky Lady Floating Casino and Hot Wings Bar.

Oh, and the second-best part? There wasn't a chocolate fountain in sight.

5

Weary Mom to Uppity Teens

At Least We Know Where the Continent of Chile Is

There's a great brouhaha brewing over the problem of poor writing among America's high school and college students.

Ain't hardly none of 'em can do it right, studies say.

Some blame the text messaging craze favored by the phone-as-umbilicus set. We've become a nation of instant messagers that has far surpassed the shorthand of my high school yearbook (motto: "not badly writ"), the uninspired 2 Sweet 2 B 4 gotten. That's right: I used 2B sweet.

As long as there've been parents and kids, the older has whined about how the younger can't write, spell, speak to elders, make fire, and so forth as good as they could at that age.

I think that instead of pointing fingers, we should help convince America's young people of the lifelong benefits of learning to write with thoughtful expression, correct grammar, and, of course, appropriate sin tax.

We should get back to basics in the classroom, teaching that conjugation isn't just something your redneck cousin wants to do when his girlfriend visits him in prison.

He hadn't oughta stole that man's bling, nohow.

According to members of the prestigious National Commission on Writing for America's Families, Schools, and Colleges (or "the Hulk" as they like to call themselves), even the English classes don't require much writing these days. And yonder lies the problem.

When I was in high school, we were not only required to read such literary masterpieces as *Beowulf* and *The Canterbury Tales,* which I believe were both written by J. K. Rowling, but we were also required to write ten-page reports about them. And while this assignment was as painful as an Arsenio comeback, there's no doubt that it built character and made my writing gooder than it had been before.

Today's students, say the Hulk, don't know that you shouldn't never end a sentence with a preposition. A way we used to remember this was to gently correct "Where you at?" with "Behind the preposition at." Hey, this is what passed for snappy rejoinder back in the day. It would also get us beat up if said to the wrong person. ("Now where you at? On the ground, that's where!")

The most important advice the experts have is to get kids to start reading more. I believe it's already working. Just last week, I saw at least a half dozen sunscreened nine-year-olds sitting around a pool reading the latest Harry Potter book.

While their parents pleaded with them to come swim, they waved them away without even looking up except to ask them please not to splash page 4,016 again.

So as you can see, there's lots of hope for a new generation of great writers.

The hope dwindles as the little puddin's get older, though. In a recent survey, more U.S. teens could name the Three Stooges than the three branches of the federal government, which, as those of us old enough to recall high school civics classes know to be the the legislative, the executive, and the Moe.

It's very trendy to whine about how little our young adults know about government. How many times have we seen teens draw a blank when asked to name this great nation's vice president or, for that matter, the prime minister of Kansas?

Teens today are not dumb. Quite the contrary. They have even invented their own language, an abbreviated sort of speech that allows them to chat back and forth on their cell phones using symbols and letters that cannot be deciphered by anyone old enough to remember mood rings.

Thus, *I'm looking forward to seeing you again soon* (which, now that I write it, has all the appeal of sitting in the parlor and listening to 78s on the family Victrola) becomes simply *ltr*.

I'm not so sure this is a gd thg. Still, you must applaud today's young people for their technological savvy. Most can download an entire library of music in less time than it takes me to pit my prunes.

I believe we will see a nation in which Speaker of the House Jack Osbourne will say, "All we want is some frickin' respect. Buttholes."

But, dear Jack, respect must be earned. Those who refuse to remember the mistakes of the past are doomed to end up on shows like *I'm a Celebrity—Get Me Outta Here!*

What I'm saying is that it's possible to be cool and to know a little bit about history. If you ask a teen today to locate Vietnam on a map, there is not a doubt in my mind that he will say, "I dunno, dawg, but I'm pretty sure it's one of the blue ones."

Young people today have an abysmal knowledge of geography. They can't recall the names of the continents (and, hey, nobody's perfect—I almost always forget Chile).

So what's the solution to a nation filled with young people who honestly believe that Springfield is home to Bart Simpson, not Abraham Lincoln?

The return of civics classes (which, by law, must be taught by the same guy who teaches driver's ed *and* dates the homely but kind school librarian)?

Mayhaps. Otherwise, and I hate to say this, we may be looking at a future that includes two words that should never, ever be put together: President Britney.

While it's easy to act as if we grown-ups have all the answers, we don't. Witness what happened when I tried to help my second-grader with a science project.

Scrambling into the backseat of the car at the end of school, she paused long enough to look me in the eye. Was that disgust I saw in the eyes of my precious?

"You're fired!" she growled with a dismissive flick of her hand. All that was missing was the famous Trump hair turban.

Okay, so I "helped" her with a couple of school projects and they didn't go so well. It was late, the project was overdue, and who really cares if a sea turtle is a mammal or a rodent or whatever, anyway?

Here's a flash: They're not mammals. Not even close. But they come under the heading of "sea creatures," so that was good enough for me. While other, smarter mommies had assisted in constructing dioramas of rain forests, working volcanoes, and battery-operated solar systems, we chose a mammals-from-the-sea theme housed in a shell-lined shoebox. Which would've been killer if we had left out the turtle. This, coupled with my "help" on two math homework problems that turned out to be wrong, resulted in my firing.

Of course, I know that turtles aren't mammals. They are ambivalents, which can live on air or underwater and write with their right or left flippers. They also almost never vote.

Although the science project ended poorly, it wasn't a waste of time, because we also got to learn about the dwarf sea horse. These tiny creatures have a colt's head, a monkey's tail, and a chameleon's independently roving eyes. ("You talking to me? *You talking to me?* Oh, I give up.")

While all that is fascinating, the coolest thing we learned is that the dwarf sea horse doesn't have a stomach. That's right! It has what is called "a continuous gut." This anomaly is only found in the Florida Keys and, occasionally, the nation's finer Golden Corral restaurants.

The dwarf sea horse searches constantly for food, all day and into the night. Although I don't have the head of a colt, I must have some dwarf sea horse in me.

Another cool thing we learned about these weird little creatures is that the male gives birth. That's right! The female, who is desperately out there trying to find a late-night drive-through, deposits the eggs in the male's pouch, and he takes care of them, presumably giving up caffeine and highlights just to be on the safe side.

Studies have shown that although the males carry the babies, they actually invest about half as much metabolic energy as females do in producing offspring. Everybody say duh-huh.

So, in conclusion, turtles are not mammals, Donald Trump is a mammal but not warm-blooded, and I am, at least in the eyes of one elementary school student, toast.

6

Hilary Duff & Us

When Motherhood Hits Those Inevitable Valleys, We'll Always Have "the Hils"

Hons, I am finally a hero in my daughter's eyes. Not because I snatched her from the jaws of a rabid dingo or plucked her from a deadly riptide. No, no. I'm a real hero because I have secured tickets to the Hilary Duff concert.

To those of you who don't know Hilary Duff from Howard Duff, this is a Very Big Deal. It's like if you were a parent back in '64 and came home one day waving tickets to *The Ed Sullivan Show* and asking, "Hey! Who'd like to see four mop-topped cuties from Liverpool perform tonight?"

Hilary is a squeaky-clean teen queen with a passable voice who plays to sold-out audiences of "tweens." My daughter and her best friend adore Hilary. They sleep in Lizzie McGuire nightgowns (Hilary's TV show character—try to hang here, will you?), they wear Lizzie tennis shoes, they carry Lizzie purses.

As role models go, Hilary's okay. There was that reported flap between her and the tiresomely tough Avril Lavigne (Hil said Avril didn't appreciate her fans enough—sigh) and a spat with Lindsay Lohan at the *Freaky Friday* premiere (Hil stole her boyfriend, hunkette Aaron Carter), but generally, she's no diva. I know it's true 'cause I read it in *Bop* magazine.

At forty-seven, I knew I'd probably be the oldest mom in the Bi-Lo Center in Greenville, South Carolina, and even as the tears of joy spilled like tiny diamonds down my precious daughter's cheeks, she managed to choke out, "Uh, can you maybe sit behind us or maybe somewhere in the back?"

Ouch.

Just for that, my friend and I intend to do as our foremothers did before us and embarrass the dookie out of our little girls. I'm going to jump up and down and make those hand signals that the kids all make, the ones that I'm not sure whether they're gang signs or mean *I love you* in Hawaiian. I'm going to sing along to all of Hilary's songs, wear a belly shirt that says MRS. TIMBERLAKE, and get something unprintable pierced.

Although I'm whining a bit about the long drive, the high ticket prices, the inevitable purchase from the Duff Stuff kiosk, and so forth, I'm actually pretty excited.

Your first concert is something you never forget, and I'll be right there, in Section 6, Row D, to see my baby's reaction. I got a little misty recounting to her my first time: a two-hour trip to see Humble Pie and King Crimson with my sorta-boyfriend's kindly daddy driving six of us and waiting in the parking lot for three hours.

"He was a hero just like you, Mom," she said.

Word.

Fast-forward a few weeks, and there I am, crouching behind the wheel well of Hilary Duff's tour bus. It's so big and gorgeous that it brings tears to my eyes.

From a distance, I must've looked like the world's oldest tween queen stalker. Not like that crazy-eyed one who just got arrested for harassing Catherine Zeta-Jones because Michael Douglas is her soul mate, but a kinder, gentler stalker who just wants a cool picture for her kid.

As I stood with my friend and our daughters on a sweltering sidewalk in Greenville, six hours from home, I wondered aloud if we should hang out in the lobby at the Hyatt in case "the Hils" was staying there. We'd heard that earlier in the day in the breakfast buffet, and I'd immediately lost my appetite and started squealing and flapping.

Duff stalkers were everywhere that day. It's just that most of them were size 0 and looked eerily like Duff herself. I, on the other hand, was wearing my official Mommy big-shorts, the khaki ones that make my ass look eight axhandles across, and carrying two cameras and a camcorder, just in case. I was also seized with an irrational urge to tell every kid walking by to "stand up straight, and get your damn bangs out of your eyes." The world's oldest and most uncool Duff stalker.

Sophie's friend Emeline had won backstage passes to meet Hilary, so we were feeling pretty smug as we walked from our hotel to the arena, where we saw many thousands of other little girls dressed in short pleated skirts, jeans jackets, and hair adornments, most trailed by tired moms.

We were whisked to the side with the other "meet and greet" winners—an intimate gathering of about two hundred, as it turned out—and escorted to the rear of the convention center, where we passed roadies cooking hamburgers. Someone squealed at the sight of an enormous suds-filled washing machine: "I'll bet Hilary's clothes are *in there!*" Sophie said I was embarrassing her. Well. It *could've* been her clothes.

When Hilary appeared from behind a blue curtain, well, I 'bout died. I have met the Queen of England and Dan Aykroyd in my day. Once, Melanie Griffith filmed a movie right across the street from my house, and I found Antonio Banderas standing on my very own sidewalk. And, yes, it's true, he's really short, but it didn't matter because how many times are you going to walk out to your car and go, "Oh, hi, Antonio!" and have him smile back and wave. I tell you this so you don't think I'm like some hick who's never seen a celebrity up close and personal.

And here stood Hilary Duff, way tinier than she looks on TV.

We got pictures of Sophie and Emeline with Hilary before being shooed out by a very large bodyguard. The concert was fun. At sixteen, Hilary was all high-energy pop/rock without a hint of naisty. There was something unexpectedly touching about all those little girls sitting beside their mommies, singing all the words of all the songs together.

I wanted to hold on to the moment because I know that the future holds awful arguments about dates, driving privileges, and general distrust. But like every other mom at that concert who found herself holding up a glow-stick instead of a Bic lighter, I know that there's a good chance that it will be healed just a little when we turn to each other and say, "Remember the time we met Hilary Duff?"

7

Field Trips, Fornification, and a Shit-Eating Giraffe

Who Says School Can't Be Fun?

School field trips to celebrate the end of the school year are better than I remember. My daughter's recent trip to the zoo sure topped my own memory of a two-hour bus ride to the maximum-security Central Prison in Raleigh, North Carolina, where we were given a less-than-PC tour. ("Now over here, you got yer crazy-eyed serial killers. . . . Over yonder, you got yer habitual fornificators.")

I'm fairly confident that the reason crime is on the increase is that nobody takes those field trips anymore. That's why you have your fornificating going on right and left.

The annual field trip to prison had the desired effect, which was to scare the livin' crap out of every little Southern boy and girl so that they would never go astray. It worked, too. To my knowledge, not a single kid in my fifth-grade class ever pursued a life of crime, and I can tell you it's because none of us ever truly recovered from seeing those prisoners waving good-bye, tattooed arms stretching through the bars, giving us the finger.

I realize now that having hundreds of North Carolina school children file by and gawk at you is a violation of all kinds of prisoner privacy and personal rights and so on, but bottom line, we were so scared after that ritual, we just wanted to go home and hug our mamas and never so much as jaywalk.

It was an incredibly effective deterrent but not the sort of thing you can do today with entire busloads of children. A parent today could sue, claiming that their kid was posttraumatic-stressed by the whole thing.

It would be cheaper and just as effective to force school kids to watch every season of HBO's *Oz* on DVD.

After a few hours of seeing what can happen if you get the wrong cellmate (the creepy white supremacist who makes you wear mascara and lipstick, for example), you'd be scared straight, all right.

Of course, the prison field trip wasn't the only one we took. There was the annual trek to the local wastewater treatment facility, or as we called it, "the dookie factory."

Sure, it was a small school in a poor, rural county, a hundred miles from, well, anywhere. It wasn't exactly like we could dash over to MoMA for the Diane Arbus retrospective, so we had to make do with what we had.

Still, it's hard to imagine why anyone thought it was a good idea to give sewage plant tours to snickering adolescents. The highlight was observing the trap that catches the condoms.

A lot of colors and styles were evident, which made us all look at our boring little town in a whole new light. Apparently, there was a steamy side to life out there beyond the rows of corn, tomatoes, and soybeans.

A lot of people were gettin' some. Maybe more than some.

Big Eugene, who could usually be found smoking beneath the pecan trees on the schoolyard while the rest of us in fifth grade played hopscotch, announced that the wilder condoms were something called "French ticklers." We said, "I know *that,*" but Big Eugene, who had flunked an ungodly number of grades and already had a pencil-thin mustache, merely scowled dismissively at us through the haze from his Benson & Hedges. He knew we were lying, and even though we knew deep in our hearts that one day Big Eugene would be flipping off schoolchildren from his jailhouse window, we felt the need to impress him.

All of which is to say that I have some degree of field-trip phobia.

When my daughter announced her class was taking a field trip, I involuntarily shrieked "No!" but then had to realize that it was doubtful the kindergarten classes were going to prison or the dookie factory.

Indeed, it was the zoo. This would be safe and fun, I thought. Animals frolicking—what could go wrong?

Well, for starters, the baboon, who was frankly obsessed with amorous activities that didn't require a partner.

"What's he doing?" a few of the kids asked.

My husband, who was the only man who had come along to chaperone, decided he would deal with this question, and deal with it he did.

"That's just the traditional baboon way of waving hello," he said, sounding remarkably poised and knowledgeable.

"Oh," a little boy in the class said. "Should we wave back?"

"Oh, God no."

Next up: the "desert habitat" where an ancient camel proceeded to amuse the children by leaning down to eat his own shit. Without even moving his legs, the giraffe savored every bite as if it were the Christmas ham.

"*Oooh, icky gross!* I think I'm gonna *hurl!*"

"It's just nature," said one of the kids, trying to comfort my husband.

Not only are field trips different these days, but the very games that kids play on the playground are actually designed to prevent competition.

I know this because, at my daughter's elementary school "activity day," there wasn't a single game of Kill or Red Rover in evidence, much less Kill's kinder, gentler cousin, dodgeball.

And gone was the highly sexist game that we used to play back in the Wonder Years, the one that required all us girls to wait coyly for the arrival of a line of boys who would loudly announce, "Bum-bum-bum, here we come, all the way from Washing-*ton*." I forget most of it except that when the boys shouted "Where are you from?" (or, actually, "Where y'all fum?") we had to shout out, "Pretty Girls Station!" then squeal and run away from those baaaad boys from Washing*ton*. Perhaps they were future lobbyists.

The boys then chased the "pretty girls," and the game ended with a lot of bloody knees and general playground mayhem. No mayhem is allowed these days. Ditto "horseplay" and "roughhousing."

Kill has been banned from public school playgrounds for quite some time. Apparently the message of throwing a ball as hard as you could at an opponent who was then locked in "prison" but could get "paroled to kill again" was just a tad un-PC. Unless you were the kind of kid who longed to play on Chuckie Manson's T-ball team, Kill wasn't real appealing. After all, the game ended only when everyone on one team was "officially dead."

I was vastly relieved to see that Red Rover had also disappeared. As the smallest kid in first grade, I dreaded Red Rover and pined to sit in the shade beside my classmate Michelle, a plucky little girl who had to wear a clunky metal back-and-neck brace and read during recess, looking up only to sigh in disgust as the limbs of her classmates were snapped in the name of "fun."

In Red Rover, the biggest, burliest boy would try to break through the weakest link (Yoo-hoo! That would be *me*) of knotted-up arms and elbows. I would always just shake my arm away and let him come through, much to the horror of my teammates.

Of course, I was also the first one "called over," as in, "Red Rover, Red Rover, send the shrimpy kid over!" I would then pitifully pretend to break through the linked arms of the other team before going, "Oh! You got me. I'll just sit over here with the girl with the screws in her skull."

When I asked my daughter who won the egg-on-a-spoon race, she said she didn't know 'cause it was "just for fun."

Okay. But would it have killed 'em to keep score?

Although playground games aren't allowed to be competitive, we parents find ways to compete, such as with homework. Parents love to complain about how much homework their kids have to do every night. It's our generation's equivalent of the old walking to school, uphill both ways, in the snow, with *rickets!*

You think *your* kid has too much homework? Please, they say, waving a hand dismissively in your face: "My kid spends an average of eight-point-six hours per night just on *math*. Hell, he hasn't had a bath since 1998. There is simply no time."

To hear most parents tell it, Little Johnnie is so devoted to his homework studies that he breaks only long enough to accept a tray of soup and cold cheese sandwiches slipped through the slot in his bedroom door.

Soccer practice? Ha!

Scouts? Who's got the time?

Karate? Piano? Birthday parties? You must be kidding.

There must be too much homework. What else could explain those horrid wheeled backpacks that zip through school hallways at breakneck speeds, slicing ankles and tripping those unfortunate enough to be in their path? (If I get tripped by one more Diva Starz suitcase on wheels, I'm going to *lose it!* Oops, too late.) These backpacks the size of Guam (which, as I recall from my own geography homework days, is a small country somewhere between Chile and Mustard) must surely contain all the papers and books vital to completion of the night's homework.

These days, to hear the parents tell it, it's all homework, all the time.

Except, well, actually, it isn't.

We know this now, thanks to a study by the Brookings Institution, a famous Washington think tank. (Motto: "Well, yes, as a matter of fact, you *are* stupider than us.")

The researchers found that, in most cases, too much homework is, uh, a myth, and that truthfully, the great majority of kids have less than one hour of homework a night.

Not only that, but homework has actually decreased every year since 1984. At this rate, pretty soon your kid should be able to finish homework for five classes in a SpongeBob commercial break.

This is great news for the parents who actually do all that homework. Anybody who's ever been to a typical school science fair will quickly deduce that it's incredibly difficult for most seven-year-olds to build a scale model of the space shuttle complete with astronauts that pee real Tang.

So how did we get the idea that American kids are "over-studying"? (As I write this, a Japanese seventh-grader is laughing hysterically somewhere.) Well, some of them are, but just one in ten, and, yes, we know that's probably *your* kid and we should just shut up.

Face it. We can't credibly whine about homework anymore. I know. I'm going to miss it, too.

So what do we do if we can't compete on the playground or in homework?

We resort to Terrific Kids competitions.

To tell the truth, I was never real fond of those "I've got a terrific kid!" bumper stickers you see on the steroidal SUVs in the carpool line.

I mean, everybody's kid is terrific, right?

What kind of insecure weirdness is at work when we must have a bumper sticker on our car just so everybody else will believe it, too?

Who cares? Should we drive more carefully in the presence of a vanload of Officially Designated Terrific Kids?

("Watch 'em, Marvin; that's the future of our country ridin' in that Yukon.")

What kind of a parent believes that this "terrific kid" endorsement is an accurate tool for predicting future successes?

Yoo-hoo! Over here, everyone! That would be me.

It's not easy to admit that at the Terrific Kids assembly at my daughter's school, I was as green as a toad when two of her friends were designated "terrific" and stepped to the stage to receive their stickers and certificates.

The very, very smallest part of me wondered, "What's so terrific about them?"

They're adorable, sure. Good students, absolutely. Helpful and obedient? Check.

So where's *our* bumper sticker?

Oh, this is just so embarrassing. I've now officially become one of the people I used to make fun of. What's worse, I'm not sure it won't rub off on my kid. Will she take on my awful competitive nature and begin to say things like, "Hmmmm, sure would be a shame if something were to happen to Little Susie to make her somehow less 'terrific'!"

I don't think I have to worry about that just yet. So far, my kid seems oblivious of any of this and prefers to concentrate on her poetry studies, which are frankly limited these days to *Girls go to college to get more knowledge / boys go to Jupiter to get more stupider.*

Parents show up for the Terrific Kids assembly with

camcorders and *bouquets of flowers*. So now, the kids who don't get flowers from their parents pout, and the ones who did get flowers have won the unspoken "My parents love me better than yours love you" contest.

I swear it almost makes me long for Red Rover.

8

The One and Done Club

Sure, I Could've Thrown a Litter
Like You, but How Much Ballet Can a Mom Take?

My mom-friends and I have decided that it's going to be a looooong summer now that the kids have been out of school for eighteen days, eleven hours, and twenty-six minutes. Not that we're counting.

There's one mommy in the group, okay, me, who crudely scratches lines, diagonally crossing every four, to show how many days of "summer vacation" have passed. I feel like Tom Hanks's character in *Cast Away*, only I haven't started talking to a soccer ball wearing a face drawn with my own blood. Yet.

There's a noticeable difference between my mom-friends who sagely scheduled summer camps for their kids and, uh, the rest of us.

"After book-publishing camp," one said smugly, "Sallie Jo

will do one week each of Tuscan cookery and Tae Bo, and then we'll round out July with horse camp, cursive hand-writing camp, and pre-Olympic diving."

Those of us who rejected the notion of a rigidly sched-uled summer of activities (that's right, the *crazy* ones) are cursing that we said, a mere eighteen days, eleven hours, and twenty-six minutes ago, "Children don't need all this organized activity! They need free play time!"

Well, no. That's why they call them children. They need a nice, paid instructor to show them pipe cleaner crafts and oversee relay races all day. What they apparently *don't* need, much to my shock, is a ham sandwich in front of *Days of Our Lives* with Mommy.

When my daughter complained of boredom the other day, I said, as lovingly as possible, "Shhhh! Lexie's gettin' ready to tell Abe that Brandon's the father of her love child. Don't you know nothing about a story arc?"

She sighed heavily and retreated to her room to read a book. Freak.

I guess the thing I hadn't counted on was that, even on a day like yesterday, which included a three-hour playdate with a friend, a T-ball game, and a birthday party at an amusement park, my daughter would actually say, "I'm booorred" in the twenty-three-odd minutes we had be-tween rushing from place to place.

My daughter and her friends are under the delusion that they're tiny passengers on an invisible cruise ship, and we moms are the cruise directors. ("First up, Styrofoam peanut tower construction, followed by Slip'N Slides and slushies on the Lido deck at fourteen hundred hours!")

My friend, also the mother of an only child, promised to wave to me from the back of the white van after she gets her arm out of the straitjacket that she'll surely be wearing by summer's end.

I'm sure she's exaggerating. I don't think you can really get an arm out of one of those things.

One of the only camps I did sign up for was ballet camp. I've always wanted to be one of those dedicated and cheerful "ballet moms" who researches summer dance camps for months and even sells cookie dough and Christmas wrapping paper for ballet school fund-raisers.

Ballet is beautiful, but I'm a new soul, incapable of appreciating scene after scene of young girls standing on their toes and mincing about and then standing on their toes and mincing about some more. And the plots? Sneaky fairies and magic feathers and stuff. Oh, just let me eat my own flesh till I quietly disappear. Still, the princess likes it a lot, so off we went to see her school perform something called *Coppélia*.

Now for those of you who don't know pointe from pintos, *Coppélia* is a famous comedic ballet. Like most ballets, the plot is paper thin but, hell-o, what can I say? The male lead gave me new interest in ballet. On account of he was FG. Fully gorgeous, I mean. I saw Baryshnikov perform years before he was reduced to playing one of Carrie's many boyfriends on *Sex and the City,* so I know a little about how a well-placed man in tights can give you a, uh, deeper appreciation of ballet.

Coppélia is pretty to watch, I suppose, but the plot is maddening: handsome dude falls in lust with a mannequin, thinking she's real (he's purty, but he's dumb); his fiancée finds out and gets jealous; fiancée exposes mannequin for the fake she is; handsome dude and fiancée have huge church wedding and live happily ever after.

Okay, how stupid do you have to be to go ahead and marry a man who just dumped you *for a mannequin?* But this is ballet, friends, and it's all part of the damn magic.

I don't "get" ballet. Take *Giselle,* for instance. In this one, a simple peasant girl named, well, Giselle, falls in love with a nobleman in disguise. When she finds out who he really is, and that he's betrothed to another, she has, like, a giant hissy fit and dances herself to death. Literally! Of course, because it's ballet, nothing is as it seems, and Giselle's love survives being buried. Unfortunately, she never manages to shake the Evil Queen. (Ballet is real big on Evil Queens.) She goes back to the grave, and her true love grieves for her forever and ever. This doesn't exactly put us all in the mood for pie, now, does it?

Or what about *Firebird,* another famous ballet, in which a guy named Ivan wanders into a "mysterious forest" inhabited by a magical firebird. Ivan cons the bird out of a "magic feather" that will keep him safe from the evil in the garden, including spells by mad magicians and such. I know. I'll bet you could've used a magic feather the last time you were "enchanted" by a mad magician, too, huh? Anyway, the firebird returns to help and lulls the forest monsters to sleep. In return, Ivan agrees to smash the magic egg that has cast a spell of evil over the forest forever. In the end, life gets really good in the forest, though there is no mention of cable.

All of this is fine if you're into it, but I'd much rather watch Denzel in *Man on Fire* for like the bazillionth time. That part where he puts the explosives up the bad guy's ass and then sets the timer and hands it to him? Now *that's* entertainment!

The princess loves ballet, though, so I attempt to be supportive.

Over the years, I've discovered that there are two kinds of ballet moms at our school: First, there's the kind that stays the whole hour watching anxiously through the cut-out window, enjoying every inch of little Cherish Rae's progress while monitoring the student—teacher ratio in case she needs to complain to the director. Which she will.

And then, there's the other kind, like me. We use that same hour to buy an entire week's worth of groceries, careening back into the parking lot just as class ends and the kids are getting their hands stamped with cute little red-ink ballerina figures.

When she was really little, I used to try to con my kid. "You were great!" I gushed, trying desperately to hide the eighteen bags of groceries that had magically overflowed into the backseat. Well. Her father believes there's a grocery fairy—why can't she?

There's also the carpool fairy, which would be me, if you can envision any fairy being twenty pounds overweight and wearing a shirt her kid tie-dyed over UNC sweatpants.

I've chauffered my daughter all over town this summer, not just to ballet. I have to admit that I'm going to miss, sort of, the backseat chatter that has kept me amused and confused.

You see, little girls have a ginormous capacity to giggle at things that no one over ten would ever "get." My personal least favorite is the game where one says, "I one an elevator," and the next one says, "I two an elevator," and, ohmigod, we can see where this is heading, eventually: "I eight (ate) an elevator." Hilarity ensues. They never get tired of this game, even though the "joke" is pretty obvious after the first ten or twelve items.

This summer, much of the backseat banter has concerned teen idols, or as we like to call them in our household, Chad Michael Murray.

DAUGHTER SOPHIE: Oh, Chad Michael Murray is *really* cool. A girl in my arts camp said she knows somebody whose cousin lives next door to him, and she can get his autograph for us!

FRIEND: (Brain-piercing squeal) *Eeeeeeee!* That. Is. So. Totally. Cool.

SOPHIE: That's right, and guess what?

FRIEND: What?

SOPHIE: I forget!

FRIEND: Yeah! Me, too!

(Loud, prolonged giggles for roughly eight minutes while you wonder if constant exposure to high-pitched noises can sever your brain stem. I do know for a fact that certain noises can make you nuts. A kindly woman at church once gave my daughter a "talking prayer bear" that recited the Lord's Prayer. Sadly, it was with a thick Japanese accent. You haven't really lived until you've tucked your baby into bed and heard her recite what sounds like a badly dubbed Jackie Chan movie ending with a karate-chop "Ahhh-*men!*" Back in the car, though.)

SOPHIE: I like Bratz but not Yasmin. Mommy says Yasmin looks too skanky.

FRIEND: What's skanky?

SOPHIE: It means pretty. But in a grown-up way. Like Mommy's kinda skanky, not young or anything.

FRIEND: I get it. My mommy's skanky, too!

SOPHIE *(pausing for effect)*: Well, is she stanky, too?

FRIEND: *Eeeeeeeeee!* (squealing and uncontrolled spewing of McDonald's chocolate milk all over backseat of trusty Taurus)

And, while we're on the subject, memo to Morgan Spurlock, who made the fabulous and shocking documentary *Super Size Me,* in which he almost dies after eating McD's food three times a day for a month. Dude—thanks for *ruining my life*. No more fast food after watching that one. Now I have to "plan menus" and "buy groceries" and, ohmigod again, "cook."

It could be lots worse, I guess. At least I don't stank.

Chauffeuring my kid around town has gotten harder now that there's a new law requiring kids under eight to use booster car seats for safety's sake.

Have you ever tried to tell a kid who's been out of a car seat for more than a year that she must get back in one because it's the law?

ME: Honey, remember that car seat that you were so happy to get out of when you were six? The one that your eight-year-old friend used to laugh at?

SEVEN-YEAR-OLD *(warily)*: Yeeessss?

ME *(very quickly)*: Well, they changed the law, and now you're going to have to get back on that booster seat until you weigh eighty pounds, so if you don't like the idea, you better start eating a *lot* of macaroni and cheese really quick.

KID: So let me get this straight. Fat kids don't have to use a booster seat?

ME: Honey, *fat* is a very negative word. In the South, we prefer to use words and phrases such as *big-boned,* or *prosperous,* but never fat. It's quite rude."

KID: Are you serious? I have to ride in a car seat again? *Like a baby?* Why don't you just rent me some Wiggles videos and make my humiliation complete?

ME: Hon, all your friends will be in booster seats, too. Well, I mean, except for the fat ones. Oh, sorry! And look, it's not like the car seat really little kids use, the one with the vomity-smelling padded bar in front and all those dried Cheerios in the cushions. It's just the booster seat. No one will even know you're sitting on it.

KID: How long do I have to do this?

ME: Well, like I said, you have to hit eighty pounds or until you're eight years old.

KID: My life is over.

ME: Oh, honey, don't be so dramatic. It's for your own good.

KID: Can't we just say that I'm eight years old in case you get pulled over?

ME: That's lying!

KID: What about the time we went to the circus and you said I was five when I was really six so you could save five bucks on admission?

ME: Well, that's different. You were acting five that day.

KID: It's not fair. How can they change the rules?

ME: Dunno, sweetie. You got two choices. Suck it up for a few months or gain twenty-three pounds by January first.

KID: Was that a Krispy Kreme we just passed?

Getting out of the car seat is a rite of passage that's right up there with losing a tooth.

It means that your baby's growing up. I'll never forget

when my daughter, then five, held her fist out to me, then opened it slowly.

There, in the palm, was one perfect, pearly tooth that had inexplicably escaped its rightful home in her mouth.

"The Tooth Fairy's gonna come tonight!" Sophie squealed and danced around the kitchen clutching the tiny tooth while pointing to the hole where it used to be, bottom front and center.

"Swell," I said, finishing my coffee and dabbing my eyes. This was more in-your-face proof that my baby was growing up. I launched into a pathetic recitation of all the wonderful meals that little tooth had chomped on, the zillions of chicken nuggets, the pizzas, the broccoli and carrots. Yeah, okay, I made up those last two.

Then it dawned on me. Trying to be cagey, I said, "Hmmm, by the way, how much does the Tooth Fairy pay for teeth these days, do you know?"

"Well, Lucy got *seventy dollars*."

Lucy's my daughter's rich friend. Every kid should have one. Lucy's mother would never shriek, "I told you we ain't paying for that shit" if she gave away all her Lifetouch school pictures, including the "Bonus Little Patriot" flag-embossed keychain before she even got home like my kid did.

This was a Teachable Moment, though. It was time, once again, for a reminder of How Things Used to Be.

"Darling, when Mommy was a little girl, I got a shiny quarter from the Tooth Fairy, right under my pillow."

"You're kidding, right?"

"Well, back in Mommy's day, that was about half of what you'd need to buy the latest forty-five from Creedence Clearwater Revival."

"Huh?"

"CCR. You know, 'Bad Moon Rising'?"

"Were they better than Maroon Five?"

"Uh. Well, actually, no."

Later that day, I decided to poll the mommies on how much the Tooth Fairy brings.

Most said between five and ten bucks for a first tooth. I decided the tooth fairy would bring five dollars and a disclaimer that all future teeth would bring one dollar.

"What's a dis-claim-er?" my daughter asked, reading the letter the next morning.

"Well, it's like those things at the bottom of ads for prescription drugs that tell you in little print that there's a halfway decent chance that if you take the pill, it'll cure you but you'll also get excessive ear hair and a craving to eat dirt."

"Oh."

Later, I discovered there's no pleasing the mommies. One said five bucks was ridiculously high; another said she wouldn't consider giving less than twenty dollars for a First Tooth. But she's the one who dressed as the fairy and made little fairy dust footprints on her daughter's carpet so we all know she's a nut job, right?

Having an only child means that we get only one chance to do it right. There isn't going to be a do-over, and there's always some well-meaning person to point that out.

The perky hostess at the family-friendly restaurant looked at our little party of three, still wearing church clothes and thinking only of cinnamon pancakes.

"Just one child?" she asked, digging into a basket for crayons and a kiddie menu containing enough activities for a cross-country drive.

"Well, yes," said my husband, a trifle defensively. "Of course, there are days when she *seems* like more than one, but, no, it's just one. I mean we were kind of late getting started, if you know what I mean, and we're not getting any younger and so we just decided—"

"Oh, for God's sake, shut up," I hissed. "She just wants to know how many kid menus to grab."

"Oh."

As parents of an only child, we're used to the "just one child" comment. There's never any malice in it; at least I don't think there is.

Occasionally, well-meaning friends will beam and say things like, "I know *she's* not spoiled!"

Well, of course she is. And if I'd thrown a litter like some of them did, they'd all be spoiled, too. What's your point?

Very occasionally, someone will tsk-tsk and say things like "I bet you want a little brother or sister" to our daughter, and my jaw just drops.

"I'm forty-six years old!" I want to scream at them. I mean, sure, I don't look it. . . . Anyway, where am I supposed to get one of those? It's not like they're hanging out on an end cap at Target, and I don't want to be one of those freaks you read about in the *Enquirer* that had a kid with "borreyed" eggs at age eighty-six or some such.

Besides, there are plenty of folks who should have stopped at one kid. Or none. Like Michael Jackson, who, when he's not fighting child molestation charges busies himself playing with the Elephant Man's pelvis.

Frankly, I don't have the patience for more than one kid. I have plenty of mom-friends who smile dreamily and Madonna-like as their many children crawl on them, draw on the walls, and throw up on the carpet.

Still, it's surprising when strangers take it upon themselves to comment on the sad state of the only child.

"I had a friend who was an only child," the lady in line at the drugstore volunteered. "She used to spend all her time talking to her imaginary brothers and sisters, poor little thing."

Save your pity, toots. One is only the loneliest number in bad Three Dog Night songs. Believe it.

9

Toyland, Joyland

Is That a Bratz Boot in Your Sofa Cushion, or Are You Just Glad to See Me?

My daughter says that what she really wants for Christmas is an American Girl doll named Nellie. Sophie even circled the picture in the catalog and scribbled *Please!!!* in blue Magic Marker.

For those who don't know, every American Girl doll represents a specific time in our nation's history. Nellie, it turns out, is the cute-but-economically disadvantaged waif friend of rich American Girl doll Samantha. She costs $108.

Some waif.

The American Girl catalog is beautifully photographed. Heck, by the time I finished looking at it, I could barely stifle an urge to order Kit, Molly, and especially the plucky Josefina complete with her authentic reproduction New Mexico sleigh bed.

Thank heavens I was reminded by the big, bold letters of the catalog's very first page: "True friendship is the greatest gift."

Indeed it is, and that's why my little girl is going to become good friends with the Nellie look-alike I found on sale for twelve bucks last week and slyly named K-Martha.

K-Martha is absolutely gorgeous and, although she doesn't come with her own line of books, bedding, and matching human-size clothing, I think she's going to be a hit.

Although they're undeniably beautiful, AGs are way too fancy and expensive to play with, so you put them up on a shelf or in a glass case and admire them. K-Martha, on the other hand, you can drag by the feet and use for the cat's pillow and it's no big deal.

Each American Girl doll comes with her own bio. Kit, who represents 1934 in our nation's history, "went from rich to poor overnight but still has spunk!" says the catalog. Oh, those wacky poor kids; at least they make us laugh!

Samantha, the most famous AG, is "a generous girl with a curious nature living in 1904." She's the one who just starred in her own TV special, so I imagine the other dolls have taken to hissing and sniping and calling her Miss Thang behind her back.

Molly represents 1944 and, for ninety-eight dollars plus shipping, comes with a "pretend steel penny." Oh, you shouldn't have.

If you get tired of watching them look historic, you can

take the Girls for a pretend ride on the official American Girl horse. He costs sixty dollars, but he looks just like a horse from the Family Dollar Store to me.

There is only one lonely American Girl boy-doll, and he's no Ken, let me tell you. Even on the catalog pages, Bitty Boy Twin looks as if he wants to scream.

I wonder why. Perhaps it's because he's sick of being dressed by chubby little hands that don't take proper care of his Fall Frolic outfit or his Festive Plaid knickers. Or maybe it's because he just read his "biography" and realizes that the high point of his life is going to be having "not-so-clean fun making cookies" with his twin sister. Hey! Who needs PlayStation?

Truthfully, I suspect Bitty Boy looks so horrified because he just read his own shipping charges or maybe he learned that all his siblings are on back order. Again.

What could possibly be more American?

How about the Easy-Bake Oven, which Sophie has begged for this year, no surprise to any mother of a little girl. But when I actually went out to buy one, I felt that awful mix of panic and disappointment I'd felt earlier in the day when I discovered they'd taken beets off the Pizza Hut salad bar. *Is nothing sacred?*

The new Easy-Bake Oven looks nothing like the one I remember as a tot. It's a microwavey "snack center" contraption. At least it still operates on a 100-watt bulb that every parent forgets to buy. It's a parental rite of passage to spend most of Christmas Day trying to figure out which bulb in the house can be unscrewed and substituted so you can watch a single "brownie" cook in just under eight hours.

The hot toys this year talk a lot more than the ones in the past, and I'm not sure this is a good thing. Diva Starz dolls, we're told, "speak fashion-related phrases!"

What the hell is a fashion-related phrase? Oh, I get it. Stuff that supermodels say. Stuff like, "I'd like a single leaf of arugula on a Wheat Thin, please, and then I'll go throw it up" or "I'd like to act, but I have no talent!"

There's also the Lil Chefs Talking "Smart" Kitchen, a seventy-dollar plastic kitchen programmed with fifty sounds and phrases "typically heard in the kitchen." I'm hoping that includes the mantras from my kitchen: "Let's just throw out this slop and go to Wendy's" or "Don't answer that; it's a telemarketer!"

Maybe your kid aspires to be a fry cook. The McDonald's Food Cart comes with a little headset just like the drive-through guy wears, presumably so you can pretend to mutter unintelligible gibberish to whoever you're playing with and they can scream, "What? What did you say?" just like the real drive-through.

There's even a talking Lemonade Lisa who dispenses lemonade-type product to a pretend customer while uttering "10 fun phrases!" Personally I'd prefer a mini-Starbucks stand where pretend customers would complain nonstop about spending nearly five bucks for a large latte.

I may settle for a Fisher-Price Sweet Magic Kitchen, which has pretend food that turns colors to let you know it's done. Ohhhhh. So that's how you can tell.

Of course, the best toys at this stage always seem to involve Barbie & Co. My daughter's little friend gave her a pregnant Midge doll for her birthday this year. It was a regular stroll down memory lane, I tell you. When I was a kid, I had Barbie and my sister had Midge, a perky, freckle-faced redhead with a Dutchboy hairdo. She was the girl next door, the pretty-in-pink-plaid pal, the also-ran to her hottie friend, the Barbster.

I always felt a bit smug that I had Barbie while sis had Midge. You just knew things were going to be harder for Midge. And now she's knocked up.

The funniest thing is the brouhaha from the freaks that are offended by this sort of thing. Turns out some Wal-Mart stores, exposing retail spines of Jell-O, have taken to hiding the massive Midge behind the counter during the Christmas season so shoppers wouldn't be "offended" by the bun in the oven.

Wonder what they do with those pictures of Mary riding the donkey into Bethlehem and great with child. Is that okay, you think?

Frankly, we love pregnant Midge. The baby's daddy, says a rather defensive Mattel, is her longtime husband, Alan, who has been chronically inferior over the years to the buff Ken.

While Barbie and, to a much lesser degree, Ken have been carving out careers in everything from aerospace engineering to professional surfing, Midge and Alan have just been getting by, shopping the sales and buying extras for their tacky-but-clean singlewide with S & H Greenpoints. And now, the blessed event!

Turns out Baby Doctor Barbie (yes, there is one) is rumored to have delivered Midge's baby, at least so says Mattel in a press release. Oh, it just always has to be about Barbie, doesn't it? You just know she patted Midge's swollen fingers and said condescending things about how she'd get her shape back just like she did. Why, Midge, says Barbie, you'll be back to winning Olympic gold medals in no time, just like me.

Of course, she's Midge, so we know that she's Everywoman, operating on real-world rules that mean her butt will remain as lumpy as undercooked grits for the rest of her polystyrene life.

The pregnant Midge doll, much to Sophie's delight, actually delivers the baby sans soap-opera squealing scenes and similar unpleasantness. No "Push! Push!" words of encouragement from Alan, just lift up the rounded belly flap, and out drops the curled-up infant! What could be more fabulous? (Having had a C-section, I can relate to Midge. I should warn her that, for the next three days, nosy Dr. Barbie will be in her face demanding to know if she's "passed gas yet" while Alan uses this as a chance to invite the nurse to pull his finger, so very Alan.)

I have to wonder what Midge and Alan must make of Barbie's recent, uh, dalliance.

It was *très* shocking when we learned recently that Barbie had actually given Ken the old "I need some space" speech and taken up with Blaine, a "hunky Australian surfer dude" several years her junior.

At the time, those of us who have applauded Barbie's enviable ability to morph from movie star to pet doctor to airline pilot were worried about her mental stability.

After all, Ken, whose only downside was waxy buildup on his hair, was always supportive of Barbie's myriad career changes. Only adult ADHD, or perhaps a movie-star acceptable level of manic depression, could explain this compulsion to try so many different careers. No matter what she undertook, Ken was always there, in his cardigan and khakis or swim trunks or dinner jacket, championing his beloved's latest lark.

Blaine, on the other hand, just doesn't seem that reliable. He's the type who would cheat on Barbie with one of those Bratz sluts and then lie about it in the morning, even as Barbie discovered the creepy telltale amputeed boot in Blaine's sofa cushions.

Barbie didn't pick a great time to start thinking outside the (cardboard) box. Blaine, it turns out, isn't selling all that well. The only question left is, now that third-quarter earnings are down 26 percent, will Barbie reconcile with Ken?

Ken, if you're reading this, don't take the ho back. You're too good for her. Don't let the suits at Mattel try to put you back by Barbie's side. She dumped you after forty-three years for a tanned boy toy in board shorts, and you're gonna come crawling back?

Dude.

Those of us who have looked up to Barbie for her career achievements recognized Ken as the wind beneath her wings. And not just professionally. Ken would be the one who would lovingly wipe the rice pudding from Barbie's perfect chin when the two of them eventually relocated to adjoining rooms at Mattel's assisted living complex. Blaine? He's too busy chasing other Sheilas, pounding Foster's lager, and hanging out with his surf buddies, all of whom look depressingly like Ashton Kutcher.

Barbie's new beau is, from sales figures and appearances, simply not working out.

So, what to do? First, hire a publicist to handle the inevitable media hordes that will want to know where their love went. An immediate "they will remain good friends" press release must be distributed.

Ken and Alan should start hitting the bars together. Alan, as we all know, probably has a tab at every watering hole in Mattelville. Maybe with Ken in the mix, he'll actually be allowed back inside one or two of them.

Expect Ken to play hard to get for a while, but I predict he'll be back. After four decades, he's proved to be a capable lapdog. I only hope that he reminds Barbie every now and again that he could've had Midge any time he wanted.

But then, again, who couldn't?

10

Slacker Moms Unite!

Say *Adios!* to All That Guilt

Everywhere I turn lately, there's a magazine cover, newspaper headline, or book jacket screeching about how the modern mom is trying to do it all and failing miserably.

Shuttling her kids from soccer to fencing to swim class to flute lessons, today's Supermom is frazzled, resentful, and depressed. In interview after interview, she wonders why motherhood isn't the fun gig she imagined.

Maybe because I came to motherhood a bit later in life than most, I've never really tried to overachieve and now, at last, my slackness has been rewarded.

Slacker moms are in!

Pulitzer Prize–winning columnist Anna Quindlen wrote glowingly about her own slacker mom recently. The woman couldn't even drive, and she usually answered, "I dunno, he's around here somewhere" when one of Anna's brothers went missing, but "wherever she was, was home."

She didn't worry about her kids not getting accepted in the town's best gymnastics class; she just told them to get out from under her and play outside. Radical!

Ever since I gave birth, I've watched with a mix of horror and admiration those mommies who do it all. They work full-time, lead Scout troops, and volunteer to host foreign exchange students. They exercise for an hour every day, shuttle their kids all over town, cook nutritious meals, and collapse every night for five hours of tortured sleep.

Finally, they've gone from a low hum of discontent to a full-fledged whine. And all I can say is this: It's About Damn Time.

It turns out that "slacker moms" like me are considered to be the ones who are truly mentally healthy. I know—scary isn't it?

The mantra of the slacker mom should always be: "Do just enough to get by." Try saying it, supermoms. It's really quite exhilarating.

Here's how we do it.

ANNOYING WELL-INTENTIONED PERSON: Hi, Celia! I was just wondering if you'd be willing to organize (host, train, serve as, volunteer, mentor, etc.) so-and-so?

ME: No.

See how easy?

At first you'll no doubt feel guilty, but stand firm. Your sanity is at stake. Put your feet up; watch *Oprah*. Let your kid play. Do Just Enough to Get By.

I'm sure that a few of you diehards are saying, "Well, that's fine for you, but that leaves us to do all the work!"

I know! Isn't it fabulous? Look, martyrdom's overrated. If you resent it, stop the hell doing it.

Here at Slacker Mom Central, I will continue to do just enough to get by on the extracurricular front.

Okay, to be honest, as soon as my one term as Spanish coach is over.

See even we hardcore slacker moms can get sucked in occasionally.

After telling everyone that slacking off and refusing to volunteer for anything is fabulously freeing, I heard myself say, in a small voice, yes, when I was recruited to help with the after-school Spanish club.

I don't even know how it happened, so just let this be a lesson to all of you aspiring slackers. Perhaps an exact transcript of the conversation can help us figure out what went wrong.

NICE MOM: Celia, will you help with the new Spanish Club after school? I know your daughter's signed up, and we desperately need volunteers.

ME *(snorting)*: You must be desperate, toots. The only Spanish I know is Nachos Bell Grande and Jose Cuervo.

(See, so far, so good. I'm standing firm. So why am I

now riding around with a backseat full of piñata-making materials?)

NICE MOM *(cheerily)*: Oh, that's okay! You don't have to speak Spanish to help out.

(Now here's where I should have sniffed el rat-o. She's killing me with kindness, and I'm falling for it. See what happens next.)

ME: You don't? (I thought this was strange. Does this mean that I can finally perform surgery without having to attend that pesky medical school?)

NICE MOM: Heck no! (Okay, here's a bad sign; never trust cheery women who say Midwesterny-sounding things like "heck!" There's just something not right about them.)

NM: Really, we just need people to help pass out materials and maybe keep the kids from getting too loud.

ME: Uh, okay, I guess.

I have no idea what hit me. Was it because she was so relentlessly cheerful? Was it the thought of being able to jerk a knot in somebody else's kid for a change?

The next day, I reported for duty at the school cafeteria, where one of the mom-leaders came over and asked if I'd mind reading a book or two in Spanish to the kids.

I'd been hoo-doo'ed by the chipper Midwesterner. Of course they expected me to speak Spanish.

"No hablo español," I said weakly.

"Oh, good! You're fluent!"

Another corralled volunteer looked at me helplessly. "I've had six years of French," she said.

"No problemo," I assured her. "It's probably a lot the same. Just substitute a lot of choppy sounds for that jeh-jeh-jeh-joosh stuff the French say. Oh! And be sure to add an *o* to the end of everything. I seem to remember that from high school."

"Okay-o," she said gamely.

Once the kids learned to count to twenty in Spanish, it was time to play Spanish Bingo, which is a lot like English Bingo except with a lot less cigarette smoke and black hair dye.

I looked at my watch and realized that we'd been at it for about twelve minutos. What on earth were we going to do for the rest of the hour?

Thank goodness, our fearless leader ("I had to learn Spanish cuz I married me a Mexican") was on the case. Everyone would learn how to say his or her name in *español*.

This reminded me of Spanish 1 class when we did the same thing. While I had fantasized that my Spanish name would be exotico, it turned out to be exactly the same as it was in English.

"But I want to be Rosalita or something," I had whined to the beleaguered teacher.

"Oh, yeah?" she asked. "Well, I wanna be Doris Day, but that ain't happening either."

Muy harsh.

So, I've lost some of my slacker mom street cred, but not all of it. A few days after Spanish Club ended for the year, a coven of Supermoms approached me about helping with a new Brownie troop.

"No @##$ way," I said, feeling the smug surge of power that comes from being such a committed slack-ass. The only Brownies I had any interest in, I told them, came out of a Duncan Hines box.

They skittered away to hassle some other victim, no doubt hissing the whole time about my "lack of commitment" and my "refusal to be a team player" and my "really wide brownie-eating ass."

Those Supermoms can be real bitches when you think about it.

We could all take a lesson from men, if you ask me. Because no matter how slack a dad is, if he does the least little thing, people gush over him.

When I went on a business trip a while back, everyone marveled at the "good job" my husband did.

Why is that? Is it like seeing a chimpanzee play the clarinet? Sure, it's possible, but you don't honestly expect to ever see it in your lifetime.

Or is it like the Arkansas rooster I remember from childhood? The one that could take your dollar bill, punch a cash register, and give you change back? He even had his own *postcard*. Is someone, somewhere, printing a postcard with a similar apparent freak of nature? The caring daddy who managed to not completely screw up a week of single parenthood?

"Your husband did *such* a good job," cooed a teacher at our daughter's elementary school.

"You should have seen how, when he realized it was PE day, he just flew out the door and went home so he could get her tennis shoes!" gushed another. "She's one lucky little girl!"

A woman whom I don't even know stopped to tell me that my husband "sure was a great dad while you were gone!"

What was next? A memo from the central office announcing that the school's name would be changed to honor him?

Again, I ask, Why is it a man performs the minimal task of getting his kid to and from school dressed in anything that's not Hello Kitty pajamas and he's all of a sudden frickin' Keanu dismantling a bomb on a city bus?

Feeling ridiculously guilty, I renounced my slacker mom status temporarily and immediately signed up to take pecan tartlets to the teachers' tea. Where was my ticker tape parade? Who judged the schoolwide essay contest every year? Who had been class mom for three years in a row? (Okay, y'all know it wasn't me but it *could* have been.)

Clearly, after a week away, my stock was low. Plus, I'd gotten into a fight with the carpool Nazis that morning.

"We just want it safe for the children," one hissed at me.

Because I was holding my daughter's hand and we were *on foot,* I failed to see a threat here. What were we in danger of doing? Taking out a few roly-polys before their time?

"You shouldn't walk here! You should walk there!" the second carpool Nazi screeched, sounding rather like a hostile Dr. Seuss and pointing to a space approximately two feet away.

Jesus. Give somebody a Day-Glo vest and they think they rule the world.

That night, I told my husband that his favorite slacker-mom had once again gotten it wrong. I'd offended the carpool volunteers.

"You didn't?" he fairly shrieked.

"Yeah, so what?"

"I have to *live* with these people," he moaned.

"Not anymore. Slacker mom's back on the job now, remember?"

"Oh, yeah," he said, brightening. "What's for supper?"

PART II

Celebrities

11

Celebrity Moms

Don't Hate Them Because They're Beautiful
(When There Are So Many Other Reasons to Hate Them!)

I'm sure that y'all are just as relieved as I am that actress Denise Richards had her baby and it weighed, like, five pounds or some similar celebrity-baby weight.

Our long national nightmare is over. Denise was starting to rival Kate Hudson for the longest gestation. Celebrities announce their pregnancies through their publicists on the morning after conception and thus begins the very long season of photos in the park of them wearing ball caps, their two-hundred-dollar tank tops stretched tight over blossoming tummies.

Celebrities generally don't give birth to big, fat, standard American babies. They tend to work out during their pregnancies, drinking wheat grass shakes and nibbling on sun-dried particleboard. Then, immediately after the birth, they hire a full-time personal trainer to whip them back into their prepregnancy weight of roughly ninety-four pounds.

If there was any way they could insert a tiny home gym into the womb and encourage the baby to start working out *now,* they would. ("Hush now, little Artemis. No pain, no gain!")

Celebrities are not like you and me, my hons. And not just because they eat with their feet. No, no, it's because they don't even call babies what they are. They call them *bumps.* An entire cover story in *People* magazine was devoted to showcasing the bumps of Gwyneth Paltrow, Carnie ("Would somebody please tell me again why the hell I had gastric bypass surgery?") Wilson, and "double bumpers" Marcia Gay Harden and Julia Roberts.

Celebrities also tend to wear skin-tight clothing throughout pregnancy, a look that is, as I have said before, just plain wrong. Yes, we get it, you're pregnant and you're fabulous! But we find it hard to relate. Instead of waddling into the IHOP twice a week to order "lemon crepes and keep 'em comin'" like those of us out here in the Real World, they are instead stepping up the yogilates sessions with Simone and Rafiki. Makes me want to snap their twiglike celebrity necks like a Cheeto.

Mmmm, Cheetos. Sorry. Where was I?

Oh, yes. Britney Spears. See, here's the thing about that celebrity mama. Britney is, at heart, just a good ol' Southern girl. I'm sure that her rich friends were horrified by her wearing that shirt that said BABY with an arrow, but I thought she was just being fashionably retro. Either that or she wanted to make sure nobody thought it was just some rogue goiter.

God bless Britney for naming her baby Sean Preston, a nice, normal name that sounds like it came straight off *The Young and the Restless,* which is where decent regular folks get their baby names. We don't name our kids things like Coco or Mosaic or some such, because we know they'd get their ass kicked on the playground. At church.

I also loved Brit for gaining, like, a gazillion pounds while pregnant. Girlfriend ate fried okra and spoonbread and mac and cheese the whole time, and I know that the other L.A. moms must've been horrified.

(Note to Britney: If Kevin starts saying you need "to drop some elbees," remind him that you could lose 140 pounds right quick with the right divorce lawyer. Hell, you've done it before. And I don't want to say Kevin Federline isn't smart. I mean, just because he believes that Geena Davis is really the president doesn't mean he's dumb, does it?)

Britney had a C-section, which is terribly un-celebritylike.

You know, it's the celebrity moms-to-be who first popularized the doula movement. Doulas are like uppity midwives; they hate drugs and forceps and anything else truly useful. They are *très* chic! I'm sure that I will now get very earnest mail from doulas and their, uh, doulettes, about how I don't understand the incredible level of support they bring to the birth process. Then again, who cares?

I suppose if I sound bitter, it is because I've seen too many photos of Denise with her baby moments after delivery, not a hair out of place, luminescent skin and tastefully understated eye makeup. You want to see what a real woman looks like moments after birth? Watch *A Baby Story* on The Learning Channel: sweat-soaked, bloodshot eyes, doula-less.

And knowing that bump isn't going any-damned-where for at least a year.

Once baby arrives, celebrities have a new dilemma. What to do with them while mom's on the set or in the recording studio.

Well, thank goodness for a new whiz-bang video program created just for the celebrity who must be away for many hours at a time. The system allows the celebrity babies to watch a computer screen that plays a slide show of the many faces of the famous mom, accompanied by a caption identifying her as MOMMY.

Hollywood moms are crazy about this because it's tiresome to constantly have to say, "No, no, little Zeitgeist, that's not Mommy; that's Nanny. Mommy just got paid many millions of dollars to simulate the devil's aerobics with Brad Pitt. Isn't Mommy a-ma-zing?"

Of course, to a six-week-old, the caption on the video might as well say *potato* or *egomaniac,* but let's not quibble here. The intention is to make sure that there is no confusion about just who the mommy is.

This way, the procession of starched and background-checked nannies will never be mistaken for the actual birth mother. I should think it might also be helpful to switch the video to have a picture of the nanny with the words NOT THE MOMMY or ILLEGAL ALIEN as caption.

Speaking of aliens, as I write this, Tom Cruise and Katie "I'm With Crazy" Holmes are expecting a celebrity pod-baby. Yes! The seed has been successfully planted and now is growing and flourishing in the formerly Catholic womb of Ms. Katie.

I say "formerly Catholic" because, as we all know, Tom Cruise is a huge Scientologist, and he likes his women like his coffee, hot and full of beans just like him.

Let's not sugarcoat this one, hons. I don't think Tom is the baby daddy. I'm not convinced that he, uh, has it in him, so to speak. My friend Courtney agrees and repeatedly refers to the Cruise kid as "that fake-ass baby." Well, I didn't say she was my nice friend.

Tom and Katie are planning a Scientology-approved method of birthing, which consists of "silent contemplation and no drugs."

Funny thing, I don't remember childbirth as a time of silent contemplation so much as a time to turn my head all the way around in a perfect 360 spin. Hey, you say *to-mah-to*.

Celebrities love Scientology, apparently because they

don't have any decent Baptist churches out in Hollywood, so they must cling to the teachings of some guy named Ron. Scientologists believe in mind over matter. One of its biggest fans is actress Kirstie Alley. So am I the only one who thinks it's funny that she finds the gospel according to Jenny Craig much more useful than that of L. Ron Hubbard in shedding all those mind-over-matter pounds?

John Travolta (maybe *he's* the baby daddy) is a huge Scientologist and his wife, Kelly Preston, is always yammering about her Scientology birthing style.

Scientologists believe that words spoken during birth are recorded in a baby's subconscious mind and can cause irrational emotions later in life.

Ooops. Do you think the phrase, "You did this to me, you scum-sucking sack of shit" screamed repeatedly over the course of nine hours counts? If so, my bad.

I think it's hilarious that the only damn time Hollywood celebrities don't do drugs is when they're giving birth. What's wrong with this picture?

Tom Cruise says that you don't need drugs to birth a baby, because drugs are the evil spawn of the pharmaceutical industry's marriage to mainstream medicine.

He is so adamant about this that he even blames psychiatry—in a crazy-man-screaming-on-the-subway kind of way—for the Holocaust. Yes, that Holocaust.

The whole *Rosemary's Baby* feel of this particular celeb coupling is just indescribably delicious. And the tabloids have a new staple: Tom dipping Katie, apparently in a rather awkward height-compensation gesture. I'm guessing poor Katie can't even walk across the kitchen for a bowl of corn-flakes without Tom springing out and dipping her.

He dips her at the supermarket, the soccer game, walk-ing the dogs, everywhere. At last we have a replacement for the stock photo of Angelina Jolie with that eighty-pound Maddox glued to her hip or Paris Hilton with seventy-five-pound Nicole Richie glued to hers.

Oh, and speaking of Paris, she has said that she is ready to have a child. I guess this means that the future is in good hands. Of course, we don't know where they've been.

Why does Paris want kids?

"I know that kids complete your life," she said in an in-terview with *People* magazine. "I think having kids will make me happier than I am. Plus, I already treat my three puppies like kids!"

Yes, well, as long as you have a realistic notion of moth-erhood. The goal of any baby should be to bring happiness to his shallow-as-a-pie-pan mother. And if you can train that baby to eat on all fours from a five-hundred-dollar bowl bought at a Rodeo Drive boutique and shaped like a giant bone, well, so much the better!

Holy God, where is Dr. Phil when you need him? He needs to have one of those knee-touching sessions with Paris, look straight into her soulless eyes and say, "Paris, if you think raising up young'uns is the same as hauling around that

Gucci dog carrier of yours with a two-pound mutt that looks like a toilet brush with eyes, you're crazier 'n cactus juice."

Paris Hilton having a baby is just a bad idea. Parenthood is about sacrifice, and I don't mean having to choose between the dead sea mud treatment and the high colonic at your private spa.

Oh, and one more thing. If Paris is really serious about her desire to have a baby, she should probably know that if she thought that Brazilian wax was painful, she might want to hire a surrogate for the actual birthing. They're *hot*.

12

Something Stinks

And I'm Pretty Sure It's Tonya Harding

This Christmas, it seemed to me that every celebrity introduced a "signature fragrance." If all you want for Christmas is to smell just like Donald Trump, you're in luck. I haven't seen it yet, but I'm guessing that Trump Cologne smells like money. At sixty bucks for less than an ounce, it should be called Sucka. I'm sure *Apprentice* fans would love a gift set featuring Trump flanked by (much) smaller vials of George, which smells vaguely like crotchety old man, and Carolyn, which comes with its very own stick to insert up your ass, never to be removed.

Also just in time for holiday gift-giving: Britney Spears's flirty floral, Curious, rumored to attract scruffy, ill-dressed man-boys whose skills are limited to fathering children out of wedlock and—oh, sorry, that was all.

Also new this season, a citrusy mix from the folks at Adidas. Right. I'm going to buy perfume made by a company known for products that combine rubber and sweaty feet. Pass.

Paris Hilton (insert your favorite joke here) was supposed to introduce her new signature scent for the masses later, but her handlers felt that she's so hot right now that there was no sense in waiting. No name yet, but I'm rather fond of Mattressback!

Jessica Simpson has a huge line of smell'um, including a "threesome of deliciously kissable Taste." Gawd, it must be true what they always said about preachers' daughters.

Kim Cattrall, who's not really a ho but just played one on TV, has introduced Spark Seduction, and Boston Rob Mariano, a second-place finisher in TV's *Survivor,* has unveiled Foreman, which "combines scents of juniper and clean sweat." Mariano said he chose the name because he used to be a construction foreman before becoming Mr. Am-buh. Cool. I used to work in a restaurant; meet my new scent, Fry Cook.

Perhaps the weirdest celeb scent I've encountered is Full Throttle, from father-son team Paul Teutul Sr. and Jr., of *Orange County Choppers,* a cult hit on The Discovery Channel. Both Teutuls look kinda scary but, as we're reminded every year at Christmas until we just wanna puke, hardcore bikers are all just gentle giants wanting to deliver gifts to poor kids. Whatever.

The entire cast of *All My Children* has teamed with Wal-Mart to introduce Enchantment. I presume that with just one spritz you'll be transported to a fictional town where women wake up with flawless hair and makeup in the arms of their husband's best friends.

That doesn't smell; it reeks.

Of course, those are all real products available in real stores. But I believe there are so many more celebrities who could be tapped for perfume pitches. How's about Rehab, a clean new scent from Whitney Houston? (Free gift-with-purchase: Bobby Brown's spicy scent, Jail Thyme.)

Skater-turned-professional-wrestler Tonya Harding loves to talk tough, so I'm thinking her perfume might be called Smells Like Ass.

Okay, that could hurt sales.

Although the endless celebrity perfume is tiresome, it's still not so irksome as the celebrities thinking that just because they had a cameo on *Baywatch* one time, they're now ready to write for kids.

Madonna's leading the pack with an entire series of children's books. Whose idea was it to give Madonna a five-book kids' book deal? What next? A parenting book by Michael Jackson? *(What to Expect When One of Us Is Painfully Weird at Best or a Child Molester at Worst?)*

Why does every celebrity think they should write a children's book? Usually they're still feeling the last bliss of the epidural when they bark at the nurse, "Call my agent! The world *needs* my children's book!"

Sometimes it works. Fergie transformed her tattered toe-sucking image by writing a sweet series of children's books about a talking helicopter. I'm less optimistic about new poppa-of-three Jerry Seinfeld's foray into kid lit. I mean what's that gonna read like? I'm guessing: "What's the deal with porridge? I mean, is it oatmeal or is it Cream of Wheat?"

But Madonna? Does the world really need her take on Puss 'n Boots? (Then again, the original features a velvet-vested cat wearing nothing more than the vest, a smile, and some fetching thigh-high leather boots, so perhaps we have nothing to fear.)

Still, this is the woman who created a coffee table book that was so scorching, it was shrink-wrapped before it hit the stores.

One wonders what Dr. Seuss would think of Madonna's literary pursuits if he were still alive.

Perhaps something like this . . .

I would not, could not read this book
Not on a plane or by a brook
Not in a boat or on a float
So I ask you, Thing One and Thing Two
What would you, should you, have me do?
Read it? No! You ask too much!

I don't like bondage, sex, and such
What? It's sweet, it's good kids' stuff?
It's nothing nasty or even rough?
Okay, then, I shall give it a try
But keep the smelling salts standing by

Am I being harsh? Maybe. But would you let Madonna babysit your toddler? ("I spy with my little eye . . . a transvestite nun and a dozen choristers wearing nipple rings!")

I thought not.

Of course, celebrities aren't just spending their idle hours developing dubious perfumes and writing children's books. They have so much to give us all.

For instance, convicted felon and rap diva Lil' Kim has introduced a line of luxury watches that cost up to $3,500. I suppose marking time is weighing heavily on her mind these days, bless her tiny little heart.

Scruffy country crooner Willie Nelson sells BioWillie, an ecologically correct fuel that I'm guessing is composed entirely of old whiskers and sleep boogers.

You can even get a MasterCard debit card with Usher's face on it or, for the old-school types, Elvis, who continues to make huge amounts of money from the grave.

If you're having a party, don't forget the Erik Estrada gourmet chips. Did you say "Erik who?" Tsk-tsk. How could you forget his dramatic stylings as a motorcycle cop in *CHiPs*? Get it now? The chips have the bitter aftertaste of fleeting fame and broken dreams. Or maybe that was just the potassium gum.

Serve those chips with a side of Cheech Marin's Gnarly Garlic Hot Sauce. Cheech, of Cheech and Chong fame, used to be hilarious when they riffed on pot, but now he plays the gardener on *Judging Amy*. The judge better take a closer look at the plants in her mama's yard, I say.

And, finally, there's the rubber-bracelet craze ignited by Lance "Bubba" Armstrong. His Live Strong yellow rubber bracelets have raised millions for cancer research, and good for him. But don't you think we've all gotten a little carried away with the whole rubber-bracelet thing?

The other day I saw one that read ADOPT A SNIPER: ONE SHOT, ONE KILL, NO REMORSE, I DECIDE.

Kinda makes you feel all warm and gooshy inside, doesn't it.

Admittedly the sniper bands aren't nearly so popular as the ones that say DREAM and BELIEVE and even I ♥ KITTENS but it's out there.

There's even one that says NO BULLYING. I have this awful mental picture of a bespectacled, wedgie-prone, undersize middle-schooler showing that one off like Wonder Woman to the creepy bully who inevitably will steal his iPod. "But wait!" he will moan, crumpling to the floor. "Didn't you see my bracelet?"

What would Lance Armstrong think of the bracelets

that say simply BEER and SLACKER or the steel-gray one that says FBI?

Here's a hint, J. Edgar Doofus: It's unlikely that a real FBI agent would wear a rubber bracelet identifying himself that way. It would be like that fuzzy-haired undercover agent at the high school showing up in the lunchroom with a nifty tie-dye version that says NARC.

The rubber bracelets can cause confusion. If you see one embossed with a rainbow, does this mean that the wearer is gay or simply a lover of bright colors and, God forbid, unicorns?

Somewhere Lance Armstrong must be sitting in a restaurant and wondering why the teenage waitress is wearing bracelets that say HIGH MAINTENANCE, SPOILED, and DRAMA QUEEN.

And, as she turns to walk away, the faint musk of Tonya Harding trails behind her.

13

Montel's Smoking Weed

(But Will He Share with Sylvia the Psychic?)

I just read where TV talk show host Montel Williams has come out in support of legalizing marijuana for medical use. Turns out that Montel has been smoking dope for years to ease his MS symptoms. While I am happy that he has found pain relief, I have to admit that this certainly explains a lot. Everybody knows Montel's show is just one redneck family paternity test after another, with only the occasional relief of dwarf wrestling or chats with that creepy psychic lady, Sylvia something. Now we know why: The brother was high!

This should lay to rest any notion that marijuana actually makes one think more creatively. I'm picturing Montel firing up a big ol' doobie at the morning staff meeting and saying,

"A'ight, dawgs, let's do a show where we test some guy's DNA to see if he's really the father!"

While his yes-men staffers nod and say, "Great idea!" you know they're all thinking, *Tel needs to stop smokin' the chronic and give the people what they want: More Midget Weddings!*

Most of Montel's most popular shows involve repeat visits by psychic mediums. I'll admit Miss Sylvia is better than most because she just comes right out with stuff. ("Yes, your brother's in heaven and he's also sitting beside you right now. Next!") To hear Miss Sylvia tell it, we're surrounded by dead relatives, which always makes me nervous when I think about getting undressed.

Some of the TV mediums sound as if they've been getting high with Tel, though.

MEDIUM: I'm getting a message from someone named Harry. Your late father?

AUDIENCE JOE: Nope, no Harrys.

MEDIUM: Oh, my bad! Did I say Harry? I meant John.

JOE: No Johns either—sorry.

MEDIUM: He's telling me he is a pianist, this John.

JOE: Nope. But I do have a dead aunt named Clarissa who played cards a lot.

MEDIUM: Clarissa! That's who I meant, of course! (Audience cheers wildly.)

Talking about Montel getting high, wouldn't you hate to be the one in charge of bringing the little chocolate doughnuts to the morning meeting? Talk about your never-ending jobs. ("Dang I'm hawn-gry!")

Learning that Montel has basically been high since 1999 is kinda funny when you consider all those "scared straight" lectures and teen boot camps he sponsors. All he wants to do, turns out, is puff some cheeb legal-like.

And so do Walter Cronkite and Hugh Downs. That's right! I found their names, along with Montel's, on a list of celebrities who support legalizing marijuana for sick folks. And did I mention that my bunions have been driving me kuh-razy?

Says the grandfatherly Cronkite, "At the end of the day, me and the missus like to burn a coupla buddha-sticks and stare at the sunset. Dude." Okay, not really, but a girl can dream.

And Hugh "Ganja-man" Downs? Who knew? Of course, there were some nonsurprises on the list, namely Susan Sarandon and Tim Robbins, who define Hollywood hipness with their hybrid cars and illegitimate children, and Woody Harrelson, who—hello!—wears only clothes made out of hemp.

In an interview, Montel said that there are days when he doesn't even want to get out of bed.

I feel ya. The irony is that when the rich and powerful get sick, politics can get pretty strange. Witness the militaristic Montel and the conservative Nancy Reagan bravely fighting her own kind for stem-cell research. When illness hits home, it's amazing how marijuana becomes less reefer madness and more "compassionate access." Either way, I'm glad Montel's feeling groovy. Sick people should be able to find relief where they can. Word.

14

Reality Bites

Super Skanks Lewinsky and Hilton Are Fun to Watch, but Those 100-Pound Toddlers Rule!

When I first read about Fox's new reality series *The Simple Life*, I knew I wouldn't be able to resist the show about two vapid Beverly Hills honeys dumped on a rural Arkansas pig farm. I tried to fight it, hons, but, before I knew it, it was back to the Barcalounger with a box of Smart Ones éclairs, clicker in hand.

I can't resist reality TV, although I do have some standards. How's about a tiny little shout out for my refusal to watch *The Littlest Groom*?

To say that the stars of *The Simple Life*, famous ick girls Paris Hilton and Nicole Richie, appear to be shallow and self-absorbed is like saying that Joan Rivers appears to have had some cosmetic surgery.

Paris and Nicole (dumb and dumber) haven't got enough

meat on their bones to make a poor man a pot of soup, but that's not why I love to hate them. Although it certainly helps.

Of course, it doesn't take a genius to figure out why we like these Dumb Rich People shows that are sprouting up faster 'n toadstools after an Arkansas thunder-buster. They're fun to watch because we get to do a little superior dance.

I may not inherit a $360 million hotel chain, but I have sense enough to know that (in the most famous Paris pronouncement) Wal-Mart doesn't "like, uh, just sell walls."

Nicole is clearly the second banana in this show, and I'm waiting for the poor thing to figure that out. She's Gilligan to Paris's Skipper. I fully expect Paris to grab Nicole's hat and hit her over the head with it repeatedly. Nicole is the noxious wind beneath Paris's wings, limited to sighing and squealing as soon as she sees Paris sigh or squeal. The scene in which both girls recoil at the notion of plucking a chicken while Arkansas granny just shakes her head and huffs about the layabout Hollywood harlots is simply television at its finest.

Paris, whose nudie video continues to cause a stir, likes to visit the local eight-aisle Superette wearing jeans cut so low that she resembles a plumber more than a runway model. Classy!

In the earliest episodes, there appeared to be some small amount of chemistry between the Justin Timberlake–ish oldest brother in the host family and Paris, who is obsessed with discovering new ways to expose her "coin slot."

So, yes, we watch this show because it makes us feel good. We may never have enough money to casually spend $1,500 on a Gucci dog carrier like Paris (and one wonders if she really wants to buy a Nicole carrier for her little hanger-on buddy), but we can drive a straight shift without ripping the transmission out.

Yeah, we can.

Of course, some reality TV is too bad even to enjoy as a guilty pleasure. I'm thinking about the sincerely awful vehicle featuring Monica Lewinsky as the perky/wise hostess of a romantic reality and dating show. Yes, that's right. Monica Lewinsky dispensing dating advice to the lovelorn.

I was hoping we'd seen the last of the D.C. strumpet when she tearfully ran off the set of her own HBO special and into the arms of her Nutter Butter–brained mama, but nooooo. Monica has grabbed her fifteen minutes of fame, wrassled them to the ground, and is holding them—and us—hostage. She, like a bad burrito, simply won't go away.

Who can we blame for Monica's TV show, *Mr. Personality*? Could it beeee Satan? No, but you're close: the Fox Network.

In Episode One, an attractive stockbroker named Hayley must choose her ideal date from among twenty masked men. Get it? She can't see what they look like, so the guys must rely on their personalities to win her over. Personally,

I'm pulling for the troll with the one eye in the center of his forehead. As we say in the South, that oughta learn her.

Fox, in its own twisted way, probably thought the show was actually virtuous, even high-minded. After all, female contestants would be forced to date a guy based on his inner beauty.

Memo to Fox: Any guy with even an ounce of "inner beauty" wouldn't participate in this dreck.

As hostess, it would be Monica's job to act as Hayley's confidante, sharing dating advice.

If only I had had a chance to take Hayley aside, I would've told her that I know it's been a bad year for stockbrokers. (I know this because I just got the quarterly statement for my ever-dwindling 401-Kiss my money good-bye Plan and have spent most of the year mapping out a Fancy Feast retirement with my own Mr. Personality.)

But, girl, please. You do not want to take dating advice from Monica Lewinsky. Perhaps you've forgotten: Monica didn't get the guy. What's your next move? Acting classes from Mariah Carey?

Seeing Monica back in the news after so much time reminded me of a theory that I have about her: She is really an Osmond. No, really. The big black hair, the chipmunk cheeks, the Chiclets teeth. She is the Missing Osmond, the one they never talk about. The, as Donnie might say, "one bad apple."

Monica says her new job shouldn't surprise people. She

told *Newsweek* that her affair with President Clinton had made her a public figure and, "I've come to realize that I've already had my own reality show."

I can't see how to make this any tawdrier unless Fox makes Monica wolf a bowl of wriggling beetle larvae at the end of every show.

Memo to Fox: Settle down. I thought of it first.

The best reality shows are the ones that feature ordinary people. How much do we really want to watch of Farrah Fawcett carping at her bloated boyfriend, Ryan O'Neal? Give me *The Amazing Race* any day.

The thing that blows my mind is how many people will do anything to get on TV.

I have spent hours I can never get back watching TLC's trademark shows: *A Dating Story, A Wedding Story, A Baby Story*, and the like, and I can only hope that a *He Cheated and Now I'm Divorcing His Triflin' Ass Story* is in the works.

One of TLC's most popular shows is *What Not to Wear,* and, hons, it's as mean as Star Jones on Day Five of the Atkins Diet.

The premise is creepsome. Two "celebrity stylists" watch videotapes of women who dress poorly that have been *supplied by their friends and families.* (More on this later.) The stylists then confront the justifiably horrified bad dresser as she weeps into her plaid poncho with pom-poms, circa 1977, and promises to try to dress better, with their help.

The "stylists" have changed over the years. In the first

season, the show starred a flamboyant Fabio-haired Wayne Scot Lukas, who played off the diminutive and chatty Stacy London.

Mr. Lukas, who has since left the show, favored a signature look that mixed puka shells and buckskins. On camera, he was too easily distracted by the beauty of his own hair and spent much of the show flipping and tossing it about like a rather hard-faced Breck girl. In an interview, he explained that the show's important because "We all have body issues and all of our body issues are huge and all of our body issues are secrets."

Say what?

Stacy, who remains on the show with the milquetoast Clinton Somebody, dresses well enough but is as annoying as nail fungus with her constant squeals of "Shut *up!*" She says the show is all about confronting one's lack of style.

Or as Wayne Scot once put it, "When me and Stacy get you naked in a room, and we say, 'What do you hate about your body?' When they have to say it, their world crumbles."

As we vacuum the remnants of shattered self-esteem off the dressing room floor, let's consider the show's real villains, the family and "friends" who supply the humiliating videos of dear ol' Mom wearing her beloved fuzzy housecoat and bunny slippers in the privacy (ha-ha!) of her own home.

Reality TV is addictive, though. How else do you explain this disappointing vignette of my married life?

Not long ago, there was a moving and provocative documentary on PBS that detailed, in a most compelling way, the horrible racial strife in 1950s Mississippi. I knew it would be excellent, the kind of programming that makes even the no-TV nuts get their heads out of their subtitled "films" and rethink their position.

Of course, I didn't watch it. I had to see *Joe Millionaire*, in which a muscle-bound and rather vacant cutie pie courts greedy women who *think* he's a millionaire when, in fact, he's a bulldozer operator.

Oh, hons, I am *so* ashamed.

Joe Millionaire? My husband walked through the living room just as I flipped to the documentary so he'd think I was smart instead of the kind of person who secretly enjoys those awful fat baby shows on *Maury* and *Dr. Phil*. (And speaking of which, am I the only one to make the fat baby–fat mama connection? Hell-oooo.)

But I flipped channels too late. I was so busted. The moment had that kind of awful shame attached to it that is usually reserved for wolfing the last piece of cold pizza over the sink (where calories never count).

"Joe Millionaire?" he said. His tone hovered somewhere between disapproval and pity. I guess he felt like Connie Chung, who probably tells her girlfriends, "I thought I was

marrying a serious journalist, and now he has this show where he has contests to see who can pull the fat baby off the tricycle. I can hardly hold my head up at the network correspondents' dinner every year."

What is wrong with me? With our nation? Why, during a sneak preview of Fox's *Bridezilla,* which follows the weddings of the nation's most whiniest bitches, did I think, "Oh, baby, I am *so* TiVo-ing that."

Or Fox's *High School Reunion.* Typically, Fox likes lots of skin, so they plan to keep reunions to ten years, instead of, say, thirty, when it's doubtful anyone wants to bounce around the hot tub in a thong and conversations might revolve around who drove what route to get there and how steel-cut oatmeal had turned their lives and colons around.

Taking a tip from Fox, NBC's *Fear Factor* selects only female contestants with exceedingly large fake breasts and no measurable amount of body fat. These women are the kind who can convincingly make suggestive comments while devouring a plate of pig rectum. Hey, it's a gift.

I'm not proud of my viewing habits, but I can quit anytime I like. Well. Almost anytime. Dr. Phil has a 180-pound two-year-old toddler coming up, and I think he's looking for a wife.

15

Does Addiction to "Days of Our Lives" Mean That I Don't Actually Have One?

(A Life, That Is)

It's time to fess up: I have been imprisoned by a serious addiction for more than twenty-five years. The prison is in effect only from 1 to 2 p.m. Eastern Standard Time, but still.

My addiction to the idiotic *Days of Our Lives* is hugely embarrassing. I mean on the order of the time I had a big fight with my bank and emerged victorious only to discover that I had spinach glued to *every single one of my teeth*. Damn those veggie burritos.

Anyway, yes, I know that it is a stupid, stupid TV show full of cardboard cutout characters and poorly acted "plots." No matter. I find *Days* as irresistible as Horton family matriarch Grandma Alice's homemade doughnuts, which the poor ol' thing trots out for weddings, funerals, and serial killings.

HOPE BRADY: Gran, the Salem serial killer has just struck again! My father, my mother-in-law, and my stepfather-in-law are all dead!

MRS. H.: Have another doughnut, dear.

But, lately, something strange has been happening on *Days:* It's gotten interesting.

See, the serial killer who is killing off the cast one by one, sometimes as many as two a week, is none other than Salem's most esteemed psychiatrist, Dr. Marlena Evans, the sincere-faced long-legged beauty who has been the heart and soul of this show for decades.

Marlena—Doc to us—has counseled all of Salem at one time or the other, and now she's, *ick,* stabbing them with a letter opener to the carotid, outsmarting her buddies who spend much of every show saying, "We're going to get the killer. This won't happen again," but before we even go to a commercial break, oopsie, there's another body.

Truthfully, most victims have been, well, expendable. I was mildly miffed when she killed her ex-husband, Roman Brady, on his wedding day. I was hoping Roman would find true happiness with reformed whore Kate Roberts, but no.

After murdering him at his wedding reception, Marlena even comforted the grieving sorta-widow, patting her and offering the earnest-faced consolation we've come to expect.

Marlena's especially good at killing the goodhearted, dull ones like Caroline Brady and Doug Williams.

Doug was one-half of the famous DougandJulie, long-time annoying *Days* soul mates. I think they signed their checks just like that: DougandJulie. (True story: Back in the '80s, I entered a contest to win breakfast with the actors who play DougandJulie and won! They were lovely and boring just like on the show. I think I asked Doug if I could have the rest of his hash browns, and he said, "I guess.")

I know Doc's going to get caught, but it won't be anytime soon. The only one who's figured out it's Marlena is nineteen-year-old Sean, who's dating Doc's daughter, Belle, Salem's only virgin.

"Let the police handle this, son," said Sean's idiot cop father. But his cell phone crackles alive: "Oh, no! Another body!"

And time for another doughnut.

Sadly, I was forced to go cold turkey for two weeks without seeing *Days* when it was preempted by the Olympics.

Sure, you think that's pathetic, but that's just because you don't watch it. Otherwise you'd know that you can't expect people to just go on with their lives like normal when the last episode was a cliffhanger with Jennifer out there having a baby in the wilderness, Sean busting out of the house where he's been held prisoner by a psychotic wannabe girlfriend, and don't even get me started about Marlena and Roman (miraculously alive again!) making out in the jungle while his foot gets more gangrenous by the second. On top of that, Mimi thinks she's got cancer, Uncle

Mickey, 106, is gettin' some from a barmaid, and Sami just found out that her mama clawed her way out of her coffin. (You gotta love a show where the character says with a note of superiority and utter calmness, "See? I told you that Mom was buried alive, and you didn't even believe me.")

I get that it's unspeakably shallow to miss *Days* to the point of tears when the real heroes were over there in Greece, sprinting and wrestling and fencing and underwater-checkers playing and whatnot.

So I tried to really get into the Olympics and after I finally, sort of, succeeded, they ended. My life could resume, and I need never hear the painfully earnest preachings of the Rev. Bob Costas or see serious journalist Katie Couric giddily pretend to master the balance beam.

Low moment of viewing? When I simply didn't get the pole vault miscue and saw the woman sprint under the pole and told my husband, "Heck, I could do *that*."

Because I'm not a guy, I won't miss the barely there bikinis worn by the Olympic volleyball chicks. My husband says it has to do with wind resistance and improving their aerodynamic jumping abilities. He is so full of sand.

I think it has to do with them being hoochie mamas. Talented, sickeningly fit hoochie mamas, but hoochies nonetheless.

I came to the Olympics embarrassingly late and so missed the big ruckus caused by the American who won the gold, although it was later discovered, after the judges sobered up, that the guy from Taiwan was the rightful winner. There's a fascinating debate about this, but it's not nearly so fascinating as watching Bo Brady of *Days* try to decipher signals his kidnapped family is trying to transmit from a mysterious island.

Now *that's* gold-medal TV.

PART III

Vanity Flares

16

This Blonde Isn't as Dumb as You Think

Online IQ Test Proves I'm a Visionary
(Whatever the Hell That Is)

Probably the last people who are unapologetically joked about and ridiculed in public are blondes. People think we be stupid just because our hair is yeller, and they're not too shy to say so. Most folks think the average blonde doesn't know the difference between come 'ere and sic 'um.

If you don't believe it, consider that there are entire Web sites devoted to collecting and distributing dumb blonde jokes. Which reminds me, how many blondes does it take to change a lightbulb? Two. One to hold the Diet Coke and the other to call "Daaady!" I love that one.

Or this one: What do you call it when a blonde dyes her hair brunette? Artificial intelligence.

Har-dee-har-har.

The stereotype of the dumb blonde is as old as that, uh, really dark stuff that grass and trees and stuff grow in.

I started out blond. Then something strange happened in my thirties, and my hair started getting darker and darker. Call it hormones, call it genetics, call it really bad luck, but I knew immediately that I couldn't accept not being blond.

A trip to my beloved hairdresser, Brenda (pronounced "Branda" in the South), remedied the problem. It wasn't painless, my hons. No, far from it. Brenda tied a plastic rain bonnet tight on my head, then used what looked like a crochet hook to pull wisps of formerly blond hair through holes in the cap. I cried and flapped my hands and endured the pain, all in the name of being blond again. Finally, she zapped the wisps with purple goo, and two hours later, I was blonder than ever.

Naturally, I was ecstatic, but as y'all know, a few weeks later, I was *Roots: The Next Generation*. It was horrible realizing that this would have to be an ongoing process. So, for the past fifteen years, I've faithfully trotted to Brenda, who now, mercifully, uses little foil strips.

All that said, imagine my shock when Britney Spears, our national spokesmodel for all things blond, decided to go brunette, literally and figuratively returning to her roots. One week, she's blond as God and Preference by L'Oréal intended and doing things like marrying and divorcing in a day, and the next, she dyes her hair, becomes a brunette, and starts studying Jewish mysticism.

On behalf of blondes everywhere, what up?

Oh, Britney, must we turn to Christina Applegate or—horrors!—Courtney Love as our leader now?

As a blonde in mind, spirit, and bottle, I'm not worried. The ability to do math and chew gum at the same time is highly overrated. Britney'll be back.

As if losing my blondeness isn't bad enough, lately something strange has been happening with my eyeballs.

For a year or so now, I've gotten lots of snickers from friends who think it's odd that I read my menu at arm's length.

"Arms too short?" Heh, heh, heh.

"Isn't it time you got some reading glasses?"

"The same thing happened to my eyes when I turned fifty."

Fifty?!

I'm not fifty, although I can sort of make it out as a blurry image in the not-so-distant future. Yes, yes, I realize that "getting older beats the alternative," but I am a vain creature.

When I recently asked the waiter at a fancy restaurant for a pair of "house reading glasses," he looked at me with the same disdain as if I had asked for a foam doughnut to sit on.

My friend who is a little younger than me recently had a miniature nervous breakdown after a department store clerk cheerily deducted an extra 15 percent "because today is Senior Day!"

"What does that have to do with me?" my friend asked innocently, still not understanding the full horror of what had been bestowed on her forty-two-year-old self.

"Well," continued the smiling and clueless clerk, "see, on Tuesday, everybody fifty-five or older gets an additional discount!"

"You think I'm fifty-five?" she asked, an edge of hysteria creeping into her voice.

"Well, uh, uh, well."

Although I haven't been offered the Senior Day discount, I have experienced a sad, nostalgic tug as the grocery store clerk doesn't even bother to look up to okay my wine purchase.

Oh, of course, I don't look twenty-one, or even double that, but it would just be so much fun if she would falter, just for a nanosecond, before punching the override key.

When it's time to write the check and I fumble for the reading glasses that now live in the bottom of my purse in complete denial, I could swear she sighs and rolls her eyes.

Not long ago, as I stood in the grocery line, a nice man in his seventies, I'd guess, noticed my giggling six-year-old as she completed the joyous task of choosing between Gummi Savers and Nerds.

"Lord-a-mercy, don't we love our grands!" he said with a kindly chuckle.

I thought he meant the biscuits, so I nodded enthusiastically. I was halfway to my car with the bag boy ("Ma'am, do you need help with that? I mean what *is* your bone density these days?") before the full impact hit. Grands? *Grands?* Bring on the Botox, hons. I'm not going down without a fight.

The awful truth is that, if I have to choose between being a dumb cute blonde or a smart mousy brown, I'm going with cute every time. Fortunately, I don't have to choose. Although I've always thought that smarts-wise, I'm somewhere between the two Simpsons—Jessica and Marge—it turns out I'm a genius.

At least that's what the on-line IQ test I took said.

It turns out that there are like a million of these on-line IQ tests out there in cyberspace. (That's ten hundred thousand to the rest of you.) Some are sponsored by Mensa, the worldwide organization of smart people. In my experience, Mensans tend to be a bit belligerent about how smart they are. (I say belligerent, but I could also have said haughty, pugnacious, or quarrelsome. See how smart I is?) They're also disproportionately fond of medieval fairs and *Star Trek* conventions and living in their mamas' basements.

So, anywho, I took the IQ test, and guess what? I'm, like, a *genius!* Right. I already told you that. Okay, technically, they didn't use the G-word once my score was computed, but they did say that I fit the profile of a "visionary philosopher." Well, roll me up and call me curly! Who knew?

I was so excited with my score (it's tacky to brag, but let's just say it was in the, ahem, 140s) that I shoved the printout under hubby's nose at breakfast the next morning.

"Read it and sleep," I said triumphantly.

"You mean weep?" he asked.

"Whatever."

So he read the analysis and damned near choked on his Cheerios when he read the part about me having "a powerful mix of skills and insight, like Plato."

"You sure they don't mean Pluto?" he joked.

Now wasn't that an odious, repugnant thing to say?

I suppose the reason he questioned my test results was a single sentence that referred to my "exceptional math and verbal skills."

This phrase did not have the ring of verisimilitude because I am famously bad at math. If I'm in charge of tipping at a restaurant, the waiter will either fall to his knees in gratitude or slash my tires. There ain't no Mr. In Between.

The results of my IQ test said that as a visionary philosopher, I can "anticipate and predict patterns." It's so true. Don't I know, instinctively, every time the clearance at Stein Mart is going to jump from 50 to 75 percent? It's God-given; you can't learn it.

You're probably worried that, from now on, I'm going to write about just boring visionary stuff, but I'm not. One must bloom where one is planted. I think Pluto said that.

17

The Butcher's Great, the Baker's Suffering

But How Is the Anti-Carb Frenzy Affecting the Candlestick Maker?

It's official. Every human being I know is now on the Atkins Diet. Sure, they look kind of silly, sitting there eating puddles of spaghetti sauce without the noodles underneath like God and Emeril intended, but they're *serious*. No side of garlic bread for them. But, yes, please, another eight-pound meatball!

Like most women my age who eat a lot of fudge and don't exercise, I've gained a bit of weight recently, and so I decided that the Atkins Diet was worth a try. Any diet that encourages mass consumption of T-bones and kielbasa sausages can't be all bad, right?

Wrong. I lasted exactly thirty-two hours on the Atkins Diet and have no intentions of ever trying it again. Without carbohydrates—and lots of them—I discovered that I really did have the capacity to take another's life. And *enjoy* it.

Particularly if the "other" was eating a big, fat yeast roll in front of me. In which case we would, once again, trot out the "but, Yer Honor, he needed killin' " defense so popular in our South.

Carbohydrates, from the Latin, *carbo* which means "yummy" and *hydrates* which means "cinnamon bun," are not something I can eliminate or even drastically cut back on.

There is no joy in a steak without a baked potato, a hot dog without a bun, a casserole without noodles, a movie starring Jimmy Fallon.

The late Dr. Atkins believed that restricting carbs would cause the body to burn up its stored fat faster. Ha! That might work for most people, but I can assure you that my body, in thirty-two hours, was already plotting new and more embarrassing places to store fat.

I don't dispute that the Atkins Diet works for most people. I've seen women shed fifty pounds in a matter of weeks using this diet. The only bad part is that if you slip up and eat, say, a single French fry or a saltine, you will wake up twenty pounds heavier. It's cruel that way.

Weight Watchers makes more sense to me, and that would be my first choice of diets except they assign "points" to food, and this involves a lot of math, calculating the dietary fat grams divided by the calories and then converting it all into these "points."

According to WW, I am entitled to a measly 23 points a day but I'd use up 18 of them in just one order of Taco Bell's Nachos Bell Grande, or, as I like to call it, heaven on a cardboard plate.

The South Beach Diet is similar to the Atkins Diet in that carbs are a huge no-no in the beginning. Bill Clinton lost lots of weight on the South Beach Diet, but then he had heart bypass surgery, so I'm not so sure about it. Also, South Beach has a *lot* of rules. The book weighs, like, eight tons or so. I think most South Beachers lose the weight not by following all the instructions so carefully but simply by lugging that stupid book around.

The Zone delivers steady weight loss that's not so quick or so visible as Atkins and South Beach, but it also has a lot of rules, and the supplements and exotic Zone-sanctioned meals (fillet of froufrou with a side of pistachio-encrusted doodahs) ain't cheap. The Zone believes that you can best lose weight if you balance protein and carbs in a 40–30–30 mix. That's 40 percent protein, 30 percent carbs, and 30 percent of something else that I can't remember, so just substitute fried Snickers bars for that one.

With all these diets around, we've all become completely carb-phobic. The other day, I was in Subway eating my favorite Jared-sanctioned six-inch veggie on whole wheat when a rather portly *total stranger* walked up and asked, "Do you realize how many CARBS are in that thing?"

He couldn't have looked more horrified if I'd been sitting there eating a shit sandwich. He then took a seat across the aisle from me and unwrapped what appeared to be turkey, bacon, ham, pepperoni, and a leg of lamb all wrapped up in a strange little scrap of brown crepe so thin you could read your Atkins Diet book through it.

One after another, customers came in and ordered "Atkins sauce" on their "sandwiches." I can only imagine that this is actual blood from a meat-producing animal.

The thing about Atkinsians is that they are a trifle high and mighty, aren't they? "Oh, I can't eat that. I'm doing Atkins!" Don't get so uppity, fool. It's not like you're becoming a missionary or something.

A waiter friend says he's regularly berated by women who scream "Get that out of here!" I mean it's hot bread, not a rabid possum, he's bringing to the table with cute little shell-shaped butter pats on a doily.

The stranger who had criticized my veggie sub finished his whatever-it-was and stopped by my table to tell me that his mother—*his mother*—was about my age, and she was losing a lot of weight with Atkins.

Okay, here's the thing. Don't assume that a woman is on a diet. My husband likes me just the way I am. He points out that he doesn't have to "shake the sheets to find me," and that's the way it's going to stay.

The Atkins lingo is confusing, too.

"We're in the induction phase now," a friend confided over two pounds of bacon the other morning.

"I'm so sorry," I said, missing her meaning. "But y'all can try again or even get a surrogate."

What the hell are they talking about?

Carbohydrates have become the new embodiment of evil. Did you know that if you rearrange the letters in the word *Carbohydrate,* it spells "Cameron Diaz can't act"? Yeah, I know I made it up, but that's what we crazy carbmonsters do. We lie! Don't blame us: It's the gluten. Makes a girl do strange things.

Men and women both diet, of course, but men don't take it as seriously as we do. My friend Lisa came home from work the other day to a horrific sight.

There was her loving husband, still wearing his suit and tie from work, holding a just-opened bottle of Miller Lite and . . . weighing himself.

That's right. Standing on the scales in front of God and everybody, *casually* checking his weight at the end of the day.

"What are you *doing?*" Lisa shrieked.

Her husband looked at her curiously, as if she were, somehow, the crazy one. Then he cocked his head a bit, which as every woman knows, can actually make you weigh three ounces more.

"I'm checking my weight," he said. "Something wrong?"

Oh, yes, my friend. Something is very, very wrong. No

woman on the face of the earth would actually stand, fully dressed at the end of the day, on a set of scales. I mean besides Renée Zellweger, who, let's face it, practically has HELP ME! scrawled across her bony little chest these days.

For Lisa's husband to weigh himself while holding a beer is too much to bear. Might as well spit into my "burns more fat" yogurt.

Women know that there are some essential guidelines to the proper weigh-in. For starters, you weigh only in the morning, before breakfast and after all bodily functions have been attended to. Women weigh after flossing, Q-tipping their ears, and even blowing their noses. Every possible source of added weight must be eliminated.

Also, and this should go without saying, you have to weigh yourself buck nekkid. I have seen grown, professional women (okay, me) sob in protest at stepping on a doctor's office scale while fully clothed.

ME: This dress is heavily beaded; you'll need to deduct at least twelve pounds.

NURSE: I don't see any beads.

ME: What are you? The frickin' *bead police?*

So I told my husband about Lisa's insensitive lout of a husband, but he didn't get it. "What's the big deal with women and weight? I mean, why are you so worried? What do you weigh, anyway? One twenty? One twenty-five?"

Suddenly, I felt much better. "Yes," I said. Well. Maybe in outer space.

18

Fashion Forecast

Run, Run Rudolph, Nipple Jewelry for Morons, and Get Thee a Behind, You!

My closest friends have warned me that I don't have the guts to write about this subject, but that's what they said when I wrote about artificial testicles for neutered dogs, so who's laughing now? Well, probably not the dogs.

A dedicated humor writer doesn't shy away from the tough stories, the ones that might even make a few enemies. And that's why it's time to take on a subject that is hallowed to many women, even a religion of sorts. I speak, of course, of the holiday sweater cult.

Those of you who are reading this whilst fingering the delicate silver bells attached to the meticulously embroidered reindeer tableau that is dancing across your chest might want to bail now.

I never noticed the cult until my daughter started

kindergarten, although I'm not a big fan of "character wear" in general. There's just something not quite right about those grown women who wear Tweety Bird sweatshirts over their leggings at the mall. I mean unless you run a daycare center, isn't it time to move on and get Road Runner off your chest? And nobody over the age of ten should ever wear any article of clothing that announces I TAWT I TAW A PUDDYTAT. Talk about a cry for help.

But I digress. It's the holiday sweater cult that has got me in a swivet. At the kindergarten Fall Festival, I apparently didn't get the memo that I must wear an elegant themed sweater painstakingly adorned with pumpkins, ghosts, and bats.

Some of these sweaters are insanely expensive. One cult member confided to me that she once spent $250 for a butter-soft wool sweater with dancing candy canes and nutcrackers prancing around her neck. Her eyes danced, her voice became high-pitched—she wanted me to drink the Kool-Aid, no question.

Class wars are evident. You've got your $14.98 Frosty the Snowman from Wal-Mart versus your $200 Brighton version from the prissy boutique with the size 0 sales staff, and don't think the cult members won't know the difference.

Far be it from me to question another's sense of fashion (I did, after all, wear a mod paper dress in junior high during an unfortunate Carnaby Street phase) but this whole cutesy-wootsy, elves-are-eating-my-brain thing where you own an entire wardrobe of sweaters with buttons that can be pushed to play "The Twelve Days of Christmas" is beyond me.

One friend told me she has enough sweaters to wear a different Christmas sweater from December first to twenty-fifth. My only response was, "Why?"

Fashion is a hobby for me. I'm fascinated by women who spend five hundred dollars on a single pair of high heels. Even if I had that kind of dough, I wouldn't do it, because somewhere in the back of my noggin sits Sally Struthers pitifully imploring me to "Please help Save the Children." (And the awful, shameful me always thinking, *Whoa, Sally, if you'd ease up on the Toaster Strudels, you could save a few right there.*)

So, no, I can't spend five hundred dollars for shoes. Guess I'm just too much of a hick. Here's another confession: I don't own a single piece of nipple jewelry.

I read recently where Janet Jackson's personal stylist spent hours perusing nipple jewelry before he found that now-legendary sunburst design that was revealed during the Super Bowl halftime show.

Who the hell has enough money to hire someone to shop for her nipple jewelry? It makes me feel downright dowdy for getting excited about finally buying one of those shirts with my initial on it. Shopping for nipple jewelry? Doesn't Janet ever need just, you know, socks?

My daughter, a huge Justin Timberlake fan who even has a little silver 'N Sync cell phone that is programmed to call her and say good night every night from J. T. himself, was eager to watch the Super Bowl halftime show.

So while hubby showered, as he does during all Super Bowl halftime shows, even if we're at other people's houses (what can I say—the man hates pageantry), the princess and I settled in to see her beloved Justin perform.

I like to consider myself a modern mom, capable of handling discussions of sex and stuff without blushing and flapping. Still, I was unprepared for the big rip-off. I stopped my Dorito in midcrunch. What was that?

I didn't even notice the, uh, boob. I was wondering what that thing was attached to it, and I don't mean Justin's paw.

"Mommy," pondered Precious, "why did Justin rip that lady's top off?"

Channeling the wisdom of my foremothers (who am I kidding—all they had to worry about was not dying in childbirth, making homemade soap out of cow ear wax, and doing the nasty in the same bed where your eleven children are trying to sleep), I decided to answer her question honestly.

"Ratings, sugar. It's all about shock and awe, corporate greed, and a culture that is increasingly morally challenged."

"You talk funny, Mommy."

All was forgiven that night when her 'N Sync phone rang right at bedtime with a cheery "Sleep tight, and don't let the bedbugs bite!" from Justin. Amazing how he can do all that *and* find time to expose Janet Jackson's dinners on national television.

Thank heavens the NFL issued an official statement condemning the halftime show antics as "embarrassing, offensive, and inappropriate" and all but called for its smelling salts and shawl. I can only assume that this means that from now on, all NFL cheerleaders will be wearing burkas and shimmying only slightly suggestively.

Right. That'll happen.

All I want is for someone to please tell Janet Jackson where Talbots is.

She might want to focus on another part of her admittedly buff body. According to fashion insiders, "The boob, it's been done. It's old, but the butt is new!" Only fashionistas can say something like that without cracking themselves up.

What are they talking about? Buttocks cleavage, you fashion Neanderthal. BC is taking over the nation. Open your eyes and see for yourself. The look once popularized by jovial plumbers everywhere is now hotter 'n fish grease.

Not blessed with an audacious onion? Fear not, Jane Hathaway! Buttocks implants are the new must-have accessory for the true fashionista. Just ask Paris Hilton. But remember to speak very slowly.

In case you still don't get the picture, let plastic surgeon Bruce Nadler of New York City explain it to you: "You want two mounds that are very discrete so you have a valley in between them. It's like having the perfect push-up bra," except for the fact that it's on your ass.

This is all, of course, another example of plastic surgery following fashion. All those low-rise jeans out there, the ones with the quarter-inch-long zippers, means a lot of butt gets exposed in the process. With surgery, you can actually have your butt puffed up to make rear-end cleavage to keep your pants more interesting. I know! I know! I'm dizzy with the possibilities myself!

It should be only a matter of time before the "front butt" look popularized by overweight women who prefer very tight pants while cruising the aisles of Wal-Mart becomes the new must-have accessory. ("You wanna see some front butt, honey? When I wear my orange stretch capris, you can't tell whether I'm a-comin' or a-goin'!")

To go along with all this low-rise, puffed-up-butt trend, you'll want to add a very large tattoo. Turns out that a tattoo that shows just, like, the top third of an eagle, sunset, or some such before disappearing into the jeans completes the look. As explained by one excited New York tattoo artist, "The lower back is what the ankle was!"

Okay, let's see if I got this straight. The butt is the new breast, and the lower back is the new ankle. Now if only we could figure out where the brain has moved.

19

Ass-Lifting, Face-Tightening, Boob-Bustin' Products

Right On or Rip-Off? You'll Have to Ask My Pantyhose

I hate to admit it, but *The Swan* has gotten inside my head, and I can't get it out. Every time I look in my mirror, I hear the velvety voice of the hit reality TV show's fancy-pants Beverly Hills plastic surgeon saying, "She will, of course, need a brow lift, upper and lower face lift, liposuction on the cheeks, buttocks, chin, inner and outer thighs, calves, ankles, and eyelids, breast augmentation, nose job, tummy tuck, gum tissue recontouring, Zoom bleaching, dental veneers, a lip lift, hair extensions, and—oh what the hell—a brand new head."

I know that *The Swan* has made a lot of thoughtful people ponder the disturbing shallowness of a culture that pursues, at all costs, some random notion of "beauty." But not being a thoughtful person, it just made me wonder if I shouldn't apply for the next installment.

The only bad part would be that *Swan* contestants are allowed only three ten-minute phone calls home a week for four months. That's not nearly enough time to explain, in painstaking detail once again, where I "hide" the laundry detergent (on the shelf above the washer—call me devil-may-care!) or the princess's SpongeBob macaroni and cheese (the pantry!) or, naturally, the car keys.

One of the biggest complaints critics of *The Swan* have is that the show deliberately selects sad sacks with zero self-esteem just to boost ratings. Hons, that's just good story-telling, if you ask me. When one aspiring *Swan* was being wheeled into a seven-hour surgery, she tried three times to call her husband for a few last-minute words of encouragement only to be told he was on a smoke break.

Ewww.

On the final night, when an ultimate Swan was crowned, I had a chance to look at the husbands, who were all in the range from extremely ordinary to butt ugly. Of course, it was a little hard to see through the veneer of drool during the cheesy lingerie competition, when the contestants trotted out their new "full D" figures.

It was some consolation that pageant winner Rachel Love-Fraser chose not to enhance her smallish bust, a curiously satisfying victory for those of us who just dream of being a "full A."

Lest you think Fox was insensitive to every need of these women, consider that they hired a "life coach" to help counsel the women during their four months of mirrorless isolation.

Still, I was underwhelmed by Coach Nely Galan's approach to at least one weepy and bandage-wrapped contestant: "Do you realize how many people would love to have this chance? I'm honestly disappointed that you're not trying harder."

Like they say, with a life coach like that, who needs flesh-eating bacteria?

We women do crazy things to make sure that we look our best.

My friend Patsy Jo is getting ready to attend her thirtieth high school reunion, and she has prepared for it in a sane and sensible way: She has ordered Face Lift in a Bottle.

Apparently you paint the stuff on your face, and the goo has a tightening, lifting effect that makes you look years younger. The only thing is, it lasts only about six hours, so you could be taut and fabulous at cocktail hour and seem to have aged horribly by the end of dessert.

I'd like to try it for my next reunion, but I'm afraid I'd screw up the application and come out looking like a cross between Joan Rivers and the Elephant Man. Or I'd use too much and end up looking like one of those raku crackle pots.

Although I'd never heard of Face Lift in a Bottle, I have tried a few beautifying remedies of my own that smacked of quackery. The weirdest one was something called the Amazing Disappearing Double Chin-Strap, a sweaty band of very tight latex that you strapped on in hopes of eliminating the dreaded midlife double chin. The ads made it sound so easy: "Wear Amazing Disappearing Double Chin-Strap while you do your household chores!"

Friends who dropped by were treated to quite a sight. "What *happened?*" they'd shriek. "Were you in a car wreck?"

"No, silly!" I would say. "It's going to get rid of my double chin."

Actually, I had to sign most answers because my lips had been pushed up to my nose, making normal conversation difficult.

After weeks of faithfully wearing the gizmo, I had to admit there was no difference, and I tossed it. The only good news was that I could finally stop doing household chores.

There was also a failed experiment in do-it-yourself breast augmentation. I have a number of friends who have gotten boob jobs from a licensed plastic surgeon, but that stuff costs money. Nope, I decided I would try Beauti-Breast instead. The way it works is that you place your tatas inside two funnel-shaped cups that attach to "any household faucet or spigot." (I don't know the difference either, except I think spigots are usually outside, and this was definitely not going to be something I did in my driveway.)

Once hooked up, you turned on the water and, according to "scientific research," the tremendous volume of water shooting through the funnels would somehow lead to what scientists refer to as "really big tits."

It was a rip-off, of course. It would've been much cheaper to strap myself, topless, to the hood of my car next time it went through the Auto Spa.

All this just proves there is no magic fountain—or even spigot—of youth and beauty, sister-hons. Only through rest, exercise, and healthy diet can we help ourselves look our best.

I know; I crack myself up.

The latest national beauty obsession is to have teeth so bright that we can use them to read at night. ("Aim your choppers over here, Martha, I can't see the *TV Guide* crossword.")

Don't get me wrong. I like white teeth as much as the next person. Someday, I even hope to own some, although there's a better than even chance that they'll be the kind that must sit, grinning maniacally, from the confines of a watery glass beside my bed.

The real thing just seems like too much work. For example, those ubiquitous whitening strips that brag that you can discreetly brighten your smile while you go about your life, even while working out! But I don't want to work out. Do they have any that work if you just want to sit on your ass and watch *Judging Amy*?

"I'm getting a whiter smile," says the smarty-pants spokesmodel on the commercial, as she, like, jumps from a plane or something else more exciting than my typical day: folding laundry while simultaneously eating the last of the mini-Snickers from Halloween.

People have become so obsessed with whiter teeth that those of us who don't use strips, gels, brush-ons, and trays are starting to look like Austin Powers in comparison.

I actually met a young woman the other day whose teeth were so white, they were blue.

"Your teeth are amazing," I said, though it was hard for her to hear me because I was speaking from behind my hand, suddenly ashamed of my own teeth, less knockout than Niblets.

"I know," she said, smiling even wider.

"I think you just put my eyes out."

A check of some of the teeth-whitening products out there reveals that you can actually get your teeth eleven shades whiter if you have them professionally bleached. Eleven shades! What are they using? Clorox? I think I'll take my wine-stained best tablecloth to the dentist next time I go.

Recently, I read a testimonial for a professional bleaching product from a young couple who spent the month before their wedding getting their teeth custom-bleached so their smiles would match on their big day. Haven't these idiots ever heard of Photoshop? Hons, if I got married today, I'd have those wedding photos shave off my hips, whiten my smile, and give me the bust that I have so richly deserved all my life.

And to think, the only thing we used to worry about was making sure the bridesmaids' dresses matched the punch.

Everything's so complicated now, what with all these products to make us gorgeous. Even the simple act of buying pantyhose is maddening. Gone are the days when you could just buy that little L'Eggs egg, size B, nude, sheer toe.

When I went pantyhose shopping recently, I discovered that a lot has happened, not much of it good.

Did I want pantyhose infused with microencapsulated caffeine or grapefruit scents?

No thanks. The way my thighs rub together, I'd smell like Starbucks all day, and that would just lead to me and everyone around me craving triple-fat mochaccinos, and then where would we all be? Size C, that's where.

The theory behind injecting grapefruit and caffeine into hosiery is that it makes it last longer, even after repeated washings. This is, to use the technical term, utter crap.

Some pantyhose boast of chemical additives to make you feel better as you walk. I'm guessing the nude, size B, Vicodin pantyhose are particularly popular with movie stars.

The rest of us must settle for pantyhose injected with things like "jojoba." I'm not sure what jojoba is, but I'm pretty sure I don't want it anywhere near my noonie.

I also discovered something called "bum boost" pantyhose by Pretty Polly for sagging buttocks. (And, yet again, I'm struck by what a terrific name that would be for a rock band: Sagging Buttocks.) This is great! Next time hubby asks why I'm acting like I have my ass on my shoulders, I can just smile and say, "I do, and it's all thanks to Pretty Polly!"

The most popular of the new breed of pantyhose promises to reduce cellulite. As you walk, tiny encapsulated anti-cellulite lotions are working to massage your dimpled thighs into smoothness. (See "utter crap," above.)

Look. Cellulite is a hereditary curse. Some friends and I once spent six months dutifully rolling our thighs with rolling pins every morning and evening to "break up the cellulite." It was a dismal failure, so we eventually came to our senses and went out for pie.

There's also "age-defying" pantyhose. Now this is exciting, indeed. I love the idea of defiant pantyhose getting themselves all worked up over every little thing. What's that, Officer? You think I was speeding? Well, let's just see what my pantyhose have to say about that, mister.

"Let your pantyhose work hard for you!" says the advertisement. I couldn't love this more. I'm taking a break and letting my new pantyhose write for a while.

As long as the caffeine's in 'em, they should do just fine.

The truth is, no matter how much we primp and preen and how much we spend on cosmetics (I once accidentally spent forty-eight dollars for a La Prairie lip gloss and, trust me, this is nothing Laura Ingalls Wilder ever used), you're still going to have spinach-teeth or, in my case, a third breast.

When you have a book published, a funny thing happens: People who know perfectly well that you write for a living suddenly expect you to also be able to do radio and TV shows, spin plates on a stick, whatever! Writers are used to working alone. We sit around in our pajamas, watching the world go by from a small upstairs home office whose windows really need cleaning and whose psychedelic curtains that seemed so cool five years ago now look stupid, like Marilyn Manson's idea of a nursery window topper.

To push your book, you must do dozens of radio and TV shows. Recently, while being interviewed on a half-hour TV show, I thought things were going swimmingly until, during the break, one of the cameramen walked over and said, "Uh, could you adjust your shirt? It kinda looks like you got a third breast in there."

Okay, so *now* I'm completely relaxed. While my jaw drops at this horrible revelation, I hear the host say cheerily, "And we're back!" The camera cuts to me, but I can't be bothered. Suddenly, I'm pulling and jerking on my puckered sweater like it's a straitjacket. When the host asks a question, I don't even look up, just mumble, "Huh? Yeah, okay, just let me fix this."

And then there was the time that my cat fell asleep on my face (don't ask) and gave me poison ivy just two days before I was supposed to go on the road for a book tour.

This is incredibly ironic when you're telling everybody

that your book is called *We're Just Like You, Only Prettier*. Scratching my cheeks raw and covered in oozing red sores and patches of white calamine lotion, I made small children run from me. "Wait!" I cried. "Come back! I don't usually look like this. Come back! Wanna see my third breast?"

PART IV

Huzzzbands

20

The Paradoxical Male

Smart Enough to Find "Me Time," but Dumb Enough to Get Stuck Buying the Tampons

My husband took advantage of our state's "tax-free" weekend as only a man can. While I sat home clipping coupons to save seventy-five cents on Cinnamon Life cereal, he was out buying a computer, something called a wireless broadband router (I have no idea), a PC bundle pack that includes lots of stuff we already have, and . . . a shiny new bicycle!

You have to love that after a tough morning of computer buying, doggone it, he deserved some "me time" on his very own new bike. Men.

"I didn't know bikes qualified for tax-free," I huffed.

"Oh, it didn't," he said. "But it was so big and red and shiny."

Apparently lobotomies were on sale, too. Hubby then

explained that, thanks to his smart, tax-free shopping, we had actually saved $136 in sales tax.

Whoa, now. This is *my* argument, the old spend-money-to-save-money one that he always refutes when it comes to truly useful stuff like a butter-soft leather trench in teal that matches my eyes.

"There's more!" he said, practically dancing about the room. "There's a rebate on everything—well, except the bike, of course."

Oh, goody. Now I get to experience that particular circle of hell known as rebate redemption.

That afternoon, I gathered together the rebate forms, including lengthy rules for redemption, and a box cutter that would be used to either carve the original UPC from the boxes or to end my life, whichever seemed more appealing.

After an hour or so spent looking for the serial number for one product, I called the toll-free "rebate question hotline for doofuses." A computer-generated voice told me where to find it, and let's just say I felt pretty stupid, like the kind of person who couldn't find her serial number in the dark with both hands and a flashlight. It was right there in tiny print beneath the bottom quarter flap of the third perpendicular.

I wanted my mommy.

Next, I started to work with the box cutter to remove the UPCs. Except there were lots of them. Those little barcodes were everywhere, and they all looked different.

Which was the right one? Another call to the hotline resolved that, too—although was it my imagination or was the computerized voice growing impatient with me?

Finally, I needed a legible copy of the store sales receipt with appropriate items circled in ink, a copy of the ESN (who knows?), my college transcript, voter registration card, and Penney's bra-and-panty-club membership card.

Well, almost.

By nightfall, I'd driven to the copy shop twice and was only halfway through the paperwork. I needed help, but hubby had gone for a bike ride "to unwind."

Men just don't take things as seriously as women do. It's not just that we do all the rebates, Mother's Day gift-buying, and so on, but they just don't think anything's all that serious.

If you don't believe me, consider these two words: Hooters Air.

Men are the brains (sort of) behind the nation's newest and orangest airline. Up in those ultrafriendly skies, I'm guessing every cloud has a silicone lining.

Only a man could dream up an airplane full of attentive, buxom, chirpy Hooters girls wearing barely there tangerine hot pants serving drinks and snacks.

The "airline's" press people have been very careful to point out that, in the event of an emergency, you will not be expected to rely on a Hooters Girl to save your sorry self. That's right; not even by grabbing one to use as a flotation device, tempting as that might be.

The real flight attendants will be doing all the safety drills and such. Great. It's high school all over again, with the bookish, flat-chested women trying to get you to listen and respect us—er, them—while the cheerleader with the stupendous tatas is happily doing cartwheels in the background and getting all the attention.

What a Hooters Air passenger should hear: "Please place your tray tables in an upright and locked position."

What he does hear: "Hi, my name is Tawny, and I like spring mornings and newborn puppies."

So far, business is good—and it's no wonder. Whoever filed this business plan was no boob. Cheap fares, golf packages, *and* big balambas? That's like the holy trinity to most of the men I know. Throw in a bottomless bowl of Doritos, *SportsCenter* on the overhead TV monitors, and a case of Coronas, and you've pretty much got the recipe for Complete Male Bliss.

It's unlikely that Hooters Air, with its fleet of gently used 737s that are probably way older than the average Hooters Girl, will ever need to file for bankruptcy, unlike its snooty, humorless competition. I predict no need for a "federal bailout" or similar silliness.

I think that US Airways and the rest of the bankrupt airlines should take a lesson from Hooters Air. Stop taking yourselves so seriously with your "business class" and your blah-blah-blah endless CNN Headline News. Put a little fun back into flying. Pilots, show us some chiseled calf muscles!

There's something delightfully, guiltily un-PC about Hooters Air. Oh, sure, I know I'm supposed to be all of-fended and indignant (further objectifying women, what*ever*) but, try as I might, I can't even work up a mild, powdered-cappuccino froth on this one.

It's the same reaction I have to the annual slew of let-ters from outraged school librarians canceling subscriptions to *Sports Illustrated* after the swimsuit issue comes out. "Well, I never!" they always huff. Probably not. But I'll bet Tawny has.

Men aren't really pigs, of course. They just know what they want (see shiny red bike, above), and they aren't ashamed of it.

Men, as my husband continues to remind me, are ex-tremely simple creatures. Still not convinced? Then maybe you need to read a study that found that male geniuses make their greatest scientific discoveries all because they want to get laid.

The study of male scientists has discovered that geniuses do their best work in their early thirties (before their brains shrivel to the size of a grape tomato) and that work stems from a need to impress a member of the opposite sex. *New Scientist* magazine reported that "the male competitive urge to attract females is a driving force for scientific achieve-ments."

This explains why Albert Einstein, who, bless his heart, had a face that would stop a clock and raise hell with small watches, didn't sweat the personal grooming stuff. He knew that the way to get the babes was to, like, invent something. ("Won't go to the Scientists' Pot Luck Supper with me? Well, would you go with the inventor of the theory of relativity? I thought so.")

Louis Pasteur, famous for discovering a way to heat liquids to prevent the growth of bacteria, a process known as Louisization, I believe, was all in it for the babes, although his favorite pickup line could've used a little work. ("Come upstairs, and I'll show you an explosion of activity in my petri dishes!")

Jonas Salk was just another unmotivated Generation A'er until he discovered the vaccine for influenza while trying to attract the attentions of any future Mrs. Salks.

The study said that genius men (loosely defined as any man who can close a kitchen cabinet door) "do what they do to win the sexual attention of women."

Sure, it all seems less noble when you realize that all the genius scientists are out there fiddling with cancer cures just to score with the hot new girl scientist in the lab, but I say the end justifies the means.

If you put singer and lingerie model Kylie Minogue actually in the lab, we'd probably see a battle that would make *Freddy Vs. Jason* look like a meeting of the Women's Missionary Union.

Unfortunately, such hormone-driven genius doesn't last very long. The study found that, as the competitive drive decreases with age, men geniuses shift their priorities from "competing for women to taking care of their offspring."

This means that once a male genius nears forty and has children, his once-great mind loses its ability to do much of anything except argue with T-ball coaches and carp about the price of gasoline.

The report also found that marriage significantly dampens the male genius's desire for scientific achievement, perhaps because he must now accept the fact that he will occasionally be dispatched to the grocery store for diapers and tampons. It's a place where, his wife assures him, "nobody cares about your big ol' brain."

So he will wander the aisles, remembering past glories. And he'll be inexplicably drawn to the grape tomatoes.

21

Animal Instincts

Meet My New Rock Band—
The Cancer-Smelling Dogs!

When I sent my husband and daughter to "look at the cute kittens" at the pet store one Saturday morning, I have to admit it was just to get them out of the house so I could finally watch the finale of *For Love or Money 2*.

Thirty minutes later, my six-year-old was calling on the cell phone.

"Please, Mommy," she started slowly; then the rest came spilling out: "He's-so-cute-he-lets-me-hold-him-and-he-purrs-a-lot-and-I-wanna-name-him-Button."

Oh, for shit's sake. Good thing I hadn't sent them to the Lexus dealership or we'd be living off mayonnaise sandwiches. Again.

"Honey," I said, freeze-framing that little swamp slut Erin on the TV screen with my magic PAUSE button. "We already have two very old, mostly senile cats. It wouldn't be fair to them."

"Waaaaah! I don't see why we can't get just one little kitten! *You're mean!*"

I told my husband to put our daughter back on the phone.

"Oh, okay. Bring Button home, and we'll make it work." They gushed with gratitude and I hung up, wondering exactly what had just happened.

Thirty minutes later, Sophie raced in and shoved a shaking Button into my lap. For the first few days, things went great. Button was *no* trouble. In fact, he never, actually, moved. He lay in a tight ball, sleeping, while Sophie and her friends squealed at him to "get up and play!" It was like he was stuffed.

Finally, after he roused long enough to pee on my nightgown, I decided to take him to the vet.

"He's stressed," the vet said.

"*He's* stressed? What about me?" The two big fat liars who'd sworn they'd take care of him had barely been seen since.

As it turned out, Button was suffering from an intestinal ailment. For this, I had to push his little face back tight like Joan Rivers, pry his jaws open with my finger, and shove a pill down his throat.

"Wow, can you make him stop yelping like that?" Hubby asked. "I don't think he wants to take that pill."

Five spit-outs later, the pill was safely lodged in Button's tummy to work its wonders. The next day, he was much better; a week later, he was climbing up the draperies and pooping earnestly about the house in every possible location except the two litter boxes I'd bought for him.

Two more vet visits (I went to one with paw-print poop stains on my shirt, and *I didn't even care*) and Button was all better. I, however, wasn't sleeping well, because he'd taken to chewing on my toes all night long, forcing me to dream of tenement rats.

I thought that Button might finally earn his keep the day the lizard arrived.

I know that one of the worst things a parent can do is to pass silly phobias on to their children but, in the case of the lizard, I couldn't help myself. Lizards terrify me.

When Hubby got home from work, I was standing on the couch, calling to Button to come catch the lizard, but he was way too busy taking a dump on my dining room rug and could not be disturbed.

"What's up?" Hubby asked Soph, who was standing on the coffee table.

"Mommie saw a lizard in the living room," she explained calmly.

"A lizard? Inside the house? Are you sure?"

"Of course we're sure," I said. "Why else would I be standing on this couch?"

"That's no help," he said smugly. "They're excellent climbers."

"That's no help; they're excellent climbers," I mock mouthed him. *"Get a broom and find him!"*

Lizards severely creep me out. Once, I went to a little boy's birthday party, and his grandpa had two of them latched to his earlobes. The children loved Paw-Paw's cool party trick; I fainted.

So when our unwelcome visitor sashayed across the floor *like he owned the place,* I felt light-headed again. Thank goodness my neighbor heard my screams.

"It's just a little fella," she cooed, holding a Tupperware container open to catch him. He dodged to the left and scampered under the chair that I will never be able to sit in again.

"Get your cats in here," she advised cheerily on the way out, brushing aside my pleas to come live with her. "He won't last long when they find him!"

Clearly, she didn't understand that any instinct my cats ever had has been snuffed by three squares a day from our friends at 9Lives. Unless I could figure a way to lure the lizard into a can labeled "Now tender and meatier!" no help there.

A man doing yard work next door was summoned. I offered him all the money in the house—five dollars—to find and remove the lizard.

"He won't hurt you," the man said slowly, as though he

were talking to some sort of half-wit standing on a couch. "They are actually wonderful at eating flies and mosquitoes."

He tried for about fifteen minutes, but the lizard skittered all over the room, eventually returning to the chair that I will now have to burn.

"We have to sleep at a motel tonight," I told Hubby later. "Make the arrangements."

"Don't be silly. Did you know that the lizard's waste products actually inhibit the growth of certain household bacteria?"

Okay, it's official. Everybody is on the lizard's side. Somewhere, he was under a chair grinning from creepy non-ear to non-ear.

We never found the lizard, but I'm afraid it's only because he's hiding in my closet, changing his colors to match my clothes.

I suppose things could be worse than having your house taken over by a shit-slinging kitten and a maniacal lizard.

Near the top of a long list of things I'm grateful for is that, as far as I know, not a single one of my neighbors owns a pet tiger. Hey, it's not as far-fetched as you may think. I just read where there are between five thousand and seven thousand tigers living in private homes in this country. And I'm guessing that they pretty much hog the remote.

Even people who don't have yards are buying exotic wild animals as casually as a baggie full of goldfish from Wal-Mart.

Recently, I read about a guy in Florida who used to play

Tarzan in B movies and whose 750-pound tiger escaped from his home. Presumably watching him walk down the street were the actor's other pets: two lions, a leopard, and a cougar.

Steve Sipek had his own mini-jungle at his home near Palm Beach, perhaps in an attempt to relive his sort-of glory days as Tarzan. We can only hope that Tobey Maguire doesn't start trying to sling webs from his fingertips if his career falters. It's just so J. J. Walker sad when people confuse the characters they play with the people they are in real life. Think about it. No one really says "Dy-no-mite!" with any degree of enthusiasm anymore.

Of course, most of the owners of wild animals aren't aging movie stars but regular people like you and me except they've been sprinkled with what I like to call "the stupid dust."

What other explanation for a normal person to buy a wild animal? One story I read while doing a (very) little research on this subject suggested that owners of wildcats like that edge, or "spunk," of living with a wild animal. The "rush" of all this "spunk" was said to be "awesome." As I said, stupid dust. A woman in Washington State said her wildcat routinely runs off with her clothes whenever she gets dressed. Great. Now they're cross-dressing, too.

Sadly, like those pitiful dyed green and pink chicks that used to sit in dime store incubators like little punk rockers on a stage every Easter, cute doesn't last.

The experts are always warning these big-cat collectors that trouble can surface in the animal's adolescence when the formerly cuddlesome cub takes to growling, lunging, slamming doors, and sarcastically making little *L* shapes on its forehead every time you leave the room.

Well, almost.

As much as I adore my normal-size cats, you'd think that I might also enjoy the company of a dog, right? The truth is, I don't like 'em. Never have; never will. When you tell someone that you don't like dogs, they usually give you a look that falls somewhere in between pity and outright disgust.

They just don't get why I wouldn't want to be hanging around an animal that has been known to eat not only its own poo but the poo of others it finds in the yard.

This is not rocket science to me. It's a simple household rule: If you're a shit-eater, you're not living with me.

Naturally, since I don't like dogs, they sense this intuitively and totally respect my feelings. This respect is demonstrated by jumping on me, often knocking me to the ground, licking me, and doing unspeakable things while wrapped around my leg. The more I back away and mumble, "Nice doggie, now go play in the street," the more they seem to love me.

The only dog we ever had when I was growing up was a mutt who lived with us just long enough to rip everything on the clothesline to shreds and eat my favorite Davy Jones poster. I can still remember Davy's cute brown eyes dangling in a soggy mess from the corner of the beast's jaw.

The last time I saw Blackie (hey, nobody ever said we were particularly original dog owners), he was headed toward the woods behind our house wearing my training bra on his backside and chewing the remains of a mood ring.

That said, I accept that most dogs are plenty smart. I've always been impressed by how they can sniff drugs and even bombs using their keen sense of irony, I mean smell.

Unfortunately, I'm kind of freaked out about the newest revelation about dogs. There is indisputable scientific evidence that dogs can actually smell cancer on you. Now, I'm sure your first thought is the same as mine: *What a cool name for a rock band: Cancer-Smelling Dogs.*

After that thought passed, I realized that, because I am a profound hypochondriac, now I have to fret every time I visit my friend down the street and her enormous rug of a retriever lunges for me. Does Colby do this because he loves me or because he's trying to alert me to a life-threatening medical condition? Is he saying, as he slobbers onto my shirt and nuzzles my earlobes, "Timmy's trapped in the well, oh, no, what I meant to say is that you really should have that pancreas checked out." Well, is he?

Not long ago, I learned about a local service station that uses the services of an elderly hound to "sniff" tires. He can pinpoint a leak before you even know it's there. Amazing!

I hate to admit this, but it's obvious: Dogs have it all over my beloved but totally useless housecats.

I could drive up to the house on four flat tires, with a ticking bomb and a kilo of cocaine in the trunk, tumors hanging off me as big as pie plates, and my selfish cats would just yawn, stretch, and go back to sleep.

In the case of a woman with skin cancer, the dog not only detected the problem but set about trying to remove it himself! That's cool, although it's going to be a billing nightmare for her HMO. I can picture the back-of-the-phone-book ads: The doctor is *in* and it's Rin Tin Tin!

22

What Women Want

If You Can't Be Imprisoned for Life, Could You Maybe Act Just a Little Gay?

Suddenly, being a housewife is downright trendy. In two of this season's biggest TV hits, housewives are either "desperate" or "swapped." My, oh, my, what a refreshing change from the days when a housewife's only virtue was that she might "have the magic of Clorox 2."

Finally, housewives are hot—whether they're living lives of loud desperation on Wisteria Lane as in ABC's megahit *Desperate Housewives* or they're raising fat, pampered brats over on *Wife Swap*.

Long ignored by everyone except peanut butter manufacturers, housewives are finally getting some ink for being sexy, complicated creatures that are too often underestimated. In other words, we're here, we leer, get used to it.

Having dinner with my stay-at-home mom friends the

other night, we had to wonder why we don't look like the babes on *Desperate Housewives*. I feel a little like most of New York City's female population must've felt while watching *Sex and the City* for the first time. Who were these gorgeous women wearing five-hundred-dollar Manolos and little else as they bedded most of Manhattan? Doesn't anybody have to get up in the morning?

To be fair, there is one harried *Desperate* housewife who is raising the World's Worst Little Boys. Even wearing jam, though, she's still beautiful and loves to show off those chiseled work-out arms that I've grown to hate in other women. Whither the batwings that we get from having too little time to work out and too much time to finish little Sally's *Shark Tale* Happy Meal?

I take *Desperate Housewives* for what it is: a fun, fluffy farce with a slight *Twin Peaks* edge to it. Still, I feel insecure when I compare my housewifely look to theirs. Around the house, I wear a Kathie Lee floral shift that has seen better days. It's fabulously comfortable and ideal for vacuuming. But it's nothing like the put-together look modeled by Marcia Cross of *DH* as she toothbrush-scrubs her toilet while wearing a scarf tied jauntily around her graceful neck.

On the surprisingly poignant reality show *Wife Swap*, we see women more like ourselves: a little chubby, a little loud, a lot loving.

The great thing about *Wife Swap* (settle down, right-wingers; there's no hanky panky among spouses here) is that there's no hero or villain. Granola mom and SUV mom are right some of the time. And mercifully neither one believes that a bottle of bleach contains anything approaching magic.

But both shows do illustrate, in an over-the-top way, that American women are getting a little screwy when it comes to picking our mates. And increasingly, mind-bendingly desperate.

How else do you explain the hundreds of sacks of love letters that show up at Scott Peterson's San Quentin cell every week?

Murder conviction? Oh, nobody's perfect. To these women, Peterson is just as cute as a bug's ear. They apparently assume that if you're good-looking and famous, even if it's for murdering your wife and kid, then you'd be a great catch.

But you never see men doing this, hons. You never hear about men writing Andrea Yates or Susan Smith in prison, do you?

That's because men are statistically more likely to read about heinous family-killing crimes committed by a woman and say, "Damn, that bitch is crazy!"

A California criminal justice professor who was asked to explain the mail-to-murderers phenomenon said it usually happens when women don't believe the accused is guilty and they want to come to the rescue of someone whom the whole world is against, someone who is "beleaguered."

For my money, beleaguered beats dead any day.

Yep, Scott Peterson is a prize catch, all right. And now, he's single!

O. J. Simpson, who has finally suspended his exhaustive personal crusade to find "the real killer" of his wife on finer public golf courses throughout the state of Florida, never has a problem finding willing and wonderfully attractive women to date.

What up?

Not only do we "desperate" women want to date murderers, but we also want to date gay men.

Why else would we invite *Queer Eye for the Straight Guy*'s Fab Five into our homes to "make over" our husbands? I know I'd like to.

Why can't our straight-guy husbands understand that we're sick of fighting about where to hang the velour rug depicting the poker-playing dogs? I want to drape it lovingly over the top of the garbage can on Monday morning just before the truck comes rumbling down the alley. He wants to hang it over the buffet like it's some kind of rare tapestry from the Moron Dynasty.

While I don't want to correspond with murderers just because they would never leave their undershorts on the floor, I also don't want to be married to a gay man. I couldn't take the fault-finding.

It would take a nanosecond for *Queer Eye*'s menswear counselor Carson to dis my husband's "Got Duckheads?"

approach to fashion, but I wouldn't have time to feel superior once Thom, the decorator, spotted our ironing board as nightstand. Culinary expert Ted would sniff and make gagging noises over our grocery-store wine. And, sure, grooming guru Kyan would lecture my husband about proper shaving ("It's not a race, bro!"), but we'd both suffer when culture expert Jai examined our pitiful collection of CDs. ("The Eagles? *The Eagles!* Get this couple some Beyoncé, *stat!*")

Every woman I know is gaga about these five gay men who "makeover" the looks, and the lair, of a particularly needy straight guy. In the end, the gays got the girls. It's high school all over again, but look who's kicking butt! Sure, Bubba may have snickered at the sensitive young man who sewed sequins on his cousin's wedding gown back in the day, but who's laughing now? I can't *hear* you!

The beauty of *Queer Eye* is its ability to reduce a huge, hulking straight construction worker into the kind of guy who waxes his back hair, quotes John Donne, and literally weeps with gratitude for a makeover, hugging his five new friends until they have to pull away.

When the Fab Five's work is complete, straight guy usually turns, teary-eyed, to survey his redecorated crib, transformed from messy, dorm-room mishmash to a sleek yet warm tribute to the wonders wrought by Thom let loose with the Bravo credit card in Pottery Barn, Urban Outfitters, and Pier 1.

Although ratings are huge among the straight set, some members of the gay community have protested the show's "perpetuation of gay stereotypes." As one gay activist told public radio recently, "Gay men can dress sloppy, waste a weekend watching sports on TV, and not know how to cook, too."

Note to gay activist: These are not good things. Learn how to take a compliment, would you?

They say that the show's flamboyant gay stars make it seem as though every gay man is a boa-wearing oversexed weirdo.

I don't get that. With the exception of the always-randy Carson, whose wit is eat-your-young mean, the rest just seem like very smart, very kind guys who just want to help a unibrowed brother out.

In the words of Rodney King, can't we all just go to the spa, slap on some eucalyptus exfoliating cream, and learn how to shave with something besides a Bic disposable? I thought so.

23

Bush on Marriage

"Bin Laden, Bin Schmaden! 50 Cent and Vivica Fox Are in Crisis!"

I received one of those Mr. Wonderful dolls as a gag gift for Valentine's Day. If you haven't seen one yet, allow me to explain. Mr. Wonderful is small enough to fit on a key chain and depicts a square-jawed neatly dressed man who, when pressed in the tummy, says some pretty hilarious things. Things like, "Let's just cuddle" or "You've worked hard today—let me cook dinner tonight" or "Awwww, can't your mother stay at least one more week?"

While I'm quite taken with Mr. Wonderful (who can resist a soothing male voice saying, "Here, you take the remote. As long as I'm with you, I don't care what we watch"?), it occurred to me that men have every right to expect a Mrs. Wonderful to be in production, too.

I mean it's not as if we women are perfect. Well, at least

most of y'all aren't. So I've come up with my own list of Mrs. Wonderful's possible utterances. Feel free to think up some of your own.

Things a "Mrs. Wonderful" Might Say

"What? There's a new episode of *Grey's Anatomy* on tonight? Oh, let's watch that some other time. I'd much rather make love."

"You know, I really like the speed limit you have chosen and I wouldn't dream of telling you the best way to get to Chip and Susie's house. I'll just sit here and be a thoughtful, considerate passenger."

"Oh, honey, do you really think your mom would give me some pointers in the kitchen? I would love to be able to cook for you and serve you just the way she did! Oh, and shouldn't we be making love right about now, mister?"

"*SportsCenter* is on again? Why it seems as if it comes on every hour on the hour. Aren't we lucky to live in a country like this? ESPN truly separates us from the savages!"

"Sweetheart, do you think you could wear that old Carolina sweatshirt with the tung oil stains and the holes in it to have dinner with my family just one more time? We all just *love* you in it!"

"Now, honey pie, you don't need to know where the car keys or the milk and bread are. That's what you have me for!"

"Oh, fudge! You forgot our anniversary again? Well,

heh-heh, I know something we could do to celebrate that wouldn't cost a thing!"

Marriage would be easy if we all acted more like our key chains, wouldn't it?

With the U.S. divorce rate at 57 percent, you have to wonder why President George Bush has decided to spend $1.5 billion of your tax dollars to develop programs that will encourage people to get married instead of just live together.

Bush's "healthy marriage initiative" calls for gobs of federally funded counseling on the benefits of marriage through mentoring and instruction in how to make a marriage work. (Short version: "Just let her win.")

The notion of the government getting into the business of matchmaking is a hoot. What next? TV spots with Dick Cheney as a caftan-wearing marriage voodoo priestess? Condoleeeeeza offering tips for the lovelorn via those eight-bucks-a-minute "love hotlines"?

Making healthy marriages is a laudable goal, but it's a notion that needs a high-profile test case like, say, Britney Spears and Jason Allen Alexander, a prime example of a couple who never gave their marriage a fair chance. Under the Bush plan, there would never have been any time for Kevin Federline.

Under the Bush plan, Britney and Jason would have been given orders to work on their fifty-five-hour marriage and iron out their differences. (He thought "gravy train with old high school buddy"; she thought "Face it, after five sour appletinis I'd pretty much marry Christina Aguilera, who is hairier, by the way.")

In Bush's world, Brit and Jason wouldn't just be able to go before a judge and whine for a quickie annulment.

No, no. It happened too fast. What God and a half-dozen really wasted witnesses hath put together, let no judge put asunder in just a few minutes. Under the Bush plan, a federal bureaucrat could have been dispatched to the scene of the breakup and convinced the couple that it was purely possible for Britney, one of the richest and most popular entertainers in the world, to give it all up in order to settle down and make fat Louisiana babies with a, uh, college student.

Can we be far removed from a divorce requiring an official letter from the President of the United States to be final?

We get it. Marriage should not be entered into lightly. But Bush should know that most couples already get premarital counseling for free from their minister. Admittedly, in Las Vegas, this is probably reduced to an Elvis impersonator advising the couple, "Don't be cruel." Then again, what more is there to say, really?

The president's weird marriage-or-bust program could also have helped those headline-grabbing former shackmates

Ben Affleck and Jennifer Lopez. If only they could have had a sit-down with the leader of the free world before deciding to split. J. Lo could've expressed her frustration with Ben's gambling and womanizing, and Ben could've said, "Look, we all know that I'll never be truly happy with anyone except Matt Damon, so let's just stop pretending."

Y'all know I'm right.

I worry about Bush's "save the marriage at all costs" mentality. One couple I'd like to nudge into divorce court would be Mr. and Mrs. Kobe Bryant.

I have to admit it: I was on Kobe Bryant's side till he bought his wife an eight-carat purple diamond that cost more than four million bucks to atone for that pesky rape charge. Hallmark, which has a card for almost everything, must not have had one in the "Sorry I Strayed, But It Was Consensual" category.

On the other hand—yep, the one that sports my modest three-quarter carat diamond ring bought from a pawnshop, no less—maybe Kobe's wife had the right idea.

Next time Hubby forgets to take out the garbage? Let's seeee, that's one pair of sapphire earrings. If he eats the last Eskimo Pie (again), that's one tennis bracelet on the Kobe Scale of Remorse.

My heart goes out to Kobe's wife, with her sad Precious Moments doll eyes. As I watched her stroke his hands during the World's Most Humiliating Press Conference when the news first broke, I had to wonder how she could sit there while he described her as his "backbone," "soul mate," and similar gibberish.

She did "her duty" on live TV. But sister-hon should have accepted that ring only long enough to hold it under Kobe's nose and say something on the order of, "Fool, you need to put that hunka junk where the sun don't shine."

While I don't think it's smart to force people into marriage through a guvmint program, I'm actually a big fan of weddings—old-fashioned ones, that is. That's why I'm so distressed to see the disturbing trend of tacky engagement announcements. You know the ones I'm talking about. The bridal page picture where He is tightly wrapped around Her in their best impersonation of a couple desperately in need of a room.

Now I realize that we live in an age in which most people actually believe you can—heck, you *should*—meet your soul mate on a TV show catfight filmed in a borreyed castle somewhere. Therefore, maybe we've let a lot of wedding customs go by the wayside.

Still, I must speak out against the "modern" engagement photos of couples wearing bathing suits or tube tops and muscle shirts looking slightly hungover. And, at the risk of offending more than a few friends and relatives, I don't think grooms belong in engagement photos at all.

One reason is they're impossible to pose. How many

times have you seen the studio portrait where she is standing behind her beloved, arms wrapped around him like a
sumo chokehold? They sure look happy.

Call me old school, but I think engagement portraits
should be of the bride only. Men have no business being in
the picture. Just show up at the chapel and remember not
to smash cake in her face on the big day. You're a guy, for
heaven's sake. No one cares what you look like, and neither
should you.

The tacky wedding write-up is another pet peeve. There
is simply no need to advise us, as one wedding announce-
ment did recently, that "two have become one during a
spectacular Maui honeymoon trip."

Oh, precious Lord.

Ditto the fact that your children served as your junior attendants. We know you've shacked since Clinton's first term;
just don't rub our noses in it.

As a native Southerner, it's possible that I am irrationally
traditional on such matters. We Southerners cling like kudzu
to our traditions. Every so often, though, things go awry.
I'm remembering a bridal shower I helped host in which a
friend thought it would be a good idea to have tiny plastic
cherubs frozen in the punch bowl ice ring. Instead of evok-
ing the image of merry cupids that we had hoped for, more
than a half dozen guests gasped in horror and demanded to
know, "Why are there dead babies floating in the punch?"

Like picking a wedding photographer based solely on which one of your redneck cousins has the biggest lens and best chance of staying sober, the floating cupids seemed like a good idea at the time.

And speaking of wedding photography, y'all show some love to Catherine Zeta-Jones, who has gone to court, repeatedly, to claim that her wedding day was ruined by unauthorized photographers.

Oh, how I have cried myself to sleep thinking about how CZJ has had to suffer. And Michael Douglas, too. They're outraged that the paparazzi snapped unauthorized pictures of their wedding at the Plaza Hotel years ago.

My heartless friend Susan thinks it's ridiculous. "I mean," says Susan, "doesn't this woman know there are people with real problems out here in the real world?"

What can I tell you? Susan clearly can't comprehend deep pain. After all, as I pointed out, CZJ said that both she and Michael broke down and cried in phone calls to friends about how tacky tabloid photos ruined their most special day. At least the most special since Michael's last wedding.

One gets the impression that Michael Douglas would say just about anything to keep the missus happy, and for that he gets major props. But it does tarnish his macho image a bit to see him wringing his hands in public about how "devastated" and "emotional" he is about photos that "made the reception look like a disco."

The Zeta-Jones–Douglases did allow that the pain and

stress of the wedding day ordeal, while irreparable, could be mollified somewhat by $800,000.

Big of them.

To the two of them I'd say, that having a wedding at the Plaza Hotel doesn't entitle you to a lot of privacy. Hell, even I have had tea at the Plaza and roamed its hallways, so that should tell you those folks are about as discriminating as a pre-Trimspa Anna Nicole Smith at an all-you-can-eat chitlins buffet.

Marriage isn't easy, even with federal grants and lawsuits to help. Perhaps the Zeta-Jones–Douglases can bravely soldier on, despite this numbing tragedy of disco receptions and allegations of matching chicken necks on bride and groom. Perhaps some of Bush's counseling could help them work through the stages of grief: denial, anger, greed, and a new house in Bermuda.

Works for me.

PART V

Southern-Style Silliness

24

Illness and Death, Southern Style

(Or Why I Will Never Eat London Broil Again)

I've always been an obituary junkie. If there's a long, fabulous obit accompanied by a picture obviously taken at least forty years earlier while wearing a sailor hat, then I'm hooked. If there's a nickname in quotes, say, Red Eye, Tip Top, or simply, Zeke, then my entire day is made.

I don't like obituaries that don't list the cause of death. Even if the newly dead was ninety-six, one can't assume. I crave details. I must know whether death resulted from accident, disease, or simply an unfortunate tuna casserole.

I don't like obituaries that don't list charities. Not long ago, I read about a Wisconsin mother of six who died at seventy-one and specified that, in lieu of flowers, donations be made to any organization supporting the impeachment of President Bush. You just know she died with her little fists all curled up, mad as a mule chewing bumblebees.

I don't like obituaries that just list the bare facts: name, age, place of death, relatives, funeral details. No, no. I want to know that the deceased loved the Atlanta Braves, Reese's Pieces, Dale Jr., and going to Mr. Tang's Imperial Wok on all-you-can-eat crab legs night. People, is this too much to ask?

Occasionally, readers are rewarded with a list of survivors that includes beloved family pets: "Joe is also survived by his faithful standard poodle, Rhett, and a somewhat sickly betta fish he purchased at Wal-Mart only a week before he died and had named Stumpy for reasons unknown to anyone else."

I like obituaries that aren't afraid to let loose a little bit. "Crossing Jordan," "racing into the arms of the Almighty," and "leaving all earthly cares behind" (including, perhaps, an unpaid Belk charge card and that nagging thumpa-lumpa-lump noise that had been coming from beneath the hood of the LeSabre for a couple of months now) are powerful descriptions, all.

I love obituaries that take the time to point out that the deceased died "peacefully, surrounded by his entire family." Celebrities appear to be especially good at this. Not only are they rich and famous, but their families can assemble dutifully and peacefully from around the globe on a moment's notice. I hate them.

Still, it's a tremendous accomplishment for any family to be assembled in one room *and* peaceful! But, unlike the Thanksgiving table, in which all manner of grievances tend to spill out over the creamed onions, deathbed etiquette demands that Aunt Pearl refrain from calling Uncle Gene "that lying apostate of hell who cheated on me back in '57."

I'm too young to be talking about death and dying, I guess, but it's a Southern thing to obsess over these matters. Funeralizing is second only to hospital visitation in occasions that call for you to dress in your best Jaclyn Smith for Kmart Collection.

I did an inordinate amount of hospital-visiting when my friend Lula was admitted.

The best part of our visits was listening to this wiry little redneck woman who was her roommate on the other side of the curtain.

Here's something you need to know: Little old Southern redneck women are always pissed off. They can't help "theyselves." Maybe it's from a lifetime of living with a man who thinks a talking bass plaque is a suitable fortieth anniversary gift.

Lula's roommate was one of the most hardcore little old rednecks I've ever encountered, so naturally I just pulled up a chair and listened while Lula just scowled.

Azelene had started firing questions as soon as Lula got settled into her bed.

"What're *you* in for?" she snapped.

"Oh," said Lula, "we thought it was my heart, but it turned out to be my gall bladder, so I'm going to be just fine."

"Hmmmph!" Azelene snorted. "Don't you let 'em tell you you didn't have no heart attack, honey. When I had my first heart attack, they tried to tell me it was just indigestion. They don't know *nothing!* Damn thing like t' have blowed the whole back of my heart off!"

Lula gasped.

"That was almost as bad as the time I had to call 911 on account of my backbone was a-poking outside of my skin. They said it wasn't, but they don't know pea turkey squat. You don't believe me? Just feel this scar on my back ratch 'ere. Go on! Feel of it, honey. You know, I've lost all the feeling in all my arms and laigs ever since I got the sugar."

Redneck vocabulary tip: A good Southern redneck doesn't know from diabetes. It's always *the sugar.* They also call Alzheimer's *old-timer's* and don't know that's funny. (In a related vocabulary note, redneck old people always call SUVs *SOBs,* and they really don't know what they're saying. You haven't lived until you've heard old Aunt Bettisue say, quite innocently, "That there SOB's gonna run right over us, he's so big.")

Redneck Southern women of all ages love to dress up any ailment, no matter how minor. My redneck friend Verna-Lynn is particularly blessed with a colorful vocabulary when it comes to her "ladies' time."

"I swear I'm flushing clots the size of a London broil," she announced one day over lunch.

Check, please.

Elderly redneck women will go to dramatic lengths to get attention. My friend's mama used to look both ways down the street before carefully lying down in the shrubbery near her front door with just her legs showing from the kneecaps down.

The first time I saw this, it was naturally quite upsetting, and I raced to help. My friend stopped me. "Oh, hell, hon, that's just Mama's way of getting attention. She's forever hiding in the shrubbery and pretending to have blacked out. Come on in and borrow that casserole dish you needed; she'll crawl out directly."

I tell you this so you'll have a bit of context when you consider Azelene's conversations.

During a break in a long discussion about her latest bout of hemorrhoids ("I swance they're as big as sofa cushions"), I noticed a spit cup surface from under Azelene's bedcovers.

For a few moments, all you could hear in the hospital room was the sound of an old woman's spit hitting the side of a Tar Heels 1993 National Champions mug. The relative peace was disrupted, as it always is when the Southern Redneck Woman has company in the hospital.

A friend had dropped by to visit but confessed he was nervous. "I haven't been in a hospital since my brother shot hisself in the leg on account of trying to commit Hare Krishna."

Somebody brought fried chicken.

Lula and I, bored by the *Falcon Crest* reunion that was taking place on the TV overhead, just soaked it all up, including a lengthy visit from Azelene's preacher, a thunder-voiced Pentecostal who sold double-wides by day. He'd come straight from his weekly visit counseling all the lost sheep in the "pentenchurary."

"Did you see my Edwin?" Azelene asked.

"Shore did. He said he didn't rob that Kangaroo Mart, and he can prove it."

"Course he can! My baby's innocent as the day he was born. Which like t've killed me. He weighed damn near sixteen pounds, you know. They had to remove all my internal organs just to prize him out. They say you can't live without a liver, but I been doin' just fine. I knew they didn't put everything back. Saw it sittin' on the counter just like it needed some fried onions with it."

"Merciful heavens," Lula half groaned.

The next day, rolling out of Azelene's life forever, Lula waved good-bye. Azelene, not a sentimental sort, just yawned. "On your way out, tell that bony little hank o' hair out at the desk I need a pan. Did I tell you about my hemorrhoids?"

25

Want to "Talk Southern"?

Here's Some Advice from My Abode to Yours

I had to call the phone company after a small hurricane passed through, ripped the line down, and left it in a mangled mess on my deck.

This didn't go well. See, I live in North Carolina, and the phone company representative—who for some inane reason began every sentence with "Now, Miss Riventybarky, we understand that you are frustrated" while simultaneously adding to my frustration—was elsewhere, like Bangalore.

Not that there's anything wrong with that. Some of my best friends are Bangaloreans. Okay, not really. I'm from the South, where when we say, "The phone line's down, and y'all need to get a truck over here to put it back up," this is somehow greeted by the Bangalorean as completely unreliable.

"Miss Riventybarky," she began, "have you considered that perhaps the phone is unplugged or there is a problem with the, uh, [sound of shuffling translation guides] jack inside the [shuffling again] abode?"

I distinctly remember grabbing an unopened bottle of wine at this point and considering banging it open on the side of the kitchen counter, thus bypassing the more time-consuming corkscrew method.

"I don't live in an abode; I live in a house, a house without any telephone service and my name is *not* Riventybarky!"

"Miss Riventybarky, now I do understand that you are frustrated—"

"Arrrgggh!"

Long story short, I finally convinced my almond-eyed friend on the far side of the world that I really did have enough sense to recognize a tattered phone line on the ground. She finally agreed to believe me, and we all gave peace a chance. The very next morning, a fabulous crew from the local phone company showed up in whipping rains and "got 'er done."

I was thinking about this because I just learned that my Southern hometown is now a major "call center" for Verizon, a telecommunications giant whose name comes from the Latin *Veri,* which means "bladder" and *zon,* which means "elongated." I don't care; it still sounds cool.

Anywho, the funny part is that here we are, in the Deep South, and we're the call center servicing, get this, Metropolitan New York City! What elongated bladder genius thought this would be a good match?

NY CALLER: My phone's broken and you need to fix it today.

US: Todaaaay? Do what?

NY CALLER: Yes, today, Gomer. I'm a very busy and important person wearing way too much hair product.

US: I understand your, uh, frustration—

NY CALLER: "I'll give you somethin' to be frustrated about. Now get the grits outta your mouth and fix my f-ing phone."

US: I bet you wouldn't talk like that in front of your mama. *Click.*

Thing is, we don't talk like the rest of the country, and we're frankly relieved.

Remember this above all else: Southerners despise bad news and loathe sharing it without some gloss. We invented that classic joke about the beloved cat that was killed while his owner was away from home. It's the one where the neighbor bluntly says "Your cat's dead," and his devastated friend says, "Couldn't you tell me nicer? Ease me into it? Tell me the cat got up on the roof and then tumbled down and died instantly and without any undue suffering?" A few weeks later, the same neighbor is forced to relay some sad news again. Remembering his friend's request, he begins, "See, your grandma was on the roof. . . ."

This near-pathological avoidance of bad news has led to such famous Southernisms as using "the late unpleasantness" to describe the War Between the States. We don't just come right out and say something; we have to cozy up to it like the cat to the cream jar.

One of the best examples of classic Southern understatement is found in the word *unfortunate,* which, in the South, can describe anything from losing all one's earthly possessions in a house fire ("Selma and Jim-Bob experienced a most unfortunate fire") to describing your exceedingly homely girl-cousin as having "a most unfortunate nose."

Unfortunate, you'll notice, is usually paired with *most* for purposes of emphasis. Don't use *very,* or you will be revealed to be the outsider that you truly are and told to go back to sprinkling sugar on your grits and similar abominations.

Here's a quick checklist for dos and don'ts down South. No thanks are necessary; it's thanks enough that I am able to help.

DON'T say *yous.* Practice saying *y'all, y'all's,* or *yalls'es* without sneering. Get over yourself.

DON'T discuss how much money you make or how much you paid for your leaf blower, standing mixer, lawn tractor, shoes, and so on. Southerners don't do that, because it's tacky.

DO realize that tacky is the worst label that can be applied to any person, behavior, or event in the South. As in, "Mama said Raylene's bridal shower coming three months after she had the baby was as tacky as those Sam's Club mints she served right out of the carton."

DON'T criticize our driving. We know where the turn lane is and what it's for. We're just messing with you.

DON'T accuse us of being "thin-skinned" or lacking a sense of humor. We laugh plenty behind your back.

DO remember that *barbecue* is a noun, never a verb, and it's a holy noun at that.

DON'T question the superiority of Atlantic Coast Conference basketball. This could lead to a most unfortunate coma.

Of course, as is often the case, we in the South can be our own worst enemy. I recently learned that there is a course being taught at the University of South Carolina that helps Southerners lose their accents. Can you believe it?

My ox is gored, my tater fried, and, yes, the red has indeed been licked off my candy.

You see, I have a dog in this fight. The notion that you should try to get rid of your Southernisms makes me madder'n a wet setting hen.

The professor, Erica Tobolski, says that she is teaching her students how to stop talking Southern and start using Standard American Dialect (or, appropriately, SAD for short). This way, we can all sound exactly alike. Isn't that just gooder'n grits and finer'n frog's hair?

Of course it's not. The truth is, I wouldn't give Ms. Tobolski air if 'n she was trapped in a jug. Which it sounds to me like she may have been. For some time. How else do you explain such oxygen-deprived plumb foolishness? I swear if that woman's brains were dynamite, an explosion wouldn't even ruffle her hair on a windy day.

"Many students come to see me because they want to sound less country," Ms. Tobolski told the Associated Press. They want to be able to turn their native Southern accent on and off so it doesn't embarrass them when they travel or go on job interviews.

Y'all want to know what embarrasses me? That any right-thinking daughter or son of Dixie would sign up for this insulting course. Do we really want to sound like the "You've got mail" guy or the android who tells us to "Press One for Customer Service"?

Answer me. *Do we?*

Oh, "hail" no.

I have a friend who travels to the Northeast a lot on business. She's a high-powered, successful executive, and she takes pride in her Southern accent.

Going toe-to-toe with Boston lawyers on their turf, she refers to them as *y'all,* but they have learned that to question her brainpower would just prove that they're the ones dumber'n a sack of hammers.

What we need to do is celebrate our accent and nevah, evah try to change it. If we try to get rid of it so others will think better of us, we will have lost our Southern soul, trading the essence of ourselves for what?

So take that course, if you must. But don't be surprised if you end up spending your empty little life stumbling around just as lost and prone to misery as a blind horse in a punkin patch.

Y'all know I'm right.

26

Flu Strikes at Christmas

(And Nobody Had a Silent Night)

If you're going to go and get yourself a really noisy, nasty intestinal virus, it's always best to do it while visiting your in-laws for the holidays. That way, the entire extended family, which is staying overnight in the small brick ranch house that your husband grew up in, can be treated to a cacophony of sounds that they will long remember.

And that way, one by one, they can step, in their bathrobes, to the closed door of the one full bath in the house and shout, with a mixture of pity and fear, "You doing all right in there?"

To which you scream a loving *"Go away!"*

Maybe I'll write about my Christmas night "song" one day in one of those tiny little volumes with treacly prose that sells so well during December. As I snuggled into my husband's boyhood bed mere hours before the attack on my innards was launched, I read five of these little books, all filled with misty-eyed memories of hearth and home and angels and snowmen. None offered a memory like the one I was about to generate for all the family to snicker about for years to come.

Hours later, my humiliation complete, I lay in bed and tried to ignore the smell of frying country ham. A brother-in-law timidly offered to bring me some breakfast, but I told him to just bypass the middleman and throw it directly into the toilet on my behalf. All morning long, I could over-hear the conversation between niece and nephew, aunt and uncle and so forth.

"I heard her at about four thirty," said one.

"Naw, it was closer to two thirty. You must've slept through the first round."

Oh, sweet Jesus, make them stop.

It didn't take a genius to figure out that this was going to permanently scar the younger members of the family who, mere hours before, had happily been playing with a whoopee cushion brought by Santa himself. Now the sound wasn't all that funny.

"Do you think she's gonna die?" I heard one ask.

"Sure sounds like it," another said solemnly.

A relative in Texas called with holiday greetings, and I heard my husband cheerfully announce that I couldn't come to the phone because "She's busy at both ends!" Great. There's one less state I can show my face in again.

The rest of the morning, I heard the relatives leave, cheerfully reminding my mother-in-law to "Lysol the doorknobs!" My husband's family believes that Lysol solves everything. I was deathly afraid they might sneak in and try to spray me from top to bottom while I slept. And dreamed of writing "Upheaval at the In-Laws': A Christmas Song."

Yeah, that'll sell.

I'm not sure a flu shot would've helped in my case, but I couldn't get one anyway, because I was too young. I told everybody that and enjoyed it mightily. It's the most fun I've had since I told the nurse running the church Bloodmobile that "I can't donate on account of I don't weigh enough."

Oh, settle down. I've signed away my organs and, frankly, the way that guy at the Optimist Club booth stared at me when I was signing away my dead corncas, I was a little scared he was going to take 'em right then.

But give blood? Uh, not so much. So instead of being the weenie that I am, fainting in front of an entire basement full of people, I said I didn't weigh enough.

Because this is the South, where people are civilized to your face, there were no follow-up questions such as, "Honey, your ass appears to need its own area code, so I'm guessing you do weigh more than ninety-five pounds."

She sure was thinking it, though.

When I took my octogenerian dad to the drugstore to get his flu shot, I couldn't believe the crowd. The line snaked through eight—count 'em, eight—aisles. For the first hour, it barely moved. When we finally saw one man walk by, pointing to his arm and then making a *V* for victory sign, we burst into spontaneous applause.

The funny thing about getting in line for a flu shot is that, if you are not of a certain age, you get dirty looks. I was just there for moral support, but I could see the raised eyebrows: *Hmmm, she better be missing some kidneys or something.*

I recognize the look because it's the same one I use when I see someone park in a handicapped space and then cheerily skip into the mall having figured out that sometimes it's cool to borrow Great-gran's Taurus.

"It's not for me," I stammered. "I'm just here with my dad. I don't want a flu shot. In fact, I wish I could give back the one I got seven years ago so that others might be helped."

Ahhh. Their faces relaxed, and they put down their torches. I had been afraid that I was one step away from the old "witch test," where they would dunk me in a vat of NyQuil to see if I would sink.

When you're in a drugstore for that long, you gotta read something, so I selected Dr. Phil's weight-loss cookbook. It wasn't a great choice, because it's so big and heavy that I had to pretty much kick it ahead on the floor with my foot like luggage while reading it. Dr. Phil's diet consists of meals like *Lunch:* Grilled salmon, steamed asparagus and leeks, and sweet potato soufflé. *Dinner:* Roasted chicken, steamed vegetable medley, and fat-free polenta cakes.

Yeah. Let me just call my personal chef and have her whip that shit up. Is Dr. Phil *on the pipe?*

Frankly, after a few hours in the flu line, I was convinced that what we'd have for supper that night would be stackable Lay's, Altoids, and some stationery with kittens on it. Yum!

This past winter, there was such a flu-shot frenzy that I wondered why there wasn't a Flu Channel. ("All Flu, All the Time!") complete with Weather Channel studs wearing yellow slickers and reporting live from the scene of Joe and Joan's four-poster mahogany bed. I can just see 'em clinging to the bedposts as they battle gale-force sneezes and wet hacking coughs while assuring us that "There's . . . not . . . much . . . time!"

It seems a cruel irony that flu season coincides with the busiest shopping season. At the mall, I desperately want to wear a surgical mask and gloves but I'm too chicken, fearful that shoppers will mistake me for Michael Jackson, who has been notoriously germ-phobic since he was just a small nut job growing up in Encino.

Post-flu, there are three types of antibacterial lotions in my purse these days and, like the in-laws, I've taken to spraying doorknobs with Lysol, sometimes while my guests are still touching them.

Even if I'd had a flu shot, there's no guarantee it would have been the right one. At least that's what everybody at the CDC (the Cootie Detection Center) down in Atlanta says. That's because every year there is a "new strain" of flu out there, mostly representing ominous sounding parts of the world like the Haiku Province, the Kung Pow Shrimp, and the Moo Goo Gai Pain. You never know which one's going to strike.

So somebody at the drug company has an office pool or a lucky dartboard and finally picks one and bazillions of Moo Goo vaccines are shipped out. But just when you start to relax, you discover that, as it turns out, that guess was completely wrong. That this year's flu strain was more of a Knockwurst–Type A, and epidemiologists around the world were left with egg foo yong on their faces.

I'd like to talk more about this, but I have to boil my mail. You just can't be too careful, hons.

27

Knitting, Boy Dinosaurs, and Chipotle

What Is a Category You Will Never See on *Jeopardy!*

Get this. Knitting is hip. In fact, knitting is almost as hip as chipotle these days. Women are forming "stitch 'n' bitch" clubs where they sit around and knit. This sounds like a giant step backwards to me. What's next? Getting together to make our own spray starch?

Knitting. You've got to be kidding. Before I hear from all the rabid pro-knitting nuts (oops, too late—more on that in a minute), let me say that I actually know a little something about knitting. I used to knit little purses for my friends in junior high, but then I *got a life*.

And about chipotle. Don't get me started. Nobody even knows how to pronounce this stuff, and now every restaurant you go to wants to put chipotle all over everything.

It reminds me of the old Monty Python skit where the

diner asks his waiter about the dessert specials, which turn out to be "rat pudding, rat pie, and strawberry tart." The customer looks perplexed. "Strawberry tart?" "Well," says the server, a tad apologetically, "there's *some* rat in it." Same with chipotle. I don't even know what it is, but it's on everything. Chipotle sauce, chipotle butter, chipotle beer. What next? "New, improved Hamburger Helper: Now with 50 percent more chipotle!"

Anyway, I was sitting around not knitting or eating chipotle the other night when I stumbled across a fascinating article about dinosaurs. See, it turns out that the real reason dinosaurs died out sixty-five million years ago was because a series of asteroid hits caused the skies to go dark and the Earth to grow cold.

This had a more serious effect than just making the dinosaurs hang out in the garages of their friends trying to get some cheap spray-tanning.

No, no. The real problem was that, as it turns out, boy dinosaurs are born more often when temperatures drop. After a while, there was little suspense in the dinosaur waiting room. It was, always, a boy.

And he was eating chipotle. No, no, just kidding.

For a while, I imagine this was a lot of fun. Dinosaurs all over the earth got to put their hooves up on the coffee table without being yelled at and could sit around with their buddies without being nagged to mow the rocks or whatever.

While I'm sure this was cause for great prehistoric merry-making, after a while, the old men's club just got kind of dull. All they ever did was hang out, eat way too many leaves, and just, generally, discuss Republican politics.

So, now you know how dinosaurs disappeared. Let's just hope that knitting and chipotle won't be far behind.

Okay, maybe just chipotle.

Knitters, I have discovered, don't have much of a sense of humor. Every time I crack on the knitters, I get irate letters. Who knew?

Judging from the, uh, passion, with which these people write letters, I have to say that it would not surprise me in the least to find a large hand-knit horse's head on the foot of my bed one day. Here was a typical letter from a woman I will simply call "Purl."

"Who do you think you are to put down knitting? I knit all the time. You should learn to knit. I bet if you did learn to knit, your stuff would look as stupid as you do."

Well, all righty, then.

And then there was the scorching mail from a nameless someone who wrote, "You should be fired for saying that knitting is for losers." (Just for the record, I did *not* say that. I implied it. Now crocheting and tatting? That's for losers. And don't even get me started on macramé. *Kidding!*)

Another writer took a more ominous approach: "You said knitters should 'get a life.' That wasn't very nice. You are a very crappy person, and maybe you shouldn't even have a life. Signed, Tony Soprano." (Okay, maybe not, but that's who it sounded like. Is there some kind of knitting Mafia out there? And, if so, do they stitch tiny little cozies for their Uzis? ("You have spoken disrespectfully of my hobby. And now you must pay. . . . Oh, criminy! How do I get this thing *off?*")

And this from another nutty knitter: "I suppose when you want to give a sweater to someone you love, you just go to the store and buy one!"

Well, uh, yes, Mrs. *Colonial House,* and your point would be?

The whole thing makes me wonder if I've tapped into some kind of Angry Knitters alternate universe. ("Don't mess with me. I *knit!*") I thought that knitting was supposed to relax you, rather like how watching an aquarium can lower your blood pressure. Although I'm not sure I believe that. I watch an aquarium and just get hungry for something yummy with slaw and hushpuppies.

Finally, I heard from a male knitter who said that he knits tiny little caps for premature babies, and he wanted to know what exactly I do for tiny little babies.

Well, admittedly, there's not much market for sarcasm among newborns, but, if it makes you feel better, I shall be happy to read aloud portions of my work to the unborn in wombs across America, rather like those Mozart tapes you're supposed to play to make your kid smart.

Just don't blame me if he comes out a smart-ass. You *so* asked for it, dude.

28

OnStar Hotline

Sure, They Can Help with Car Emergencies, but Can They Make a Decent Gravy?

"OnStar Hotline, may I help you?"

"Oh, thank God! *[panicky]* I need help with my Christmas list."

"Okay, ma'am, please calm down. I can see from your location that you are in the mall parking lot and your blood pressure has just spiked to a rather dangerous level."

"Well, that's because some doofus just took my parking space. *[sobbing]* You don't know what it's like out here, OnStar."

"Right, ma'am, we also see that it appears that your credit card has maxed out, so perhaps shopping isn't a good idea today. Ma'am."

"OnStar, I thought you were here to help."

"Right, ma'am, sorry to editorialize. Have your airbags deployed?"

"It's not a wreck, you ninny. It's a shopping emergency."

"Sorry again. Now, ma'am, it appears that, in fact, the pants you are wearing today do make your butt look too big."

"OnStar!"

"Sorry again, ma'am. We're really much better when it comes to auto emergencies, of which this doesn't seem to be one."

"Oh, right. Like the commercial where the woman has locked her keys in the car and her baby's inside and she's crying. That one always makes me cry when y'all unlock the doors."

"Me, too, ma'am."

"Really?"

"Of course not."

"OnStar, you're so good at helping everybody. Can you or can you not help me with my Christmas list?"

(Pause)

"OnStar, are you there?"

"Thinking, ma'am. Are you sure you don't have any kind of auto emergency? We're really quite well-trained to say things in comforting tones like, 'Sit tight! Help is on the way.'"

"And I love the commercial where you ask if the person in the wreck would like you to stay on the line until help arrives. That's just so sweet. I mean you're like a best friend in a box, on selected GM models, that is."

"Oh, now, keep going on, ma'am, and you're gonna have me bawling!"

"Right. What about help with my Christmas list—can you do it, OnStar?"

"Hmm. You know, fragrance is always nice. We at On-Star are partial to anything in the pine tree line or perhaps new car scent."

"I dunno, OnStar. Look, let's change subjects. Since you are so calm and comforting and knowledgeable, can you give me some advice so my turkey gravy isn't lumpy this year?"

"Whoa. You're asking the impossible now, ma'am. Everyone knows you make terrible gravy."

"They do? Everyone? How do you know?"

(Irritated sigh)

"Oh, right. You know everything."

"Now you're starting to get it, ma'am. Although, just between you and me, it wouldn't kill you to use cornstarch instead of flour. Oh, and, two words, Kitchen Bouquet. That shit is awesome!"

"OnStar! Did you just say *it-shay?*"

"Forgive me, ma'am. I got caught up in the moment. It won't happen again."

"Sure, fine. One more question, though. If you know so

much, can you tell me why people still pay money to hear Ashlee Simpson sing when everyone knows she lip-synchs?"

(Silence)

"OnStar? Are you there?"

"Thinking, ma'am. Frankly, we at OnStar are surprised at all the nepotism in the entertainment world. Another caller wanted to know why Jamie Lynn Spears has her own TV show. It's not as if there's a giant talent pool coming out of Bigfoot, Louisiana, or wherever."

"Exactly, OnStar! I've been thinking the same thing myself. Look, I know I've taken too much of your time already—"

"Well, ahem, that's okay, ma'am. Martha Stewart will have to wait."

"*Martha Stewart?!* Is she on hold now?"

"Oh, dear. I didn't mean to name-drop like that. But, yes, while you've been fretting over your gravy and your Christmas list, a certain Connecticut homemaking mogul has been waiting, it says here, rather impatiently for some OnStar assistance."

"Oh, OnStar! Go help her! Martha needs you! I mean I just love Martha and I think it was horrible that she went to the big house, the pokey, stir, Oz, up the river—"

"Yes, we get it, ma'am."

"I'll admit, though, that I used to want to be just like Martha, but then I read where she gets up before dawn, and I was like, *screw* that! I mean you gotta love a woman who gets up every Christmas morning at three a.m. just to wring the neck of her pet duck and stuff it with a mix of lightly braised shallots and human hearts. I mean, don't you?"

"Ma'am, I really have to go now. Ms. Stewart is starting to get upset. My GPS shows that she is going into a bit of a rage. Frankly, ma'am, I'm about to wet myself."

"Oh, of course. I understand. Just one more thing. This isn't going to turn into one of those OnStar commercials, is it, where y'all use the real-life emergency calls to sell your service?"

"Dream on, ma'am."

29

If It Ain't on eBay, It Ain't Worth Having

Whoa! Is That Willie Nelson's Face in Your Grits?

I read that Britney Spears's pregnancy test is for sale on eBay, perhaps inspired by the success of the sale of a wad of chewed gum she tossed during a London concert three years ago that went for fifty-three dollars.

One wonders why Britney can't just use a trash can like the rest of us, but apparently she just tosses and spits and flicks like crazy. Her cast-off Kleenexes and cigarette butts were also on eBay, in case you think the gum and pregnancy test are tacky. There's also a used bar of soap and a soiled hand towel deemed "priceless" by its owner, hmm, a Mr. J. Timberlake out of Memphis, Tennessee, perhaps?

People magazine reported that a cameraman at one of Britney's Canadian concerts snagged the wad of gum discarded backstage to show his friends and, after their interest waned (approximately three seconds later), he decided to try his luck on eBay.

Although there's no real way to prove that the gum has Britney's actual dried saliva and teeth impressions on it, short of calling in Marg Helgenberger and the rest of those *CSI* freaks, the seller offers "sorta proof" such as ticket stubs that show he attended a Britney concert sometime somewhere and perhaps a picture of Britney chewing actual gum.

Because Britney is such a prolific gum-chewer, it's a good idea to consider quitting your day job and just stalking her, waiting for the next wad of Juicy Fruit or Big Red to come flying across the hedgerow and into your waiting, gloved hands.

I, for one, won't be spending my hard-earned cash on Britney's alleged nose-blow. Not when I could be saving it up for something truly valuable like, say, spinach, flung from the tooth of The Rock (or "The," as I like to call him), my secret crush. Now *that's* money well spent.

Of course, you don't have to be famous to have something worth sharing with eBay. Diane Duyser of Florida made twenty-eight thousand dollars from the sale of a partially eaten ten-year-old grilled cheese sandwich that she said bore the image of the Virgin Mary.

The half-sandwich had spent the past decade nestled among a dozen cotton balls in a clear plastic case on Ms. Duyser's nightstand. Ms. Duyser, a devout woman with deeply held religious beliefs, said in a prepared statement that she wants all people to know that she believes that "This is the Virgin Mary, Mother of God." Still, apparently practicality won out. I mean, having the Mother of God on your nightstand along with your Jergens lotion and *TV Guide* is cool, but it doesn't really get that upstairs bathroom renovated, now does it?

Of course, it's not for me to judge Ms. Duyser's sincerity. I've seen the holy sandwich in pictures and, while there is definitely the blackened crumb outline of a woman's face in the bread, it really looks a whole lot more like Delta Burke to me.

But face it. Who's going to pay twenty-eight thousand dollars for a sandwich with Delta Burke's face on it? Believe me. Next time I splash cat food onto that Styrofoam plate and it looks even an itsy-tiny bit like the Virgin Mary, I'm alerting the media.

Thing is, these "miracles" tend to happen when you least expect them. Just last week, I sprinkled some Bugles on a paper towel for my daughter and her friend, and the way they fell out, they looked exactly like Johnny Depp.

Religious icons sell better, probably. Give me time. Today Johnny Depp, tomorrow Jerry Falwell, and then right on up to the Blessed Virgin. I once spotted Franklin Graham's face in a puddle of ranch dressing, but I was too hungry to do anything about it like the savvy Ms. Duyser.

One reason many people consider this a real miracle is

that the sandwich has never sprouted a single mold spore in ten years. This has got to be divine intervention. If I accidentally leave a lone Frito out overnight, it'll be covered with more hair than Robin Williams's forearms by morning.

The biggest mystery to me was how Ms. Duyser could eat just one bite of a grilled cheese sandwich and then have the willpower to put it aside. But then I found out it was made without any butter or oil. Hell-o. That's *not* a grilled cheese sandwich; that's blasphemy.

The winning eBay bidder turned out to be the owners of an on-line casino, who declared they'd spend "as much as it took" to own the holy toast.

Something tells me they've already gotten burned.

And, finally, let's consider the case of burly computer technician Larry Star of Seattle, who sold his ex-wife's wedding gown on eBay after writing a long and hilarious portrait of their married life together and posing for the photo wearing the gown.

Since the gown sold for $3,850 (about three times what he says it cost him five years ago), Larry might be on to something. He certainly surpassed his stated goal of making enough money for "beer and a couple of Mariners tickets."

Inspired by Larry's success, I went up into the old attic myself and found an autograph book with David Soul's autograph (the original Hutch, you know, and he drew a little peace sign inside the *o* in his last name—outtasite!), my black sequined prom dress, circa 1974, and what appears to be a possum skeleton. Let's start the bidding!

Larry, whose French-braidable back hair would probably send *Queer Eye* grooming guru Kyan Douglas reaching for his smelling salts, poked fun at his ex and her family and thanked the sweet Lord above that at least they hadn't had children. (Oopsie, well, yes, they did have a son as it turns out but it's a lot funnier the other way.)

After all the media attention—Larry was on talk shows more often than that psychic who wears the blue eye shadow—he's decided that he should write humor for a living.

To which I say, good luck, my furry friend. Larry could easily become the male counterpart to fictional but fabulous Carrie Bradshaw, relationships columnist on the old *Sex and the City*. A one-trick pony (chick-bashing), perhaps, but if it's funny, I'm in.

A word of warning to Larry, though. Be prepared for people to take you seriously. That line about how you will be wearing "a hairy, flesh-toned ensemble" for your next wedding because you'll be "buck naked with a toe tag lying on a slab in the morgue because I would have killed myself " will provoke a bunch of earnest letters from folks who bash you for making light of suicide.

It's all part of the job, Larry, and I won't lose any sleep fretting that you might get your feelings hurt. If you can laugh off the woman who told you she wished that she had her ex's testicles to sell on eBay, you're obviously not the sensitive sort.

At any rate, I appreciate you getting me thinking, Larry. Somewhere there's a couple out there with our names who would just love to have some more personalized wedding-bell cocktail napkins. Heck, I'll even throw in the possum skeleton. What am I bid?

30

Marketing Madness

It's Enough to Make You Lose Your (Poli)Grip

I don't recall when the big corporations started slowly, insidiously renaming the stadiums and arenas across this great nation, which, incidentally, is brought to you by Pepsi. But I do remember when it hit home. Just up the road from where I live, the pastoral concert venue Walnut Creek Pavilion was changed to the Alltel Pavilion thanks to a fat cash infusion from the cell phone giant. I still call it Walnut Creek. This is still a free (Dodge Ram) country after all.

The economic reality is that there are scores of renamed and rehabbed stadiums and concert halls all over the country. And aren't those shiny new skyboxes worth the humiliation of admitting that you actually bought tickets to the

Frito-Lay Bean Dip Rose Bowl or the Dr. Scholl's Corn Pads Fiesta Bowl?

It's hardly news that big money can change everything, but every now and then, say, while watching the WNBA's Light Days Panty Liner play of the game, I think that things have gone too far.

Oh, I was just kidding. Nobody watches the WNBA.

On the other hand, maybe if absolutely everything is for sale, why not me? Baby needs new shoes, as they say, and what I need is some corporate sponsorship. Why not the fruit-juicy Hawaiian Punch—line of the day? Are you listening PepsiCo?

For a little extra dough, I could insert into my books, talks, and humor columns veiled, subliminal messages that would be great free advertising for my corporate sponsors. My doctor says Mylanta. Okay, maybe more subtle than that.

Don't blame me. This is, like cross-country two-way communications by Nextel, the way of the future. Hons, you know it won't be long before Brian Williams thanks us for watching NBC's continuing coverage of the Sonic Jalapeño Poppers War in Iraq.

We're so conditioned to corporate sponsorship, who among us would be all that surprised to see the Swiffer WetJet "moppin' up the terrorists" moment of the day? The Toilet Duck "tank roll of the hour?" The Monistat "Yes, Geraldo was a fungus among us" field report?

The possibilities are as endless as the relief I always get

from Icy Hot. Purina could sponsor those moments when *American Idol* judge Randy Jackson affectionately calls someone "dawg."

As in Mighty Dog! Now with more tender kibbles and bits.

Although stadiums have sold out across the country, surprisingly, sanity prevailed when Major League Baseball decided (after allegations of monumental tackiness) not to place red-and-yellow *Spider-Man 2* promo ads on the bases at a Yankees game. At first MLB officials didn't seem to get it. They did, after all, pinkie-swear not to put anything on the hallowed home plate.

But they did plan to transform the on-deck circles into huge spiderwebs for the game.

It's small wonder that companies like Sony warmed to the idea. Sony is the parent of Columbia Pictures (and a rather permissive parent at that, the kind that never minded if you, heh-heh, had an underage beer when you visited your buddy on Hamburger Helper night). With so many people zapping commercials these days by using digital video recorders like TiVo, you have to be creative in promoting your product.

Maybe that explains the ham-handed product placement in *Cheaper by the Dozen,* a two-hour Crate & Barrel ad starring Steve Martin and Bonnie Hunt. Empty boxes with the nifty and unmistakable C & B logo were scattered in every room of the Baker house. Sure enough, when the brood moved uptown, the moving van was followed closely by the huge Crate & Barrel delivery truck. I think it backfired; now I associate owning C & B stuff with having twelve children. I'd rather eat my own eyeballs.

Subtle product placement is a thing of the past. If *Gone with the Wind* were made today, Clark Gable would pull Vivien Leigh close to say, "Frankly, Scarlett, I don't give a damn, but if I did, I'd choose Cingular Wireless with no roaming fees or activation costs."

For the first time in its hundred-year history, the Kentucky Derby is allowing jockeys to wear advertisements on their silks.

It's one thing to see Dale Jr. and his ilk coating themselves shamelessly in Viagra and Tide detergent decals but the Derby?

I don't blame the jockeys, who don't make all that much money, if you believe Spider-Man. Sorry, wrong Tobey Maguire movie. After all, they could be paid thirty thousand dollars to wear a little Wrangler jeans logo. Still, it tackies up everything and makes the world just a little bit more crass, a little less decent. Then again, what's my point? Did I mention that I'm for sale?

Major League Baseball officials changed their minds thanks to the pressure of fans, those oft-forgotten families who shell out ninety dollars for so-so seats and overboiled hot dogs.

Only a few days earlier, MLB had boasted that "*Spider-Man* is a natural fit for baseball," a wacky statement that made about as much sense as "Why, yes, Mr. Billy Joel, I'd be delighted to let you drive me home!"

It's been tough times for a lot of big business, so I guess they're getting desperate. Telemarketers can't hassle us anymore now that we've got the Do Not Call registry. I was one of the first of an estimated ten million angry Americans who signed up to have their phone number removed from telemarketers' call lists. Within months, some sixty million were signed up. The rest, I presume, are clinically insane.

The process is blissfully simple. With a few computer keystrokes, I could practically see the legions of telemarketers, with their offers of "free" water-quality testing, home security systems, groceries, and so forth fleeing like those zombies in the low-interest credit card commercial.

And that's not all. Now that I'm registered, I can sue any telemarketer who calls me for eleven thousand dollars per harassing call. This is going to be some fun, particularly if that perky pest from the time share group in Williamsburg, Virginia, calls again. The last time she woke me on a Saturday morning to tell me that Williamsburg was waiting for me to see firsthand the "magical marriage of perfectly preserved history and modern-day fun," I told her that if I ever meet her in person, she better make sure there aren't any loaded muskets lying around.

Sadly, the don't-call list doesn't filter out all household pests, just 80 percent of them. Charities are exempt, even the phony ones.

This means the Quasi Fraternal Benevolent Lovers of Law Enforcement, who harass me more than anyone else, can legally call me. These people are the most persistent, interrupting my dinner preparations nightly with "Hello, we'd like to keep drug dealers off the street, and we need your help."

This has led to the unbecoming sight of me standing at the stove as my young daughter quietly colors at the kitchen table while I scream into the phone "Leave me alone! I love drugs!" Nothing else has worked, so I have high hopes for this approach.

While there is some concern that the new don't-call laws will put many thousands of telemarketers out of a job, causing a serious jump in the nation's unemployed, I think I speak for many millions of Americans when I say, "So?"

31

My Last Meal?

That's Easy: A Clam Roll and a Dozen Krispy Kremes (Oh, Hell, Keep 'Em Coming)

My friend Lisa, whom I always call Liser because she's from South Carolina (aka South Cackalackie), has a theory about the so-sad plunging of Krispy Kreme's fortunes.

Liser and I have spent an inordinate amount of time lately fretting about the fate of Krispy Kreme on account of *we can't live without them.*

If Keith Richards had gotten hooked on KKs instead of that pesky and harder-to-find heroin, he could've gone through life with actual cheeks.

Liser says that KK forgot its base, its core, its down-South faithful, and I think she's on to something. At first, we Southerners were excited and proud when we read about those über-bored, sophisticated Manhattanites dizzily lining up for "two glazed," flicking the inevitable shower of sugar from their black uniforms en route to their glamorous jobs. Maybe this would be the one thing that could unite Southerners and Northerners. After all, grits haven't worked out like we'd hoped. I still blush at the memory of ordering grits in Atlantic City, New Jersey, and having the waitress look at me, laugh heartily, and finally say, "Grit? What is grit?"

"It's not singular," I'd said with as much Southern pride as I could assemble on short notice. "It's grits."

She laughed even harder.

Although the Yankees who move down South find plenty of fault with much of what we do and how we act, they have never failed to understand, once they taste one, that Krispy Kreme doughnuts are the finest things on God's green earth.

No sane person would dis KKs once they've tried a hot one. A recent transplant once told me that Dunkin' Donuts tasted better, but I knew there was only one plausible explanation for that kind of foolish talk.

"You haven't actually tried a hot Krispy Kreme, have you?" I asked.

"Well, no, but Dunkin' Donuts has always been the best."

"Try one, and get back to me," I said with more kindness than I felt. Truthfully, I was nearly as angry as I was the time a Yankee woman who was visiting a Southern friend of mine announced that our pork barbecue "tastes just like vomit."

I wanted to kill her with my bare hands but it wouldn't have been Christian.

A few days later, there was an e-mail from Mr. Dunkin' Donuts: "I'm so sorry about what I said. We tried them and have been back every night since."

Well, of course.

So when we in the South kept hearing about the phenomenal success of Krispy Kreme up north and beyond, we wondered: Could this be the bridge between cultures that we've been missing ever since the Waw-wuh? Would our Northern neighbors pay proper homage at first bite as all good Southerners do by saying, "Mmmm-mmm. Now *that's* what I'm talkin' about!"

But something went wrong, and Krispy Kreme, the business, is in a severe downward spiral for inflating sales figures and other Martha Stewarty crimes. Thinking they were Starbucks (the coffee's okay, but you'll chip a tooth on that biscotti), they overbuilt stores like crazy, borrowed too much, and used some accounting techniques that would make Donald Trump blush to keep stockholders happy.

Although nobody's come out and said it, you could summarize KK's problems with a simple and oft-used Southernism: They got above their raisin'.

All that success made them forget their simple roots: wonderfully tacky green-and-white stores in small Southern cities where local high school students could buy cartons at the back door to raise money for the yearbook, band uniforms, lights for the stadium, whatever.

I remember loading my old Chevy II with dozens of boxes and driving them forty miles home, where they sold in about twelve seconds at the gas station.

But then Sarah Jessica Parker got caught eating one and acting like she *discovered* them. My Aunt Fannie.

As movie stars raved, KK stores sprang up like dollarweed across the whole country, and we Southerners watched with a mix of pride and trepidation.

Liser says, wisely, that Krispy Kremes are special because every Southerner has a memory of them. Mine mostly involve highly illegal traffic maneuvers such as jumping a median and making a U-turn after seeing that sacred moment when the HOT DOUGHNUTS NOW! sign flickers on.

Did Moses ignore the burning bush? Did the wise men say, "Nice star, but we've really got some laundry to do?" I think not.

Sadly, with mass production came a drop in standards. Doughnuts sold up Nawth came with instructions for reheating. Say who? Any right-thinking Southerner knows that Krispy Kremes must be eaten hot, preferably at the cash register while you're still fishing for change.

It's not that they're bad cold; it's just that they're ordinary, which is something they should never, ever be.

Liser's theory that we love Krispy Kreme because of the

memories must be the reason that I'm so devastated at the closing of a decidedly un-Southern restaurant chain.

Howard Johnson represented the very best of my childhood: road-trip vacations that always included a stop at HoJo for "frankfurters grilled in butter," fried clam strips in a butter-soaked roll shaped like a boat, and a kids' menu that was perforated so that, after ordering, you could punch out the lines and wear it as a hat.

Howard Johnson, with its iconic orange room, turquoise trim, and Simon the Pieman logo, was the first place I ever ate coconut ice cream, and it was love at first bumpety bite. I've had it plenty of times since, but it has never tasted so good.

Howard Johnson in Boston was the first place my young Southern eyes saw a tableful of nurses, still in their uniforms and just off work, happily swilling beer and cussing up a storm.

Whoa. The only nurse I knew was the one who took my temperature and patted my hand at the doctor's office in my tiny hometown.

Because this was the South, the doctor's office had a few unfortunate furnishings. Aside from the distressing "colored" and "white" waiting rooms that remained all the way into the 1970s, there was a terrifying display of jars containing malformed cow fetuses and the like.

That nurse from my childhood had steel-gray hair and

never cussed or drank anything stronger than a Dr Pepper, although I can tell you if I had to stare at those cow fetuses all day, I'd probably be on the pipe in less than a week.

So I watched these strong workingwomen with booming laughter like they were some new life-form, which, to a Southern tadpole, they were.

I was so busy eavesdropping, I could barely concentrate on another staple in the long HoJo list of weird favorites: Boston baked beans and brown bread, sitting in a steaming trademark brown crock in front of me.

On the way out, you could always buy the brown bread in a can with the HoJo logo on it. Bread in a can? Cussing nurses? Let's just say my world was rocked.

Howard Johnson's in Winston-Salem, North Carolina, was the place where I saw Roger McGuinn and some of The Byrds enjoying what I now realize was preconcert "high food."

I marveled at the good fortune of seeing somebody famous and double-marveled at how they could eat that many French fries. Yes, well. I was very young.

At Howard Johnson's in Jacksonville, North Carolina, I celebrated an engagement that (mercifully) never got off the ground. You could question the wisdom of choosing Howard Johnson's for such a lofty occasion, but this was the '70s, and things were different then. We didn't have pesto.

So, yes, I'm devastated that HoJo has closed all but eight of its original 850 restaurants. The experts say it's no surprise, because of the chain's old buildings, a menu that never changed, and too much competition from those noisy box restaurants that brag about serving margaritas in a fish bowl. To hell with them. They can't make a decent clam roll.

With all the diet hysteria, I guess we shouldn't be surprised that these old-school chains like Krispy Kreme and HoJo are suffering. Maybe it's just as well that they go out gracefully. I'd have hated to see HoJo have to change its famous Indian pudding to Native American pudding or transform its beloved $1.49 fish fry night into a sushi special.

Can I get an Amen?

32

Politicians Serve Up McValues

(With Extra Cheese on the Side)

Why is it that every election year, politicians on both sides insist on trying to convince me that they share my "values." Usually, they don't get specific but rather toss out big, dumb puffy-cloud piffle that doesn't mean much of anything.

Yeah, yeah, I get that every time you trot out the V-word I'm supposed to get a rumbling in my chest that has nothing to do with that unfortunate burrito decision made earlier in the day and everything to do with old-fashioned purple mountains' majesty patriotism.

Of course they must share my values because there they are in the campaign ads, shirt-sleeves rolled up neater than *Queer Eye*'s Carson, happily hugging perky soccer moms and gooey-perfect round babies. (And speaking of soccer moms, how do they all know how to do that knotted sweater thing where the sweater just casually flows from their shoulders? I tried that and damn near hanged myself.)

With all the crowing about values, it won't be long before the candidate coos "I share your values, yes, um do" into the ear of yet another overweight American toddler. Memo to politician: This kid eats Legos and sand all day. Is this really someone you want to cozy up to?

So what are our Values? What do we truly hold dear in a nation where you can actually order off the McValue menu? Once we've gotten past the Big Three—faith, family, and *Fear Factor*—we get to the nittus-grittus, and that, my hons, is where I come in.

I made a little list of things of things I value that I'd like to see the politicians embrace.

Banana pudding as the National Dessert. I don't know if we have a national dessert, but if we do, it's probably something stupid and moldy that Dolley Madison whipped up back when everything was made with raisins and wood.

Sweet iced tea, even at Starbucks. Take that infernal, overpriced mango-infused goo you're pretending to like so much and flush it down your ergonomic potty. (P.S. What the hell is a *barista*? This is America, you idiots, call them what they are: counter help.)

Children who scream in public places for no good reason. If your kids can't behave in public, for heaven's sake do what your grandmother did, and give 'em some Benadryl. Hey, it's not rocket science. A sleepy kid is far less likely to have the energy to chase his sister around the Target rounders with a newly mined booger, as I witnessed recently.

Immediate firing of any restaurant employee who says "No problem" when I ask for something. No problem? Well, one would hope not since *it's your job and all*.

People who don't get the joke. Any joke. I hate to tell you how much heat I took for suggesting that Hong Kong scientists could make more progress on SARS if they'd use actual PETA members for their experiments.

Those inane privacy notices that come with every piece of mail these days. The other day I received one with a bill from a doctor's office. It said: "We do not sell your private information to anyone!" Rather than using a tone that implies that medals and pie should be awarded for this, shouldn't we be able to assume that? I would hope that they also don't kick old people and small dogs in the face "just because."

But, most of all, I want to live long enough to see elections where candidates give me more than a bunch of patriotic platitudes. Is that really too much to ask?

Maybe yes. I met William J. Bennett seven years ago at a naturalization ceremony for several dozen brand-new American citizens. Even for a jaded newsie, it was hard not to choke up while watching them file by a huge, flag-draped trash can and ceremoniously toss in little flags representing their native countries.

In the speech that followed, Bennett extolled the virtues of the Good American: honesty, hard work, self-discipline, and the ability to successfully double down without looking like a monkey at the blackjack tables.

Bennett, a former "drug czar," which, in actual fact, does *not* require him to wear a funny pointy hat, is the self-appointed King of Virtues. So imagine my surprise to learn that he'd lost $8 million playing video poker. *Video poker.* Not even a classy James Bondian game like baccarat, which requires shirt and shoes. Video poker? It reminds me of those old men I used to see in Atlantic City who'd spend all day betting quarters on motorized plastic horses racing around an Astroturf-covered table.

I don't know. For a former U.S. Secretary of Education, it's just so, well, un-czarlike.

You could argue that Bennett spent his own money pursuing a leisure activity in legally operated casinos. He even pointed out that he didn't put his family "at risk" or "spend the milk money."

Hell, I know the guy's insanely rich. He probably didn't even spend the "ski retreat in Vail" money. The rich, hons, are not like you and me. They have never known the sweaty anticipation of scratching off the numbers on the tic-tac-dough lotto tickets after driving ninety minutes to the Citgo station just across the state line in South Carolina. I mean, not me, of course, but friends of mine.

So what if Bennett lost more than $500,000 in Vegas one day? It was his to lose, right?

I don't know. Maybe I'm just bitter. After all, nowhere in my daughter's copy of Bennett's bestselling *Children's Book of Virtues* does it mention anything really useful. Instead of the blather about how "a brave heart will always persevere as long as it takes to get the job done," why not tell us something we can truly use, like how to persevere to get the best five-card hand so we can earn the bonus with our payout?

Instead of the heartwarming tale of the little Dutch boy saving his town by holding his finger in the dike, why not tell us how to sniff out the best slots at Harrah's?

Education schmeducation. As long as you work on your Joker Poker playing skills, you might as well use that high school diploma to wipe the wing grease off your chin at drink-free-till-you-pee night at the casino.

Virtue is its own reward, as they say. But you don't get your room comped with virtue, right, Billy boy?

If I sound jaded about politicians, is it any wonder? I mean, they're just so abominably ordinary. Except maybe for Strom Thurmond, who finally died, but I hear they had him stuffed and he's working as a greeter at the North Myrtle Beach Wal-Mart. What with fathering out-of-wedlock children with his African American mistress while spouting segregationist politics, you could never call him dull.

Ditto Dick Cheney, who knew his microphone was working and still invited a political rival to perform an unnatural anatomical act on himself. Cheney didn't apologize but did say he felt better for having said it.

I feel ya, Mr. Vice President. Who among us hasn't let fly with a few well-chosens in times of deep stress. When I do this, I'm a good enough Methodist to feel automatically ashamed of myself. Apparently, Cheney is just a manly man blowing off some steam.

While Cheney sparked a furor with his "ugly talk," Teresa Heinz Kerry got pounded by the mommies after she appeared to fairly jerk poor little Jack Edwards's thumb from his mouth during a campaign stop. I joined other mommies across the nation in a bobble-headed chorus of "Oh, no, she *did-unt.*"

Teresa crossed the Mommy Line when she swatted at the four-year-old's hand while his own mom stood just inches away. It's not like she's his memaw, which, as we all know, is the only universally recognized "stand in" administrator of parental discipline.

Mommies get squirrely when somebody tries to discipline their kids, even if that somebody is right. Most of us resist the urge, though powerful at times, to point out that Little Johnny was surely raised by wolves.

As a Southern mommy, Elizabeth Edwards should have felt free to say, "Back off, ketchup queen, this doesn't concern you." Perhaps Teresa would have invited her to "shove it," and then the real fun would begin!

The truth is, it's strangely refreshing to hear people in

power say what they really think, no matter how crude. It has provided some comic relief from the pious values and virtues pabulum. What's that? You think civil political discourse that adheres to the rules of living in polite society is all that separates us from the savages? Oh, just go Cheney yourself, I say.

Cussing politicians. Meddling mamas. Gambling-addicted moral authorities. Just when you think politics can't get any weirder, you find yourself saying three words that you thought you never would: Governor Arnold Schwarzenegger.

Although he's no longer the darling of his constituents, Ahnold is said to be eyeing the Oval Office if he can just get around that bothersome Constitutional thingy that prevents "furriners" from being president.

I'm envisioning a cabinet that might include Secretary of State Jean-Claude Van Damme or perhaps Attorney General Jackie Chan.

When Arnold was elected governor of his beloved "Cally-fawn-ee-ya," I thought they had to be kidding. He had so many sexual harassment lawsuits filed against him, it was just too Kobe-licious to consider.

I couldn't believe that Californians elected a guy whose résumé listed his greatest political achievement as "marrying famous Kennedy chick." It didn't even hurt him when somebody dug up an old interview in which he essentially said Adolf Hitler was as cute as a basket of kittens.

California's historic switching of gubernatorial horses in

midstream has led other states to wonder if they should follow suit, asking, "Hey, why can't we have a muscle-bound, knuckleheaded movie star to lead us into the future and shit?"

I live in a state with a decent enough governor. He's earnest and hardworking, but let's face it, he's no George Clooney. I like the man, personally, but, truth be told, what we really need in North Carolina is native son Andy Griffith, who was wise as both Sheriff Andy Taylor *and* Ben Matlock. If he's too frail, we've still got Michael Jordan, who would make damn sure we'd finally get our lottery. (Are you listening, Bennett?)

As crazy as it sounds, Californians clearly confused Arnold's tough Terminator-speak with the real person. Who better to open up a can of whup-ass on high taxes and a limp economy than an action hero? The worm turned, as it often does in politics, and Arnold's approval ratings dived when everyone found out that he wasn't close to superhuman and he'd never be able to save the world.

At least not unless he could get those Charlie's Angels to help him.

Epilogue

Oh, don't y'all just love this part of a book? Sometimes I read it first because I want to make sure everything turns out okay. Whether it's a novel or nonfiction, the epilogue is that fabulous little business at the end that tells you, with great authority and certainty "whatever happened to . . ."

Loose ends are tied up, questions are answered, and you can close the book with a satisfying *thwump* and get on with your life feeling as merrily stuffed as if you'd just eaten a dish of warm peach cobbler. Well, almost.

If my life were a novel—and, really, what Southern life isn't?—I'd want the final epilogue to say something like, "She moved to a big old house on the beautiful Battery in Charleston, where she lives with her adoring husband, devoted daughter, plumber son-in-law (it's an old house in the South, remember?), and three excruciatingly attractive and well-mannered grandchildren. She eats Lowcountry Shrimp and Grits at least four days a week and twice't on Sundays and, as far as regrets, only wishes she could take back that time when she yelled at her six-year-old so loudly that a huge pecan tree limb shattered and landed between them.

The incident, which might have been interpreted by some as a sign from the Almighty to lighten up a bit, merely made her consider a new career path. She considered hiring herself out, making extra money by going to people's houses and screaming at their unwanted limbs: "Pick up your toys!" "Don't yank on my clothes while I'm talking on the phone!" "Finish your math homework!" "Stop eating all my Cheez Waffies!"

Southern women are notoriously resourceful, and screaming at foliage is a whole lot better than yelling at your kids. Even if they did eat all your Cheez Waffies.

When you write about your life, you have to be willing to own up to the stuff that isn't so flattering, especially if it's funny.

When all my friends made noble-sounding New Year's resolutions this year, I simply pledged to upgrade my TiVo by year's end. I should have, instead, resolved to have a stronger work ethic. Okay, any work ethic would do.

Why can't I be more like Stephen King, famous for finishing thirty pages every day before a breakfast of, I'm guessing, a monkey-brain-and-bat's-blood omelet?

Or more like Dave Barry, whose clever use of words like *muskrat, boogers,* and *underpants* earned him a Pulitzer? For years, people have asked me why my newspaper columns aren't syndicated like Barry's, and I always tell the truth: Dave Barry is a once-in-a-lifetime talent who has honed his craft over many, many decades and who is also rumored to have an outstanding collection of photographs of newspaper syndicate executives committing unspeakable acts with farm animals.

What? What'd I say?

That's me, though, a frequent traveler on life's low roads. When I gave my sweet husband a T-shirt for Christmas that said I LIKE MY WOMEN LIKE MY COFFEE, GROUND UP AND IN THE FREEZER, he looked, well, frightened.

If I'm ever going to get that house on the Battery, y'all are going to have to step up and buy a bunch of these books. Hey, I'm not asking for me; think of the grandchildren.

It's not like success would ruin me, hons. I would still be the same bitchy chick with a heart as big as a slop jar that y'all have been kind enough to put up with through three—count 'em, three—collections of Southern strangeness.

I'm not going to be one of those eccentric Southerners who lets a little success go to her head. Never! And rumors that I once showed up for a book signing and demanded a dressing room stocked with 12 cases of Diet Mountain Dew, 60 cans of squeeze cheese, and 118 boxes of Waverly Wafers are just hateful lies!

With fame should come an entourage, and I positively can't wait for mine! True story: One time I saw Martin Lawrence in person. He was making a movie on my street and he had a *huge* entourage, including a muscular man whose only duty was to answer Martin's cell and gently hold it to his ear and two women who allowed him to rest his noggin on their huge chests in between takes like they were a collection of Koosh pillows.

Okay, never mind the entourage. I don't need a bunch of hangers-on tending to my every need. Just one will do, as long as his name is Mr. Matthew McConaughey.

That's it. You can *thwump* now. Peace out.

Acknowledgments

This book wouldn't exist without two people who continue to have faith in the funny: Jenny Bent, my incomparable agent, and Jennifer Enderlin, my brilliant editor. Their wisdom and support sustain and nurture me, and I thank them from the bottom of my heart.

I'm indebted to the entire team at St. Martin's Press, including John Karle, my adorable publicist and an excellent listener; talented designer Sarah Delson; Kim Cardascia, who answers all my silly questions; media escorts Pat Speltz (who introduced me to Memphis ribs, the best food on God's earth), "Kentucky" Barb Ellis (who sniffed out the Talbots outlet for me and I've got the eight-dollar sandals to prove it!), Michelle Dunn, and Lenore Markowitz; and the hardworking, dedicated sales and distribution staff. Bless you all.

Acknowledgments

Special thanks to Mark Kohut, who introduced me to the spectacular folks at Ingram in Nashville, Tennessee. I've never had a better audience!

Over the years, so many booksellers have offered encouragement, advice, and, best of all, a nice, tall stack of books right beside the cash register. I'm especially grateful for the enthusiastic support of Nicki Leone of Bristol Books in Wilmington, North Carolina, who has helped me in more ways than I can list and who reminds me that anything's funny as long as you can insert the word *monkey* somewhere. She's right, of course. Because of Nicki, I am tinkering with the idea for my first novel, *The Da Vinci Monkey*.

I'm deeply grateful for the support of booksellers Cathy Stanley of Two Sisters Bookery as well as Deborah Goodman and the staff of Barnes & Noble in Wilmington, North Carolina, whose awesome wall-of-books display was so amazing, it made me cry.

Other booksellers who have gone above and beyond to promote my work include Nancy Olson and Renee Martin at Quail Ridge Books & Music in Raleigh; Lynn Payne, B & N, Charlotte; Larry Tyler, B & N, Myrtle Beach; Deon Grainger, Waldenbooks, Myrtle Beach; Kathy Patrick, Beauty & the Book, Jefferson, Texas; Katherine Whitfield, Davis-Kidd, Memphis; and Jamie Kornegay and all the fabulous folks at Square Books and Thacker Mountain Radio in beautiful Oxford, Mississippi.

Acknowledgments

Special thanks also to Wanda Jewell, executive director of the Southeast Booksellers Association, and the many members of SEBA who hand-sold my books to sunburned tourists from Virginia to Florida saying, "This is what we're about in the South."

I am deeply indebted to my newspaper, TV, and radio friends especially Colin Burch and the late Mike Morgan at the *Myrtle Beach Sun-News;* Amber Nimocks, Jeff Hidek, Amanda Kingsbury, Ben Steelman, and Allen Parsons at the *Wilmington Morning Star;* Robie Scott at the *Charleston* (SC) *Post & Courier;* Carolyn Gibson of WYPL FM, Memphis; and Betty Ann Sanders and Diane Stokes, TV hostesses extraordinaire.

Hugs and MoonPies to generous and talented authors Lee Smith, Jill McCorkle, Laurie Notaro, Haven Kimmel, and Haywood Smith, who have been kind enough to support me in front of God and everybody.

Keeping me nourished, body and soul, are my wonderful friends Lawton and Mabel Halterman, who share the bounty of their garden, including the best new potatoes and butterbeans on earth, and Lawrence Shadrach and his daughter, Bess, who keep me in gardenia bouquets every June. Their daylily garden next door is a vision I savor all summer long.

Thanks also to the delightful Ronda Rich for so graciously sharing her knowledge of the speakers' circuit with a rookie who still feels like throwing up right before.

Acknowledgments

For making me laugh, or making me think, this year, I give thanks to an assortment of friends, new and old, including Tim Russell, Courtney Grannan, Kara Chiles, Debbi Pratt, Susan Reinhardt, P. D. Midgett, Laura Mitchell, Vance Williams, and Bill Atkinson.

And, finally, especially and most of all, I'm grateful to my wonderful husband, Scott Whisnant, who would be perfect even if he didn't think that Angelina Jolie with her big ol' futon lips is overrated, and to our precious daughter, Sophie, who is smarter, funnier, and kinder than I and who is patiently teaching me how to swim and raise crickets. I love you big.

Don't Miss Celia's Other Books!

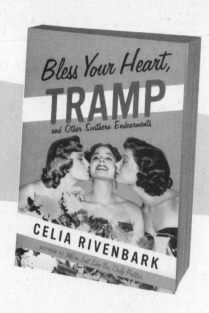

Available wherever books are sold.
www.celiarivenbark.com

 St. Martin's Griffin

ROBIN HOOD

Robin Hood

HENRY GILBERT

WORDSWORTH CLASSICS

This edition published 1994 by Wordsworth Editions Limited
8b East Street, Ware, Hertfordshire SG12 9HJ

ISBN 1 85326 127 0

4 6 8 10 9 7 5

Typeset by Antony Gray
Printed and bound in Great Britain by
Mackays of Chatham plc, Chatham, Kent

CONTENTS

PREFACE

Once upon a time the great mass of English people were unfree. They could not live where they chose, nor work for whom they pleased. Society in those feudal days was mainly divided into lords and peasants. The lords held the land from the king, and the peasants or villeins were looked upon as part of the soil, and had to cultivate it to support themselves and their masters. If John or Dick, thrall of a manor, did not like the way in which the lord or his steward treated him, he could not go to some other part of the country and get work under a kinder owner. If he tried to do this he was looked upon as a criminal, to be brought back and punished with the whip or the branding-iron, or cast into prison.

When the harvest was plenteous and his master was kind or careless, I do not think the peasant felt his serfdom to be so unbearable as at other times. When, however, hunger stalked through the land, and the villein and his family starved; or when the lord was of a stern or exacting nature, and the serf was called upon to do excessive labour, or was otherwise harshly treated, then, I think, the old Teutonic or Welsh blood in the English peasant grew hot, and he longed for freedom.

The silence and green peace of forest lands stood in those days along many a league where now the thick yellow corn grows, or the cows roam over the rich pastures, or even where today the bricky suburbs of towns straggle over the country. Such forests must have been places of terror and fascination for the poor villein who could see them from where he delved in his fields. In their quiet glades ran the king's deer, and in their dense thickets skulked the boar, creatures whose killing was reserved for the king and a few of his friends, the great nobles, and princes of the

Church. A poor man, yeoman or peasant, found slaying one of the royal beasts of the forest was cruelly maimed as a punishment. Or if he was not caught, he ran and hid deep in the forest and became an outlaw, a 'wolf's-head' as the term was, and then anyone might slay him that could.

It was in such conditions that Robin Hood lived, and did deeds of daring such as we read of in the ballads and traditions which have come down to us. Because his name is not to be found in the crabbed records of lawyers and such men, some people have doubted whether Robin Hood ever really existed. But I am sure that Robin was once very much alive. It may be that the unknown poets who made the ballads idealised him a little – that is, they described him as being more daring, more successful, more of a hero perhaps, than he really was; but that is what poets and writers are always expected to do.

The ballads which we have about Robin Hood and his band of outlaws number about forty. The oldest are the best, because they are the most natural and exciting. The majority of the later poems are very poor; many are tiresome repetitions of one or two incidents, while others are rough, doggerel rhymes, without spirit or imagination.

In the tales which I have told in this book, I have used a few of the best episodes related in the ballads; but I have also thought out other tales about Robin, and I have added incidents and events which have been invented so as to give a truthful picture of the times in which he lived.

HENRY GILBERT
London, July 1912

CHAPTER ONE

How Robin Became an Outlaw

It was high noon in summer-time, and the forest seemed to sleep. Hardly a breeze stirred the broad fans of the oak leaves, and the only sound was the low hum of insects which flew to and fro unceasingly in the cool twilight under the wide-spreading boughs.

So quiet did it seem and so lonely, that almost one might think that nothing but the wild red deer, or his fierce enemy the slinking wolf, had ever walked this way since the beginning of the world. There was a little path worn among the thick bushes of hazel, dogberry, and traveller's joy, but so narrow was it and so faint that it could well have been worn by the slender, fleeting feet of the doe, or even by the hares and rabbits which had their home in a great bank among the roots of a beech near by.

Few, indeed, were the folks that ever came this way, for it was in the loneliest part of Barnisdale Forest. Besides, who had any right to come here save it was the king's foresters keeping strict watch and ward over the king's deer? Nevertheless, the rabbits which should have been feeding before their holes, or playing their mad pranks, seemed to have bolted into their burrows as if scared by something which had passed that way. Only now, indeed, were one or two peeping out to see that things were quiet again. Then a venturesome bunny suddenly scampered out, and in a moment others trooped forth.

A little way beyond the bank where the rabbits were now nibbling or darting off in little mad rushes, the path made a bend, and then the giant trunks of the trees were fewer, and more light came through from the sky. Suddenly the trees ceased, and the little sly path ran into a wide glade where grass grew, and bushes of holly and hazel stood here and there.

A man stood close by the path, behind a tree, and looked out into the glade. He was dressed in a tunic made of a rough green cloth, open at the top, and showing a bronzed neck. Round his waist was a broad leathern girdle in which were stuck at one place a dagger, and at the other side three long arrows. Short breeches of soft leather covered his thighs, below which he wore hosen of green wool, which reached to his feet. The latter were encased in shoes of stout pig's leather.

His head of dark brown curls was covered by a velvet cap, at the side of which was stuck a short feather, pulled from the wing of a plover. His face, bronzed to a ruddy tan by wind and weather, was open and frank, his eye shone like a wild bird's, and was as fearless and as noble. Great of limb was he, and seemingly of a strength beyond his age, which was about twenty-five years. In one hand he carried a long-bow, while the other rested on the smooth bole of the beech before him.

He looked intently at some bushes which stood a little distance before him in the glade, and moved not a muscle while he watched. Sometimes he looked beyond far to the side of the glade where, on the edge of the shaw or wood, two or three deer were feeding under the trees, advancing towards where he stood.

Suddenly he saw the bushes move stealthily; an unkempt head issued between the leaves, and the haggard face of a man looked warily this way and that. Next moment, out of the bush where the hidden man lay, an arrow sped. Straight to the feeding deer it flew, and sank in the breast of the nearest doe. She ran a few feet and then fell; while the others, scared, ran off into the trees.

Not at once did the hidden man issue from his hiding-place to take up the animal he had slain. He waited patiently while one might count fifty, for he knew that, should there be a forester skulking near who should meet the scampering deer whose companion had been struck down, he would know from their frightened air that something wrongful had been done, and he would search for the doer.

The moments went slowly by and nothing moved; neither did the hidden man, nor he who watched him. Nor did a forester show himself on the edge of the shaw where the deer had fled. Feeling himself secure, therefore, the man came from the bush, but there was no bow and arrows in his hand, for these he had left secure in his hiding-place to be brought away another day.

He was dressed in the rough and ragged homespun of a villein, a rope round his brown tunic, and his lower limbs half covered with loose trousers of the same material as his tunic, but more holed and patched. Looking this way and that, he walked half-bent across to where the doe lay, and leaning over it, he snatched his knife from his belt and began almost feverishly to cut portions of the tenderest parts from the carcass.

As the man behind the tree saw him, he seemed to recognise him, and muttered, 'Poor lad!' The villein wrapped the deer's flesh in a rough piece of cloth, and then rose and disappeared between the trees. Then with swift and noiseless footsteps the watcher went back through the path and into the depths of the forest. A few moments later the villein, with wary eyes looking this way and that, was passing swiftly between the boles of the trees. Every now and then he stopped and rubbed his red hands in the long, moist grass, to remove the tell-tale stains of blood.

Suddenly, as he came from behind the giant trunk of an oak, the tall form of the man who had watched him stood in his pathway. Instantly his hand went to his knife, and he seemed about to spring upon the other.

'Man,' said he in the green tunic, 'what madness drives you to this?'

The villein recognised the speaker at once, and gave a fierce laugh.

'Madness!' he said. ' 'Tis not for myself this time, Master Robin. But my little lad is dying of hunger, and while there's deer in the greenwood he shall not starve.'

'Your little lad, Scarlet?' said Robin. 'Is your sister's son living with you now?'

'Ay,' replied Scarlet. 'You've been away these three weeks and cannot have heard.' He spoke in a hard voice, while the two continued their walk down a path so narrow that while Robin walked before, Scarlet was compelled to walk just behind.

'A sennight since,' Scarlet went on, 'my sister's husband, John a' Green, was taken ill and died. What did our lord's steward do? Said, "Out ye go, baggage, and fend for yourself. The holding is for a man who'll do due services for it." '

' 'Twas like Guy of Gisborne to do thus,' said Robin; 'the evil-hearted traitor!'

'Out she went, with no more than the rags which covered herself and the bairns,' said Scarlet fiercely. 'If I had been by I could not have kept my knife from his throat. She came to me; dazed she was and ill. She had the hunger-plague in truth, and sickened and died last week. The two little ones were taken in by neighbours, but I kept little Gilbert myself. I am a lonely man, and I love the lad, and if harm should happen to him I shall put my mark upon Guy of Gisborne for it.'

As Robin had listened to the short and tragic story of the wreck of a poor villein's home, his heart burned in rage against the steward, Sir Guy of Gisborne, who ruled the manor of Birkencar for the White Monks of St Mary's Abbey with so harsh a hand. But he knew that the steward did no more than the abbot and monks permitted him, and he cursed the whole brood of them, rich and proud as they were, given over to hunting and high living on the services and rents which they wrung from the poor villeins, who were looked upon merely as part of the soil of the manors which they tilled.

Robin, or Robert of Locksley, as he was known to the steward and the monks, was a freeman, or socman, as it was termed, and he was a young man of wealth as things went then. He had his own house and land, a farm of some hundred and sixty acres of the richest land on the verge of the manor, and he knew full well that the monks had long cast covetous eyes upon his little holding. It lay beside the forest, and was called the Outwoods. He and his ancestors had held this land for generations, first from the lords to whom the manor of Birkencar had been given by King William, and for the last generation or so from the Abbey of St Mary, to which the last owner, the Lord Guy de Wrothsley, had left it in his will.

Robin held his land at a rent, and so long as he paid this to the monks they could not legally oust him from his farm, much as they would have liked to do this. Robin was looked upon by the abbot as a discontented and malicious man. He had often bearded the abbot in his own monastery, and told him to his face how wickedly he and his stewards treated the villeins and poorer tenants of their manors. Such defiance in those days was reckoned to be almost unheard of, and the monks and Guy of Gisborne, their steward at Birkencar, hated Robin and his free speech as much as Robin hated them for their tyranny and oppression.

'Pity it is I was away,' said Robin in reply to Scarlet's last words. 'But you could have gone to Outwoods, and Scadlock would have given you food.'

'Ay, Master Robin,' said Scarlet, 'you have ever been the good and true friend of us all. But I, too, have been a freeman, and I cannot beg my bread. You have made enemies enough on our behalf as it is, and I would not live upon you to boot. No, while there is deer in the greenwood, I and the little lad shall not starve. Besides, Master Robin, you should look to yourself. If your unfriends had known how long you would be away they would – it hath been whispered – have proclaimed you an outlaw, and taken your land in your absence, and killed you when you returned.'

Robin laughed. 'Ay, I have heard of it while I was away.'

Scarlet looked at him in wonder. He thought he had been telling his friend a great and surprising secret.

'You have heard of it?' he replied; 'now that is passing strange.'

Robin made no answer. He knew well that his enemies were only looking out for an opportunity of thrusting him to ruin. Many a man going on a long journey had come back to find that in his absence his enemy had made oath to a justice that he had fled on account of some wrong-doing, and thus had caused him to be proclaimed an outlaw, whose head anyone could cut off.

Scarlet was silent, thinking of many strange tales which the villeins, when they sat together at ale after work, had spoken concerning their great friend Robin.

Suddenly, from a little way before them, came the sound as if a squirrel was scolding. Then there was silence for a space; and then the cry, a lonely sad cry it was, as of a wolf. Instantly Robin stopped, laid the long-bow he had in his hand at the root of a great oak, together with the arrows from his girdle. Then, turning to Scarlet, he said in a low stern voice:

'Place the deer's meat you have in your tunic beside these. Quick, man, ere the foresters see your bulging breast. You shall have it safely anon.'

Almost mechanically, at the commanding tones Scarlet took the rough piece of hempen cloth in which he had wrapped the flesh of the doe from the breast of his tunic and laid it beside the bow and arrows. Next moment Robin resumed his walk. When they had gone a few steps, Scarlet looked round at the place where they had placed the things. They were gone!

A cold chill seemed to grip his heart, and he almost stopped, but Robin's stern voice said: 'Step out, man, close behind!' Poor Scarlet, sure that he was in the presence of witchcraft, did as he was bidden; but crossed himself to fend off evil.

Next moment the narrow path before them was blocked by the forms of two burly foresters, with bows at their backs and long staves in their hands. Their hard eyes looked keenly at Robin and Scarlet, and for a moment it seemed that they meditated barring their way. But Robin's bold look as he advanced made them change their minds, and they let them pass.

'When freeman and villein are found together,' scoffed one, there's ill brewing for their lord.'

'And when two foresters are found together,' said Robin, with a short laugh, 'some poor man's life will be sworn away ere long.'

'I know ye, Robert of Locksley,' said the one who had first spoken, 'as your betters know ye, for a man whose tongue wags too fast.'

'And I know thee, Black Hugo,' replied Robin, 'for a man who swore his best friend to ruin to join his few poor acres to thine.'

The man's face darkened with rage, while the other forester laughed at his discomfiture. Black Hugo looked at Robin as if he would have thrown himself upon him; but Robin's fearless eyes overawed him, and he sullenly turned away without another word.

Robin and Scarlet resumed their walk, and in a little while had issued from the forest, and were tramping through the bush and thick undergrowth of the waste lands which divided the farms of the manor on this side from the forest.

At last they came to the top of an incline, and before them the land sloped down to the cultivated fields and the pasture which surrounded the little village of villeins' huts, with the manor-house at a distance beyond the village half-way up another slope. Scarlet looked keenly about him, to see if anyone in the fields had seen him coming from the forest; for he had run from his work of dyke building to shoot the deer, and wondered whether his absence had been discovered. If it had, he didn't care for the scourging-post and the whip on his bare back, which might be his portion tomorrow when the steward's men came round to find his work only half done. At any rate, his little lad, Gilbert of the White Hand, would have a king's supper that night.

Would he? He suddenly remembered, and again fear shook him. Where had Robin's bow and arrows and his venison disappeared? Had some goblin or elf snatched them up, or had he really looked in the wrong place, and had the foresters found them by now? He clenched his jaw and looked back, his hand upon his knife, almost expecting to see the two foresters coming after him.

'Hallo,' said Robin carelessly, 'there are my bow and arrows and your venison, lad.'

Turning, Scarlet saw the things lying beside a tussock of grass at a little distance, where he was certain he had looked a moment before and seen nothing!

'Master,' he said in an awed voice, 'this is sheer wizardry. I – I – fear for you if unfriends learn you are helped by the evil spirits that dwell in the woods.'

'Scarlet,' said Robin, 'I thought thou wert a wiser man, but, like the rest, thou seemest to be no more than a fool. Have no fear for me. My friends of the woods are quite harmless, and are no worse than thou or I.'

'Master,' said Scarlet, sorry for his hasty speech, 'I crave pardon for my fool's words. My tongue ran before my thoughts, for the sight of those things where nothing had been a moment before affrighted me. But I know there cannot be worse things in the woods than there are in strong castles and abbots' palaces whose masters oppress and maim poor villeins. Say, master, is that which has helped us but now – is it a brownie, as men call it – a troll?'

Robin looked quietly into Scarlet's face for a moment or two without speaking.

'Scarlet,' he said, 'I think I see a time before us when thou and I will be much together in the greenwood. Then I will show thee my friends there. But until then, Scarlet, not a word of what has passed today. Thou swearest it?'

'By the gentle Virgin!' said Scarlet, throwing up his hand as he took the oath.

'Amen!' replied Robin, doffing his cap and bending his head at the name. 'Now,' he went on, 'take thy meat and hand me my bow and arrows. For I must back to the greenwood. And tell thy little man, Gilbert, that Robin wishes him to get well quickly, for I would go shooting with him again on the uplands at the plovers.'

'Ay,' said Scarlet, and his haggard, hungry face shone with a gentle look as he spoke, 'the little lad hath ever loved to speak of you since you took such note of him. Your words will hearten him bravely.'

When the two men had parted, Robin turned and plunged into the thick undergrowth, but in a different direction from that in which he had come with Scarlet. He looked up at the sun and quickened his pace, for he saw it was two hours past noon. Soon he had reached the trees, and threading his way unerringly among them, he struck southwards towards the road that ran for many a mile through the forest from Barnisdale into Nottinghamshire.

With a quick and eager step did Robin pass through the glades, for he was going to see the lady he loved best in all the world. Fair Marian was she called, the daughter of Richard FitzWalter of Malaset. Ever since when, as a boy, Robin had shot and sported in Locksley Chase, near where he had been born, Marian had been his playmate, and though she was an earl's daughter, and Robin was but a yeoman and not rich, they had loved each other dearly, and sworn that neither would marry anyone else.

This day she was to journey from her father's castle at Malaset to Linden Lea, near by Nottingham, to stay a while at the castle of her uncle, Sir Richard at Lee, and Robin had promised to guard her through the forest.

Soon he reached a broad trackway, carpeted with thick grass and with deep wheel-holes here and there in the boggy hollows. He walked rapidly along this, and did not rest till he had covered some five miles. Then, coming to where another road crossed it, he paused, looked about him keenly, and then disappeared among some hazel bushes that crowned a bank beside the four ways.

Proceeding for some distance, he at length gained a hollow where the ground was clear of bushes. On one side was a bare place where the sand showed, and to this Robin walked straightway. On the bare ground were a few broken twigs which to the ordinary eye would have seemed to have been blown there by the wind; but with hands on knees Robin bent and scanned them keenly.

'One bent at the head and eight straight twigs,' he said under his breath; 'a knight on horseback, that will mean, with eight knaves afoot. They are halted on the western road not far from here. Now what means that?'

He stood up, and turning away, quickly crossed the road by which he had come, and dived into the forest which skirted the right-hand road. Very cautiously he made his way between the trees, taking care not to step on a twig as he walked rapidly over the grass, his quick eyes meanwhile bent in every direction, trying to pierce the twilight of the thick forest round about.

Suddenly he dropped on his knees, and began working away farther into the trees. He had heard the tiniest noise of a jingling bridle before him. In a little while, peering from between the branches of a young yew tree, he saw, drawn up into the deepest shadow of the trees, a band of armed men, with a knight in chain mail on horseback in their midst.

Eagerly he scanned each, in the endeavour to learn to what lord they belonged; but the men on foot were dressed in plain jerkins, and the knight bore a blank shield, kite-shaped. For some moments he was baffled in his attempt to learn who these men were, and why they lay hid in the wood as if about to set on some travellers whom they expected to pass by. Then the knight swept his glance round the forest, and with a gesture of impatience and an oath quieted his restive horse.

At the sound of his voice Robin recognised him, and his face went stern, and a fierce light came into his eyes.

'So, Roger de Longchamp,' he said to himself, 'you would seize by force my lady, whose favour you cannot get by fair means!'

For this Sir Roger was a proud and tyrannical knight, who had asked for the hand of Fair Marian, but her father had refused him. FitzWalter loved his daughter, and though he laughed at her for her love of Robin, he would not give her to a man with so evil a fame as Roger de Longchamp, brother of that proud prelate the Bishop of Fécamp, and favourite of Duke Richard.

Often, when Robin had thought how Sir Roger de Longchamp or any other man, however evil he was, could visit Sir Richard FitzWalter and speak openly with Marian, he became moody, and wondered whether indeed there was any truth in the tales which old Stephen of Gamwell, his uncle, had told him concerning his noble lineage. He had said that, three generations before, Robin's ancestors had owned broad lands and many manors, and had been lords of Huntingdon town. But that, for having taken part in some revolt of the English against the Norman conqueror, their lands had been seized by the king, the earl slain, and his kinsmen hunted this way and that into obscurity.

Everyone knew now, that the earldom and lands of Huntingdon were in the hands of the king himself, and that the title had been given to David, brother of the Scottish king. But Robin had often wondered whether he could regain something of the former honours and rank of his family. If so, then he would go and claim Marian boldly, and take no denial.

A movement among the lurking men before him caused him to cease his thinking. A man came running through the trees towards them, and going up to the knight, said in a low voice:

'They are coming! The lady and one varlet are on horseback, the others are walking. There are nine in all, and they are mere house-churls.'

'Good!' said the knight. 'When they come near I will ride against them and seize the lady's bridle. Should the churl who is riding seek to follow me, do you knock him down.'

Robin smiled grimly as he listened, and slipped an arrow from its fastening at his belt. Almost immediately the voices of men were heard coming along the grassy road, with the beat of horses' hooves, and in a little while Robin's heart warmed as he saw through the leaves the gentle womanly figure of Marian on a horse, with her hood thrown back from her face. She was conversing with Walter, the steward of her father's house, who rode beside her.

Next moment the knight had burst through the trees, followed by his men. The brave Walter instantly pushed his horse before that of his mistress, and with a stout staff which he carried prepared to defend her, while the others of her guards also ran before her. Sir Roger struck at the steward with his sword, which sliced a huge splinter from the staff which the other held. With a quick turn of the staff, however, Walter beat on the knight's sword hand, and so shrewd was the blow that the weapon fell from the knight's fingers. It was hung by a strap at his wrist, however, and with a furious cry he regained the haft again.

In a second more the sword would have pierced the body of the brave steward, but suddenly he was jerked from his horse by one of Sir Roger's men, and fell senseless on the ground. The struggle between Marian's men and those of the knight was now becoming hot, but the poor villeins with their staffs or short spears had little chance against the swords of the robbers.

Already the hand of Sir Roger was on the reins in Marian's fingers, and with flashing eyes she was trying to back her horse away, when suddenly there came a sound like a great bee, and as she looked at the bars of the knight's visor she was aware that something flew into them, and next moment she saw the long yellow shaft of an arrow quivering before them.

The knight gave a deep groan, swayed, and then fell from his horse. Instantly his men ceased fighting; one, the chief among them, ran to the dead knight, drew the ruddily tipped arrow from his master's eye, and then all looked swiftly up and down the broad track and at the dense green forest at their sides.

' 'Tis but one man!' said one of them. 'It came from the left side here.'

'Ay, but I know the bolt! It is – ' began he that still held the arrow, but he never ended his words. Again came a swift sound through the air, but this time like the low whistling of a forest bird, and he sank to the ground with a small black arrow-shaft jutting from his breast. The bolt had been shot from the right side, showing that more than one bowman observed them.

Instantly the others scattered and ran into the forest, but ere the last could reach its shade an arrow, no larger than a birding bolt, issued from the trees on the right and sank into the shoulder of the last fugitive, who shrieked, but still ran on.

Next moment Marian saw Robin, with cap in hand, issue from the wood beside her. He came to her side, and with flushing cheeks she bent to him and said:

'Sweet Robin, I knew thou wouldst not fail me. That was a brave shot of thine which struck down that felon knight. But, dear heart of mine, if he be he whom I think he is, his death will work thee much harm.'

She gave him her hand, and fondly Robin kissed it.

'He is Roger de Longchamp, sweetheart,' replied Robin; 'but if it had been King Henry himself lurking thus to do you harm, I would not have saved my bolt.'

'But, Robin dear,' went on Marian, and her eyes were soft yet proud, 'the bishop his brother will pursue thee and outlaw thee for this. And thou wilt lose lands and name for my sake! O Robin! Robin! But I will take counsel of Sir Richard at Lee, who loves thee dearly, how best to get thee pardon from the bishop.'

'Sweet Marian,' said Robin, and very stern was his look and voice, 'I will have no pardon from any proud prelate for any ill I do the evil brood of priests. Come soon, come late, I knew that ere long I should do some deed against the doers of evil who sit in strong castles or loll in soft abbeys and oppress and wrong poor or weaker folk. It is done at last, and I am content. Trouble not for me, dear heart. But now, let us get thee to a safe place ere those runaway rogues raise the hue and cry after me. Walter,' said Robin to the poor steward, who, dazed and faint, was now sitting up in the road, 'gather thy wits together, brave man, and see to thy mistress. Lads,' he said to the villeins, most of whom were wounded, 'think no more of thy wounds till thy lady be safe. The knight that is slain hath friends as evil as he, and they may be down upon us ere long, and then you may not escape so lightly. And now trot forward to where the roads fork, and I will join thee anon.'

Robin helped Walter on his horse, and Fair Marian and her faithful villeins went forward. When they had passed, Robin pulled the dead knight out of the track and far into the forest, then raised the visor of the helm, placed the dead man's sword-hilt on his breast, and folded the limp arms over it, so that it seemed as if the dead were kissing the cross of the sword. Then, with bared head, kneeling, he said a short prayer for the repose of the knight's soul. He did the same with the dead body of the marauder who had been slain by the second arrow, and then, picking up both his own bolt and the smaller arrow, he slashed the knight's horse across the loins and saw it go flying down a forest drive that would lead it quite away from the spot. All this

The death of Sir Roger de Longchamp

he did so as to put pursuers off the track as long as possible.

Then, going a few steps into the forest in the direction in which the knight's men had fled, he put a horn to his lips and blew a long shrill blast with strange broken notes at the end. Afterwards he hastened to rejoin Fair Marian, and with his hand upon the bridle of her horse he led the way from the beaten track, and passing by secret ways and tiny paths only half visible, he rapidly pushed on, and very soon they were in the deeps of the forest where none who were with him had ever passed before.

Fair Marian, content to know that Robin was with her, saw nothing to fear in the silence and sombre shadows about them; but many of the villeins, as they walked in single file along the narrow way made by the hooves of the horses, often crossed themselves as they passed along some gloomy grove of trees, or wound across the solitary glades where everything was so silent and grey that it seemed as if no life had stirred there since the beginning of the world.

To their simple minds they were risking the loss not only of their lives, but of their immortal souls, by venturing into these wild places, the haunts of wood demons, trolls, and witches. They kept close together, the last man in the line looking ever behind him in dread; while all glanced furtively this way and that between the close trunks of the mossy trees, expecting every moment to see the evil eyes of elves gleaming out at them, or dreading that warlocks or witches, with red grinning mouths, would dart from behind some great screen of ivy or dodder which hung from some of the old trees.

The only sounds to be heard were the soft padding of their own footsteps over the thick grass or the snap of a twig here and there. Sometimes far up through the dense leaves above their heads they could hear the cry of a bird, or from a thicket here and there would come a strange, uncanny cheep! cheep! but nothing could be seen. Once or twice they heard the murmur of water, and they would come upon a little lonely brooklet half hidden beneath the undergrowth.

Once they passed through a wide glade, and in the middle thereof were two green mounds close to each other, and at the sight of them the poor churls were exceeding afraid.

'Trolls' houses!' they whispered to each other, and pointed and hurried on.

'I doubt we 'scape with our souls this day,' said one in a half whisper.

'Why doth he that leads us bring us by those places of dread?' growled another. 'The trolls will spy us as we pass, and work some wizardry upon us, and the bones of all of us will be left to whiten in this unholy forest till the crack of doom.'

So closely, in their terror, did they press upon the haunches of Walter's horse that he had to warn them.

'Keep back, thou fellows,' he said. 'Thou knowest my horse is mettlesome, and if he lash out at thee, thy heads, though thick, will not be thick enough to withstand his hoof.'

By this time the light from the sky showed that the afternoon was drawing to even. Little had Robin spoken since he began the swift flight through the forest, but now he turned to Marian, and with a smile said:

'Forgive me, sweet lady, for my seeming churlishness. But Roger de Longchamp's friends at his castle of Evil Hold are men not to be despised. Their cruel deeds are not fit for thy ears, and I have hastened to escape them speedily. Have I taxed thee beyond thy strength?'

'Nay, nay, Robin dear,' said Marian, with a sweet look. 'I knew what was in thy heart, and therefore I troubled thee not with talk. But what mean you by the Evil Hold? I knew not Roger de Longchamp's castle of Wrangby was so named.'

'That is how it is named by the poor folk who own him lord,' replied Robin, 'because of the nameless deeds that are committed there by him and his boon comrades, Isenbart de Belame, Niger le Grym, Hamo de Mortain, Ivo de Raby, and others.'

Marian shuddered and paled at the names.

'I have heard of them,' she said in a low voice. 'Let us push on,' she continued. 'I am not tired, Robin, and I would fain see thee safe in Sir Richard's castle.'

'Have no fear for me,' laughed Robin. 'While I have my good bow, and the greenwood stands to shelter me, I can laugh at all who wish me ill. In a little while now you shall be greeting your uncle, and safe within his strong walls.'

Suddenly from somewhere in the twilight forest before them

came a scream as of some animal or bird in the talons of a hawk. Robin stopped and peered forward. Then there came the lonely cry of a wolf, causing the villeins behind to shudder as they, too, strained their eyes into the murky depths of the trees.

Robin stepped forward, and as he did so he gave a cry as if a blackcock called his mate; then he led Marian's horse forward at a slow pace. In a little while they came to rising ground, and approaching the top they saw the sinking sun gleaming redly through the trees. At the summit they found the trees gave place to a gentle slope of greensward, and before them, beyond some meadows, lay a castle, and on a trackway not far from the forest were two riders passing towards the castle.

'I think,' said Robin, 'that yonder horsemen are Sir Richard and his kinsman, Sir Huon de Bulwell.'

'It is in truth they,' replied Marian; 'I think they have been to meet me by the highway, and are no doubt wondering what hath befallen me. Give them a call, dear Robin, and do you, Walter, ride forward and tell them that, thanks to my friend, Robert of Locksley, I am safe and well.'

Robin blew a blast on his horn. The horsemen turned their heads at the sound, and Marian, pushing her horse away from the trees, waved a kerchief at them. Instantly they recognised her, and waving their hands in greeting, began to ride towards the party.

'Tell me, Robin,' said Marian as, having dismounted to rest her stiffened limbs, she walked beside her lover, 'what meant those cries we heard but now? It was as if someone signalled and you answered them.'

'It meant, sweetheart,' replied Robin, 'that a friend of mine in the greenwood there saw these horsemen and thought they might be our enemies. But I guessed they could not have reached this spot so quickly as we, and that they whom he saw were some of Sir Richard's meinie [followers] come to look for thee. Then I warned him that I thought all was well, and so came on.'

'Who are these friends who guard you thus when you pass through the forest?' she asked. 'Is it the same who shot those smaller arrows at Sir Roger's men?'

'I will tell thee, sweeting,' replied Robin. 'They are dwellers in the forest whom once I rescued from a fearful death at the hands of evil and cruel men. And ever since they have been my dear friends, to guard and watch for me when I am in the greenwood.'

'I am glad thou hast such friends, dear Robin,' said Marian. 'It lightens my heart to think thou hast such faithful watchers. For I fear me that thou wilt have need of such ere long.'

But now Sir Richard at Lee and his kinsman had come up, and great was their joy to find Fair Marian was safe, for they had been much troubled to find no sign of her upon the road by which she usually came; and were riding back to the castle to collect a body of retainers to search the forest roads for her.

When Sir Richard and Sir Huon were told of Sir Roger's attempt to kidnap Marian, and of how Robin had slain him, they looked grave, and Sir Huon shook his head. But Sir Richard, a grey-haired man with a noble countenance, turned to Robin and shook him by the hand heartily.

'Thou hast rid the earth of a vile oppressor and a felon knight,' he cried, 'and I for one thank thee heartily. The evil that he hath done to poor folks, the robbery of orphans, the cruelties to women – all his crimes have cried long to heaven for vengeance. And I rejoice that your good bolt hath pierced his evil brain.'

'Ye say truth,' said Sir Huon gravely, 'but I think me of what Robin may suffer. The bishop will not let his brother go unavenged, nor will the comrades of Roger rest in their efforts to capture Robin and take him to their crucet-house [torture-house], which men rightly call the Evil Hold.'

'Fear not for me,' said Robin, with a quiet yet firm voice. 'I doubt not I shall escape all their traps and snares. But do you and the father of my dear lady take care that, in despite, those evil knights do not capture Fair Marian and wreak their vengeance upon her. As for me, I will do all I may to shield her.'

'Ye say truth,' said Sir Richard. 'I had not thought on that, but of a surety Isenbart de Belame and Niger le Grym will wish to seize our fair niece as a prize. God and Our Lady forfend us all from their evil wiles.'

'Amen,' said Robin; 'and meanwhile I will keep a watch upon Castle Wrangby and its villainous lords.'

For the next three days Robin and Marian, with Sir Richard and the Lady Alice, his wife, spent the time merrily together, hunting with hawks along the leas, or hunting the wild boar in the woods. At night in hall they played hoodman blind, or danced to the viols, or sat at draughts or chess, or heard minstrels sing to them or tell them tales of Arthur's knights, of Roland, and of Oliver his dear friend, or of Ogier the Dane, or Graelent, and how they had all vanished away into the realms of the Fairy Queen.

But on the fourth day Robin went into the forest to shoot small birds, and as he sat on a bank he heard the tapping as of a woodpecker. Looking up into the limbs of the wych-elm above him, he saw a little man's face peeping out through the leaves.

'Come down, Ket the Trow,' said Robin, 'and tell me thy news, lad.'

Next moment the little man had dropped from the tree and stood before Robin. Ket was no taller than a medium-sized lad of fourteen, but he was a man full grown, with great breadth of chest, long hairy arms and legs, the muscles on which stood up like iron bands. His hair was black, thick, and curly; he had no shoes on his feet, and the only covering he wore was a stout leather jacket laced in front, and close-fitting breeches of doe-skin that reached to his knees. His face, broad and good-natured, was lit up with a smile as he returned Robin's kindly gaze, and his eyes, bright and keen, yet gentle as those of a fawn, rested on Robin's face with a look of respect that was almost reverence.

'You followed the men that fled. Where went they?' asked Robin.

'Through the forest north by west went they, till they came to the burn,' answered Ket. 'They forded it at the Stakes and crossed the moor to the Ridgeway. Through Hag's Wood they wended, and through Thicket Hollow, and then I knew where they would go; by the Hoar Tree and the Cwelm stone, over Gallows Hill and by the Mark Oak, till they came to the Dead Man's Hill, and so by the lane of the Red Stones to the Evil Hold. All night I watched in the Mark Oak, and at dawn I saw three knights ride from the castle. One went south by east, and with him on horses were two of the knaves I had followed. Two went east, and these I followed. They had ten horsed knaves with them. They went through Barnisdale Wood, and I left them on the wide road which leads to Doncaster.'

'You did well, Ket,' replied Robin. 'And then?'

'I went to thy house, Outwoods, by Barnisdale Wood,' replied Ket, and Scadlock thy man I met in Old Nick's Piece, and sad was he, for he said that he saw Guy of Gisborne and two monks riding by thy land the day before, and they spoke together, and stopped and pointed at thy fields. And he thinks the curse of that Judas, Sir Guy, is on thy land, and that ruin cometh quickly to thee, and full was he of woe, and much he longed to see thy face.'

Robin was silent for a while, and he was sunk in thought.

'Heard you aught else? What of Scarlet and the little lad?'

'I saw them not, but at night I crept down to the village and stole beside the cot with the bush before the door [the village alehouse], and leaned my ear against a crack and listened. And much woe and anger was in the mouths of the villeins, so that they drank little.'

'What said they?' asked Robin. 'How many think you were there?'

Ket lifted up both hands and showed ten, then he dropped one hand and showed five fingers, and then two more.

'Were they the young men or the older?'

'Most were full of fiery words, and therefore young I guess,' went on Ket. 'They that had the sorest backs spoke most bitterly. Cruel had been the beatings at the post that day, it seems; one was yet in the pit, too sore to move; one had been burned that day with the branding-iron because the steward swore he was a thief – and he was most fierce of all; and many said their lives were too bitter to be borne. The work they must do on the lord's land was more than was due from them, and their own fields were left untilled, and therefore they starved. Some said they would run away to the town, where, if they could hide for a year and a day, they would be free men; others said the plague and pestilence could be got in a village cot as easily as in a town hovel, and they would prefer to live on the king's deer in the greenwood.'

'Ay!' said Robin, in a bitter voice, 'poor folks have no friends in these days. The king's own sons rebel and war upon their father, the lords and monks fight for power and wider lands, and grind the faces of their villeins to the soil which they delve and dig, and squeeze from them rents and services against all rightful custom. Ket!' he said, rising, 'I will go home this day. Find Hob, your brother, and when I have said farewell to my friends I will come anon.'

Saying these words, Robin picked up the birds he had shot and went back to the castle of Sir Richard, to say farewell to Marian. Ket the Trow or Troll glided among the trees and disappeared.

That day, when the shadows of the trees cast by the sinking sun lay far over the fields, and in the warmth and quiet of the departing day there seemed no room in the peaceful world except for happy thoughts, Robin with quick soft steps came to the edge of Barnisdale Forest where it marched with his own land.

The forest side was on high ground, which then sank gently away to his fields. Long and earnestly he looked at his house, and beyond to the cots of the five villeins who were part of his land. His own house, and the garth or yard in the low quickset hedge about it, seemed quite peaceful, as indeed it should be at that time. Perhaps Scadlock, his bailiff, was inside, but the villeins must still be at work in the fields. Then it struck him that perhaps it was too quiet. There were no children tumbling and playing about in the dusty space before the villeins' cottages, but every door was fast closed, and no life stirred.

He was about to continue his walk under the trees to gain the footpath which led to the front of his house, when he saw a woman, a serf's wife, steal from the door of her hovel and creep along to the end of the hedge. There she stood, and seemed to watch for someone coming across the fields on the other side of the house. Suddenly he saw her with both hands gesticulating, as if signing to someone to keep away. For a long time she stood thus, but from where Robin stood he could not see who it was to whom she made her signal.

At length the woman, having apparently succeeded in giving her warning, stole cautiously back into her house and quietly closed the door.

Something was wrong. Of that Robin was certain now. Glancing warily this way and that, he went farther among the trees, and approached the head of the footpath with every care. Suddenly as he looked from behind a tree he dodged down again. A man-at-arms stood beneath the next tree, which threw its broad branches over the footpath.

From behind the beech trunk Robin keenly observed the man, whose back was towards him. He had evidently been put there to guard the approach from the forest. From where he stood the soldier could see the front of the house, and something that was happening there seemed to hold his attention. Sometimes he gave a laugh or a grunt of satisfaction.

Robin's eyes went hard of look. He knew the man by his tunic of red cloth and his helm to be one of the guard of armed retainers which the abbot of St Mary's, lord of the manor, had formed for his own dignity and to add to his retinue of lazy and oppressive menials. Very cautiously Robin crept along between the two trees, keeping himself hidden by the trunk against which the man leaned.

With the stealthiness and quietness of a wild-cat, Robin covered the space, until only the trunk of the tree separated him from the unsuspecting soldier. He rose to his full height, but as he did so his leg snapped a twig jutting from the tree. The man half swung round at the noise, but next moment Robin's fingers were about his throat, and in that grip of iron he was powerless.

The man swooned, and then, laying him down, Robin quickly bound his hands and feet and placed a rough gag in his mouth, so that when he revived, as he would shortly, he would be unable to do any harm.

When Robin turned to see what had drawn the man's attention so much, a groan burst from his lips. Tied to posts in front of the house were Scadlock and three of the poor villeins. Their backs were bare, and before each stood a burly soldier with a long knotted strap in his hand.

A little way from them stood others of the men-at-arms and their chief, Hubert of Lynn, a man whom for his brutal insolence and cruelty Robin had long hated. In the still air of the afternoon Robin's keen ears could catch the laughter which came from Hubert and his men. At length, when all seemed ready, the voice of the leader rang out:

'A hundred lashes first for these dogs that would resist the servants of their lord, and then an arrow for each. Now – go!'

Almost as if one man moved the four whips, they rose in the air and came down upon the bare backs which, since Robin had been their lord, had never been wealed by the cruel whip.

Robin, under the beechen boughs, picked up his longbow and the long deer-bolts or arrows, which he had laid down when he had prepared to creep upon the man at the top of the path. He twanged his bowstring, saw that it was well set to the bow, and laid each arrow apart before him.

Then kneeling on one knee, he whispered a prayer to Our Lady.

'The light is bad, fair and sweet Mother of Christ,' he said, 'but do thou guide my arrows to the evil hearts of these men. Six bolts have I, and out of the pity I have for my poor, folk I would slay first him with the bitterest heart, Hubert of Lynn, and then those four with whips. Hear me, O our sweet Lady, for the sake of thy Son who was so stern against wrong, and pitiful for weak folk. Amen.'

Then he notched the first shaft, and aimed it at the breast of Hubert. Singing its deep song as if in exultation, the great arrow leaped through the air upon its way. When it was but half-way across the field, another, with as triumphant a song, was humming behind it.

With a cry, Hubert sank on one knee to the ground, the shaft jutting from his breast. Feebly he tried to pluck it forth, but his life was already gone. He fell over on his side, dead. At the same time the place seemed full of great bees. First one man dropped his whip, spun round with his hands upon a bolt in his side, and then fell. Another sank to the ground without a murmur; a second leaped in the air like a shot rabbit; and the other, with one arm pinned to his side by an arrow, ran across the field swaying this way and that, until he dropped in a furrow and lay still.

There were four who remained untouched, but filled with such consternation were they, that they broke and fled in all directions. So dazed was one that he came flying up the field path at the head of which Robin still kneeled, terrible in his wrath, with his last bolt notched upon his string. The fellow ran with open arms, terror in his eyes, thinking not at all of whither he was going.

He pulled up when he came within a few yards of Robin, and yelled:

'O master, be you fiend or man, shoot not! Thy witch bolts spoke as they came through the air. I yield me! I yield me!'

The man fell before Robin, crying: 'I will be your man, lord. I was an honest man two days ago, and the son of an honest man, and my heart rose against the evil work I was in.'

Robin rose to his feet, and the man clutched his hands and placed his head between in token of fealty.

'See to it,' said Robin sternly, 'that you forget not your plighted word. How long have you been with Hubert and his men?'

'But two days, lord,' said the man, whose simple and honest eyes were now less wide with terror. 'I am Dudda or Dodd, son of Alstan, a good villein at Blythe, and forasmuch as my lord beat me without justice I fled to the woods. But I starved, and for need of food I crept out and lay at the abbey door and begged for bread. And they fed me, and seeing I was strong of my limbs said I should bear arms. And I rejoiced for a time till the cruel deeds they boasted of as done upon poor villeins like myself made me hate them.'

'Get up, Dodd,' said Robin. 'Remember thy villein blood henceforth, and do no wrong to thy kind. Come with me.'

Robin went down to the garth of his farm, released poor Scadlock and his other men, then entered the house and found salves wherewith he anointed their wealed and broken backs.

' 'Twas but yesterday, master,' said Scadlock, in reply to Robin's question as to what had happened, 'that they proclaimed you an outlaw from the steps of the cross at Pontefract, and this morning Hubert of Lynn came to possess your lands for the lord abbot. We here – Ward, Godard, Dunn, and John – could not abear to see this wrong done, and so, like poor fools, with sticks and forks we tried to beat them back.'

'Ay, poor lads, foolish and faithful, ye had like to have paid with your lives for it,' said Robin. 'But now, come in and feed, and I will take counsel what must needs be done.'

By this time it was dark. One of the women was called in from the serfs' cottages, a fire was lit in the centre of the one large room which formed Robin's manor-house, and soon bowls of good hot food were being emptied, and spirits were reviving. Even the captured man-at-arms was not forgotten; he was brought in and fed, and then lodged securely in a strong outhouse for the night.

'Master,' said Scadlock, as he and Robin were returning to the house from this task, 'what is in your mind to do? Must it be the woods and the houseless life of an outlaw for you?'

'There is no other way,' said Robin, with a hard laugh. 'And glad I shall be, for in the greenwood I may try to do what I may to give the rich and the proud some taste of what they give to the poor men whom they rule.'

'And I will go with you, master, with a very glad heart,' said Scadlock. 'And so will the others, for after this day they can expect no mercy from Guy of Gisborne.'

Suddenly they heard across the fields towards the village the sound of many voices, and listening intently, they could hear the tramp of feet.

'It is Guy of Gisborne and his men-at-arms!' said Scadlock. 'Master, we must fly to the woods at once.'

'Nay, nay,' said Robin, 'think you Guy of Gisborne would come cackling like so many geese to warn me of his approach? They are the villeins of the manor, though what they do abroad so late is more than I may say. They will smart for it tomorrow, I ween, when the steward learns of it.'

'Nay, master,' came a voice from the darkness at their elbow; 'here'll be no tomorrow for them in bondage if you will but lead us.'

It was the voice of one of the older villeins, who had stolen up before the crowd. It was Will of the Stuteley, generally called Will the Bowman – a quiet, thoughtful man, whom Robin had always liked. He had been reeve or head villein in his time.

'What, Will,' said Robin, 'what would they with me? Where should I lead them?'

'Give them a hearing, Master Robert,' said Will. 'Their hearts are overfull, but their stomachs are nigh empty, so driven and stressed beyond fair duty have they been this winter and summer. First the failure of harvest, then a hard winter, a hungry summer, and a grasping lord who skins us. I tell thee I can bear no more, old as I am.'

'Well, well, Will, here they are,' replied Robin, as a crowd of dark forms came into the yard. 'Now, lads, what is it you want of me?' he cried.

'We would run to the greenwood, master,' some cried. 'Sick and sore are we of our hard lot, and we can bear no more,' cried others.

Unused to much speaking, they could not explain their

feelings any more, and so waited, hoping that he who was so much wiser, yet so kind, would be able to understand all the bitterness that was in their hearts.

'Well,' said Robin earnestly, 'and if you run to the woods, what of your wives and children?'

'No harm can come to them,' was the reply. 'Our going will give them more worth in the eyes of the lord and his steward. We do not own them. They are the chattels of the lord, body and soul. There will be more food for them if we go.'

There was some truth in this, as Robin knew. The lord and his steward would not visit their vengeance upon the women and children of those villeins who ran away. The work on the manor lands must go on, and the women and children helped in this. Some of the older women held plots of land, which were tilled by their sons or by poorer men in the hamlet who held no land, and who for their day's food were happy to work for anyone who would feed and shelter them.

'How many of ye are there?' asked Robin. 'Are there any old men among ye?'

'There are thirty of us. Most of us are young and wiser than our fathers,' growled one man. 'Or we will put up with less these days,' added another.

'So you will let the work of the manor and the due services ye owe to the lord fall on the shoulders of the old men, the women, and the youngsters?' said Robin, who was resolved that if these men broke from their lord they should know all the consequences. 'Come, lads, is it manly to save our own skins and let the moil and toil and swinking labour light on the backs of those less able to bear the heat of the noonday sun, the beat of the winter rain?'

Many had come hot from the fierce talk of the wilder men among them as they sat in the alehouse, and now in the darkness and the chill air of the night their courage was oozing, and they glanced this way and that, as if looking how to get back to their huts, where wife and children were sleeping.

But others, of sterner stuff, who had suffered more or felt more keenly, were not to be put off. Some said they were not married, others that they would bear no more the harsh rule of Guy of Gisborne.

Suddenly flying steps were heard coming towards them, and all listened, holding their breath. The fainter-hearted, even at the sound, edged out of the crowd and crept away.

A little man crashed through the hedge and lit almost at the feet of Robin.

' 'Tis time ye ceased your talking,' he said, his voice panting and a strange catch in it.

' 'Tis Much, the Miller's son!' said they all, and waited. They felt that something of dread had happened, for he was a fearless little man, and not easily moved.

' 'Tis time ye ceased plotting, lads,' he said, with a curious break in his voice. 'Ye are but serfs, of no more worth than the cattle ye clean or the grey swine ye feed – written down on the lawyers' parchments with the ploughs, the mattocks, the carts, and the hovels ye lie in, and to be sold at the lord's will as freely!'

Tears were in his voice, so great was his passion, so deeply did his knowledge move him.

'I tell thee thou shouldst creep back to the sties in which ye live,' he went on, 'and not pretend that ye have voice or wish in what shall befall ye. For the lord is sick of his unruly serfs, and tomorrow – tomorrow he will sell thee off his land!'

A great breath of surprise and rage rose from the men before him. 'Sell us?' they cried. 'He will sell us?'

'Ay, he will sell some ten of thee. The parchment is already written which shall pass thee to Lord Arnald of Shotley Hawe.'

'That fiend in the flesh!' said Robin, 'and enemy of God – that flayer of poor peasants' skins! But, lads, to sell thee! Oh, vile!'

A great roar, like the roar of maddened oxen, rose from the throats of the villeins. Oh, it was true that, in strict law, the poor villeins could be sold like cattle, but on this manor never had it been known to be done. They held their little roods of land by due services rendered, and custom ruled that son should inherit after father, and all things should be done according to what the older men said was the custom of the manor.

But now, to be rooted out of the place they and their folk had known for generations, and sold like cattle in a market-place! Oh, it was not to be borne!

'Man,' said one, 'where got you this evil news?'

'From Rafe, man to Lord Arnald's steward,' replied Much. 'I

met him at the alehouse in Blythe, and he told it me with a laugh, saying that Guy of Gisborne had told the steward we were an unruly and saucy lot of knaves whom he knew it would be a pleasure for his lordship to tame.'

'Ye say there are ten of us to be sold?' asked a timid voice in the rear. 'Do ye know who these be?'

'What matter?' roared one man. 'It touches us all. For me, by the holy rood, I will run to the woods, but I will put my mark on the steward ere I go.'

'Rafe knew not the names of any,' said Much. 'What matter, as Hugh of the Forde says. There are ten of ye. They are those who have given the hardest words to Guy of Gisborne, and have felt the whip most often across their backs at the post.'

'How many of us are here, lads?' said Will the Bowman in a hard voice.

'We were thirty a while ago,' said one with a harsh laugh. 'But now we are but fourteen, counting Much.'

'Where is Scarlet and his little lad?' asked Robin. He had suddenly remembered that his friend was not among these others – yet Scarlet had been the boldest in opposing the unjust demands and oppressive exactions of the steward.

'Will Scarlet lies in the pit!' said Much, 'nigh dead with a hundred lashes. Tomorrow he will be taken to Doncaster, where the king's justice sits, to lose his right hand for shooting the king's deer.'

'By the Virgin!' cried Robin, 'that shall not be. For I will take him from the pit this night.' He started off, but many hands held him back.

'Master, we will go with thee!' cried the others.

'See here, Master Robin,' said Will the Bowman, speaking quietly, but with a hard ring in his voice. 'We be fourteen men who are wearied of the ill we suffer daily. If we do naught now against the evil lord who grinds us beneath his power we shall be for ever slaves. I for one will rather starve in the greenwood than suffer toil and wrongful ruling any more. What say you, lads all?'

'Yea, yea! We will go to the greenwood!' they cried. 'Whether Master Robin leads us or not, we will go!'

Robin's resolution was quickly taken.

'Lads,' he cried, 'I will be one with you. Already have I done a deed which I knew would be done ere long, and I am doubly outlaw and wolf's-head. The abbot's men-at-arms came hither while I was away and claimed my lands. Scadlock and my good lads resisted them, and were like to suffer death for doing so. With my good bow I shot five of the lord's men, and their bodies lie in a row beneath that wall.'

'I saw them as I entered,' said Will the Bowman, 'and a goodly sight it was. Had you not slain Hubert of Lynn, I had an arrow blessed by a goodly hermit for his evil heart, for the ill he caused my dear dead lad Christopher. Now, lads, hold up each your hand and swear to be true and faithful till your death day to our brave leader, Robert of Locksley.'

All held up their hands, and in solemn tones took the oath.

'Now, lads, quickly follow,' said Robin.

In a few moments the garth was empty, and the dark forms of Robin and his men were to be seen passing over the fields under the starlit sky.

There was not one backward look as the men passed through Fangthief Wood and came out on the wold behind the village. From here they could dimly see the little group of hovels lying huddled beside the church, the dull water of the river gleaming farther still, and the burble and roar of the stream as it flowed through the mill-race came faintly up to their ears.

In those days, whenever the villein raised his bended back from the furrows, and his eyes, sore with the sun-glare or the driving rain, sought the hut he called home with thoughts of warmth and food, he was also reminded that for any offence which he might commit, his lord or the steward had speedy means of punishment. For, raised on a hill as near as possible to the huts of the serfs, was the gaunt gallows, and, near by, lay the pit. Gallows or Galley Hill is still the name which clings to a green hill beside many a pretty village, though the dreadful tree which bore such evil fruit has long since rotted or been hewn down. In the village street itself were the stocks, so that he who was fastened therein should escape none of the scorn, laughter, or abuse of his familiars.

It was thus with the village of Birkencar. On the wold to the north were the gallows and the pit, only a few yards from the manor-house, in the parlour of which Guy of Gisborne dealt forth what he was pleased to term 'justice'. The manor-house

Robin Hood

was now dark and silent; doubtless Guy was sleeping on the good stroke of business he had done in getting rid of his most unruly, stiff-necked serfs.

Over the thick grass of the grazing fields the steps of Robin and his men made no noise, and, having arrived at a little distance from where the gallows stood, Robin bade the others wait until he should give them a sign. Then, passing on as quietly as a ghost, Robin approached the prison built under-ground, in which serfs were confined when they awaited even sterner justice than that which the lord of the manor could give.

The prison was entered by a door at the foot of a flight of steps dug out of the soil. Robin crept to the top of the steps and looked down. He did not expect to find any guard at the door, since the steward would not dream that anyone would have so much hardihood as to attempt a rescue from the lord's prison.

As Robin scanned keenly the dark hole below him, down which the starlight filtered faintly, he was surprised to see a small figure crouching at the door. He heard a groan come from within the prison, and the form beneath him seemed to start and cling closer to the door.

'O uncle,' said a soft voice, which he knew was that of little Gilbert of the White Hand, 'I thought thou didst sleep awhile, and that thy wounds did not grieve thee so much. Therefore I kept quiet and did not cry. Oh, if Master Robin were but here!'

'Laddie, thou must go home,' came the weak tones of Scarlet from within the prison. 'If Guy or his men catch thee here they will beat thee. That I could not bear. Laddie, dear laddie, go and hide thee somewhere.'

'O Uncle Will, I can't,' wailed the little lad. 'It would break my heart to leave thee here – to think thou wert lying here in the dark with thy poor back all broken and hurt, and no one near to say a kind word. Uncle, I have prayed so much this night for thee – I am sure help must come soon. Surely the dear sweet Virgin and good Saint Christopher will not turn deaf ears to a poor lad's prayers?'

'But, laddie mine, thou art sick thyself,' came Scarlet's voice. 'To stay there all night will cause thee great ill, and – '

'Oh, what will it matter if thou art taken from me,' cried the little boy, all his fortitude breaking down. He wept bitterly, and pressed with his hands at the unyielding door. 'If they slay thee, I will make them slay me too, for my life will be all forlorn without thee, dear, dear Uncle Will!'

'Hallo, laddie, what's all this coil about?' cried Robin in a hearty voice, as he rose and began to descend the steps.

Little Gilbert started up half in terror; then, as he realised who it was, he rushed towards Robin, and seizing his hands covered them with kisses. Then, darting back to the door, he put his lips to a crack and cried delightedly:

'I said so! I said so! God and His dear Saints and the Virgin have heard me. Here is Robin come to take you out.'

'Have they scored thee badly, Will?' asked Robin.

'Ay, Robin, dear man,' came the answer with a faint laugh; 'worse than a housewife scores her sucking pig.'

'Bide quiet a bit, lad,' replied Robin, 'and I'll see if what axe has done axe can't undo.'

With keen eyes he examined the staples through which the ring-bolt passed. Then with two deft blows with his axe and a wrench with his dagger he had broken the bolt and pulled open the door. The little lad rushed in at once, and with a knife began carefully to cut his uncle's bonds.

Robin gave the cry of a plover, and Scadlock with two of his own villeins hurried up.

'Quick, lads,' he said. 'Bring out Will Scarlet; we must take him to Outwoods and bathe and salve his wounds.'

In a few moments, as gently as was possible, they brought poor Scarlet forth and laid him on the grass. A hearty but silent hand-grip passed between him and Robin, while little Gilbert, his eyes bright, but his lips dumb with a great gratitude, kissed Robin's hand again and again.

'Where are the others?' asked Robin of Scadlock, when two of the men had raised Scarlet on their shoulders and were tramping downhill.

'I know not,' said Scadlock. 'They were whispering much among themselves when you had gone, and suddenly I looked round and they were not there. I thought some wizard had spirited them away for the moment, but soon I saw some of them against the stars as they ran bending over the hill.'

'Whither went they?' asked Robin, a suspicion in his mind.

'Towards the manor-house,' was the reply.

'Go ye to Outwoods,' Robin commanded. Do all that is needed for Scarlet, and await me there.'

With rapid strides Robin mounted the down, while the others with their burden wended their way towards Fangthief Wood. When Robin reached the top of the down the manor-house stood up before him all black against the stars. He ran forward to the high bank which surrounded it, and met no one. Then he found the great gate, which was open, and he went into the garth and a few steps along the broad way leading up to the door.

Suddenly a form sprang up before him – that of Much, the Miller's son.

'Ay, 'tis Master Robin,' he said in a low voice, as if to others, and from behind a tree came Will Stuteley and Kit the Smith.

'What's toward, lads?' asked Robin. 'Think ye to break in and slay Guy? I tell ye the manor-house can withstand a siege from an armed troop, and ye have no weapons but staves and your knives.'

'Master Robin,' said Will the Bowman, 'I would that ye stood by and did naught in this matter. 'Tis a villein deed for villein fowk to do. 'Tis our right and our deed; in the morn when we're in the greenwood we'll do thy biddin' and look to no one else.'

A flame suddenly shot up from a heap of dried brush laid against a post of the house before them, then another near it, and still another. The sun had been shining fiercely the past two weeks, and everything was as dry as tinder. Built mainly of wood, the manor-house would fall an easy prey to the flames.

'But at least ye must call out the women,' urged Robin. 'There is the old dame, Makin, and the serving-wench – would ye burn innocent women as well?'

Already the inmates were aware of their danger. A face appeared at a window shutter. It was that of Guy. A stone hit the frame as he looked out, and just missed him as he dodged back.

Huge piles of brushwood had been heaped round the house, and these were burning furiously in many places, and the planks of the walls had caught fire, and were crackling and burning fiercely.

'Guy of Gisborne!' came the strong voice of Will the Bowman, 'thy days are ended. We have thee set, like a tod [fox] in his hole. But we've no call to burn the women folk. Send 'em out, then, but none o' thy tricks.'

They heard screams, and soon the front door was flung open and two women stood in the blazing entrance. One of the men with a long pole raked the blazing brushwood away to give them space to come out. They ran forward and the door closed. Next moment it had opened again, and a spear came from it. It struck the villein with the pole full in the throat, and without a groan he fell.

A yell of fury rose from the others who were standing by, and some were for rushing forward to beat down the door.

'Ha' done and keep back!' came the stern level tones of Will the Bowman. 'There's nobbut the steward in the house and he'll burn. Heap up the wood, and keep a keen watch on the back door and the windows.'

An arrow came from an upper window and stuck in a tree near which Will was standing. Will plucked out the quivering shaft and looked at it coolly.

'Say, Makin,' he said to the old woman who had come from the house, 'are there any of the abbot's archers in th' house?'

'Noa,' replied the old housekeeper; 'nobbut the maister.'

'I thought 'twas so,' replied Will. 'Yet he should shoot a bolt better than that.'

'You're no doomed to die by an arrow,' said the old dame, and laughed, showing her yellow toothless gums.

'No, maybe so,' replied Will, 'and maybe not. I lay no store by thy silly talk, Makin.'

'Nor will the maister die by the fire ye've kindled so fine for un,' went on the old woman, and laughed again.

Will the Bowman looked at the fiercely burning walls of the house and made no answer. But he smiled grimly. Who could escape alive from this mass of twisting and whirling flames?

Suddenly from the rear of the house came cries of terror. Robin, followed by Will, quickly ran round, and in the light of the burning house they saw the villeins on that side with scared faces looking and pointing to a distance. They turned in the direction indicated, and saw what seemed to be a brown horse running away over the croft.

Glancing back they saw that the door of a storehouse which adjoined the manor-house was open, though its wood and frame were burning. With a cry of rage Will the Bowman suddenly started running towards the horse.

'Come back! come back!' cried the villeins in terrified voices. ' 'Tis the Spectre Beast! 'Twill tear thee to pieces!'

But he still ran on, and as he ran they could see him trying to notch an arrow to the bow he held in his hand.

'Whence did it come?' asked Robin of the villeins.

'It burst on a sudden from the house, with a mane all of fire and its eyes flashing red and its terrible mouth open,' was the reply. It ran at Bat the Coalman there, and I thought he was doomed to be torn to pieces, but the Bargast turned and dashed away over the croft.'

'I think Guy has escaped you,' said Robin, who suspected what had happened.

'How mean'st tha?' asked Bat the Charcoal-Burner.

'I doubt not that Guy of Gisborne has wrapped himself in some disguise and frightened you, and has now got clear away,' replied Robin.

'But 'twas the Spectre Mare!' the villeins asserted. 'We saw its mane all afire, and its red flashing eyes and its terrible jaws all agape.'

Robin did not answer. He knew it was in vain to fight against the superstition of the poor villeins. Instead, he went back to where he had left Makin, the old woman.

'Makin,' he said, 'did thy master flay a brown horse but lately?'

'Ay, but two days agone.'

'And where was the hide?'

'In th' store beyond the house.'

'Thou saidst thy master should not die by fire, Makin?'

'Ay,' replied the old woman, and her small black eyes in a weazened yellow face looked narrowly into Robin's.

'Will the Bowman hath gone to shoot thy master,' went on Robin; 'but I think he will not catch him. I think thou shouldst not bide here till Will comes back, Makin. He will be hot and angry, and will strike blindly if he guesses.'

The old woman smiled, and gave a little soft laugh. Then, with a sudden anger and her eyes flashing, she turned upon Robin, and in a low voice said:

'And could I do aught else? A hard man he's been and a hard man he'll be to his last day — as hard to me as to a stranger. But these arms nursed him when he was but a wee poor bairn. 'Twas I told him what to do wi' the hide of the old mare. Could I do aught else?'

'Ay,' said Robin, 'I know thou'st been mother to a man who has but a wolf's heart. But now, get thee gone ere Will of Stuteley comes.'

Without another word, the old woman turned and hurried away in the darkness.

A little while later Will the Bowman returned, and full of rage was he.

'The dolterheads!' he cried. 'Had ye no more sense in thy silly heads as not to know that so wily a man would be full of tricks? Spectre in truth and in deed! Old women ye are, and only fitten to tend cows and be sold like cows! Could ye not see his legs beneath the hide of the horse which he'd thrown over himself? – wolf in horse's skin that he is. Go back to thy villein chores; ye're no worthy to go to the greenwood to be free men.'

He went off in great anger, and would say no word to anyone.

It was only later that he told Robin that he had run after the horse-like figure, and had distinctly seen the human legs beneath the hide. He had tried a shot at it, but had missed, and the figure ran forward to the horse pasture on the moor. There his suspicions had been proved to be true, for he had seen Guy of Gisborne pull the hide off himself, and jump on one of the horses in the field and ride away, taking the hide with him.

'Now, lads,' said Robin to the villeins, ' 'tis no use wasting time here. The wolf hath stolen away, and soon will rouse the country against us. You must to the greenwood, for you have done such a deed this night as never hath been done by villeins against their lord's steward as far back as the memory of man goeth.'

'Thou'rt right, maister,' they said. ' 'Tis for our necks now we must run. But great doltheads we be, as Will said truly, to let the evil man slip out of our hands by a trick!'

No more, however, was said. All made haste to leave the burning manor-house, most of which was now a blackening or smouldering ruin. Rapidly they ran downhill, and having picked up Scadlock and the other villeins with Scarlet and the little lad, Robin led the way under the waning stars to the deep dark line of forest which rose beside his fields.

CHAPTER TWO

How Little John Stole the Forester's Dinner, and of His Meeting with Robin Hood

'Ay, lads, but this be bliss indeed!'

The speaker was Much, the Miller's son. He gave a great sigh of satisfaction, and rolled himself over on the grass to make himself even more comfortable than he was. Grunts or sighs of satisfaction answered him from others of the twenty forms lying at full length under the deep shadow of the trees. Some, however, answered with snores, for the buck they had eaten had been a fine one, and the quarterstaff play that morning had been hard, and for ringing heads slumber is the best medicine.

It was in a small glade deep in the heart of Barnisdale Forest where the outlaws lay, and was known to them as the Stane Lea or Stanley. At one side of it a little rivulet gurgled over its pebbles, and at the other end stood a great standing stone, green with moss, where, doubtless, ages before, the skin-clad warriors of the forest had come with their prayers to the spirit of the great chief who was buried beneath it. Beside the brook knelt Scadlock and his fellow cook, cleaning the wooden platters which had just been used, by the simple process of rubbing them with sand in the clear running water.

The sunlight of the hot July day fell on the water through spaces between the slowly bending leaves, and in the deep green gloom the rays shone like bars of gold. Most of the villeins lay on their backs, feeling pure enjoyment in looking up into the weaving masses of leaves above their heads, through which, like flaming spear-heads, the sunlight slid now and then as the gentle summer breeze stirred the deeps of the trees. After a full meal, and with the soft air blowing upon their cheeks, these poor outlaws tasted such happiness as had never before been their lot.

Little Gilbert, his cheek now ruddy with health, sat beside Scarlet shaping arrows with a knife.

Seated with his back against the trunk of a fallen elm was Robin, his bearing as bold, his eye as keen and fearless and his look as noble now as when a short month ago he was not an outlaw, a 'wolf's-head' as the phrase was, whom any law-abiding man could slay and get a reward for his head.

Strict had been his rule of these twenty men who had come to the greenwood with him and had chosen him as their leader. Slow of step and of movement they were, but he knew that the lives of all of them depended upon their learning quickly the use of the quarterstaff, the sword, and the longbow. Every day, therefore, he had made them go through set tasks. Chapped and hard with toil at the plough, the mattock, and the hedge knife, their hands took slowly to the more delicate play with sword, quarterstaff, and bow; but most of them were but young men, and he had hopes that very soon they would gain quickness of eye and deftness of hand, besides the lore that would tell them how to track the red deer, and to face and overcome the fierce wolf and the white-tusked boar in his wrath.

'What should us be doin' now,' murmured Dickon the Carpenter, 'if we were still bondsmen and back in the village?'

'I should be feeding the lord's grey swine or ploughing his domain lands,' said Long Peter, 'while my own fields grew rank with weeds'

'I,' said Will Stuteley bitterly, 'should be cursing the evil abbot who broke my poor lad's heart. When I feel I should be happiest, I think and grieve of him the most. Oh, that he were here!'

No one spoke for a few moments. All felt that although all had suffered, Will the Bowman had suffered most bitterly from the heartlessness of the lord abbot of St Mary's and Sir Guy of Gisborne's treacherous dealing. Will had had a son, a villein, of course, like himself. But the lad had run away to Grimsby, had lived there for a year and a day in the service of a shipman, and thus had got his freedom. Then he had saved all he could, toiling manfully day and night, to get sufficient money to buy his father's freedom. He had scraped and starved to win the twenty marks that meant the end of his father's serfdom. At length he had saved the amount, and then had gone to the lord abbot and offered it for his father's freedom. The abbot had seized him and cast him into prison, and taken the money from him. Then witnesses were found to swear in the manor court that the young man had been seen in his father's hut during the year and a day, and by this the abbot claimed him as his serf. As to the money he had saved – 'All that a serf got was got for his lord' was an old law that none could deny. The young man, broken in health and spirit, had been released, had worked in the manor fields dumb and dazed with sorrow, and at length one night had been found dead on his pallet of straw.

'And I,' said Scarlet, leaning on his left elbow and raising his clenched right hand in the air, 'I should be reaping the lord's wheat, and with every stroke of my sickle I should be hungering for the day when I should sink my knife in the evil heart of Guy of Gisborne, who made me a serf who was once a socman, because of the poverty which came upon me.'

This, too, was true. Scarlet had been a freeman, but harvests had failed, the lord's steward had forced him to do labour which it had never been the custom for a freeman to do, and gradually his fields had run to waste, and Scarlet had lost his land, and sunk to the level of a common serf.

'Master,' said Much, the Miller's son, 'it seemeth to me that we be all poor men who have suffered evil from those who have power. Surely now that we are outlaws thou shouldst give us some rule whereby we may know whom we shall beat and bind, and whom we shall let go free? Shall we not let the rich and the lordly know somewhat of the poor man's aching limbs and poverty?'

'It was in my mind to speak to you of such things,' said Robin. 'First, I will have you hurt no woman, nor any company in which a woman is found. I remember the sweet Virgin, and will ever pray for her favour and protection, and I will, therefore, that you shield all women. Look to it, also, that ye do not any harm to any honest peasant who tilleth his soil in peace, nor to good yeomen, wherever you meet them. Knights, also, and squires who are not proud, but who are good fellows, ye shall treat with all kindness. But I tell thee this, and bear it well in mind – abbots and bishops, priors, and canons, and monks – ye may do all your will upon them. When ye rob them of their gold or their rich stuffs, ye are taking only that which they have squeezed and reived from the poor. Therefore, take your fill of their wealth, and spare not your staves on their backs. They speak the teaching of the blessed Jesus with their mouths, but their fat bodies and their black hearts deny Him every hour.'

'Yea, yea!' shouted the outlaws, moved by the fire which had been in Robin's voice and in his eyes. 'We will take toll of all such who pass through our greenwood roads.'

'And now, lads,' went on Robin, 'though we be outlaws, and beyond men's laws, we are still within God's mercy. Therefore I would have you go with me to hear mass. We will go to Campsall, and there the mass-priest shall hear our confessions, and preach from God's book to us.'

In a little while the outlaws in single file were following their leader through the leafy ways of the forest, winding in and out beside the giant trees, across the fern-spread glades whence the red deer and the couching doe sprang away in affright, wading across brooks and streams, skirting some high cliff or rocky dell; but yet, though the way was devious and to most unknown, all felt confidence in the leadership of Robin.

Suddenly Much, who walked beside Robin, stopped as they entered a small glade.

'Look!' he said, pointing to the other side. ' 'Tis an elf – a brownie! I saw it step forth for a moment. 'Tis no bigger than a boy. It is hiding behind that fern. But this bolt shall find it if 'tis still there!'

He raised his bow and notched an arrow, but Robin struck down his wrist, and the arrow shot into the earth a few yards ahead of them.

'The brownies are my friends,' said Robin, laughing, 'and will be yours too, if you deserve such friendship. Hark you, Much, and all my merry fellows. Shoot nothing in the forest which shows no desire to hurt thee, unless it is for food. So shall ye win the service of all good spirits and powers that harbour here or in heaven.'

The men wondered what Robin meant, and during the remainder of their walk they kept a keen look-out for a sight of Much's brownie. But never a glimpse did they get of it, and at length they began to chaff Much, saying he had eaten too much venison, and took spots before his eyes to be fairies. But he persisted in asserting that he had seen a little man, 'dark of face and hair, no bigger than a child. A sun-ray struck him as he moved,' he said, 'and I saw the hairy arm of him with the sunlight on him.'

' 'Twas no more than a squirrel!' said one; 'and Much took his brush for a man's arm.'

'Or else Much is bewitched,' said another. 'I said he slept in a fairy ring the other night.'

'I tell thee it was Puck himself, or Puck's brother!' said Much with a laugh, who now began almost to doubt his own eyes, and so stopped their chaffing by joining in the laughter himself.

At the little forest village, set in its clearing in the midst of giant elms and oaks, the men went one by one and made confession to the simple old parish priest, and when this was done, at Robin's request the mass service was said. Before he knelt, Robin looked around the little wooden church, and saw a young and handsome man kneeling behind him, dressed in a light hauberk. In one hand he held a steel cap, and a sword hung by his side. He was tall and graceful, yet strongly built, and was evidently a young squire of good family. Robin looked at him keenly, and liked the frank gaze that met his eyes.

Mass was but half done when into the church came a little man, slight of form, dark of face. With quick looks his eyes swept the dim space, and then, almost as by instinct, they rested on Robin, where in the front row of his men he knelt before the priest. Swiftly and with the stealthy softness of a cat, the little man crept along the aisle past the kneeling outlaws. As their bent eyes caught the lithe form stealing by, they looked up, some with wonder in their eyes, while others gazed almost with terror on the uncanny dwarfish figure.

They watched it creep up to Robin and touch his elbow. Then their master bent his head, and the little man whispered a few quick words into his ear.

'Two of the four grim knights have followed thee, Maister,' were the words he said. 'They are within a bowshot of the kirk door. A churl hath spied upon thee these last days. There are twenty men-at-arms with the knights.'

'Go and keep watch at the door,' said Robin in a whisper. 'Evil men must wait till God's service be done.'

The little man turned and crept quietly back the way he had come, and the outlaws nudged each other as he passed, and gazed at him in wonder. Much, the Miller's son, smiled with triumph.

The mass went on, and the outlaws responded in due manner to the words of the priest; the last words were said, and the men were just rising from their knees, when, with a hum like a huge drone, an arrow came through one of the narrow window slits, and speeding across the church, twanged as it struck on the wall at the opposite side.

'Saint Nicholas shield us!' said the priest in affright, and shuffled away through a door at the back of the church.

'Now, lads,' said Robin, 'today will prove whether ye have at heart those daily lessons with the longbow. To the window slits with you! The knights of the Evil Hold have run us down, and would dearly like to have our bodies to torture in their crucet-house.'

The faces of the outlaws went grim at the words. Throughout the length and breadth of the Barnisdale and Peak lands the tales of the cruelties and tortures of the robber lords of Wrangby had been spread by wandering beggars, jugglers, and palmers. The blood of the villeins and poor folk whom the evil knights had hurt, maimed, or slain had long cried out for vengeance. The outlaws flew to the window slits, while Robin and Scarlet, having shut the big oaken door, kept their eyes to the arrow slits in the thick oak panels. Every church in those hard days was as much a fortress as a place of worship, and Robin saw that this little wooden building could be held for some hours against all ordinary enemies save fire.

The young squire went up to Robin, and said:

'Who are these folk, good woodman, who wish thee harm?'

'They are lords of high degree,' replied Robin, 'but with the manners of cut-purses and tavern knifers. Niger le Grym, Hamo de Mortain – '

'What!' interrupted the knight hotly; 'the evil crew of Isenbart de Belame, grandson of the fiend of Tickhill?'

'The same,' said Robin.

'Then, good forester,' said the young man, and eager was his speech, 'I pray thee let me aid thee in this. Isenbart de Belame is the most felon knight that ever slew honest man or oppressed weak women. He is my most bitter enemy, and much would I give to slay him.'

'Of a truth,' replied Robin, 'ye may help me as you may, seeing your anger is so great. Who may ye be?'

'I am Alan de Tranmire, squire to my father Sir Herbrand de Tranmire,' replied the other. 'But I love most to be called by the name which my friends give me – Alan-a-Dale.'

While he talked, the outlaw had kept one eye on the arrow slit before him, and saw how the men-at-arms on the borders of the forest were forming in a body, headed by two knights on horseback, to make a dash at the door of the church to beat it down.

'I hope, young sir,' said Robin, 'that thy sword may not be needed. For I hope with my good fellows to keep those rascals from coming so near as to let them use their swords, of which, I admit, my men are as yet but sorry masters'

'But I love the bow,' said Alan, 'and in the forest near my father's manor I have shot many a good bolt.'

'Good!' said Robin, and his eyes showed that his appreciation of the young squire was increased by what he had said. 'Ho, there, Kit the Smith! Give this gentleman, Alan-a-Dale here, one of the spare bows thou hast, and a bunch of arrows. Now,' went on the outlaw, when this had been done, 'do you all, my lads, stand at the arrow slits which command that group of rascals there at the woodside. They plot to beat down this door, thinking we are but poor runagate serfs with no knowledge of weapons, whom they can butcher as a terrier doth rats in a pit. Prove yourselves this day to be men of the good yew-bow. Mark each your man as they advance, and let them not reach the door.'

Eagerly the outlaws crowded to the arrow slits which commanded the place where, in the shade of the shaw, the men-at-arms seemed busy about something. At length they could be seen to lift some weight from the ground, and then their purpose was seen. They had felled a young oak, which, having lopped off its branches, they intended to use as a battering-ram wherewith to beat down the door.

Soon they were seen advancing, some dozen of the twenty ranged beside the trunk which they bore. Two outlaws stood at each window slit, a short man in front and a tall man behind, and each man squinted through the slit with a grim light in his eyes, and held his arrow notched on the string with the eagerness of dogs held in leash who see the quarry just before them.

'Much, Scadlock, Dickon, and you twelve fellows to the right, mark each your man at the tree,' came the low stern tones of Robin, 'and see that you do not miss. You other eight, let your arrows point at the breasts of the others. By the rood!' he exclaimed, marking how confidently the knights' men advanced over the open ground, 'they think the hunting of runaway serfs is like hunting rabbits. Hold your bolts till I give the word!' he said. 'Ye will forgive me this day the sweating I ha' given thee, good lads, when I made thee shoot at the mark nigh day-long these last weeks.'

'O master!' cried one man, quivering with excitement, 'a murrain on this waiting! If I shoot not soon, the arrow will leap from my hand.'

'Shoot not till I say!' said Robin sternly. 'Forty paces is all I trust thee for, but not eight of the rascals should be standing then. Steady, lads!'

For one tremendous moment all nerves were taut as they waited for the word. The men-at-arms, coming now at a trot, seemed almost at the door when Robin said 'Shoot!'

Twenty-one arrows leaped from the slits in the wooden walls, and hummed across the space of some sixty feet. To the men in the church peering out, bated of breath, the effect seemed almost one of wizardry. They saw eight of the men who ran with the tree-trunk suddenly check, stagger, and then fall. Of the others, three dashed to the ground, one got up and ran away, and two others, turning, pulled arrows from their arms as they too fled back to the wood. One of the horses of the knights came to the ground with a clatter and a thud, throwing his master, who got up, and, dazed with the blow or the utterly unexpected warmth of the defence, gazed for a moment or two at the church.

The other knight, who was untouched, yelled something at him, and fiercely pulling his horse round, rode swiftly back to the shelter of the forest, whither all the men who could run had already fled. Suddenly the unhorsed knight seemed to wake up, and then turning, ran as swiftly as his armour would allow him towards the forest. An arrow came speeding after him, but missed him, and soon he had disappeared.

On the worn grass before the church lay ten motionless forms and the dead horse, who had been struck to the heart by an arrow.

'Now, lads,' said Robin, 'to the forest with you quickly, and follow them.'

Quickly the door was unbarred, and the outlaws gained the forest at the spot where their attackers had disappeared. The traces of their hurried flight were easily picked up as the outlaws pushed forward. Alan-a-Dale came with them, and Robin thanked him for the aid he had given them.

'If at any time,' said Robin, 'you should stand in need of a few good bowmen, forget not to send word to Robert of Locksley, or Robin of Barnisdale, for by either name men know me.'

'I thank thee, Robin of Barnisdale,' said Alan, 'and it may be that I may ask thy help at some future time.'

'What!' said Robin with a laugh, 'has so young and gallant a squire as thou seemest already an enemy?'

'Ay,' replied Alan, and his handsome face was gloomy. 'And little chance as yet do I see of outwitting my enemy, for he is powerful and oppressive.'

'Tell me thy tale,' said Robin, 'for I would be thy friend, and aid thee all I can.'

'I thank thee, good Robin,' replied Alan. 'It is thus with me. I love a fair and sweet maiden whose father has lands beside Sherwood Forest. Her name is Alice de Beauforest. Her father holds his manor from that great robber and oppressor, Isenbart de Belame, who wishes him to marry the fair Alice to an old and rich knight who is as evil a man as Isenbart himself. The knight of Beauforest would rather wed his daughter to myself, whom she hath chosen for the love I bear to her; but the lord of Belame threatens that if he doth not that which he commands, he will bring fire and ruin upon him and his lands. Therefore I know not what to do to win my dear lady. Brave is she as she is fair, and would face any ill for my sake, but she loveth her father, who is past his fighting days and desires to live in peace. Therefore her loyalty to him fights against her love for me.'

'Is any time fixed for this marriage?' asked Robin.

'Belame swears that if it be not done within a year, Beauforest shall cook his goose by the fire of his own manor-house,' was the reply.

'There is time enow,' said Robin. 'Who knows? Between this

Fast and furious was that fight

and then much may happen. I am sure thou art brave. Thou must also have patience. I shall be faring south to merry Sherwood ere long, and I will acquaint myself of this matter more fully, and we shall meet anon and speak of this matter again. But see, who are these – knight and churl, who speak so privily together?'

Robin and Alan had separated from the main body of outlaws, and were about to enter a little glade, when at the mouth of a ride at the other end they saw a man in armour, on foot, speaking to a low-browed, sinister-looking man in the rough tunic of a villein – his only dress, except for the untanned shoes upon his feet. As Robin spoke, the knight turned and saw them, and they instantly recognised him as the man who had been unhorsed before the church. The churl pointed at them, and said something to the knight.

'Ha, knaves!' said the latter, advancing into the glade towards them. 'Thou art two of those company of run slaves, as I guess.'

'Run slaves we may be,' said Robin, notching an arrow to his string, 'but, sir knight, they made you and your men run in a way you in no whit expected.'

'By Our Lady,' said the knight, with a harsh laugh, 'thou speakest saucily, thou masterless rascal. But who have we here,' he said, glancing at Alan; 'a saucy squire who would be the better of a beating, as I think.'

Alan-a-Dale had already dressed his shield, which hitherto had hung by a strap on his back, and drawing his sword, he stepped quickly towards the other.

'I know thee, Ivo le Ravener,' he said, in a clear ringing voice, 'for a false knight – a robber of lonely folk, an oppressor of women, and a reiver of merchants' goods. God and Our Lady aiding me, thou shalt get a fall from me this day.'

'Thou saucy knave!' cried the other in a rage; and with great fury he sprang towards Alan, and the clash of steel, as stroke came upon guard or shield, arose in the quiet glade.

Fast and furious was that fight, and they thrust at each other like boars or stags in deadly combat. Alan was the nimbler, for the other was a man of a foul life, who loved wine and rich food; and though he was the older man and the more cunning in sword-craft, yet the younger man's swiftness of limb, keenness of eye, and strength of stroke were of more avail. Alan avoided or guarded his opponent's more deadly strokes, and by feinting and leaping back, sought to weary the other. Yet he did not escape without wounds. He had but a light hauberk on his body, and on his head a steel cap with a nasal piece, while the other had a shirt of heavy mail and a visored helm laced to his hauberk.

At last Sir Ivo's shield arm drooped, for all his efforts to keep it before him, and his sword strokes waxed fainter, and his breath could be heard to come hoarsely. Suddenly Alan leaped in upon him, and with an upward thrust drove his sword into the evil knight's throat.

At the same moment Robin, who had been watching intently the fight between Alan and the knight, heard the hiss as of a snake before him and then a footstep behind him. He stepped swiftly aside, and a knife-blade flashed beside him. Turning, he saw the churl who had been speaking with the knight almost fall to the ground with the force of the blow he had aimed at Robin's back. Then the man, quickly recovering, dashed away towards the trees.

As he did so, a little dark form seemed to start up from the bracken before him. Over the churl tripped and fell heavily, with the small, pixie-like figure gripping him. For a moment they seemed to struggle in a deadly embrace, then suddenly the big body of the churl fell away like a log, the brownie rose, shook himself, and wiped a dagger blade upon a bracken leaf.

'I thank thee, Hob o' the Hill, both for the snake's warning and thy ready blow,' said Robin. 'I should have kept my eyes about me. Who is the fellow, Hob?'

' 'Tis Grull, the churl from the Evil Hold,' said Hob. 'He hath haunted the forest by the Stane Lea where was thy camp these three days past. I thought he was a serf that craved his freedom, but he was a spy.'

Hob o' the Hill was brother to Ket the Trow or Troll, but in build or look he differed greatly. He was no taller than his bigger brother, but all his form was in a more delicate mould. Slender of limb, he had a pale face, which set off the uncanny blackness of his eyes, black curly hair, and short beard. His arms were long, and the hands, as refined almost as a girl's, were yet strong and rounded. He, too, was dressed in a laced leather tunic and breeches of doeskin that reached the ankles, while on his feet were stout shoes.

Robin went to Alan, whom he found seated on the ground beside his dead enemy. He was weary and faint from a wound in his shoulder. This Robin bound up with cloth torn from Alan's shirt of fine linen, after which the outlaw asked him what he would do now.

'I think I will take me home to Werrisdale,' said Alan. 'I am staying at Forest Hold, the house of my foster-brother, Piers the Lucky, but there will be hue and cry raised against me ere long for the slaying of this rascal knight, and I would not that harm should happen to my brother for my fault.'

'I have heard of Piers,' said Robin, who knew indeed some-thing of everyone who dwelt in or near the wide forests which he loved, 'and I think he would not wish thee to avoid him if he could help thee.'

'I know it,' said Alan, 'but I would not that Belame and his evil crew should burn my foster-brother in his bed one night in revenge upon me. Nay, I will get me home if I can come at my horse, which I left at a forester's hut a mile from here.'

Together Robin and Alan went on their way towards the hut of the forester.

While the events just described had been taking place, a man had been passing along a path in a part of the forest some mile and a half distant. He was a tall man, with great limbs, which gave evidence of enormous strength, and he was dressed in the rough homespun garb of a peasant. He seemed very light-hearted. Sometimes he twirled a great quarterstaff which he held in his hands, and again he would start whistling, or begin trolling a song at the top of a loud voice.

'John, John,' he said suddenly, apostrophising himself, 'what a fool thou art! Thou shouldst be as mum as a fish, and shouldst creep like a footpad from bush to bush. Thou singest like a freeman, fool, whereas thou art but a runaway serf into whose silly body the free air of the free forest has entered like wine. But twenty short miles separate thee from the stocks and whipping-post of old Lord Mumblemouth and his bailiff, and here thou art trolling songs or whistling as if a forester may not challenge thee from the next brake and seize thee for the chance of a reward from thy lord. Peace, fool, look to thy ways and – Saints! what a right sweet smell!' He broke off, and lifting up his head, sniffed the sunlit air of the forest, casting his bright brown eyes humorously this way and that. 'Sure,' he went on, 'I have hit upon the kitchen of some fat abbot! What a waste, to let so fat a smell be spent up in the air. Holy Virgin, how hungry I am! Let me seek out the causer of this most savoury odour. Maybe he will have compassion upon a poor wayfarer and give me some little of his plenty.'

Saying this, John pushed aside the bushes and stole in the direction of the smell. He had not gone far before he found himself peering into a glade, in the midst of which was a tree, to which was tethered a horse, while not far from the bushes where he stood was a hut of wood, its roof formed of turves in which grew bunches of wallflower, stitchwort, and ragged robin. Before the door of this abode a fire was burning brightly without flame, and on skewers stuck in the ground beside it were cutlets of meat. These spluttered and sizzled in the genial heat of the fire, and gave forth the savoury smell which had made John feel suddenly that he was a very hungry man, and had walked far without food.

John eyed the juicy steaks, and his mouth watered. For a moment he thought no one watched the spluttering morsels, and he was thinking that for a hungry man to take one or even two of them would be no sin; but as he was thinking thus a man came from the hut, and bending down, turned two of the skewers so that the meat upon them should be better done.

John's face gloomed. The man was one of the king's rangers of the forest, as was shown by his tunic of green and his hose of brown, and the silver badge of a hunting-horn upon his hat. Moreover, his face was surly and sour – the face of a man who would sooner see a poor man starve than grant him a portion of his meal. It was Black Hugo, the forester who had accosted Robin and Scarlet in so surly a manner when he had met them in the forest.

John thought for a few moments, and then, backing gently away so that he made no noise, he reached a spot at some distance from the glade. Then, casting caution aside, he tramped forward again, and reaching the glade, burst into it, and then stopped, as if surprised at what he saw before him. He had dropped his quarterstaff in the bushes before he issued from them.

The surly forester glared at him from the other side of the fire.

'How now?' said he; 'thou lumbering dolt! Who art thou to go breaking down the bushes like some hog? Hast thou no fear of the king's justice on all who disturb his deer?'

'I pray your pardon, master ranger,' said John, pulling a forelock of his hair, and pretending to be no more than a rough oaf. 'I knew not whither I was going, but I smelt the good smell of your meat, and thought it might be that some good company of monks or a lord's equipage was preparing their midday meal, and might spare a morsel for a poor wayfarer who hath eaten naught since dawn.'

'Go thy ways, churl,' said the ranger, and his face looked more surly than ever when he heard John ask for a portion of his meat. 'Thou seest I am no monk or lord, but I prepare my own meal. So get thee gone to the highway ere I kick thee there. Knowest thou that thou hast no right to leave the road? Get thee gone, I say!'

Black Hugo spoke in angry tones, looked fiercely at the apparently abashed churl, and started forward as if about to put his threat into action. John, pulling his lock again, retreated hurriedly as if thoroughly frightened. Black Hugo stood listening for a few moments to the peasant's heavy footsteps as he crashed through the bushes towards the highway again, and then, turning to the hut, drew from a chest a huge piece of bread, from which he cut a thick slice. Then, going to the fire, he bent down and took up one of the skewers, and pushed off the meat with a knife on the slice. He did the same to the second, and then bent to the third.

Suddenly a small pole seemed to leap like a lance from the bush nearest to him, and flying across the space to the fire, one end caught the bending forester a sounding thwack on the side of the head. He fell sideways almost into the fire, stunned, and the skewer with the meat upon it flew up into the air.

John, leaping from the bush, caught the skewer as it fell, saying: 'I like not dust on my food, surly ranger.'

He deposited the meat on the bread beside the others and then, going to the prostrate ranger, turned him over and looked at the place where the pole had struck him.

' 'Twas a shrewd blow!' said John, with a chuckle, 'and hit the very spot! An inch lower would have slain him, perhaps, and an inch higher would have cracked his curmudgeon skull. As 'tis, he'll get his wits again in the turn of a fat man's head, just in time to see me eating *my* dinner.'

He lifted the forester as easily as if he were a child, and propping him in a sitting position against one of the posts of the hut, he lashed him securely to it with a rope which he found inside. Then, with his quarterstaff beside him, he sat down beside the fire and began demolishing the three juicy venison steaks.

In a few moments Black Hugo with a great sigh, opened his eyes, lifted his head, and looked in a dazed manner before him. At sight of John biting huge mouthfuls out of the bread, all his wits returned to him.

'Thou runagate rogue!' he said, and his face flushed with rage. He strove to pull his hands from the rope, but in vain. 'I will mark thee, thou burly robber. Thou shalt smart for this, and I will make thee repent that thou didst ever lay me low with thy dirty staff. I will crop thy ears for thee, and swear thy life away, thou hedge-robber and cut-purse!'

'Rant not so, thou black-faced old ram!' said John, with a laugh, 'but think thee how sweeter a man thou wouldst have been hadst thou shared thy meat with me. See now, surly old dog of the woods, thou hast lost all because thou didst crave to keep all. Thy cutlets are done to a turn; thou'rt a good cook – a better cook, I trow, than a forester; and see, here is the last morsel. Look!'

Saying which, John perched the remaining piece of meat on the last piece of bread, and opening his huge mouth popped them both in, and gave a great laugh as he saw the black looks in the other's eyes.

'I thank thee, forester, for the good dinner thou didst cook for me,' went on John. 'I feel kindly to thee, though thou dost look but sourly upon me. I doubt not thou dost ache to get at me, and I would like to try a bout with thee. Say, wilt thou have a turn with the quarterstaff?'

'Ay,' said Black Hugo, his eyes gleaming with rage. 'Let me have at thee, thou masterless rogue, and I will not leave one sound bone in thy evil carcass.'

'By Saint Peter!' said John, with a laugh, 'art thou so great with the quarterstaff? Man, I shall love to see thy play. Come, then, we will set to.'

Rising, John approached the ranger for the purpose of unloosing his bonds, when the sound of voices was borne to him through the forest. He stopped and listened, while the eyes of Black Hugo glared at him in triumph. Doubtless, if, as was probable, the travellers who were approaching were law abiding, he would soon be released, and could wreak his vengeance on this rogue. The sounds of steps and voices came nearer, until from the bushes midway on one side of the glade there issued Alan-a-Dale and Robin, who looked at the tall form of the serf and then at the ranger tied to the post.

John bent and took up his staff, and turning to Black Hugo, said:

'I doubt thy honesty, good ranger, if, as thy evil face seems to say, these are thy friends. But fear not I shall forget. We will have that bout together ere long. Thanks for thy dinner again.'

Saying this, John disappeared among the bushes and noiselessly stole away.

Robin and Alan-a-Dale came up, and could not forbear laughing when they saw the sour looks of Black Hugo.

'What is this?' asked Robin. 'The king's forester bound to a post by some wandering rogue! What, man, and has he taken thy dinner too!'

The gloomy silence of the forester confirmed what they had gathered from the parting words of the big churl, and both Robin and Alan laughed aloud at the discomfiture of the ranger, who writhed in his bonds.

'Have done with thy laughter, thou wolf's-head!' he cried to Robin.

But Robin laughed the more, until the glade re-echoed.

'Unloose me,' cried Black Hugo, in a rage, 'and I will let thee know what 'tis to laugh at a king's forester thou broken knave and runagate rascal!'

Still Robin laughed at the futile anger of the ranger, whose face was flushed as he stormed.

'I think, friend,' said Alan gently, in the midst of his laughter, 'thou dost foolishly to threaten this bold woodman whilst thou art in bonds. 'Twere more manly to stay thy threats till thou art free. Thou'rt over bold, friend.'

'Knowest thou not who this rogue is?' cried Hugo. 'He is the leader of a pack of escaped serfs, and for their crimes of firing their lord's house and slaying their lord's men they are food for the gallows or for any good man's sword who can hack their wolves' heads from their shoulders.'

'Whatever you may say of this my friend,' said Alan coldly, 'I can say that both he and his men are bold and true men, and if they have fled from a tyrant lord I blame them not.'

Alan, with a haughty look, went towards his horse. Robin ceased his laughter, and now addressed the forester.

'My heart warms to that long-limbed rascal who tied thee up and ate thy dinner,' he said. 'Thou, who with others of thy sort live on poorer folk by extortion and threats, hast now had a taste of what thou givest to those unable to withstand thee. I will give thee time to think over thy sins and thy punishment. Bide there in thy bonds until the owl hoots this night.'

Together Robin and Alan-a-Dale moved from the glade, and the forester was left to cool his anger. The sun poured down its heat upon his naked head, and the more he strained at his bonds the more the flies settled upon him and tormented him. Then he shouted for help, hoping that one of his fellow-foresters might be near, or that some traveller on the highway would hear and come and release him.

But no one came, and he grew tired of shouting. The sunlight burned through his hose, his tongue and throat were dry, and his arms, pinioned to his side and bound by ropes, were almost senseless. The forest about him seemed sunk in silence. Sometimes across the glade a flash of jewel-like light would come. It was a dragon fly, and in the rays of the sun it would hover and swerve before the bushes, like a point of living flame. Then birds came down and hopped and pecked among the embers of his fire, and even at his feet, or from a hole beneath a tree a ferret would peep forth, and encouraged by the silence would steal forth and across the glade, running from cover to cover, until he disappeared in the forest beyond.

The afternoon wore to a close, the sun went behind the trees on the western verge of the glade, and the shadows stretched along until the grey light lay everywhere. Then the forest seemed to wake up. Bird called to bird across the cool deeps of the trees, the evening wind rustled the leaves, and a great stir seemed to thrill through the woods.

The blue of the sky became slowly grey, the darkness deepened under the trees, and strange things seemed to be moving in the gloom. There came a great bird flying with noiseless wings, and hovered over the glade. Then it sank, and a sudden shriek rose for a moment as of something from which life was being torn. Then came the weird cry of 'To whee – to whee – to whoo!'

The ranger shivered. Somehow the cry seemed like that of a fiend; besides, the cold air was creeping along the ground. He pulled at his arms, which seemed almost dead, and to his wonder his bonds fell away and he found that he was free. He looked behind and inside the hut, but he could see no one. Then with lifeless fingers he picked up the rope which had bound him to the post, and found that it had been cut by a keen knife.

He looked round affrighted, and crossed himself. Robin the Outlaw had said he should be free when the owl hooted, but who had crept up and cut his bonds so that he had not been aware of it?

Black Hugo shook his head and wondered. He believed in brownies as much as he believed in his own existence, but hitherto he had not thought that brownies used knives. He shook his head again, and began to chafe his cold limbs, and as the blood began to run through them again he could have cried aloud with the pain.

He decided that someday ere long he would be revenged upon that seven-foot rascal who had stolen his dinner and tied him up. As for Robin the Outlaw, he would earn four marks by cutting off his head and taking it to the king's chief justice in London.

Meanwhile, Robin and Alan-a-Dale had pursued their way, discoursing on many things. Both found that they loved the forest, and that never did they find more delight than when, with bow in hand, they chased the king's deer, or with brave dogs routed the fierce boar from his lair. Robin put Alan upon a short route to his home in Werrisdale, and when they parted they shook hands, and each promised the other that soon they would meet again.

Then Robin turned back towards the meeting-place at the Stane Lea, where he knew his men would be waiting for him after their chase of the men-at-arms, to share the evening meal together.

Robin was almost near the end of his journey when he came to the brook which, farther up-stream, ran beside the very glade where his men would be busy round a big fire cooking their evening meal. At this place, however, the stream was broad, with a rapid current, and the forest path was carried across it on a single narrow beam of oak. It was only wide enough for one man to cross at a time, and of course had no railing.

Mounting the two wooden steps to it, Robin had walked some two or three feet along it, when on the other bank a tall man appeared, and jumping on the bridge, also began to cross it. Robin recognised him at once, by his height, as the fellow who had tied the forester to his door-post and stolen his dinner. He would have been content to hail the big man as one he would like to know, but that he had a very stubborn air as he walked towards him, as one who would say: 'Get out of my way, little man, or I will walk over thee.'

Robin was some twelve or fourteen inches shorter than the other, and being generally reckoned to be tall, and strong withal, he deeply resented the other's inches and his bragging air.

They stopped and looked frowningly at each other when they were but some ten feet apart.

'Where are thy manners, fellow?' said Robin haughtily. 'Sawest thou not that I was already on the bridge when thou didst place thy great splay feet on it?'

'Splay feet yourself jackanapes,' retorted the other. 'The small jack should ever give way to the big pot.'

'Thou'rt a stranger in these parts, thou uplandish chucklehead!' said Robin; 'thy currish tongue betrayeth thee. I'll give thee a good Barnisdale lesson, if thou dost not retreat and let me pass.'

Saying which, Robin drew an arrow from his girdle and notched it on his string. 'Twas a stout bow and long, and one that few men could bend, and the tall man, with a half-angry, half-humorous twinkle in his eye, glanced at it.

'If thou dost touch thy string,' he said, 'I'll leather thy hide to rights.'

'Thou ass,' said Robin, 'how couldst thou leather anyone if this grey goose quill were sticking in thy stupid carcass?'

'If this is thy Barnisdale teaching,' rejoined John, 'then 'tis the teaching of cowards. Here art thou, with a good bow in thy hand, making ready to shoot me, who hath naught but this quarterstaff.'

Robin paused. He was downright angry with the stranger, but there was something honest and manly and good-natured about the giant which he liked.

'Have it thy way, then,' he said. 'We Barnisdale men are not cowards, as thou shalt see ere long. I will e'en lay aside my bow and cut me a staff. Then will I test thy manhood, and if I baste thee not till thou dost smoke like a fire, may the nicker who lives in this stream seize me.'

So saying, Robin turned back and went to the bank, and with his knife he cut a stout staff from as fine a ground oak as could be found anywhere in Barnisdale. Having trimmed this to the weight and length he desired, he ran back on the bridge where the stranger was still waiting for him.

'Now,' said Robin, 'we will have a little play together. Whoever is knocked from the bridge into the stream shall lose the battle. So now, go!'

With the first twirl of Robin's staff the stranger could see that he had no novice to deal with, and as their staves clanged together as they feinted or guarded he felt that the aim of Robin had a strength that was almost if not quite equal to his own.

Long time their staves whirled like the arms of a windmill, and the cracks of the wood as staff kissed staff were tossed to and fro between the trees on either side of the stream. Suddenly the stranger feinted twice. Quickly as Robin guarded, he could not save the third stroke, and the giant's staff came with a smart rap on Robin's skull.

'First blood to thee!' cried Robin, as he felt the warmth trickle down his face.

'Second blood to thee!' said the giant, with a good-natured laugh.

Robin, thoroughly angry now, beat with his staff as if it were a flail. Quick as lightning his blows descended, now here, now there, and all the quickness of eye of his opponent could not save him from getting such blows that his very bones rattled.

Both men were at the great disadvantage of having to keep their footing on the narrow bridge. Every step made forward or backward had to be taken with every care, and the very power

Robin meeets with Little John

with which they struck or guarded almost threw them over one side or the other.

Great as was the strength of the big man, Robin's quickness of hand and eye were getting the better of him. He was indeed beginning to 'smoke', and the sweat gathered on his face and ran down in great drops. Suddenly Robin got a blow in on the big man's crown; but next moment, with a furious stroke, the stranger struck Robin off his balance, and with a mighty splash the outlaw dived into the water.

For a moment John seemed surprised to find no enemy before him; then, wiping the sweat from his eyes, he cried:

'Hallo, good laddie, where art thou now?'

He bent down anxiously, and peered into the water flowing rapidly beneath the bridge. 'By Saint Peter!' he said, 'I hope the bold man is not hurt!'

'Faith!' came a voice from the bank a little farther down, here 'I am, big fellow, as right as a trivet. Thou'st got the day,' Robin went on with a laugh, 'and I shall not need to cross the bridge.'

Robin pulled himself up the bank, and, kneeling down, laved his head and face in the water. When he arose, he found the big stranger almost beside him, dashing the water over his own head and face.

'What!' cried Robin, 'hast not gone forward on thy journey? Thou wert in so pesty a hurry to cross the bridge just now that thou wouldst not budge for me, and now thou'st come back.'

'Scorn me not, good fellow,' said the big man, with a sheepish laugh. 'I have no whither to go that I wot of. I am but a serf who hath run from his manor, and tonight, instead of my warm nest [hut], I shall have to find a bush or a brake that's not too draughty. But I would like to shake hands with thee ere I wend, for thou'rt as true and good a fighter as ever I met.'

Robin's hand was on the other's big fingers at once, and they gave a handshake of mutual respect and liking. Then John turned away, and was for crossing the bridge.

'Stay awhile,' said Robin; 'perhaps thou wouldst like supper ere thou goest a-wandering.'

With these words, Robin placed his horn to his lips and blew a blast that woke the echoes, made the blackbirds fly shrieking away from the bushes, and every animal that lurked in the underwood to dive for the nearest cover. The stranger looked on marvelling, and Robin stood waiting and listening. Soon in the distance could be heard sounds as if deer or does were hurrying through the bushes, and in a little while between the trees could be seen the forms of men running towards them.

Will Stuteley the Bowman was the first to reach the bank where Robin stood.

'Why, good master,' said he, 'what hath happened to thee? Thou'rt wet to the skin!'

Will looked at the stranger, and glared angrily at him.

' 'Tis no matter at all,' laughed Robin. 'You see that tall lad there. We fought on the bridge with staves, and he tumbled me in.'

By this time Much, the Miller's son, Scarlet, and the others had reached the bank, and at Robin's words Scarlet dashed at the stranger, and by a quick play with foot and hand tripped up the big man. Then the others threw themselves upon the stranger, and seizing him cried:

'Swing him up and out, lads! Duck him well!'

'Nay, nay,' shouted Robin, laughing. 'Forbear, lads. I have no ill-will – I've put my hand in his, for he's a good fellow and a bold. Get up, lad,' he said to the stranger, who had been powerless in the hands of so many, and would next moment have been swung far out into the stream. 'Hark ye, seven footer,' said Robin. 'We are outlaws, brave lads who have run from evil lords. There are twenty-two of us. If thou wilt join us, thou shalt share and share with us, both in hard knocks, good cheer, and the best that we can reive from the rich snuffling priests, proud prelates, evil lords, and hard-hearted merchants who venture through the greenwood. Thou'rt a good hand at the staff: I'll make thee a better hand at the longbow. Now, speak up, jolly blade!'

'By earth and water, I'll be thy man,' cried the stranger, coming eagerly forward and holding out his hand, which Robin seized and wrung. 'Never heard I sweeter words than those you have said, and with all my heart will I serve thee and thy fellowship.'

'What is thy name, good man?' asked Robin.

'John o' the Stubbs,' replied the other; 'but' – with a great laugh – 'men call me John the Little.'

'Ha! ha! ha!' laughed the others, and crowded round shaking hands with him and crying out: 'John, little man, give me thy great hand!'

'His name shall be altered,' said stout Will the Bowman, 'and we will baptise him in good brown ale. Now, shall we not be back to camp, master, and make a feast on't?'

'Ay, lads,' replied Robin, 'we will be merry this night. We have a new fellow to our company, and will e'en bless him with good ale and fat venison.'

They raced back to camp, where over the fire Scadlock had a great cauldron, from whence arose the most appetising odours for men grown hungry in greenwood air. Robin changed his garments for dry ones, which were taken from a secret store-place in a cave near by, and then, standing round John the Little, who overtopped them all, the outlaws held each his wooden mug filled to the brim with good brown ale.

'Now, lads,' said Stuteley, 'we will baptise our new comrade into our good free company of forest lads. He has hitherto been called John the Little, and a sweet pretty babe he is. But from now on he shall be called Little John. Three cheers, lads, for Little John!'

How they made the twilight ring! The leaves overhead quivered with the shouts. Then they tossed off their mugs of ale, and gathering round the cauldron they dipped their pannikins into the rich stew and fell to feasting.

Afterwards Little John told them of his meeting with the forester, and how he had tied him up and ate up his dinner before his eyes. They laughed hugely over this, for all bore some grudge against Black Hugo and the other foresters for their treacherous oppression of poor peasants living on the forest borders. They voted John a brave and hefty lad, and said that if they could get fifty such as he they would be strong enough to pull down the Evil Hold of Wrangby, or the robbers' castle on Hagthorn Waste.

Then Robin continued Little John's tale, and told how he left the ranger in his bonds 'to think over his sins till the owl hooted.'

'What mean you, master?' said Little John. 'Did you go back and cut the rogue loose?'

It was dark now, and only the flicker of the firelight lit up the strong brown faces of the men as they lay or squatted.

'Nay, I cut not the rogue loose! But he is free by now, and, I doubt not, crying o'er his aching limbs, and breathing vengeance against us both.'

'How, then, master?' said Little John, gaping with wonder; while the others also listened, marvelling at their leader's talk.

'I have friends in the greenwood,' said Robin, 'who aid me in many things. Yet they are shy of strangers, and will not willingly show themselves until they know ye better. Hob o' the Hill, show thyself, lad!'

Then, to the terror of them all, from a dark patch near Robin's feet there rose a little man whose long face shone pale in the firelight, and whose black eyes gleamed like sloes. Some of the men, keeping their eyes on him, dragged themselves away; others crossed themselves; and Much, the Miller's son, took off his tunic and turned it inside out.

'Holy Peter!' he murmured, 'shield us from the power of evil spirits!'

'Out upon thee all!' cried Robin in a stern voice. 'Hob is no evil spirit, but a man as thou art, with but smaller limbs, maybe, but keener wits.'

' 'Tis a boggart, good maister,' said one of the outlaws; 'a troll or lubberfiend, such as they tell on. He leads men into bogs, or makes them wander all night on the moors.'

' 'Tis such as he,' said Rafe the Carter, 'who used to plait my horses' manes in the night, and drove them mad.'

'And,' said another,' his evil fowk do make the green rings in the meadows, in which, if beasts feed, they be poisoned.'

'Speak not to the elf,' said another, crossing his finger before his face to protect himself from the 'evil eye' of the troll, 'or you will surely die.'

'Old women, all of ye,' said Robin, with scorn. 'Hob is a man, I tell thee, who can suffer as thou canst suffer – hath the same blood to spill, the same limbs to suffer torture or feel the hurt of fire. Listen,' and his voice was full of a hard anger. 'Hob hath a brother whose name is Ket. They are both my very dear friends. Many times have they aided me, and often have they saved my life. I charge you all to harbour no evil or harm against them.'

'Why, good master, are they friends of thine?' asked Little John, who smiled good-humouredly at Hob. 'How came ye to win their love?'

'I will tell thee,' went on Robin. ' 'Twas two summers ago, and I walked in the heart of the forest here, and came to a lonely glade where never do ye see the foresters go, for they say 'tis haunted, and the boldest keep far from it. In that glade are two green mounds or hillocks. I passed them, and saw three knights on foot and two lying dead. And the three knights fought with two trolls – this man and his brother. Hob here was gravely wounded, and his brother also, and the knights overpowered them. Then I marvelled what they would do, and I saw them make a great fire, and creeping nearer I heard them say they would see whether these trolls would burn, as their father had burned on Hagthorn Waste, or whether they were fiends of the fire, and would fly away in the smoke. Then as they dragged the two men to the fire I saw a door of green sods open in the side of one of the hills, and from it rushed three women – one old and halt, but the other two young, and, though small, they were beautiful. They flung themselves at the feet of the knights, and prayed for pity on their brothers, and the old woman offered to be burned in place of her sons. The felon knights were struck dumb at first with the marvel of such a sight, and then they seized the three women and swore they should burn with their brother trolls. Then I could suffer to see no more, and with three arrows from my belt I slew those evil knights. I pulled the two poor hill folk from the fires, and ever since they and their kin have been the dearest friends I have in the greenwood.'

'Master,' said Little John soberly, ' 'twas bravely done of thee, and truly hast thou proved that no man ever suffers from an honest and kindly deed.'

He rose and bent his giant form down to Little Hob, and held out his hand.

'Laddie,' he said, 'give me thy hand, for I would be friend to all who love good Master Robin.'

'And I also,' said brave Will Stuteley and Scarlet, who had come forward at the same moment.

The little man gave his hand to each in turn, looking keenly into each face as he did so.

'Hob o' the Hill would be brother to all who are brothers of Robin o' the Hood,' said he.

'Listen, friends all,' went on Robin. 'Just as ye have suffered from the oppression and malice of evil lords, so hath suffered our friend here and his brother. The five knights whom they and

I slew were of that wicked crew that haunt Hagthorn Waste, and hold all the lands in those parts in fear and evil custom. I know there was some cruel deed which was done by Ranulf of the Waste upon the father of these friends of ours, and someday before long it may be that we may be able to help Hob and his brother to have vengeance upon that evil lord for the tortures which their father suffered. What sayest thou, Hob, wilt thou have our aid if needs be?'

'If needs be, ay,' replied Hob, whose eyes had become fierce, and whose voice was thick and low, 'but we men of the Underworld would liefer have our vengeance to ourselves. In our own time will we take it, and in full measure. Yet I thank thee, Robin, and these thy fellows, for the aid thou dost offer.'

The little man spoke with dignity, as if he thanked an equal.

Then came little Gilbert, and put his hand in the strong clasp of the mound man, and after him Much, the Miller's son; and all the others, putting off their dread of the uncanny, seeing that Robin and Little John and the others were not afraid, came up also and passed the word of friendship with Hob o' the Hill.

'Now,' said Robin, 'we are all brothers to the free folk of the wood. Never more need any of ye dread to step beyond the gleam of fire at night, and in the loneliest glade shall ye not fear to tread by day. Ye are free of the forest, and all its parts, and sib to all its folks.'

'So say I,' said Hob, 'I – whose people once ruled through all this land. Broken are we now, the Little People, half feared and half scorned; we and our harmless deeds made into silly tales told by foolish women and frightened bairns around their fires by night. But I give to ye who are the brothers of my brother the old word of peace and brotherhood, which, ere the tall fair men ravened through our land, we, the Little People, gave to those who aided us and were our friends. I whose kin were once Lords of the Underworld and of the Overworld, of the Mound Folk, the Stone Folk, and the Tree Folk, give to you, my brothers, equal part and share in the earth, the wood, the water, and the air of the greenwood and the moorland.'

With these words the little dark man glided from the circle of the firelight, and seemed suddenly to become part of the gloom of the trees.

CHAPTER THREE

How Robin Fought the Beggar-Spy
and Caught the Sheriff

Winter was gone, the weak spring sunlight struck its rays deep through the bare brown trees of Sherwood, the soft wind dangled the catkins on the hazel, the willow, and the poplar; and the thrush, who had lived in the glade for five winters, sat high on the top of the tallest elm, and shouted to all who chose to listen that he could not see snow anywhere, that the buds on all the trees were growing as fast as they could, that the worms were beginning to peep through the mould, and, indeed, that food and life and love were come again into a world which for long weeks had seemed to be dead, and wrapped in its winding-sheet for evermore.

A wide glade, strangely clear of all bushes, lay far down before him, and on one side of it were two great green hillocks, nearly side by side. One rose well out in the glade, but the shadows from the fringe of the forest lay on the heaving swell of the other.

There seemed no sign of human life anywhere in the vast glade. Certainly a faint path seemed to start from a particular spot on the green side of the farther mound and lead towards the forest; but that might easily be the track of a couple of hares who had made their home in the hill, and who, as is well known, always race along one beaten track to their feeding-ground.

Suddenly from the forest on the wider side of the glade the figure of a small man ran out into the open. As swiftly as a hare he raced over the grass, breasted the nearest mound, and reaching the top, seemed suddenly to sink into the ground. It was Hob o' the Hill. A few moments later, and on that side of the mound which faced the nearer forest, a portion of the green turf seemed suddenly to fall in, and the two small forms of Hob o' the Hill and Ket his brother came out. They looked keenly round, the turf behind them closed again, and with swift steps they ran along the little path. Every now and then they glanced behind to see that they kept the bulk of the mound between them and prying eyes in the forest at the point whence Hob had issued.

In a little while they gained the nearer verge of the forest, and ran forward through its shady aisles under the bare brown trees. For a space of time wherein a man might count twenty there was no movement in the glade. But then, at that part of the forest whence Hob had first run, came the sound of hooves, the flash of arms, and along a narrow path there came eight riders who, issuing from the trees into the glade stopped and gazed forward.

The foremost of these was a man of fine, almost courtly, bearing, with handsome features. On his head was a steel cap, his broad breast was covered with a hauberk, and in his right hand was a lance. Beside him on a palfrey rode a man of mild and gentle countenance, who looked like a chaplain, for he was clothed in the semi-monkish robe of a clerk. Behind them rode six men, each with lance, hauberk, and steel cap, quivers at their back, and bows slung within easy reach at their saddle-bows. They had the frank, open look of freemen, and were evidently a bodyguard of freeholding tenants.

'Well, Master Gammell,' said the clerk, looking this way and that, 'which is the way now? In this wilderness of trees and glades and downs it passes me to know where thou canst hope to find this runagate kinsman of thine.'

' 'Tis as clear as noonday,' said Master Gammell, with a laugh. ' "Beyond the two howes", was the word of the good churl at Outwoods, "through the wood for a mile till you come to the lithe. Then search the scar of Clumber cliffs beyond the stream, and – " ' Master Gammell laughed good-humouredly ' " – belike an arrow in your ribs from Lord knows where will tell you that your man has seen you, even though you have not seen a sign of him." The way is clear, therefore, good Simon,' he ended, 'to the place where Robin has wintered, so let us push forward.'

Putting spurs to his horse, the leader, Alfred of Gammell, or Gamwell, pushed forward into the glade, followed by the clerk and the six archers.

'Let us not pass too close to those green hills,' said Simon. 'Men say that fiends dwell within them, and may work wizardry upon us if we pass within the circuit of their power.'

'Thou art no countryman,' laughed Master Gammell. 'There be many such mounds scattered up and down the country hereabouts, and no man ever got hurt from them that I know of. Indeed, one was upon my waste land at Locksley, and though I remember my villeins came and begged me not to dig it up, I said I could not let it cumber land that could be brought into good ploughland, and therefore I had it digged up, and naught ill was found in it but a hollow in the midst and an old jar with a few burned bones therein, and some elf-bolts and bits of stone. Such things are but ancient graves.'

'Yet have I read,' went on the clerk, 'that it is within such high mounds in lonely places that one enters into entrancing lands of green twilight, where lovely fiends do dwell, and dreadful wizards work their soul-snatching wiles and enchantment.'

'I fear me,' said Gammell, 'that such tales are of no greater truth than the songs and stories of lying jongleurs, which serve but to pass an empty hour or two, but are not worth the credence of wise men.'

Nevertheless, the clerk kept a keen eye on the green hills as they rode beside them, as if every moment he expected something of mysterious evil to issue from them and whelm them in the chains of some strange enchantment. When they entered the forest beyond, he still kept his glance continually moving through the dim ways. Simon, indeed, loved not the dark woods. He was a man who had lived much in towns, and thought that there was no sweeter sound than the shouts of men and women chaffering in the market-place, nor more pleasant sight than the street with its narrow sky blocked out by high pent roofs.

They had ridden about half a mile through the wood, when suddenly a shrill call resounded above their heads. 'Twas like the cry of a bird in the talons of a hawk, and, almost without knowing it, all lifted their eyes to see the kill. As they did so a great voice shouted:

'Stand, travellers, and stir not!'

At these words their eyes were swiftly brought down, and looking round, they saw that where they had seen only the dark trunks of trees were now some twenty men in dark brown tunic, hose and hood, each with a great bow stretched taut, and his hand upon the feather of an arrow drawn to his very ear.

One or two of the men-at-arms riding behind their master cursed in their beards and glared fiercely about, as if to seek for a way of escape. But looking closely they perceived that the bowmen surrounded them on all sides. Their dark tunics and hose, being of the colour of the trees, made them so like the very trunks themselves that some had thought for a moment that they looked at a gnarled thorn or a young oak, until the glint of light on the keen arrow point had shown them their error.

Alfred of Gammell bit his lip, and his eyes flashed in anger; but his good-humour conquering his chagrin, he said:

'Well, good fellows, what want ye of me?'

'Throw down thy weapons,' came the answer from a tall and powerful man standing beside the trunk of an oak just before them.

Very glumly the six archers did as the robber bade them, and when all their weapons were lying on the ground, came the command:

'Ride forward ten paces!' When this had been done, the speaker gave orders to three of his men to pick up the weapons.

'Now,' said he to Master Gammell, 'thou shalt come away and see our master who rules in these shaws.'

'Who may your master be, tall man?' asked Gammell angrily, as the man seized his horse's bridle and drew him forward.

'That's for him to say,' said the robber. 'But 'tis to be hoped thy purse is well lined, for though he will dine thee and thy company well, thou wilt have to pay thy shot.'

Master Gammell was prevented from replying by a shout which came from among the trees before them. Looking in that direction, they were aware of a tall man coming towards them, with two little men walking beside him. The tall man was dressed in green, with a cloak or capote which reached to his knees, while his head was covered and his face concealed by a hood.

The robber who held the bridle checked Gammell's horse as the man in green approached, and said:

'Master, here be a party of foolish armed men blundering

through thy woods as if they had the word of peace from thee that the king himself hath not got. Wilt thou dine them, or shall we take toll of their purses and let them gang their way lighter and wiser than they came?'

For a moment the man in green stood in silence looking up at the face of the first horseman. Then, with a frank laugh, he approached with outstretched hand, and throwing off the hood so that his face was seen, he said:

'Thy hand, cousin, and thy forgiveness for my men's rough ways.'

With a start, Gammell looked keenly at the face of Robin Hood, for he was the man in green; then, clasping the outstretched hand of the outlaw, he laughingly said:

'Robin, Robin, thou rascal! I should have known that these were thy faithful fellows. Thou art the man of all men I came hither to see.'

Gammell leaped from his horse, and the two men embraced, kissing each other on both cheeks. Then Gammell held Robin at arm's length and looked at him, scanning with half-laughing, half-admiring eyes the tanned face with the fearless bright eyes, the head of dark brown hair, and the length and strength of limb.

'By the shrine of Walsingham!' said Gammell, 'I should hardly have known thee, so large of limb thou hast grown since we parted five years ago at Locksley. Robin, sorry was I to hear thou hadst been forced to flee to the greenwood – pity 'tis thou wert ever so free of speech and quick of action!'

'Now, lad,' replied Robin soberly, 'naught of that. We could never agree on it. Thou hast found it pay thee best to court the strong lord whose lands lie by thine, and to shut thy eyes to many things which I must speak and fight against. Now, tell me, coz, why camest thou here?'

'To see thee, Robin, and to thank thee,' was the reply, 'and also to warn thee!'

'To thank me?'

'Ay, for that noble deed of thine at Havelond!' said Gammell. ' 'Twas but justice that thou didst give to those traitors and robbers of our poor cousin, after she had in vain besought justice of the king's court – indeed, at his very seat!'

This indeed had been an act which, almost as much as his first flight after slaying the lord abbot's men-at-arms, had made Robin's fame spread wide through the lands of Yorkshire, Derby, and Nottingham which lay beside the great rolling forests. It had happened in the late autumn, just before winter with its iron hand had locked the land in ice and snow. Robin had a cousin, a lady named Alice of Havelond, who had married Bennett, a well-to-do yeoman who dwelled in Scaurdale in Yorkshire. Two years before, the plundering Scots and fiendish Galloway men, wild and fierce and cruel as mountain cats, had come from the north ravaging and burning. A Scottish knight had taken Bennett and held him to ransom, and shut him in prison until his ransom should be paid. In his absence Thomas of Patherley and Robert of Prestbury, neighbours of his wife's, had seized on his fields at Havelond, divided them between themselves, and pulled down the houses, even throwing Alice his wife out of the house in which she dwelled.

No justice had the poor lady been able to get, neither from the king's justices nor from the steward of the lord from whom the land was held. Then, when he had lain a year in prison, she was able to pay her husband's ransom. He returned, and full of anger on hearing of the robbery of his lands, had entered on the same lands as the rightful owner. His enemies lay in wait, and beat him so greatly that barely was he left alive. His wife went to the king's court, and after long and weary waiting was told that Bennett must make his appeal in person – though the poor man was so ill from his beating that he would be sick and maimed for life. It seemed, therefore, that Thomas of Patherley and Robert of Prestbury, having shown themselves to be strong and unscrupulous, would be left in undisturbed possession of the lands which they had robbed.

Then Alice had bethought herself of her kinsmen. She had gone to Alfred of Gammell, and he had promised to take the case again to the king's court, but the lady despaired of justice in that way. Then she had taken horse, and, with one serving-girl and a villein, had sought the greenwood where her bold kinsman, Robin Hood, was said to lurk, and after many toils had found him and told him all her trouble, and begged his help.

Robin had sent her away comforted, but she had kept word of her visit to him very secret. A few days had passed, and then one night men in Scaurdale had seen two houses burning far away on the wolds, and knew that somehow vengeance had fallen on the two robbers. Next day all knew and rejoiced in the bold deed – that Robin o' the Hood had come and slain both Thomas of Patherley and Robert of Prestbury, and thus had given back to Bennett of Havelond the fields which the evil men had wrested from him.

'I tell thee,' said Alfred of Gammell, his admiration breaking through his well-bred dislike of violent deeds, 'that deed of thine made all high-handed men dwelling beside the forests bethink themselves that if they oppress too cruelly their turn might come next.'

'I hope they think thus,' said Robin, and his face was grim. 'If men let such a wrong go unpunished and unrighted as was suffered by Bennett and our cousin, to whom can those who are oppressed look to for succour? Not to thy soft priests, cousin, who squeeze poor men as evilly as any robber baron, and who fill their purses with money wrung from poor yeomen. But tell me, against whom wouldst thou warn me?'

'Against Sir Guy of Gisborne and his evil plots,' replied Gammell. 'I was yesterday at Outwoods, which now the king's bailiff holds, until a year and a day from when thou wert made outlaw. There I sought out Cripps, the old reeve, whom I knew was thy friend, and he told me that Sir Guy hath his discomfiture by thee and thy fellows keenly at heart. A bitter man he was before thou didst burn him from his house, but now he is still more evil-minded and harsh. And he hath sworn by dreadful oaths to have thee taken or slain.'

'What plots did old Cripps speak of?'

'He hath become hand in glove with Ralph Murdach, the sheriff of Nottinghamshire, and the villeins say that wandering men have told them that, together, Sir Guy and Master Murdach are bribing evil men to dress as beggars, palmers, and hucksters to wander through the forests to find thy secret places, so that one day they may gather their men-at-arms and fall upon thee.'

'I thank thee for thy counsel,' said Robin, appearing not to treat it, however, as of any special importance; 'but now thou and thy men shall dine with me this day.'

They had by this time reached a secret place in some tree-clad hills which rose steeply up beside a river in the forest, and in a cave a feast was already spread, at which all now sat down to do full justice.

Robin and his men inquired of Gammell whether Sir Guy now treated the villeins of the manor more harshly than before.

'Men say that he does not,' was the reply; 'and for a good reason. It is said that when Abbot Robert of St Mary's heard of thy slaying the men-at-arms and of the flight of thy fellows, he was exceeding wroth with Sir Guy, and told him that he had overdriven the people of his manor, and must look to his conduct, or he would not suffer him to rule the manor. So that the folk are not so harshly overborne as formerly, yet that Sir Guy is the more hateful of them.'

'A miracle!' said Scarlet scornfully, when he heard this, 'a word of mercy from the thick-jowled, proud-lipped Abbot of St Mary's!'

'Maybe, uncle,' said little Gilbert of the White Hand, who had ever wanted to be a priest and to learn to read, 'maybe the abbot never told Sir Guy to oppress the manor folk, but that Sir Guy did it from his own heart as a tyrant.'

And this, indeed, was what many of the outlaws deemed in their hearts, and thought not so harshly of the abbot thereafter.

Soon after this, Master Gammell and his men took their departure, and Robin Hood and some of the outlaws went with him to the edge of the forest, and put him on his way towards Locksley village, which lay south-west beyond the little town of Sheffield.

Now it happened one afternoon some three days afterwards that Robin was walking along beside the broad highway which led from Pontefract through the forest to Ollerton and Nottingham. He was thinking of what his cousin had said concerning Sir Guy of Gisborne's plots to capture him, dead or alive, and as he walked beneath the trees he heard the shuffle of footsteps, and looking up, saw a beggar coming down the road.

Robin, from among the trees, could see the man, while he himself was unobserved, and as he saw the beggar stamping along with a great pikestaff in his hand, he wondered whether indeed this man was a genuine beggar, or one of the spies whom Guy of Gisborne had set to watch for him.

The man's cloak was patched in fifty places, so that it seemed more like a collection of many cloaks than one; his legs were encased in ragged hose, and great tanned boots were on his feet. Round his body, slung from his neck by a great wide thong, was his bag of meal, and in a girdle about him was stuck a long knife in a leathern sheath. On his head was a wide low hat, which was so thick and unwieldy that it looked as if three hats had been stitched together to make it.

Robin's suspicions were aroused, for the man seemed to be dressed for the part, and not to be a real beggar. Moreover, his eyes continually glanced from side to side in the wood as he walked along the uneven track.

By this time the beggar had gone past the place where Robin stood, and the outlaw shouted to him:

'Stand, beggar! why in such haste to get on?'

The beggar answered nothing, but hurried his steps. Robin ran up to him, and the man turned angrily and flourished his staff. He was a man of an evil countenance, with a scar from brow to cheek on one side.

'What want you with me, woodman?' he cried. 'Cannot a man fare peacefully along the king's highway without every loose wastrel crying out upon him?'

'Thou'rt surly, beggar,' said Robin. 'I'll tell thee why I bade thee stop. Thou must pay toll ere thou goest farther through the forest.'

'Toll!' cried the other, with a great laugh; 'if you wait till I pay you toll, thou landloper, thou'lt not stir from that spot for a year.'

'Come, come,' said Robin; 'unloose thy cloak, man, and show what thy purse holds. By thy clothes thou'rt a rich beggar – if such thou truly art, and not a rogue in the guise of an honest beggar.'

The man scowled and glanced suspiciously at Robin, and gripped his staff.

'Nay, lad,' said Robin good-naturedly, 'grip not thy staff so fiercely. Surely thou hast a broad penny in thy purse which thou canst pay a poor woodman for toll.'

'Get thy own money, thou reiving rascal,' growled the beggar. 'Thou gettest none from me. I fear not thy arrow sticks, and I

'*What want you with me, woodman?*'

would be blithe to see thee hanging from the gallows-tree – as, indeed, I hope to see thee ere long.'

'And doubtless,' said Robin, 'if thou couldst earn dirty coin by treachery thou wouldst not stop at any evil work. I thought thou lookest like an honest beggar! Rogue and traitor are written all over thy evil face. Now listen to me! I know thee for a traitor in the pay of an evil man, but I'll not be baulked of my toll. Throw thy purse on the ground, or I will drive a broad arrow through thee!'

Even as he spoke, Robin prepared to notch an arrow to the string of his bow. His fingers missed the string, and he bent his eyes down to see what he was doing. That moment was fatal. With a bound like that of a wild-cat the beggar leapt forward, and at the same instant he swung his pikestaff round and dashed the bow and arrow from Robin's hand.

The outlaw leaped back and drew his sword, but quick as thought the beggar beat upon him and caught him a great swinging blow beside the head. Robin fell to the ground in a swoon, just as shouts were heard among the trees beside the way. The beggar looked this way and that, his hand went to the haft of the keen knife in his belt, and for a moment he crouched as if he would leap upon the prostrate outlaw and slay him outright.

A man in brown jumped from some bushes a few yards away, and then two others. They looked at the beggar, who had instantly assumed an air of unconcern and began to walk forward, and a bend in the narrow track among the trees soon hid him from their sight.

Two of the men were young recruits of the outlaw band, and the other was Dodd, the man-at-arms who had yielded to Robin when the latter had slain Hugo of Lynn. As they began walking along the road, suddenly Dodd espied the bow and arrow which had been dashed from Robin's hand, and he stopped.

'Ay, ay,' he said; 'what's been doing here? 'Tis our master's bow. I know it by its size, for no other hath the hand to draw it.'

'Look! look!' cried one of the others, pushing behind a bush where Robin had fallen; 'here is a wounded man – by the Virgin, 'tis our master! Now, by Saint Peter, who hath done this evil deed?'

Swiftly Dodd knelt beside his leader, and pushed his hand into his doublet to feel whether his heart still moved. Then he cried:

'Lads, thanks be to the Saints, he's alive. Run to the brook beside the white thorn there and bring water in thy cap.'

The water being thrown upon the outlaw's face, he quickly revived. He sighed heavily, his hand went up to his aching head, and he opened his eyes.

'O master,' said Dodd, 'tell us who hath treated thee so evilly. Surely 'twas done by treachery. How many were they who set upon thee?'

Robin smiled wanly upon the three eager faces bending above him, and in a little while was sufficiently recovered to sit up.

'There was no more than one who set upon me,' said Robin, 'and he was a sturdy rogue dressed like a beggar. With his great pikestaff he dashed upon me as I fitted an arrow to my string, and ere I could defend myself he knocked me down in a swoon.'

'Now, by my faith,' said Dodd, ' 'twas that rascal beggar whom we saw as we came to the road – so innocent he looked! Go you, lads,' he said, turning to the other two men, 'show yourselves keen lads, and capture him and bring him back, so that our master may slay him if he will.'

'But,' said Robin, 'use stealth in the way you approach the rogue. 'Twas my foolishness to get too near his long staff that was my undoing. If ye let him use his great beam, he'll maim ye.'

The two young fellows promised to creep upon the beggar warily, and set off eagerly, while Dodd stayed by Robin until the latter felt strong enough to stand up and be assisted towards the camp of the outlaws.

Meanwhile, the two young outlaws, knowing the beggar must keep to the only road through the forest, swiftly ran to catch him up. But presently one of them, Bat or Bart by name, suggested that they should go by a nearer way through the trees, which would enable them to lie in ambush for the beggar at a narrow part of the road. The other agreed, and accordingly they pushed through the forest. Strong of limb they were, and if their wits had only been as keen as were their senses, all would have gone well with them. But they were only three weeks from the plough, and from the hard and exhausting labour in the fields of their lord, and they were not as sharp as they would soon become when the dangers of the greenwood had been about them a little longer.

On they ran between the trees, through the glades and the boggy bottoms, flinching at neither mire nor pool, and baulking at neither hillock nor howe. At length they reached the highway through the forest again at a place where the road ran through a dell. At the bottom was a thick piece of wood through which the road narrowed, and here they took up their place, each hiding behind a tree on opposite sides of the way.

Soon, as they crouched waiting, they heard the shuffle and tramp of footsteps coming down the hill, and peering forth, they saw it was the beggar man whom they had seen near where their master lay in a swoon.

As he came to the part of the road between them they both dashed out upon him, and before he could think of fleeing, one had snatched the pikestaff from his hand, and the other had caught his dagger from his girdle and was holding it at his breast.

'Traitor churl!' said the outlaw, 'struggle not, or I'll be thy priest and send thee out of life.'

The beggar's evil face went dark with rage as he glared from one to the other, and then looked about for a way of escape. But there was no chance of escape that he could see, and therefore he determined on craftiness to get him out of his trouble.

'Kind sirs,' he said humbly, 'grant me my life! Hold away that keen and ugly knife, or I shall surely die for fright of it. What have I done to thee that thou shouldst seek to slay me? And what profit will thou get from my rags if thou killest and robbest a poor old beggar?'

'Thou liest, false knave!' cried Bat fiercely. 'I think 'twould be better if I thrust this knife at once between thy evil ribs. Thou hast near slain the gentlest man and the bravest in all Sherwood and Barnisdale. And back again thou shalt be taken, fast bound and trussed, and he will judge whether thou shalt be slain, as a mark for our arrows, or be hung from a tree as not worthy to have good arrows stuck in thy evil carcass.'

'Kind sirs,' said the beggar whiningly, 'is it that woodman whom I struck but now that I have nearly slain? Oh, by the rood, but 'twas only in defence of myself that I struck him. Sorry I am that my awkward stroke hath near slain him.'

'Out upon thee, thou hast not slain him!' cried Bat. 'Think you his good life is to be put out by thy dirty staff. He'll live to do thee skaith [harm] within the next hour, as thou shalt see. Now, Michael,' Bat said to his comrade, 'let us truss this rogue up with his own rope girdle and push him along to our master. Thou art ugly enough now, rogue,' Bat went on, 'but thou'lt look uglier still when thou art swinging and grinning through a noose.'

The beggar saw that Bat was a determined man, and that if he thought not speedily of some wile wherewith to escape from their hands, it would fare ill with him.

'O brave gentlemen,' he said in a shaking voice, 'be kind, and spare a poor old beggar. Sorry I am if I have done any ill to the brave nobleman, your leader. But I am very willing to make a good recompense for any ill I have done him. Set me free, and I will give thee twenty marks which I have in my poke [bag] here, as well as odd bits of silver which I have hidden among my rags.'

At these words the eyes of both Bat and Michael glistened. They had never had money in their lives before, and the chance of getting ten marks each – a fabulous sum to them – was too much for their loyalty to their master.

'Show us thy money, old rogue,' said Bat. 'I believe thou liest. But show it to us!'

They let the beggar loose, and he untied his cloak and laid it on the ground. The wind was blowing gustily now as the twilight was descending, and he stood with his back towards it. Then he took off two big bags which they supposed contained meal and meat and bread, and placed them on the ground before him.

Finally he took the great belt from his neck which supported another bag by his side.

'In this,' he said, 'I hide my money for greater safety. 'Tis full of old clouts with which to stuff my clothes against the bitter wind, and my shoon to keep my feet warm.'

As he was lifting the belt over his head Bat saw that immediately under his left arm was a little pouch slung by a thin strap. This seemed so artfully hidden that the outlaw thought that it must contain something of great value, and he almost suspected that the beggar, with all the clumsy preparations he was making, must be intending to keep the richest pelf from them.

He leaned forward, gripped the thin strap, and with a quick turn of his knife cut it, and the purse came away in his hand. The beggar tried to snatch it, but he was encumbered by the great bag he had in his hands. He struggled to seize it, but both outlaws held their knives against his breast.

'Cease, ugly knave!' cried Bat, 'or we'll let out thy life and have thy booty as well. And see thou playest no tricks, or 'twill go ill with thee.'

The beggar saw that Bat was becoming suspicious, and stayed his attempts to snatch at the purse which the outlaw had now crammed into the breast of his tunic. With black looks and glowering eyes the beggar rested his big bag on the ground, and bent to undo it, the outlaws also stooping to see that he played no tricks.

He pushed his hands into the bag, and then suddenly dashed in their faces a great cloud of meal. The two outlaws were blinded at once and retreated, howling imprecations and threats upon the beggar, though they could not see a whit where he was.

Next moment, however, they felt the weight of his pikestaff upon their heads, for he had quickly seized his stick, and with fierce blows attacked them. Bat, his eyes still smarting with the meal in them, felt the beggar's hand tear at his tunic, but he slashed it with his dagger, which he still held, and dimly he saw the beggar retreat for a moment with a gory hand, and make ready to bring his pole down on Bat's head with a deadly blow.

The outlaw knew then that the purse held something of value. He dashed away just as the staff fell with a blow that, had it alighted on his head, at which it was aimed, would have cracked his skull. Bat looked no more behind, but ran as fast as he could go, followed by his comrade. For some time the beggar followed them, but he was burdened by his heavy clothes, and soon gave up the chase.

It was now almost dark, and very ruefully the two outlaws made their way back to the camp.

'We are two great fools,' said Bat, 'and I will give my back willingly to Master Robin's scourge.'

'My bones ache so sorely,' said Michael, 'from the brute beast's cudgel that I crave no more basting for a time. I think I will hide me till I be a little less sore and master's anger hath cooled.'

'Flee then, ass,' said Bat, angry with himself and his companion, 'and starve in the woods as thou surely wouldst, or run back to thy manor, thou run serf, and be basted by thy lord's steward.'

But Michael was too fearful both of the lonely woods and of the strong arm of his lord's scourging man, and chose after all to go with Bat and take what punishment Robin chose to mete out to them.

They reached the camp just as the outlaws were about to sit to their supper, and Bat told everything with a frankness which showed how ashamed he was of himself. Robin heard them patiently, and then said:

'Hast thou still the purse which thou didst take from the rogue?'

Bat had thought no more of the purse, but feeling in his tunic found it was still there, and, drawing it forth, gave it to Robin. The outlaw bade Bat bring a torch to light him while he examined the contents of the purse.

First he drew out three rose nobles wrapped in a piece of rag, then a ring with a design engraved upon it, and lastly, from the bottom of the purse, he drew out a piece of parchment folded small. This he opened and smoothed out upon his knee, and read – slowly, 'tis true, since Robin, though he had been taught to read his Latin when a lad in his uncle's house at Locksley, had had little use for reading since he had reached man's estate.

Slowly he read the Latin words, and as he grasped their meaning his face became grim and hard. The words, translated, were these:

'To the worshipful Master Ralph Murdach, Sheriff of the Shires of Nottingham and Derby, these with greeting. Know ye that the Bearer of these, Richard Malbête, is he of whom I spoke to thee, who hath been commended to me by my friend, Sir Niger le Grym. He is a man of a bold and crafty mind, stinting no labour for good pay, and blinking not at any desperate deed: of a cunning mind, ready in wit and wile and ambuscades. But keep him from the wine, or he is of no avail. This is he who will aid thee to lay such plans and plots as will gain us that savage wolf's-head, Robin, and root out that growing brood of robbers who go with him. I hope to hear much good done in a little while.'

The letter was not signed, for in those days men did not sign their letters with their names, but with their seals, and this was

sealed on a piece of blue wax with the signet of Sir Guy of
Gisborne, which was a wild man's head, below which was a sword.

Robin looked at Bat and Michael, who, with heads bent,
seemed filled with shame, and as if expecting some punishment.

'Ye are not fit to be outlaws,' he said sternly. 'Ye are but
common reivers and cutters [cut-purses], and shouldst run to the
town and lurk by taverns and rob men when they are full of wine
and cannot help themselves. When I send ye to do a thing that
thing thou shalt do, whatever temptation is placed before ye. But
as ye are but fresh from the plough, I will overlook it this time.
Go,' he ended in gentler tones, 'get your supper, and remember
that I shall expect ye to be keen and good lads henceforth.'

Bat had never before known a kind word from a superior, and
his heart was greatly moved at Robin's words.

'Master,' he said, bending on one knee, 'I have been a fool and
I deserve the scourge. But if you will not give me that, give me
some hard task to do, so that I may wipe the thought of my
doltishness from my memory.'

'And let me go with him, good master,' said Michael, 'for I
would serve you manfully.'

Robin looked at them for a moment, and smiled at their
eagerness.

'Go get your suppers now, lads,' he said at length. 'It may be I
will set thee a task ere long.'

When the meal was ended, Robin called Little John to his side
and said:

'John, hath the proud potter of Wentbridge set out on his
journey yet?'

'Ay, master,' replied John, 'he went through but yesterday,
with horse and cart laden with his pots and pans. A brisk man is
he, and as soon as the snows are gone he is not one to play
Lob-lie-by-the-fire.'

Robin asked where the potter would be lodging that night, and
John told him. Then Robin called Bat and Michael to him.

'Thou didst ask for a task,' he said, 'and I will give thee one. It
may be a hard one, but 'tis one thou must do by hook or by
crook. Thou knowest well the ways of the forest from here to
Mansfield, for thou hast both fled from thy lord at Warsop.
Now I will that ye go to Mansfield for me this night and seek the

proud potter of Wentbridge. Tell him that I crave a fellowship of him. I wish him to let me have his clothes, his pots, his cart and his horse, for I will go to Nottingham market disguised.'

'This will we do right gladly, master,' said Bat. 'We will take our staves and our swords and bucklers and start on our way forthwith.'

Little John began to laugh heartily.

'Ye speak as if thou thinkest it will be no more than to say "bo!" to a goose,' he said. 'But if thou knowest not the proud potter of Wentbridge, that lacking he will soon make up in thee by the aid of his good quarterstaff.'

'I know, Little John,' said Bat with a laugh, 'that he hath given thee that lesson.'

'Ye say truly,' said honest John; 'evil befell me when I bade him pay toll to the outlaws last harvest time, for he gave me three strokes that I shall never forget.'

'All Sherwood heard of them,' said Bat; 'but the proud potter is a full courteous man, as I have heard tell. Nevertheless, whether he liketh it or not, he shall yield Master Robin his wish.'

'Then I will meet thee at the Forest Herne where the roads fork beyond Mansfield,' said Robin, 'an hour after dawn tomorrow.'

'We will fail not to be there with all that thou wishest,' replied Bat, and together he and Michael set out under the starlight on the way to Mansfield.

Next day, into the market-place of Nottingham drove a well-fed little brown pony, drawing a potter's cart, filled with pots and pans of good Wentbridge ware. The potter, a man stout of limb, plump of body, and red of face, wore a rusty brown tunic and cloak, patched in several places, and his hair seemed to have rare acquaintance with a comb. Robin indeed was well disguised.

Farmers, hucksters, merchants, and butchers were crowded in the market-place, some having already set up their booths or stalls, while others were busy unloading their carts or the panniers on their stout nags. The potter set his crocks beside his cart, after having given his horse oats and hay, and then began to cry his wares.

He had taken up a place not five steps from the door of the sheriff's house, which, built of wood and adorned with quaint designs, occupied a prominent place on one side of the market-place; and the potter's eyes were constantly turned on the door of the house, which now was open, and people having business with the sheriff rode or walked up and entered.

'Good pots for sale!' cried the potter. 'Buy of my pots! Pots and pans! Cheap and good today. Come, wives and maidens! Set up your kitchens with my good ware!'

So lustily did he call that soon a crowd of country people who had come to the market to buy stood about him and began to chaffer with him. But he did not stay to bargain; he let each have the pot or pan at the price they offered. The noise of the cheapness of the pots soon got abroad, and very soon there were but half a dozen pots left.

'He is an ass,' said one woman, 'and not a potter. He may make good pots, but he knoweth naught of bargaining. He'll never thrive in his trade.'

Robin called a serving-maid who came just then from the sheriff's house, and begged her to go to the sheriff's wife, with the best respects of the potter of Wentbridge, and ask whether the dame would accept his remaining pots as a gift. In a few minutes Dame Margaret herself came out.

'Gramercy for thy pots, good chapman,' she said, and she had a merry eye, and spoke in a very friendly manner. 'I am full fain to have them, for they be good pots and sound. When thou comest to this town again, good potter, let me know of it and I will buy of thy wares.'

'Madam,' said Robin, doffing his hat and bowing in a yeomanly manner, 'thou shalt have of the best in my cart. I'll give thee no cracked wares, nor any with flaws in them, by the Mass, but every one shall ring with a true honest note when thou knock'st it.'

The sheriff's wife thought the potter was a full courteous and bowerly man, and began to talk with him. Then a great bell rang throughout the house, and the dame said:

'Come into the house if thou wilt, good chapman. Come sit with me and the sheriff at the market table.'

This was what Robin desired. He thanked the dame, and was led by her into the bower where her maidens sat at their sewing. Just then the door opened and the sheriff came in. Robin looked keenly at the man, whom he had only seen once before. He knew that the sheriff, Ralph Murdach, was a rich cordwainer who had bought his office from the grasping Bishop of Ely for a great price, and to repay himself he squeezed all he could out of the people.

'Look what this master potter hath given us,' said Dame Margaret, showing the pots on a stool beside her. 'Six pots of excellent ware, as good as any made in the Low Countries.'

The sheriff, a tall spare man of a sour and surly look glanced at Robin, who bowed to him.

'May the good chapman dine with us, sheriff?' asked the dame.

'He is welcome,' said the sheriff crossly, for he was hungry, and had just been outwitted, moreover, in a piece of business in the market-place. 'Let us wash and go to meat.'

They went into the hall of the house, where some twenty men were waiting for the sheriff and his lady. Some were officers and men of the sheriff, others were rich chapmen from the market.

When the sheriff and his wife took their seats at the high table, all the company sat down, Robin being shown a seat midway down the lower table. A spoon of horn was placed on the table where each sat, and a huge slice of bread, called a trencher! but for drinking purposes there was only one pewter cup between each two neighbours. Then the scullions from the sheriff's kitchen brought in roasted meat on silver skewers, and these being handed to the various guests, each would take his knife from his girdle, rub it on his leg to clean it a little, and then cut what he wanted from the skewer, laying his portion on the thick slice of bread. Then, using his fingers as a fork, the guest would eat his dinner, cutting off and eating pieces of his trencher with his meat, or saving it till all the meat was eaten.

On the rush-covered floor of the hall dogs and cats fought for the meat or bones thrown to them, and at the door beggars looked in, crying out for alms or broken meat. Sometimes a guest at the lower end of the table would throw a bone at a beggar, intending to hit him hard, but the beggar would deftly catch it and begin gnawing it. When, as sometimes happened, the beggars became too bold and ventured almost up to the table, a serving-man would dart among them with his staff and thump and kick them pell-mell out through the door.

Suddenly, a sturdy beggar came forthright into the hall and walked up among the sprawling dogs towards the high seat.

Instantly a serving-man dashed at him and caught hold of him
to throw him out.

'I crave to speak with the sheriff,' cried the beggar, struggling
with the man. 'I come with a message from a knight.'

But the serving-man would not listen, and began to drag the
beggar to the door. The noise of their struggle drew the attention
of all the guests, and Robin, looking up, recognised the beggar. It
was Sir Guy's spy, whom he had met but yesterday, and who had
outwitted the two outlaws whom Robin had sent to take him –
Richard Malbête, or, as the English would call him, Illbeast.

The beggar fought fiercely to free himself, but the serving-
man was a powerful fellow, and Malbête's struggles were in vain.
Suddenly he cried:

'A boon, Sir Sheriff! I have a message from Sir Guy of
Gisborne!'

The sheriff looked up and saw the struggling pair.

'Let the rogue speak,' he cried. The servitor ceased the
struggle, but still held the beggar, and both men stood panting,
while Richard Illbeast glared murderously at the man beside him.

'Speak, rogue, as his worship commands,' said the servitor,
'and cut not my throat with thy evil looks, thou scarecrow.'

'I come from Sir Guy of Gisborne,' said the beggar, turning to
the high table, 'and I have a message for thy private ear, Sir
Sheriff.'

The sheriff looked at him suspiciously.

'Tell me thy message, rogue,' said the sheriff harshly.

The beggar looked desperately round at the faces of the
guests, all of which were turned to him. Some laughed at his
hesitation, others sneered.

'He hath a private message for thy ear, sheriff,' cried one burly
farmer with a laugh, 'and light fingers for thy jewels.'

'Or,' added another amid the laughter, 'a snickersnee [small
dagger] for thyself.'

'Give some proof that you bear word from him you prate of,'
commanded the sheriff angrily, 'or I will have thee beaten from
the town.'

'A dozen cut-purses set upon me in the forest,' said Richard
Illbeast, 'and robbed me of the purse in which was Sir Guy's
letter to thee!'

A roar of laughter arose from all the guests. This was a likely tale, they thought, and japes and jokes were bandied about between them.

'What sent he thee to me for, knave?' shouted the sheriff. 'A likely tale thou tellest.'

'He sent me to aid thee in seizing that thieving outlaw, Robin Hood!' cried Richard Illbeast, beside himself with rage at the laughter and sneers of the guests, and losing his head in his anger.

Men roared and rocked with laughter as they heard him.

'Ha! ha! ha!' they cried. 'This is too good! The thief-taker spoiled by thieves! The fox mobbed by the hares he would catch!'

'Thrust him forth,' shouted the sheriff, red with rage. 'Beat the lying knave out of the town!'

'I am no knave!' cried Richard. 'I have fought in the Crusade! I have – '

But he was not suffered to say further what he had done: a dozen men-servants hurled themselves upon him. Next moment he was out in the market-place, his cloak was torn from his back and his bags ripped from him. Staves and sticks seemed to spring up on all sides, and amidst a hail of blows the wretch, whose heart was as cruel as any in that cruel time, and whose hands had been dyed by many a dreadful deed, was beaten mercilessly from the town along the road to the forest.

For a little time the guests at the sheriff's table continued to laugh over the beggar's joke, and then the talk turned on a contest which was to be held after dinner at the butts outside the town between the men who formed the officers of the sheriff, for a prize of forty shillings given by their master.

When the meal was ended, therefore, most of the guests betook themselves to the shooting, where the sheriff's men shot each in his turn. Robin, of course, was an eager onlooker at the sport; and he saw that not one of the sheriff's men could shoot nearer to the mark than by the length of half a long arrow.

'By the rood!' he said, 'though I be but a potter now I was a good bowman once, and e'en now I love the twang of my string and the flight of my arrow. Will you let a stranger try a shot or two, Sir Sheriff?'

'Ay, thou mayst try,' said the sheriff, 'for thou seemest a stalwart and strong fellow, though by thy red face thou seemest too fond of raising thy own pots to thy lips with good liquor in them.'

Robin laughed with the crowd at the joke thus made against him, and the sheriff commanded a yeoman to bring three bows. Robin chose one of these, the strongest and largest, and tried it with his hands.

'Thou'rt but poor wood, I fear,' he said, as he pushed the bow from him and pulled the string to his ear. 'It whineth with the strain already,' he went on, 'so weak is the gear.'

He picked out an arrow from the quiver of one of the sheriff's men and set it on the string. Then, pulling the string to its fullest extent, he let the bolt fly. Men looked keenly forward, and a shout from the chapmen went up when they saw that his bolt was within a foot of the mark, and nearer by six inches than any of the others.

'Shoot another round,' said the sheriff to his men, 'and let the potter shoot with thee.'

Another round was accordingly shot, and each man strove to better his previous record. But none got nearer than the potter had done, and when the last of them had shot his bolt they stood aside with glum faces, looking at the chapman as he stepped forward and notched his arrow upon the string.

He seemed to take less pains this time than before. The bolt snored away, and in the stillness with which the onlookers gazed, the thud, as it struck the broad target, two hundred yards away, was distinctly heard. For a moment men could not believe what their keen eyes told them. It had hit the centre of the bull's eye, or very close thereto.

The target-man, who stood near by the butt to report exactly on each shot, was seen to approach the target and then to start running excitedly towards the archers.

'It hath cleft the peg in three!' he shouted.

The peg was the piece of wood which stood in the very centre of the bull's eye. A great shout from all the bystanders rose up and shook the tassels on the tall poplars above their heads, and many of the chapmen gripped Robin by the hand or clapped him on the back.

'By the rood!' one said, 'thou'rt a fool of a chapman, but as a bowman thou'rt as good as any forester.'

'Or as Robin o' th' Hood himself, that king of archers, wolf's-head though he be,' said another, a jolly miller of the town.

The sheriff's men had black looks as they realised that they had been worsted by a plump potter, but the sheriff laughed at them, and coming to Robin, said:

'Potter, thou'rt a man indeed. Thou'rt worthy to bear a bow wherever thou mayest choose to go.'

'I ha' loved the bow from my toddling days,' said the potter, 'when I would shoot at small birds, ay, and bring them down. I ha' shot with many a good bowman, and in my cart I have a bow which I got from that rogue Robin Hood, with whom I ha' shot many a turn.'

'What!' said the sheriff, and his face was hard and his eyes full of suspicion. 'Thou hast shot with that false rascal? Knowest thou the place in the forest where he lurketh now, potter?'

'I think 'tis at Witch Wood,' said the potter easily. 'He hath wintered there, I ha' heard tell as I came down the road. But he stopped me last autumn and demanded toll of me. I told him I gave no toll on the king's highway except to the king, and I said I would e'en fight him with quarterstaff or shoot a round of twenty bolts with him to see if I were not a truer archer than he. And the rogue shot four rounds with me, and said that for my courtesy I should be free of the forest so long as my wheels went round.'

This was indeed the fact, and it was this friendship between Robin and the proud potter which had made Bat's task of obtaining the potter's clothes and gear for Robin an easy one.

'I would give a hundred pounds, potter,' said the sheriff gloomily, 'that the false outlaw stood by me!'

'Well,' said the potter, 'if thou wilt do after my rede [advice], Sir Sheriff, and go with me in the morning, thee and thy men, I will lead thee to a place where, as I ha' heard, the rascal hath dwelled through the winter.'

'By my faith,' said the sheriff, 'I will pay thee well if thou wilt do that. Thou art a brave man and a stalwart.'

'But I must e'en tell thee, sheriff,' said the potter, 'that thy pay must be good, for if Robin knows I ha' led the dogs to his hole, the wolf will rend me, and it would not be with a whole skin that I should go through the forest again.'

'Thou shalt be well paid,' said the sheriff, on my word as the king's officer.'

But he knew, and the potter knew also, that the sheriff's promise was of little worth, for the sheriff loved his money too well. But the potter made as if he was satisfied. When the sheriff offered him the forty shillings which was the prize for winning at the shooting, the potter refused it, and so won all the hearts of the sheriff's men.

'Nay, nay,' said the potter; 'let him that shot the best bolt among your men have it. It may be that 'twas by a flaw of wind that my arrow struck the peg.'

The potter had supper with the sheriff and his men, all of whom drank to the potter as a worthy comrade and a good fellow. A merry evening was passed, and then Robin was given a bed in a warm corner of the hall, and all retired to rest.

Next morning, before it was light, all were afoot again. A jug of ale was quaffed by each, and a manchet of rye bread eaten. Then the horses were brought round, together with the potter's pony and cart, and with the sheriff and ten of his men the potter led the way into the forest.

Deep into the heart of the greenwood the potter went, by lonely glades and narrow deer-drives by which not one of the sheriff's men had gone before. In many places where an ambuscade could easily be laid the sheriff and his men looked fearfully around them, and wondered whether they would win through that day with whole skins.

'Thou art sure thou knowest the way, potter?' said the sheriff more than once.

'Know the road, forsooth!' laughed the potter. 'I ha' not wended my way up and down Sherwood these twenty years without knowing my way. Belike you think I lead you into fearsome lonely places. But do you think a rascally wolf's-head will make his lair by the highway where every lurching dog can smell him out?'

'How dost thou know that the false outlaw hath wintered in the place you named?' asked the sheriff, with suspicion in his eyes.

'So the peasants tell me in the villages I have passed on my way from Wentbridge,' replied the potter. 'I will take thee to within half a mile of the Witch Wood, and then thou must make thy own plans for talking the rogue.'

'What manner of place is Witch Wood?' asked the sheriff.

' 'Tis a fearsome place, as I ha' heard tell,' said the potter. ' 'Tis the haunt of a dreadful witch, and is filled with dead men's bones. Outside 'tis fresh and fair with trees, but there are caves and cliffs within, where the witch and her evil spirits dwell among the grisly bones, and the churls say that Robin o' th' Hood is close kin to her, and that while he is in the greenwood he is within her protection and naught can harm him.'

'How so?' asked the sheriff, and the ten men glanced fearfully around and closed up together.

'They say that she is the spirit of the forest, and that by her secret power she can slay any man who comes beneath the trees, or lock him up alive in a living trunk of a tree, or cast him into a wizard's sleep.'

'What be those things there?' asked the sheriff, pointing in front of him. They had now come to an opening in the forest, where the trees gave way to a piece of open rising ground covered with low bushes. On a ridge in its midst was a great oak, its broad limbs covering a great space of ground, and beneath its shade were three tall upright stones, leaning towards each other as if they whispered.

' 'Tis the Three Stane Rigg,' said the potter. 'Men say that they be great grey stones as thou seest by daylight, but when owls hoot and the night wind stirs in the bushes, they turn into witch hags which ride about like the wind, doing the bidding of the great witch of the forest – bringing murrain or plague, cursing the standing corn, or doing other ill to men.'

Men looked in each other's eyes, and then turned their heads swiftly away, for they were half ashamed to see the fear in them, and to know that dread was in their own. All men in those days believed in wizards and witches, even the king and his wisest statesmen.

'I think,' said the sheriff gruffly, 'thou shouldst have told us these things ere we set out, and I would have brought a priest with us. As it is – '

Shrieks of eldritch laughter rang out in the dark trees beside them. So sudden and so fearful were the cries, that the horses stopped and trembled as they stood, while their riders crossed themselves and looked peeringly into the gloom of the forest. 'Let us ride back!' cried some, while one or two turned their horses in the narrow path and began to retreat.

Again the mad laughter rang out. It seemed to come from all parts of the dark earthy wood about them. More of the men put spurs to their horses, and in spite of the cries of the sheriff bidding them to stay, all were soon riding helter-skelter away from the spot.

The potter, standing up in his cart, and the sheriff, dark of look, listened as the sound of the thudding hooves became fainter and fainter in the distance.

'The craven dolts!' cried the sheriff, grinding his teeth. Yet, for all his bravery, he himself was afraid, and kept looking this way and that into the trees.

Suddenly the potter cracked his whip. Instantly the clear notes of a horn sounded away in the open glade, and next moment there came some twenty men in brown, who seemed to rise from the ground and to issue from the trunks of the trees. Some even dropped to the ground from boughs just above where the sheriff stood.

'How now, master potter,' said one tall fellow, bearded and bare-headed, 'how have you fared in Nottingham? Have you sold your ware?'

'Ay, by my troth,' said the potter. I have sold all, and got a great price for it. Look you, Little John, I have brought the sheriff himself for it all.'

'By my faith, master, he is welcome,' cried Little John, and gave a great hearty laugh, which was echoed by all the outlaws standing around when they saw the angry wonder on the sheriff's face.

'Thou false rogue!' cried he, and his face beneath his steel cap went red with shame and chagrin. 'If I had but known who thou wert!'

'I thank good Mary thou didst not,' said Robin, taking off the potter's cloak and then the tunic, which had been stuffed with rags to make him look the stouter.

' 'Tis a fearsome place, as I ha' heard tell'

'But now that thou art here, sheriff, thou shalt dine with us off the king's fat deer. And then, to pay thy toll, thou shalt leave thy horse and thy armour and other gear with me.'

And thus was it done. The sheriff, willy-nilly, had to dine off a steak cut from a prime buck, and washed down his meal with good sack, and having been hungry, he felt the better for it.

Then, when he had left his horse and all his arms with Robin Hood, and was preparing to return home on foot, the outlaw ordered a palfrey to be led forward, and bade the sheriff mount it.

'Wend thy way home, sheriff,' he said, 'and greet thy wife from me. Thy dame is as courteous and kind as thou art sour and gruff. That palfrey is a present from me to thy lady wife, and I trust that she will think kindly of the potter, though I cannot hope that thou thyself wilt think well of me.'

Without a word the sheriff departed. He waited till it was dark ere he rode up to the gate of Nottingham and demanded to be let in. The gateman wondered at the sheriff's strange return, riding on a lady's palfrey, without so much as a weapon in his belt or a steel cap on his head. The tale of the shamefaced men who had returned earlier had been wormed out of them by the wondering citizens, and the sheriff, hoping to creep home unobserved, was disagreeably surprised to find the streets full of gaping people. To all their questions he returned cross answers, but as he alighted at his own door he heard a laugh begin to arise, in cackling bursts, among the crowd before his house, and when he was inside he heard the full roar of laughter rise from a thousand throats.

Next day there was never a man so full of anger as Sheriff Murdach. The whole town was agrin, from the proud constable of the castle with his hundred knights, to the little horseboys in the stables – all smiled to think how the sheriff had gone with his posse to capture the outlaw Robin, led by a false potter who was the rogue Robin himself, and had been captured and spoiled.

CHAPTER FOUR

How Robin Hood Met Father Tuck

It was full summer again, and life was very pleasant in the greenwood. However fiercely the sun burned in the open fields where the poor serfs swinked and sweated, it was always cool and shady in the woods, and under the trees the gentle breezes blew, and the flies, swinging to and fro in their perpetual dance, kept up a soft drone that seemed to invite one to slumber.

Many a poor villein as he bent over the digging or the reaping in the hot sun, thought of the cool shadows in the shaws, and raising his aching back would look far away to the dark line of tossing trees and think of the men who had escaped from serfdom, and now were ranging there free from toil and tax and hard usage. Many such wondered whether they, too, could ever be so bold as to break away from the habits and routine of years, and put themselves outside the law, and rob their lords of a valuable piece of farming stock, which was the true description of a villein in the eyes of the law of those hard times.

For many miles up and down the country bordering on the broad forest lands, the fame of Robin Hood and his men had spread. Wandering pedlars, jugglers, and beggars told tales of his daring deeds, and minstrels already, when they found a knot of villeins in a village alehouse, would compose rough rhymes about him – how he did no evil to poor men, but took from rich, proud prelates, merchants, and knights.

Then, when times were hard, when the labours of sowing, reaping, or digging imposed upon the poor villeins seemed beyond all bearing, as they were already beyond all custom, one or two in a manor would find that their thoughts shaped for freedom, and taking the opportunity they would creep away from their village of little mean hovels and run to the greenwood.

It was thus that Robin Hood's band, which at first had numbered but twenty, had gradually grown until the runaway villeins in it numbered thirty-five, though he had only taken to the forest a full year. But there was another way in which Robin obtained good men of their hands. Wherever he heard of a man who was a good bowman, or one who could wield the quarterstaff well, or was a skilful swordsman, he would go and seek this man out and challenge him to fight.

Most times Robin conquered, but several times he came across men who were more skilful than he, or more lucky in their strokes. But, whatever the result, Robin's manliness and courtesy generally won them to become his comrades, and to join him and his band under the greenwood tree.

In this way he won over that valiant pinder or pound-keeper, Sim of Wakefield, with whom, as says the song which was made by Jocelyn the minstrel, he fought –

> A summer's day so long,
> Till that their swords on their broad bucklers
> Were broke almost into their hands,

when Robin had to confess that he had had enough, and craved of the pinder that he would join him in the greenwood. The pinder was quite willing, but being a man of honesty, he said that he had been elected by his fellow villeins to the office of pound-keeper until next Michaelmas, when he would receive his fee for his work.

'Then, good Robin,' said he, as he shook hands with the outlaw, 'I'll take my blue blade all in my hand and plod to the greenwood with thee.'

In the same way Robin fought a stout battle with Arthur-a-Bland of Nottingham, who was a famous man with the quarterstaff. In this case it was a drawn fight, and they agreed to be friends, and Arthur joined the band of outlaws. He was a cousin of Little John's, and the two kinsmen greeted each other right joyfully when they met. Ever afterwards they were almost inseparable in all their exploits, and so tall were they and skilful with staff and bow, that it was reckoned that together they were the equal of ten men.

When Robin Hood first went to the greenwood, he found

there were many bands of robbers in it – men who had been made outlaws for crimes of murder or robbery; and these had recruited their bands from runaway serfs and poor townsmen and other masterless men who were not really vicious themselves, but had had to seek the woods to escape from punishment.

Robin had had a very short way with these marauding bands of robbers, who made no distinction between rich and poor, but would as soon rob a poor serf of his last piece of salted pork or bag of meal as a rich priest of his purse of gold. Whenever Robin learned of the hiding-place of a band such as these, he would go there secretly with his men, and surprise them before they could lay hand to weapon. Then, while everyone was covered by a yard-long arrow, he would say:

'I am Robin Hood, whom ye know, and I give ye this choice. Cease your evil pilferings, wherein ye respect neither the poor nor the needy, and join my band and take our oath, or fight with me to the death, and put the choice to the ordeal by combat.'

Generally the robbers would give in, and joined Robin's band, taking the oath which all had sworn – to do harm to no poor man, honest yeoman, or courteous knight or squire, and to do no ill to any woman or any company which included a woman; but to help the poor and needy, and succour them whenever it was in their power. One or two of the robber leaders, however, had defied Robin, and had fought with him. Three of these he had slain, while four others had yielded to him and became his men.

By all these means his band, that had first been no more than twenty, now numbered fifty-five. All were dressed in Lincoln green while the leaves were on the trees, but when the leaves began to turn russet and to fall, and the forest to be filled with the sombre light of autumn, all the men assumed their tunics, hoods, and hose of brown, or long-hooded capotes of the same colour, so that they passed among the trees unseen by many of the travellers from whom they were about to take toll.

One day in July Robin and many of his band were passing the time in their caves in Barnisdale. Outside all was wet and stormy, for the rain beat down like great grey spears. Every leaf dripped like a spout, the forest ways were sodden, and the dark mist hung sombrely in the hollows and moved but slowly down the long forest drives. None that could help themselves were out on the highroads, which were no more than rivers of mud, but every beggar, pedlar, quack-doctor, pilgrim, juggler, or other traveller had fled to the village alehouse, or to the inn that at rare places could be found at the side of the highway.

In their caves on Elfwood Scar, Robin and his band sat dry and cosy, telling tales to each other, or listening to the travels of a pilgrim whom Will Scarlet had found that morning with a swollen foot, limping on his way. Gilbert of the White Hand had washed the wound and salved it, and now for payment the grateful pilgrim, a brown-faced, simple man, told of his marvellous experiences and the sights which he had seen on the long road to Rome, and the terrible days spent on the sea from Venice to Jaffa.

There were other wayfarers with them. One was a quackdoctor, a merry, wizened rogue, with a wise look which he often forgot to wear in the midst of his solemn talk. He had a muchworn velvet cloak trimmed with fur which had almost worn off, and on his hat were cabalistic signs which he asserted only the very wisest of men could read, including himself. He had with him, he asserted, a little of the very elixir which had given Hercules his godlike strength, and some of the powder which had made Helen of Troy so beautiful.

' 'Tis a marvel thou takest not some of Hercules his liquor thyself,' said Little John, laughing, 'for thy wizened frame was no good to thee when that great rogue at the Goose Fair at Nottingham downed thee with his fist for saying thy salve would cure his red nose.'

'I need not strength of arm,' said the quack; his little black eyes lit up merrily. 'Confess, now, thou big man, did not my tongue scorch him up? Did not my talk cause the sheriff's man to hustle the big fellow away with great speed! Why do I need strength of limb when I have that which is greater than the strongest thews – ' he tapped his forehead ' – the brains that can outwit brute strength?'

'Yet I doubt if thy wit availed thee much,' said a voice in a far corner of the cave, 'when thou camest across the curtal hermit of Fountains Dale. Tell this good company what befell thee that day.'

The little quack's face darkened angrily, whereat the speaker, a pale-faced man in pilgrim's robes, laughed, but not with ill-nature.

'Tell us the tale, doctor!' cried the outlaws, enjoying the quack's discomfiture, while others besought the pilgrim to relate it. But to all their appeals the quack turned a deaf ear, his face red with anger, and his mouth filled with muttered curses on the loose tongue of the pilgrim-rogue and on the curtal hermit.

'Tell us, good pilgrim,' commanded Little John, whereat the quack snapped out:

'That rogue is no pilgrim! I know the gallows face of him. He is a run thrall of the abbot of Newstead, and I could get a mark for my pains if I put the abbot's bailiff on his track.'

All looked at the pilgrim. He was big of body and limbs, but by his face he looked as if he had suffered some illness.

'Ay, he speaks truth,' said the man; 'I am Nicholas, cottar and smith of my lord, the abbot of Newstead. But,' and his voice became hard and resonant, 'I will not be taken back alive to the serfdom in which I served until yesterday's blessed morn. I seek only to work in freedom under a master who will give me due wage for good work done. I can do any smith's work well and honestly – I can make and mend ploughs, rivet wheels and make harrows, and I have even made swords of no mean workmanship. But because I fell ill and could not work, my lord's bailiff thrust my poor mother out of her holding and her land, ay, with blows and evil words he thrust her out, and while I was on my pallet of straw too weak to move, they bore me out to the wayside, and the sturdy villein whom they put in our place jeered at us with evil words. And thus against all right and custom were we cast out!'

'A foul deed, by the Virgin!' cried Robin. 'But, poor lad, thou canst not expect aught else of priests and prelates and their servants. Their hearts are but stones. And so thou hast run. 'Twas well done. But what of thy mother?'

'She is out of it all, thanks be to God,' said Nicholas solemnly, 'and under the turf of the churchyard, where no lord's bailiff can harm her more.'

'Lad, if thou wantest work in freedom,' said Robin, 'stay with me and thou shalt have it, and thy due wage every Michaelmas. Many's the brown bill or sword blade we want mended. Wilt thou come with us?'

'Ay, master, willingly,' said Nicholas. Coming forward, he put his hand in Robin's, and they grasped each other's hands in sign of agreement. Then the smith took off his palmer's robe, and his great frame in rough jerkin and hose seemed thin and worn.

'Thou'rt fallen away a bit, lad,' said Robin with a smile, 'but I can see good thews are there, and in a month our forest air, our cream and venison and good ale will fill thee out till I can see thee o'ertopping Little John here.'

Little John smiled good-naturedly, and nodded in friendly wise to the new recruit.

'But now, tell us, good Nick,' said Robin, 'who is this hermit of Fountains Dale, and how served he our friend here, Peter the Doctor?'

'Oh,' said Nick with a smile, 'I meant no ill-will to Peter. Often hath his pills cured our villeins when they ate too much pork, and my mother – rest her soul – said that naught under the sun was like his lectuary of Saint Evremond.'

'Thou hearest, good folks!' cried the little quack, restored to good-humour by the smith's friendly speech. 'I deserve well of all my patients, but – ' and his eyes flashed ' – that great swineheaded oaf of a hermit monk – Tuck by name, and would that I could tuck him in the deepest, darkest hole in Windleswisp Marsh! – that great ox-brained man beguiled me into telling him of all my good specifics. With his eyes as wide and soft as a cow's he looked as innocent as a mawkin [maiden], and asked me this and that about the cures which I had made, and ever he seemed the more to marvel and to gape at my wisdom and my power. The porcine serpent! He did but spin his web the closer about me to my own undoing and destruction. When I had told him all, and was hopeful that he would buy a phial of serpent's oil of Jasper – a sure and certain specific, my good freemen, against ague and stiffness – for he said the winter rains did begin to rust his joints a little, the vile rogue did seize me by the neck and take my box of medicaments. Then he tied my limbs to the tree outside his vile abode, and from my store he took my most precious medicines, sovereign waters and lectuaries, and did force me to swallow them all. Ugh, the splay-footed limb of Satan! He said that I was too unselfish – that I gave all away and obtained none of the blessings myself, and that when he had done with me I should be as strong and as big as Hercules, as fair as Venus, as wise as Solomon, as handsome as Paris, and as subtle as Ulysses. Then, too, did he stick hot plasters upon my body, making me to suffer great pain and travail. In a word, if it had not been that I always keep the most potent and valuable of my medicines in a secret purse, I should not only have been killed but ruined, for – '

Further words were drowned by the burst of uncontrollable laughter which greeted his unconscious 'bull'.

He was plied with many questions as to the effects which this commingling of the whole of his potent wares had had upon him, to all of which the little quack replied in good humour.

'But now tell us,' said Robin Hood, 'who is this hermit who treated thee to so complete a course of thy own medicines? Where doth he dwell?'

'I will tell thee,' replied Peter the quack. 'I have heard it said of thee that since thou hast come to the greenwood thou dost allow no one to rob and reive and fight and oppress poor folks. Well, this runaway priest is one who doth not own thee master. He is a man who shoots the king's own deer, if it were known, with a great longbow; he is such a hand with the quarterstaff that he hath knocked down robbers as great as himself. He liveth a wicked and luxurious life. He hath great dogs to defend him, who I believe are but shapes of evil fiends. He is a great spoiler of men, and would as lief fight thee, Robin Hood, as a lesser man.'

'This is not the truth which Peter saith,' said Nick the Smith angrily. 'Father Tuck is no false hermit; he liveth not a wicked life as other false hermits do. He ever comes and solaces the poor in our village, and any good he can do if one is sick, that he doth for no payment. He is great of limb, and can fight well with the bow, the staff, or the sword, but he is no robber. He is humble and kind in heart, but he can be as fierce as a lion to any that would do ill to a poor man or woman. Evil wandering knights have sometimes striven to thrust him from his hold, but with the aid of his great ban-dogs and his own strong arms he hath so prevailed that neither knight nor other lord or robber hath made him yield.'

'He is a strong and a masterless rogue, this curtal monk,' repeated Peter, 'a man that will not confess that anyone is his better. 'Tis said that he was thrust forth from the brotherhood of Fountains Abbey to the north by reason of his evil and tumultuous living, and hath come into this forest to hide. If thou art truly master of the greenwood, Sir Robin,' he said, 'thou hadst best look to this proud and truculent hermit and cut his comb for him.'

Little more was said about the hermit then, and in a little while, when the rain had ceased and the sun shone out, making every leaf dazzle as if hung with a priceless pearl, the wayfarers went on the road again, and the outlaws separated to their various tasks. Some made arrows and bows, others cut cloth for new tunics, or stitched up hose which had been torn by brambles. Others, again, took up their position among the trees along the highroad to watch for a rich convoy of the Bishop of York which they heard was on its way from Kirkstall to Ollerton, for they were lacking many good things both of food and clothing and other gear, which they could only replenish from some rich prelate's store.

It was some days before Robin found an opportunity of faring south to seek the hermit of whom Peter and the runaway workman had spoken. The boldness and independence of the hermit, Father Tuck, had excited his curiosity, and Robin was eager to put the skill of the fellow to the test. He therefore gave the word to Little John and some dozen or so of the others to follow him in the space of an hour, and then betook his way towards Newstead Abbey, near where he had learned was the 'hold' or strong dwelling-place of Father Tuck.

To make greater speed Robin was mounted, and, moreover, he wore his thick jerkin of tanned leather. A cap of steel was on his head, and at his side were sword and buckler. Robin never moved a step without his good yew-bow, and this was slung across his body, while a sheaf of arrows in a loose quiver hung from his girdle.

The sun was nearly overhead when Robin set out, and he travelled for some hours through the fair forest roads before he began to approach the neighbourhood of the curtal monk's abode. At length he reached the silent solitudes of Lindhurst Wood. As he was riding through the trees a sound made him check his horse and listen. He looked about him, peering under the giant branches flung out by the grey monarchs of the forest. All about him they stood, trunk after trunk, stretching out their gnarled and knotted arms, hung with grey moss like giant beards. In the green twilight he could see nothing moving, yet he felt conscious that something watched him. He turned his horse aside into a dim alley which seemed to lead to an opening among the trees. His horse's feet sank noiselessly into a depth of moss and leaves, the growth of ages. He reached the opening among the great grey trees, and whether it was a flicker of waving leaves or the form of a skulking wolf he was not sure, but he believed that away in the dark under the trees to his left, something had passed, as silent as a shadow, as swift as a spirit.

He turned back upon his proper path, looking keenly this way and that. At length he came to where the trees grew less thickly, and he knew that he was approaching the stream near which the hermit's hold was situated. Dismounting, he tied his horse to a tree and then gave a long, low bird's note. Twice he had to give this before a similar note answered him from a place away to the right of him. He waited a few moments, and then a squirrel churred in the thick leaves of the oak above his head. Without turning to look, Robin said:

'Sawest thou, Ket, anyone in the wood but now as I came down by the Eldritch Oaks?'

For a moment there was silence, then from the leaves above Ket answered:

'Naught but a charcoal-burner's lad, belike.'

'Art sure 'twas not someone that spied on me?'

'Nay, sure am I 'twas no one that meant thee hurt.'

This was not a direct reply, and for a moment Robin hesitated. But he did not know any reason for thinking that anyone knew of his presence in Lindurst, and therefore he questioned Ket no more.

'Keep thy eye on my horse, Ket,' said Robin; and began to walk towards the stream. Soon the trees opened out, and he saw the water gleaming in the sunlight. Looking up and down, he saw where a small low house stood beside the stream to the left. It was made of thick balks of timber, old and black with age. A wide, deep moat surrounded it on three sides, and before a low-browed door stretched a wide plank which was the means by which the

inmate of the house gained the land. This plank had chains fixed
to it whereby it could be raised up, thus effectually cutting off the
dwelling from attack or assault by all who had not boats.

'A snug hermit's hold, by my troth,' said Robin; 'more like the
dwelling of some forest freebooter than the cell of an austere
monk who whips his thin body by day, and fasts and prays all
night. Where, now, is the humble hermit himself?'

He looked more closely by the trees, and saw where a little
path came down through the trees to the water as if to a ford,
and on the opposite bank he saw where it issued again from the
stream and went like a tunnel through the trees that there came
down to the water's edge. Sitting, as if in meditation, by a tree
beside the path on this side of the stream was a man in the rough
homespun garb of a monk. He seemed big and broad of body,
and his arms were thick and strong.

'A sturdy monk, in faith!' exclaimed Robin. 'He seems deep in
thought just now, as if the holy man were meditating on his sins.
By the rood, but I will test his humility at the point of a good
clothyard arrow!'

Robin silently approached the monk, who seemed sunk in
thought or slumber. Drawing an arrow, and notching it upon the
string of his longbow, Robin advanced and said:

'Ho, there, holy man, I have business t'other side of the
stream. Up and take me on thy broad back, lest I wet my feet.'

The big monk stirred slowly, lifted his face, and looked
stolidly at Robin for a moment as if he hardly understood what
was said. Robin laughed at the simple look upon his face.

'Up, oaf,' he cried; 'ferry me over the stream on thy lazy back,
or this arrow shall tickle thy ribs!'

Without a word the monk rose, and bent his back before
Robin, who got upon it. Then slowly the monk stepped into the
stream and walked as slowly across the paved ford till he came to
the other side. He paused for a moment there as if to take
breath. Then he stepped up to the bank, and Robin prepared to
leap off. But next moment he felt his left leg seized in an iron
grip, while on his right side he received a great blow on the ribs.
He was swung round, and fell backwards upon the bank, and the
monk, pressing him down with one knee, placed great fingers
upon his throat, and said:

Robin carries Father Tuck over the stream

'Now, my fine fellow, carry me back again to the place whence I came, or thou shalt suffer for it.'

Robin was full of rage at his own trick being turned upon him in this way, and tried to snatch at his dagger, but the monk caught his wrist and twisted it in a grasp so powerful that Robin knew that in strength, at least, the monk was his master.

'Take thy beating quietly, lad,' said the monk, with a slow smile. 'Thou'rt a saucy one, but thou hast not reached thy full strength yet. Now, then, up with thee and carry me back.'

The monk released him, and Robin, in spite of his rage, wondered at this. Why had he not beaten him senseless, or even slain him, when he had him in his power? Most other men would have done this, and none would have blamed them. Already in his heart Robin regretted that he had treated the monk with so high a hand. He saw now that it was in his ignorance that he had scorned Father Tuck.

Without a word, therefore, he bent his back, and the monk slowly straddled upon it and clasped his hands round Robin's neck, not tightly, but just enough to make him understand that if he tried to play another trick the monk was ready for him. When he reached the middle of the stream, where it ran most deeply and swiftly, Robin would greatly have liked to have tipped the monk in the water; but as the odds were too much against him he went on.

When he was nearing the bank he suddenly heard a laugh come from the hermit's hold, and looking up he saw at a little window hole which looked upon the stream the face of a lady. It had a wimple about it, and she was very pretty. As he looked up the face swiftly disappeared. He did not know who the lady might be, but the thought that he was made to appear so foolish in her eyes made Robin almost mad with rage. He reached the bank, and when the monk had got from his back he turned to him and said:

'This is not the last thou shalt see of me, thou false hermit and strong knave. The next time we meet thou shalt have a shaft in thy great carcass.'

'Come when thou likest,' said the monk with a jolly laugh. 'I have ever a venison pasty and a bottle or two of Malvoisie for good friends. As to thy bow shafts, keep them for the king's deer, my pretty man. Pay good heed to thy wits, young sir, and try not thy jokes on men until thou knowest they go beyond thy strength or not.'

So enraged was Robin at the monk's saucy answer that next moment he had dashed at him, and in an instant they were struggling fiercely, each striving to throw the other into the stream. The end of it was that both slipped on the soft bank, and both, still clutching each other, rolled into the stream.

They crawled out quickly, and Robin, still blinded with rage, ran to his bow and arrows, which he had dropped on the bank, and notching a bolt, he turned and looked for the monk The latter had disappeared, but next moment he came from behind a tree with a buckler in one hand and a sword in the other, while on his head was a steel cap. Robin drew the string to his ear, and the arrow twanged as it sped from the bow. He looked to see it pierce the great body of his enemy, but instead, with a laugh, the monk caught it on his buckler, and it glanced off and stuck in the ground, where it stood and shook for a moment like a strange stiff kind of plant moved by the wind.

Three more arrows Robin shot at him, but each was deftly caught by the monk upon his shield, and the outlaw was in a rage to see that by no means could he get the better of this redoubtable monk.

'Shoot on, my pretty fellow,' cried the monk. 'If you wish to stand shooting all day I'll be thy mark, if it gives thee joy to waste thy arrows.'

'I have but to blow my horn,' returned Robin angrily, 'and I should have those beside me who should stick so many arrows in thy carcass that thou wouldst look like a dead hedgehog.'

'And I, thou braggart,' said the monk, 'have but to give three whistles upon my fingers to have thee torn to pieces by my dogs.'

As the monk spoke, Robin was aware of a noise in the trees beside him. He looked, and saw a slim youth running towards him, with a hood round his head so that his face was almost concealed, a bow slung on his back, and a staff in his hand. Robin thought the youth was about to attack him, and therefore brought his buckler up and drew his sword. At the same time came other sounds from the woods as of men dashing through the undergrowth. There came a shrill whistle, and then Robin heard a scream as of an animal or bird in the talons of a hawk.

Robin recognised it at once as the danger-signal of Ket the Trow, and knew that enemies were upon him.

He thought the slim youth who had paused for a moment at the sound of the whistle was some spy of Guy of Gisborne's who was leading an ambush upon him. Robin lifted his sword and rushed upon the youth. He was but the space of a yard from the other, and noticed how he stood panting and spent as with running. The youth raised his head, and Robin caught a glimpse of the face in the shadow of the hood.

'Marian!' he cried, for it was his sweetheart. 'What is this? What – '

'Robin,' she panted, and her face flushed as she looked at him, and laid one fair hand on his arm, 'sound thy horn for thy men, or thou art lost indeed.'

Instantly she turned and ran to the monk and said some rapid words to him. The notes of Robin's horn rang out clear and shrill, and reverberated through the dim leafy alleys. Almost at the same moment the monk raised two fingers, and putting them in his mouth, blew so shrill a whistle as almost to split the ear. As he did so, men came running from the trees, and Robin knew them for the men-at-arms of the abbot of St Mary's.

'Quick, Marian!' cried Robin, 'get thee to the monk's hold. There is still time!'

Swiftly Robin looked about for some point of vantage whence he could defend himself, and saw a spit of land where it jutted into the stream. He notched an arrow on his bowstring, shot the first man down, then ran to the spit, and notched another arrow as he ran. Marian and the monk reached it as soon as he.

'Nay, nay,' repeated Robin, 'go ye across the bridge to the monk's hold. If my fellows are not near 'twill go hard with me, and I would not have thee harmed, sweetheart.' He notched a third arrow.

'Nay, Robin,' cried Marian. 'I can bend a bow, as thou well knowest, and the good monk Tuck will aid us. Look, here are the dogs!'

The men-at-arms by this time were but some ten yards away, and already Robin had sent three arrows among them, wounding two and killing one man.

Black Hugo was leading them, and cried:

'Lads, we must get together and rush him. If he can hold us at distance with his arrows we shall all be shot down.'

Even as he spoke, the long snore of an arrow suddenly stopped, and the man beside him fell with the clothyard wand sticking through his throat. The men began to egg each other on, but the great arrows made them wary. While they hesitated, suddenly they heard a baying, and before they were aware of the cause ten great ban-dogs had leaped upon them. Fierce brutes they were, of the size of bloodhounds, with great collars about their necks in which were set keen spikes.

The men fought blindly with sword and dagger against these strange and terrible foes. Suddenly a shrill whistle sounded, a giant man in monk's form, bearing a buckler, came towards them, crying upon the dogs by name to cease. Five hounds lay wounded or dead, but the others at the sound of their master's voice ceased and drew back, licking their wounds

Black Hugo wiped the sweat from his swarthy face, and looked about him, and his face went suddenly white. Across the lea or open field, which was on the side of the monk's hold, were the forms of a score of men in green running towards them as fast as they could, and each was notching an arrow to his bow even as he ran.

'Save thyselves!' cried Black Hugo; 'here come more rogues than we can face.'

The men gave a swift look across the lea, and then, turning, they dashed for the cover of the trees. The outlaws paused for a moment, and a flight of arrows droned through the air, cutting the fans of leaves, and disappearing into the bushes. Three were slain by these bolts, but the others rushed madly on in the green twilight of the old trees, scattering as they ran, to make pursuit more difficult.

When the last of the outlaws had disappeared after the fleeing men-at-arms, Robin turned to Marian, who, with heightened colour and quick breath, tried to forestall the anger which she feared her lover would have against her.

'Be not angry with me, Robin,' she said, 'but I have feared for thee so much that I had to come to the greenwood to learn how it fared with thee. You know how many a time and often we have shot and hunted on Locksley Chase when we were boy and girl together. Why should I not do that now?'

'Why shouldst thou not, sweetheart?' answered Robin. 'Because I am an outlaw, and thou art a lording's daughter. My head is for anyone to take who may, and those who aid me run the same danger. But tell me, Marian, how long is it since thou hast donned the clothes that make thee so sweet-looking a lad, and how dost thou know this rascal monk?'

'He is no rascal, Robin, but a good man,' answered Marian. 'He is Sir Richard at Lee's good friend, and hath ever spoken well of thee, and cheered me greatly when I have sorrowed for thee. And when at last I resolved to don these clothes and come to the greenwood to learn, if I might, how thou didst live, I spoke to Father Tuck, and he promised to aid me. For he hath friends throughout the forest, and thus I got to know thy friends the trolls. And I watched thee in the forest as thou didst ride hither, and Ket knew I was there.'

While Marian had been talking, she had led Robin across the drawbridge, and they were now in the dwelling of the monk. It was a room which partook of the character of kitchen, oratory, and hall. A crucifix with a praying-stool before it stood in one corner; on another wall were coats of chain-mail, steel headpieces, a double-handed sword, two or three bright bills, and a sheaf of arrows, together with a great bow. Along a third wall were ranged rough shelves on which were bags of meal and two or three pieces of salted ham or venison. In the centre of the room was a table.

As they entered, a lady rose from a seat, and Marian ran to her with hands outstretched, and drew her impulsively forward.

'Alice, this is my Robin,' she said.

Robin recognised the lady's face. She it was who had seen him carrying the monk across the river, and had laughed at him. The lady had a bright and merry face, and looked at him with a twinkle in her eye. Then she put forth her hand and said:

'So you are that bold outlaw whose head Sir Ranulf de Greasby swears every night ere he goes tipsy to bed shall yet be hung on the walls of Hagthorn Castle.'

She gave so merry a laugh, and her eyes spoke her admiration of the handsome outlaw so eloquently, that Robin's heart was completely won. He bent his knee and kissed the lady's hand very gallantly.

'I am Robert or Robin Hood, as men call me,' he said, 'and I think you must be Mistress Alice de Beauforest, whom Alan-a-Dale loves so well.'

The lady's face flushed for a moment and then went pale, and a look of pain came into her eyes. She turned away, and Marian went to her with a tender look and put her arm about her neck.

Just then the monk entered. 'By my faith,' he said, 'but thou'rt a wasteful fellow to aid. Four of my poor hounds have barked their last bark and gnawed their last bone on thy account.'

'Good hermit,' said Robin, going up to him with outstretched hand, 'I hear thou hast been a true friend to the lady I love best in the world, and I would that thou wert my friend also.'

'Robin, lad,' replied Father Tuck with a smile on his broad good-humoured face, 'I ha' been thy well-wisher since I heard how thou didst help burn Sir Guy's house about his ears. I think we are not enemies at heart, lad, you and I. Since I ha' kept this hold these seven years with the help of my good friend, Sir Richard at Lee, I ha' never heard of a man whose doings I liked to hear o' so well as thine. How thou didst put the surly sheriff o' Nottingham to scorn! I never laughed so much since the day I trundled my holy brothers into the fish-stews at Fountains Abbey and got my wicked self expelled for the deed!'

The monk caught Robin's hand and gave it a squeeze that would have crushed a weak man's bones. But Robin's grip was almost as strong, and Father Tuck smiled admiringly.

Thereafter there was much talk between them all. Marian told how Father Tuck had been her guide through the forest ways during the summer, teaching her woodcraft, and giving her much knowledge of herbs and cures. She told him that she had also made friends with Ket the Trow and Hob o' the Hill and their mother and sisters, and through them had been kept informed of all that had befallen Robin and his men.

'Robin,' said Father Tuck, 'a proud man thou shouldst be to think so fair a maid should do all this for love of thee.'

'Proud I am,' said Robin, 'and yet I have sorrow in my heart to think that I am an outlawed man, and can offer her, who hath ever known the softest ways of living, only the bare and houseless life of the wild forest. I would not change my life for anything the king could offer me, but for my nut-brown maid here to wish to wed me against her kinsmen's wishes would be to doom herself to a life that I would not – nay, that I cannot ask her to share.'

'Robin,' said Marian, 'I love but you alone, and I will wed none but thee. I love the woodland life even as thou dost, and I should be happy, though I forsook all my kindred. You think doubtless that I should repine when the leaves fall from the trees, when the wind snarls down the black ways or the snow-wreaths dance in the bitter winter. But my heart would be warm having thee to turn to, and I would never repent leaving the thick walls of my father's castle. He is kind to me, but he scorns me and daily rails at me for my love of thee, and though I would leave him with sorrow, I will come to thee swiftly if and when thou hast need of me.'

There was a little shake in her gentle voice as she ended, and tears were in the brave eyes. Robin took her hands and, raising them to his lips, kissed them fervently.

'Almost you persuade me, sweetheart mine,' he said. 'I know thou lovest but me alone, but it is not right that a maid should run to the wood with an outlaw, to live in dread, watching day and night lest their enemies approach. But this I promise thee, Marian, that if at any time ye are in peril from those that wish ye ill, and are alone and pursued by evil men, then do ye send to me and I will come, and we will be wed by this good monk here, and then together we will suffer whatever fortune doth betide us.'

'Well said, Robin Hood,' said the monk heartily, 'and well advised ye be. I see thou art an honourable man, as indeed I knew aforetime. And indeed I think it not unlikely that ere much more water floweth under Wentbridge, the fair young maid will have need of thy strong arm and the love of a good man strong enough to protect her from evil wishers.'

The monk said this knowing that Marian's father was but sickly, and that if he should die many powerful and evil barons or prelates, desiring the lands and riches of the lady Marian, would plot to get her into their power, so that they could profit from her wealth, and sell her to a husband who would give them a good price for her rich dower.

A horn sounded from the forest outside, and going to the door, Robin espied Little John and the other outlaws. Little John reported that the abbot's men and the king's rangers had been chased to the highway beyond Harlow Wood, several having been wounded. That then two knights, who seemed to be waiting for them, had striven to rally the men-at-arms, but that the arrows of the outlaws had put them all to the rout, one of the knights riding away with an arrow in his side.

'Was there aught to show who they were?' asked Robin.

'One had a blank shield, the other had a red tower on his,' replied Little John

'The red tower was a man I did not know,' said Scarlet, 'but he with the white shield was one of those whom we beat back last year at the church at Campsall.'

'Scarlet speaks truth,' said Will the Bowman, 'he is Niger le Grym, and I think the other, by the snarl in his voice and the fire of his curses, was no other than the fiend Isenbart de Belame himself.'

'I doubt it not,' said Robin. 'It shows that their spies watch us continually. Go into the forest and keep within sound of my horn. There are two ladies here within whom we must guard to their homes.'

Within, Father Tuck was preparing a woodland meal, and Marian having changed into her proper attire, they all sat to eat. Afterwards two horses were brought forward from their hiding-place in the forest, and the ladies, having mounted, bade goodbye to the monk and set off with Robin to the castle of Sir Richard at Lee, where both were dwelling for a time.

As they rode along down the sunny forest ways, Robin saw that the lady Alice still seemed sad and thoughtful, and he asked Marian why his words had caused such sorrow in her.

'Because,' said Marian, 'she can no longer save herself from wedding the old and evil lord, Sir Ranulf de Greasby. The day of marriage is set, and her lover, Alan-a-Dale, is outlawed, and is hiding in the wild hills of Lancaster.'

'I heard not of that,' said Robin. 'Why is the young squire outlawed?'

'Sir Isenbart de Belame got him proclaimed outlaw because he slew Ivo le Ravener,' was the reply. 'Moreover, he hath got a heavy fine placed on the lands of Alan's father, Sir Herbrand, and it is likely that Sir Herbrand will be ruined and his son slain ere long. Therefore, for the misery that she suffers because of this, my dear friend Alice is sad.'

'He did in truth slay Ivo le Ravener,' said Robin, 'but 'twas in fair fight, for I was by them when they fought; but I know not how the report could have been made that Alan slew him, because there was no one of his party near him, except a churl whom Ket the Trow slew.'

Robin related what had happened at the fight in the forest between Alan and Ivo le Ravener.

'I remember now,' said Marian, 'that Sir Richard told me that word was given by a forester that on the day when the knight was found slain, Alan-a-Dale came to him for a horse which he had left in his charge, and he had a sore wound on his shoulder.'

'That was Black Hugo,' said Robin, 'who was with the men-at-arms today. Said he aught else? Said he anything of who was with Alan when he came for his horse, or of the plight in which Hugo was himself?'

'Nay, I think not.'

Robin told Marian of how they had found Black Hugo tied up to his own door-post, while a big man was seated before him eating the toasted collops which the forester had prepared for his own dinner. Marian laughed heartily at this, and said that Sir Richard would be hugely delighted to hear so merry a tale.

'See you that tall fellow there?' said Robin, pointing to where the fine athletic figure of Little John, supple and wiry, strode before them, glancing keenly here and there into the forest beside them. 'He is the villein who tied up the forester, and a jollier comrade and a finer fighter I ne'er wish to meet.'

Marian thereupon wished to speak to Little John, who was called up by his leader, and soon Little John, his face flushing, was speaking to the first lady he had ever met in his life. Yet he bore himself with the dignity of a freeman, for in the frank life of the forest and the open air, the awkward and loutish manners of a serf quickly dropped away from manly natures.

While they spoke thus together, Marian asking Little John many questions concerning the life of the outlaws under the greenwood tree, Robin rode forward to the lady Alice where she rode with her woman beside her.

'Lady Alice,' said the outlaw, 'sorry am I that those words of mine caused your sad thoughts to rise. But tell me, for I have known young Alan, and a bolder, braver squire I never met, nor one more courteous in speech and kindly in manner – how soon is it appointed that thou shalt wed the old knight whom those tyrants of Wrangby wish to be thy husband?'

'Sir Outlaw,' said the lady, and her dark eyes glowed, 'I thank thee for thy kind words concerning him I love. He hath written of thee in his few letters which I have received since, a year ago, he fled an outlaw to the woods and wilds, and ever he spoke warmly of thy friendship. My hateful marriage is fixed for three days hence on the feast of Saint James, at the church of Cromwell. My poor father can no longer resist the wicked demands of Sir Isenbart, who threatens fire and sword if he submit not to his will and weds me to the old tyrant, Sir Ranulf. And we have no great and powerful friends to whom we may appeal for protection, and my lover is outlawed and cannot save me.'

Tears were falling from the brave eyes, and they went to Robin's heart. His brow was dark with anger as he thought for some moments deeply. Then he said:

'Take heart, dear lady. There may be hope in a few strong arms and stout hearts, though the time is but short. Hast thou anyone who could take a message to thy lover from me?'

'Thanks for thy great cheer, good Robin,' replied the lady, and smiled through her tears. 'There is a serf of my father's who knoweth my lover's hiding-place and hath taken four messages from me, though the way is fearsome and long for a poor untravelled villein. Yet he is brave, and loves to do my behests.'

'How is he named, and where doth he live?'

'He is named John or Jack, son of Wilkin, and dwelleth by the Hoar Thorn at Cromwell.'

'Give me something which he will know for thine,' said Robin, 'for I will send one of my fellows to him ere the vesper bell rings tonight.'

Lady Alice took a ring from one slender finger and put it in Robin's hand.

'This will he know as from me, and he will do whatsoever the bearer telleth him to do gladly,' she said, 'for my sake.'

The waiting-woman riding beside her now put out her hand, holding a thick silver ring between her fingers.

'Bold outlaw,' said the girl, a dark-haired, rosy-cheeked and pretty lass with a high look, 'let thy man take this also to Jack, and bid him from me, whom he saith he loves, that if he do not what you tell him and that speedily, then there is his ring back again, and when I see him again he shall have the rough side of my tongue and my malison besides. For if he'll not bestir his great carcass for the love of my lady who is in such a strait, then he is no man for Netta o' the Meering.'

'I will do thy bidding, fair lass,' said Robin with a smile. 'And as I doubt not he is a brave man indeed from whom thou hast accepted this ring, I have no fear that all will go well.'

In a little while they had reached Sir Richard's castle, and the ladies were safely in hall again. By this time the afternoon light was softening to evening, and Robin knew that no time was to be lost. He called Will the Bowman to him, and giving him the two rings, entrusted him with the mission he had planned. A few moments later, on Robin's own swift horse, Will was galloping with loose rein along the forest drives that led eastward to the waters of the Trent.

CHAPTER FIVE

How by the Help of Robin Hood and Jack, Son of Wilkin, Alan-a-Dale Was Wed to the Lady Alice

Jack, son of Wilkin, as he stood in the wood, tying the last bundle of faggots on a rough cart, which he had made himself, little thought that there was hastening to him a message that would have a very great effect on all his future life. Jack was a well-built, sturdy youth of about twenty, good-looking, with quick brown eyes and freckled skin. His head of curly brown hair never knew a covering, except when snow was falling or the east wind blew shrill in the frosts of winter.

He was a villein of the manor of Cromwell, and his lord was Sir Walter de Beauforest, father of the lady Alice. The lord hardly knew that Jack existed; sometimes he saw the lad when he himself was going hawking or coming from the chase, but he did not trouble to acknowledge the pull of the front lock which Jack gave him. John the Thinne, however, steward of the lord, knew Jack as one of the most willing of the younger workers on the manor. Once on a while indeed, when Jack was a boy of twelve, the steward had looked rather sourly upon him, because the boy had been noticed by the lady Alice, then a girl of but a year or two older, and she had made the boy one of her falconers. When, however, Jack's father had died, the lad had been compelled to do his work in return for the hovel and the few square rods of land which supported his mother and himself, and Jack had seen less of the lady Alice, for whose smile or kind word he would have gone through fire or water.

On the great parchment roll of the manor, which the steward kept, and which contained the pedigrees of all the serfs on the

land of the lord, Jack was entered as John, Wilkin's son. His
father's name was Will, and as he was a little man he had been
called Wilkin, which means Little Will. But Jack's surname was
not a fixed thing, because villeins and poor folk did not usually
own them in those days. Sometimes, indeed, he was called Jack
Will's son, or, because an old hawthorn leaned beside his hovel,
Jack-a-thorn, or from his mother's name Jack Alice's son, or as
we should call it, Alison; but being a cheerful fellow and quick,
Jack usually knew when he was being called, and therefore did
not stand on strict ceremony.

Jack loved horses and dogs and hawks. He knew the name of
every horse on the manor, and many a day had he spent with
them when he went a-lea or afield, driving the long straight
furrow across the strip of the lord's land which he had to plough.
Many a happy day, too, had he spent with the lady Alice on the
wild open lands, hunting with merlin or peregrine, tiercel or
kestrel.

Every little cur in the village was on speaking terms with Jack,
but there were no large dogs, such as mastiffs, hounds, or setters,
for the village was too near the king's forest where the red deer
roamed, and all large dogs were either slain by the foresters, or
their forepaws were maimed, so that they should not be used for
hunting.

Jack's great ambition was to obtain his freedom. To be a
freeman and to work his own land, like Nicholas o' the Cliffe
did, or Simon the Fletcher, seemed to him to be the greatest
happiness a man could possess. Not that his lord was a hard one,
or that John the Steward was oppressive, but nevertheless Jack
would prefer to be free than bound to the soil as he was. His
mother explained this strange desire by saying that, four generations before, in the peaceful time of the blessed king, Edward the
Confessor, when the land had known no fierce lords and violent
robber-barons, Jack's forefathers had been free people, but that
when the evil Normans had come they had enslaved them all.

To Jack it seemed a great injustice that when his father had
died, his mother had had to give the steward the finest beast they
had, Moolie the cow, a splendid milker, besides the best
cauldron in the house and the soundest stool. These were said to
be payment to the lord for letting them still 'sit' in the land and

in the hovel which they and their forbears had possessed for generations.

Until some ten months ago, the world outside Jack's village had seemed to him to be a dark, terrible, and mysterious region. He knew the country for quite three miles from the church in the centre of the village, but far into the forest to the west he had never dared to penetrate. He had suspected all strangers, and when he had met with any coming towards the village he had hidden until they had passed.

The forest he had heard was a place of dread, for the other villeins had told terrible tales. Of monsters who flew by night and hid in dark thickets by day to snap up unwary travellers; of hills from whose tops at night the glow of fire shone forth, and within which little dark elves or spirits dwelled. Indeed, the fear of little malicious fiends was never very distant from Jack's mind in those times. These evil things might take any shape, and they dwelled in the spring or the stream, in the wood beside the road, and in the tufts of grass in the field which he was ploughing or mowing. The whole village, and thousands of villages up and down broad Britain, believed in such wicked sprites, and therefore Jack was no worse than his fellows, or, indeed, than men who were famed for their learning in those days, and sat at the council boards of kings.

That sooty old crow flapping over the furrows, or the raven who came and sat on a clod and cocked his beady eye at Jack as he was ploughing, might be a witch or wizard come to see if he could do some evil trick – not a wild bird looking for the worms or the leather-jackets which the plough turned up. Therefore Jack had to cross two fingers when he passed the bird of ill-omen and say a paternoster. In the same way, if Jack saw floating in the stream a stout piece of bough which, when dried, would boil the pot, he did not pull it out thoughtlessly, as a boy of today would do. Nay; before he touched it he made the sign of the cross over it, lest some evil water nicker might be hiding beneath it, ready to clutch him down, if he did not disarm it by means of the sacred sign.

To find a cast horse-shoe or to get hold of one which was too worn to be of further use was a great piece of good luck. Jack had a horse-shoe over the door of his hovel, to keep witches and wizards from entering his abode, and another over the

window-shutter. And Jack knew which was the proper way to
hang the shoe. On All Souls' Eve, a time when evil things are
moving much about, Jack wore a sprig of rowan in his belt.

He had never seen an elf or brownie himself, but he knew that
they lived in hollows in the hills or in secret places in the forest.
The tale went, indeed, that long ago a man named Sturt of
Norwell, a serf, had heard someone crying in a wood that he had
lost his pick. Going to see who it was that cried, Sturt found it
was a brownie. Frightened though he was, Sturt sought for and
found the pick, and the fairy had then invited him home to
dinner. Afterwards Sturt often went to the green hill in the
forest, and in a year married the fairy's daughter, and thrived all
his life. His children still lived at Norwell, and one was a
freeman, and all were lively little fellows, welcomed wherever
they went for their songs and jolly ways.

Such had been Jack's manner of thinking of the world and
things generally until some few months before; and then one day
the lady Alice, like a vision from heaven for beauty and graciousness, had met him in a lonely place, and giving him a parchment
wrapped in silk, had begged him to take it to her lover, who lay
hid at a certain place in the forests of Lancaster. He was the only
man she could trust, she had said, and her words had seemed to
make Jack's heart swell in his breast.

Jack was a brave lad, but that first journey through the great
forest, bearing his precious message, was an experience which,
for dread, he would never forget. But for sheer worship of the
fair Alice, whose love for Alan-a-Dale was known to all the
manor, his loyalty had overcome all his fear, and he had
performed his mission well and faithfully.

Three times since then he had done the journey, and every
time his dread of the strange roads and the wild waste country,
which lies between Sherwood and Werrisdale, had returned to
him, but his pluck and his shrewdness had carried him safely
through the various adventures he had met with.

He had never seen an outlaw or real robber of the woods.
Pedlars and lusty beggar men or saucy minstrels had tried to
frighten or defraud him out of his few poor possessions or his
bag of food; but never had he seen any of those terrible men who
had fled from their rightful lords, forsaking land and home and

the daily customs of their forefathers. He had often wondered what reckless and desperate men they must be, how quick they must be to slay or injure.

That evening, as he stood tying the last faggot on the little cart, he was wondering what he should have done had one dashed upon him from the thicket on one of his journeys, and demanded the precious thing which the lady Alice had entrusted to him. He would have fought to the death rather than give it up.

He clicked his tongue to the rough pony which drew the cart, and led it down the track out of the wood. He looked west, and saw far away over the shaggy line of the forest the upper limb of the huge red sun in whose light the tree stems around him shone blood red. The light dazzled his eyes. He heard a twig break beside him, a man stepped from behind the trunk of a tree and stood barring his passage.

'Art thou Jack, son of Wilkin?' said the stranger, in a sharp commanding tone.

Jack stepped back, and his hand fell to the haft of the knife stuck in his belt. He looked keenly at the man, who was short and sturdy. He was dressed in green tunic and hose, much worn in places and torn here and there as if by brambles. A bow was slung across his back, and a bunch of arrows were tied to his girdle beside a serviceable sword.

Jack wondered, as he scowled at the stranger, who he might be. He looked by his clothes to be some lord's woodman, and his face, covered with a great grizzled beard, seemed honest though stern. Yet there was an air about the man that seemed to say that he owned no one lord but himself. The stamp of the freeman was in his keen eyes, in the straight look, and the stiff poise of the head.

These thoughts took but a moment to pass through Jack's mind; then he said:

'What's that to thee who I be?'

'It's much to thee who ye be,' said the stranger with a laugh. 'Look 'ee, lad, I mean thee no harm.'

There was an honest ring in the other's laugh which pleased Jack. The stranger's left hand went to his pouch and drew something from it. Then he pulled forth his dagger and upon the point of it he slipped two rings – one of gold, the other of silver – and held the weapon up to the light. The dying rays of the sun struck a diamond in the tiny hoop of gold, so that it dazzled and glowed like a fairy light in the darkening wood.

'Do ye know aught of these, lad?' asked the man.

'Where got ye them?' asked Jack, his face dark with anger. 'Ha' ye robbed them from those who wore them? If 'tis so, then thou'lt never leave this place alive.'

'Soft, brave lad,' replied the other, watching keenly the involuntary crouching movement which Jack made as if he was preparing to spring upon the other. 'My master got them from the hands of their fair owners, with these words. The lady Alice, thy mistress, said: "Jack is brave, and loves to do my behests. He will know this is from me, and he will do whatsoever the bearer telleth him to do gladly, for my sake." '

'Said the lady Alice those words?' asked Jack. His face was flushed, the blood seemed suddenly to have swept hotly into his heart, and he glowed with the pleasure of hearing his lady's praise even by the mouth of this rugged old woodman. 'And what,' he went on, 'what would my lady wish me to do?'

'Go with me and lead me to Alan-a-Dale,' said Will the Bowman.

For a moment Jack hesitated. Go with this stranger through the wild forest and the lonely lands of the Peak! But his loyalty suffered no question of what he would do.

'I will do this, friend,' replied Jack. 'Tell me thy name and who thou art.'

'I am called Will the Bowman,' was the reply. 'Robin Hood is my master'

'What!' said Jack, and started back. 'Thou art an outlaw! One of Robin Hood's men?'

'That am I,' replied Will, 'and proud to serve so brave and wise a master.'

Jack looked in wonder for a moment. This was no desperate and reckless cut-throat, such as he had imagined; but a man with a homely face, with eyes that could be stern, but which could also smile. Jack put out his hand on an impulse, and the other gripped it.

'Thou art the first outlaw I have seen,' said Jack with a hearty laugh, 'and if thy master and thy fellows are like thee, then my heart tells me that thou art honest and good fellows. And Robin Hood will befriend my lady?'

'Ay, that will he,' said Will, 'but now let's chatter no more, but get to the forest ere the light is wholly gone.'

No more words were said. Jack led the horse and cart to the rough track which led to the village, and then gave a slash to the horse and knew as it cantered off that it would soon reach home in safety. Before sending it off, however, he tore a strip of traveller's joy from the hedge and twined it round the pony's head. By this his mother would know that again he had set off suddenly at the bidding of the lady Alice.

When the two men had left the wood a mile behind them, Will said:

'Ye asked not what message came with the silver ring, lad.'

Jack laughed. 'Nay, I did not. First, because my lady's message drove it from my head, and second, because I doubt not 'twas no soft message.'

' 'Twas a maid's message,' replied Will, 'and that's half bitter and half sweet, as doubtless ye know. Then I guess the maid Netta o' the Meering flouts thee as often as she speaks kind words?'

'Ye are older than I,' said Jack with a little awkward laugh, 'and doubtless ye know the ways of girls better than I. What was the message she sent me?'

Will told him, and Jack's face reddened at the telling. 'I needed not her rough tongue,' he said with some shade of haughtiness in his voice, 'to make me stir myself for my lady's sake.'

Thereafter he would say no more, but Will noticed that he quickened his pace and seemed very full of thought. By the time the last faint light had died from the clear sky, they were deep in the forest ways. They rested and ate food from their scrip until the moon arose, and then by its gentle light they threaded the paths of the greenwood, looking like demons as their dark forms passed through the inky blackness, and like fairies covered with magic sheen when they stepped silently across some open glade.

Two days later, in the morning, the villeins of Cromwell village stood in groups about their hovels talking of the sad fate that was to befall their beloved young mistress that morning. All knew that she had given her heart to Alan-a-Dale, but that some hard destiny which ruled the lives of knights and ladies was forcing her to wed old Ranulf de Greasby, a white-haired, evil old lord who lived in the fenlands to the east.

Some of the villeins stood in the churchyard, in the church of which the ceremony was to take place. They often looked along the road to the north, for it was from thence that the wedding party would come. Already the priest had been seen ambling along towards the manor-house, from whence he would probably accompany the bride to the church.

'He goes to take comfort to her to whom he can give none,' said one young woman with a baby in her arms. 'Poor lady!' she went on, 'why should he be denied her whom she loves best in all the world?'

' 'Twould be at the price of his head if he came here this day,' said a man near her. 'Outlaw he is, and a broken man.'

'Nay, I fear there's no help for the young lass!' said a younger man. 'She'll eat her heart out when she's wed, and never be the same bright winsome maid she has ever been among us.'

'Oh, 'tis a foul wrong!' cried a young girl. 'Is there no one of all her kin who would save her?'

'Her kin are a weak people, Mawkin,' said an old wrinkled woman, 'and they would be like mice in the jaws of Isenbart de Belame if they stood against his will.'

Just then there came the sound of horses' hooves along the rough road coming from the north, and ten mounted men-at-arms rode up wearing the livery of Ranulf de Greasby. Men of hard, coarse looks they were, and without a word they rode their horses into the gate and up to the church porch, scattering the poor villeins, who got out of the way of the horses as quickly as they could. The horsemen ranged themselves five on each side of the porch, and, dismounting, each stood by his horse and glared insolently at the villeins, who were now huddled together by the gate.

'Is it from such rubbish as these that the old man fears a rescue?' asked one man-at-arms.

The others laughed at the joke. 'Our old lord hath been flouted so long by the pretty young jade,' said another, 'that now she's almost in his hand he fears some evil hap may snatch her from him.'

'Ay, she hath flouted him overlong,' said another. 'I'd not give much for her flouts once she's in his castle by Hagthorn Waste. There be ways he hath of taming the fiercest maid, as his last wife knew, so they say.'

'Ay, she that went in a handsome, dark-eyed lass with a look like a sword one minute and as sweet as a child's the next,' said another.

'I remember her,' said the first speaker. 'She lived two years. She 'scaped from him one winter's night, and was found at the dawn in Grimley Mere frozen stiff.'

'Ye are cheerful bridesmen, by the rood,' said he who was evidently the leader. 'Let us have that minstrel to give us a rousing song more fitting for a wedding. Hi, there, varlet!'

A tall minstrel, wearing a gaudy striped doublet and patched hose, had strolled from the village up to the group of villeins, and was laughing with them, while he twanged the harp which he wore round his neck by a soiled ribbon. At the call of the soldier, the minstrel stepped to the gate, and taking off his velvet cap, swept it before him with a bow.

'What would you, noble squires? A song of war and booty, or one of the bower and loving maidens, or one which tells of the chase of the good red deer?'

'Sing what thou likest, so it be a jolly song,' commanded the chief man-at-arms.

Whereupon, with a few preliminary twangings and a clearing of the throat, the minstrel gave them a popular song called 'The Woodstock Rose'. He had a rich tenor voice, and the ditty was a rollicking one, with a chorus in which all took part. Afterwards the minstrel sang them a ballad about a wedding, which pleased them mightily. When the minstrel appeared wishful to depart, the leader said:

'Stay, jolly fellow, for I think we shall have need of thee. We are like to have a sad-faced bride here soon, and thy lively songs may brighten her, so that my lord may take cheer of her gay looks. If thou pleasest our lord this day thou shalt have good reward, I doubt not.'

The minstrel was not unwilling to stay, and was preparing to sing another lay, when four horsemen were seen riding swiftly towards the church. The tallest one was Sir Ranulf de Greasby, an old grey knight with a red and ugly face. His lips were cruel, and his red eyes were small and fierce. He was dressed in a rich cloak of red silk, his belt was encrusted with diamonds, and his sword-hilt blazed with jewels. The three men with him were younger knights, of a reckless air, well dressed but slovenly in bearing. One of them was Sir Ranulf's nephew, Sir Ector of the Harelip, a ruffianly-looking man, whose fame for cruelty was as great as that of his uncle's.

The old knight drove through the gate furiously as if in a great hurry.

'Hath the lady come yet?' he cried in a hoarse voice to the men-at-arms, and his red, foxy eyes gleamed suspiciously from one to the other.

'Nay, lord,' replied the leader.

'Plague on it!' the old knight rapped out, and turning in his saddle he glanced sourly up and down the road, then at the crowd of villeins and the hovels beyond. 'She keeps me waiting still,' he muttered into his beard, while they could hear his teeth grind and could see the fierce red eyes close to slits through which came an evil light. 'It shall be hers to wait, anon, if she speak not fair to me!'

'Who art thou, knave?' he said, suddenly glancing down at the minstrel who stood beside his horse.

'I am Jocelyn, the minstrel, Sir Knight,' replied the man, and twanged his harp.

'Thou hast a knave's face,' said Sir Ranulf suspiciously; 'thou'rt not sleek enough for a gleeman.'

'Nevertheless, Sir Knight, I am a poor gleeman come to give your highness pleasure with my simple song, if ye will have it,' said the minstrel, and twanged his harp again.

'Sing then, rascal, and let thy song be apt, or thou'lt get but a basting.'

The gleeman screwed up two strings of his harp, and began:

'Though lord of lands I sadly strayed,
I long despised my knightly fame,
And wakeful sighed the night hours through!
A thrall was I to that fair dame,
To whom long time in vain I prayed –
    The haughty lady Alysoun.

Blow, northern wind,
Send me my sweeting,
Blow, northern wind, blow, blow, blow.'

As he finished the last line, a scornful laugh, strangely shrill, rang out. Men looked this way and that, but could see naught. It seemed to come from above their heads, but there was nothing to be seen except the wooden front of the church tower. Round this a few daws were flying and crying, and in and out of the arrow-slits swallows were passing to and from their nests.

The gleeman sang another verse:

'Ah, how her cruel looks tortured me –
How like two swords her eyes of gold –
Until my cheeks waxed wan with woe!
But, happy me, though I am old,
Ah, now, she, winsome, smiles on me,
    My lady fair, my Alysoun.

Blow, northern wind,
Send me my sweeting,
Blow, northern wind, blow, blow, blow.'

Again the laugh rang out, this time with a more mocking note in it. Sir Ranulf looked at the gleeman.

'Who made that noise, knave?' he said, anger in his voice. 'Hast thou any fellow with thee?'

'No one is with me, lord,' the minstrel replied.

'Belike, lord,' said one of the men, who had fear in his eyes, 'it is a nixie in the church tower.'

'Belike, fool,' roared Sir Ranulf, 'thou shalt have a strong whipping when thou art home again. Go ye round the church in opposite ways and see if no churl is hiding. And if any be there, bring him here and I will cut his tongue from his mouth. I'll teach aught to fleer at me!'

Four of the men went round the church, while others went among the graves, lest someone was hiding behind the low wooden slabs raised over some of the burial-places; but both parties returned saying they had seen nobody. The knight was in a furious rage by now, and sending five of his men, he commanded them to scatter the villeins who stood by the churchyard gate, marvelling at the strange happening. The villagers did not wait for the blows of the soldiers, but fled among their hovels.

'Now, rogue,' cried Sir Ranulf to the gleeman, 'sing another verse of thy song, and if another laugh be heard I shall know it to be caused by thyself. Think ye that I know not the wizard tricks of thy juggling tribe?'

'As I hope to be saved,' said the jongleur gravely, 'it is not I who do make that laughter. Nevertheless, I will sing another verse and stand to the issue thereof.'

Thereupon, making his harp to accompany his tune, he sang.

> 'A gracious fate to me is sent,
> Methinks it is by Heaven lent!
> Ah now as mate she will me take,
> For ever, sweet, to be thy thrall,
> While life shall last, my all in all,
>   My gentle, laughing Alysoun.
>
> Blow, northern wind,
> Send me my sweeting,
> Blow, northern wind, blow, blow, blow.'

A shout of mocking laughter, so fierce and grim as to startle all, sounded immediately above the heads of the listeners, so that all involuntarily looked up, but there was nothing to be seen. The noise ceased for a moment; then a croaking laugh came from over the road, as if that which caused the sound was slowly passing away. Then the sound came nearer for a moment, and all heard distinctly words uttered with a fierce and threatening cry.

'Colman Grey! Colman Grey!'

At the sound of these words Sir Ranulf started back and fiercely pulled his horse so that he leaned against the very church door, at which he beat with clenched fists, and cried out: 'Avaunt! Avaunt! Keep him from me! Call the priest! Call the priest! 'Tis an evil spirit – keep it from me!'

He seemed in mortal terror. His face that had been red was now white; his lips twitched and gibbered, and while with one hand he crossed himself repeatedly, with the other he now seemed to push something from him and sometimes covered his eyes. The men standing about marvelled to see him, and stood gaping with open mouths at their lord distraught.

At length he came to himself: he saw the wonder in the eyes about him, and recovering his spirit somewhat, though he still trembled, he drove his horse forward among his men-at-arms.

'What gape ye at, ye knaves and fools!' he cried violently, and raising the whip which hung on his saddle, he slashed it at the men. They gave way before him; he charged them to stand still, but they would not, and in a mad fury he dashed his horse this way and that, beating at them, where they stood among their horses. The animals reared and began to bite and tear at each other, and an almost inextricable confusion arose. Suddenly his nephew, Sir Ector, caught the arm of the mad old lord and cried:

'Sir Ranulf, the lady comes! Cease!'

The furious man looked up the northern road and saw a party of riders coming towards the church. Instantly he dropped the whip, set his hat straight, and righted his tunic. Then he bade his sullen men mount their horses and prepare to receive the lady. Already the priest and the sacristan had entered the church by a side door, and now the great doors behind them swung open, and the darkness of the church yawned.

Sir Ranulf, seeing that all was now in order, cast a fierce eye around for the minstrel. He was nowhere to be seen.

'Where went that rogue the juggler?' he asked one of his companion knights.

'I know not,' said the other. 'I kept my eye upon him till thou didst begin to whip thy knaves, and then in the confusion he crept off, for I saw him not again!'

'Good Sir Philip,' said Sir Ranulf, 'do thou do me the greatest favour, and go search for that varlet. I shall not be happy till I have him in my hands and see him under torture. Then will I learn what the knave knows and – and – what – what – meant that cry. Thou canst take two of my men with thee, but seek him out, and when thou hast seized him take him to Hagthorn Waste, and lodge him in my hold there.'

'I will do this for thee, Greasby,' said the young knight, with an insolent laugh, 'but if I bring him to thee, thou must give me thy hound Alisaundre and thy merlin hawks, Grip and Fang.'

'Thou churlish knight!' said Sir Ranulf, in a fierce undertone; 'they are those I love best. But I must have that juggler. Go ye, and I will give thee what thou askest. Quickly go, or the varlet will be in hiding.'

A few words to two of the men-at-arms, and they and the knight rode out of the churchyard just as Sir Walter de Beauforest and a friend of his, with the lady Alice between them, rode up, accompanied by a house villein and the lady Alice's maid, both on horseback behind them. The old knight, Sir Ranulf, his crafty face all smiles now, stood at the churchyard gate doffing his hat, and with his hand on his heart, bowed to the lady Alice, greeting her. The lady Alice, with face pale and sad, hardly looked at him. She was clad in a rich dress of white silk, ropes of pearls were about her neck, her light summer cloak was sewn with pearls, and her wimple cloth was richly embroidered with gold; but this richness only showed up the dreadful pallor of her face, and her eyes that looked as if they strained to weep but would not.

Sir Walter, her father, looked no more wretched than he felt. He was a proud knight, and hated to think that he had to submit to the commands of a tyrant lord, and to marry his only daughter to a knight with the evil fame which Sir Ranulf de Greasby had possessed so long. Robbery on the highways and cruel tyranny of poor folk for the sake of their meagre hoards or their lands were the least of the crimes which report laid to the guilt of Sir Ranulf. Tales there were of a tortured wife, and of poor men and women put to cruel torment in the dungeons of his castle on Hagthorn Waste.

All rode up to the church door and then dismounted. Netta, whose eyes were red, went to her mistress, and under pretence of arranging her cloak whispered words of cheer to her while for sorrow she could hardly keep herself from weeping. Then Sir Walter, taking his daughter by the hand, led her into the church and up the dim aisle towards the altar, where already the priest stood ready to perform the ceremony.

Four of the men-at-arms stood without the church with the horses, the other four went in with Sir Ranulf and his two knights, of whom Sir Ector acted as his best man. Together they approached the altar, and then, while the others kept back, Sir Walter Beauforest placed his daughter's hand in the hand of Sir Ranulf who immediately led her up to the priest.

The old priest was as sad as any of the poor villeins who now crept into the church and sat in the back benches. He had known the lady Alice when she was brought to the font to be baptised, he had taught her to read and to write, and had loved her for her graciousness and kindness. Moreover, Sir Walter had always been a good friend to the poor priest. Nevertheless, he had to do his duty, and now, opening his service-book, he prepared to read the words that should make these two man and wife.

Suddenly from the gloom along the wall of the church came a movement, and a man stepped forth into the light of the candles which stood upon the altar. It was the minstrel, but now in his hand he bore a longbow, and his harp was carried by a fair young man – Gilbert of the White Hand.

'This is an evil and unfitting match,' he cried in a loud, stern voice. 'Sir Ranulf of the Waste, get thee gone lest ill and death befall thee. Sir Priest, this maiden shall wed him she loveth best, at a more fitting time.'

All eyes were turned to the tall figure in green. The lady Alice, her eyes bright and a flush in her cheeks, had torn her hand from the fingers of Sir Ranulf, and stood trembling, her hands clasped together.

Sir Ranulf, his face dark with passion, looked from the lady to the minstrel. He was almost too furious to speak.

'So!' he said mockingly. 'Who is this? Is this the wolf's-head, the broken fool for whom this maiden here hath flouted me and put me off this year and more?'

None answered. Sir Walter peered at the minstrel and shook his head. Sir Ranulf, with a gesture of rage, drew his sword, and made a step forward.

'Who art thou, knave, to dare to withstand me?' he cried.

From the darkness of the roof above their heads came a croaking voice:

'Colman Grey! Colman Grey!'

Sir Ranulf faltered at the name and looked up, his face white with terror. As he did so, the hum as of a bee was heard, and a short black arrow shot down and pierced his throat. Without a cry he fell heavily to the ground, twitched a little, and lay still.

The knights and men-at-arms who looked on stood motionless, too surprised to do or say aught. The minstrel placed a horn to his lips and blew a shrill blast which filled the church with echoes.

Instantly, as if the sound awoke him from his stupor, Sir Ector drew his sword and with a yell of rage dashed at Robin Hood, for he was of course the minstrel. Hardly had Robin time to draw his own sword, and soon he and Sir Ector were fighting fiercely in the gloom. At the sound of the horn, also, there came the sound of clashing weapons at the door, and the men-at-arms, who had hitherto stood too amazed to move, now seized their swords and ran towards the door, only to be stayed by three of their fellows who ran into the church, pursued by a flight of arrows which poured in like a horde of angry wasps. Two men fell dead, and another tottered away sorely wounded. Next moment into the church came some half-score men in green. The five remaining men-at-arms, knowing the hatred with which any men of Sir Ranulf's were looked upon, dashed against the bowmen and strove to cut their way through, for they knew that no quarter would be given them. The fight raged furiously at the door, the men in green striving to thrust them back, and the Greasby men struggling to win through to the open.

Suddenly a scream rang through the church. Looking quickly around, Sir Walter saw the second knight who had been with Sir Ranulf rushing towards the priest's side door, and in his arms was the lady Alice, struggling to free herself from his powerful grasp.

Behind him ran Netta the maid, screaming, and tearing at the knight's garments; but as he reached the door he turned and struck the girl a blow which laid her senseless. Next moment he had disappeared through the arras which hid the door.

At the same moment Robin Hood, after a fierce struggle with Sir Ector, slew him, though wounded himself, and then swiftly made for the door through which the other knight had dashed with the lady Alice. Looking out, he saw nobody in sight, and guessed that the knight had rushed forward to the horses which stood before the church.

This was indeed the truth. Still clutching his struggling burden, the knight reckoned on seizing a horse and escaping before anyone would recover from the confusion. When he reached the front of the church he found two men in deadly combat. One was the knight who had gone off in pursuit of the minstrel, the other was a stranger. But at sight of the latter the lady Alice, breathless and panting, cried out:

The rescue of the lady Alice

'Alan! Alan! Save me!'

Her cry was almost the death-knell of her lover, for, surprised at the voice of his sweetheart crying so near him, Alan turned his head, and the knight struck at him a deadly blow, which would most surely have sheared his head from his shoulders had not Jack, son of Wilkin, who was standing near, seen the danger, and with his staff struck a shrewd blow at the knight's shoulder. This saved Alan's life and gave him time to turn. Furiously he strove to beat down his foe, knowing that he must slay this one before he could turn upon the knight who was bearing off his lady.

But the knight, Sir Philip, was a stout and crafty fighter, and meanwhile the knight who bore the lady had reached a horse, had thrown her across the saddle, and had swung himself into the seat. Next moment he had dashed towards the churchyard gate, cutting down two poor brave villeins who, seeing their lady thus used, hoped with their staves to check the robber knight. With a yell of exultation the knight saw his way clear before him, he put spurs to the steed, and spoke mockingly to the now unconscious form of the lady lying across the horse before him.

Suddenly he felt someone leap on the haunches of the animal behind him. Ere he could think what to do, a long knife flashed in the sun before his eyes. He felt a thud on his breast and a keen pain like fire, then blackness swept down upon him. He rocked in his seat, the reins were caught from his hands, and Jack, son of Wilkin, heaving the dead knight from before him, checked the frightened horse, brought it to a standstill, and lifted the unconscious body of his mistress tenderly to the ground.

By this time Alan-a-Dale had leaped in under the guard of his adversary and by a swift blow had dispatched him, and instantly had run to the side of his mistress, for whom already Jack, Wilkin's son, had brought water. Soon she revived and sat up, and hearing who was her rescuer, gave her hand to Jack, who kneeled and reverently kissed it.

'Jack,' she said, smiling sweetly though wanly, 'for this great service thou shalt be a free man, and my father shall give thee free land.'

Jack glowed with gladness, but was too tongue-tied to say aught but 'Thank you, my lady!'

By now, too, Netta, a little dazed, came forward and tended

her mistress. Robin Hood, going into the church to fetch Sir Walter, found that of his own men two had been slain in the fierce encounter with the men-at-arms, of whom but one of all the ten had escaped alive by rushing away through the side door.

'Sir Walter,' said Robin, when father and daughter had embraced each other, 'this hath been a red bridal, and I have meddled in thy affairs to some purpose.'

'I cannot be ungrateful to you, Sir Outlaw,' said Sir Walter, who, proud and stiff as he was, knew a brave leader from a paltry one, and honoured courage, whether found in earl or churl, villein or freeman; 'I thank thee from my heart for saving my daughter from this ill-starred and unhappy match. I must stand the issue of it, for the knights you have slain have powerful aiders, and I doubt not their vengeance will be heavy upon us all.'

'You speak of Belame and the Wrangby lords?' said Robin, and his brow was dark and his voice stern.

'They are the rulers of these parts in these present unhappy times,' replied the knight. 'While the king's own sons plunge the country in civil war and wretchedness, weak men have to submit to the gross tyranny of stronger neighbours.'

'Ranulf of Greasby and Ector Harelip are two the less,' said Robin grimly. 'Mark me, Sir Walter,' he went on, 'the lords of Wrangby have already filled the cup of suffering beyond men's bearing. As I hope to be saved, by the Virgin's dear word, I swear it here and now, that ere long they shall lie as low as do these robber knights, and when I pull them down, I will root out their nest, so that not one evil stone shall stand upon another.'

Sir Walter looked at the dark glowing eye of the outlaw, and remembered the deeds of wild justice which already had spread the fame of Robin throughout the forest lands from Pontefract to Nottingham, and from the desolate lands of the Peak to the flat fen marshes of Lincolnshire.

'I will help thee all I may, Sir Outlaw,' said the knight, 'and when the time comes thou mayest call on me to give thee all aid. Meanwhile, what's to be done?'

'This shall be done, Sir Walter,' replied Robin. 'Thy daughter and the man she loves shall dwell with me in the greenwood, and when they have been thrice called in a church they shall be wedded. If thou fearest assault by the robber baron, de Belame, thou canst leave thy house and live with us also; but if thou wouldst liefer stay beneath thy own roof, twenty of my men shall stay to guard and watch with thee. Dost thou agree?'

'I will liefer stay in my own house, good Robin,' said Sir Walter, 'if thy brave fellows will aid me to repel attack. And when times of peace return to this unhappy England, I trust my daughter and brave Alan, her husband, will live with me also.'

It was thus agreed. Within the next three weeks Father Tuck, in a church near by his cell, had published the banns of marriage between Alan and Alice, and it was the valiant monk himself who married the lovers, thus making them happy once for all.

On the day when Robin thus saved Alice from wedding the evil Sir Ranulf, the cruel lord, Isenbart de Belame, sat in the high seat of his castle at Wrangby, which just men called Evil Hold, and waited for his supper. About the board sat others as evil as himself, as Sir Niger le Grym, Hamo de Mortain, Sir Baldwin the Killer, Sir Roger of Doncaster, and many others.

'Plague take him!' at length cried de Belame, 'I'll wait no longer for him. Is Ranulf so jealous of his pretty bride that he fears to bring her here for us to give her our good wishes?'

The others laughed and made jeering jests.

'And where are Ector, Philip and Bertran?' said Sir Niger. 'They were to go with the bridegroom to give the shy fellow heart and courage in the ordeal.'

'Ho! scullions,' roared de Belame, 'serve the meats! And when Ranulf comes, we'll make such game of him and his bride that he'll be – '

Whang! Something had seemed to snore through the air from above their heads, and lo! here, sticking in the board before Sir Isenbart, was a black arrow, with a piece of parchment tied to it. Only for a moment de Belame lost his presence of mind. He looked up to the ceiling of the high hall and shouted:

' 'Twas shot from the spy hole! Ho, there, knaves, up and search the castle for him that shot this!' He rose himself and hurried away, while the men-at-arms from the lower table scattered throughout the castle.

Niger le Grym drew the arrow from the wood and looked at the parchment, on which were names in red and black. But being no scholar he could read naught of them. In a while came back de

Belame, red with rage, cursing his knaves and their non-success.

'What means it?' said de Mortain. 'There are names on the scroll here?'

De Belame had been a monk in his early youth, and could read. He looked at the slip of parchment, and his face went fierce and dark with fury.

'Look you,' he said, 'there are strange powers against us! Ranulf, Ector, and the others have been done to death this day. Written in blood upon this parchment are the names of all who once made our full company and are now dead. Thus, here are the names of Roger de Longchamp and Ivo le Ravener, and now there appear those of Ranulf de Greasby, Ector de Malstane, Philip de Scrooby, and Bertran le Noir – all written in blood!'

'This is passing strange!' said some. Others looked with whitened faces at one another, while one or two even crossed themselves.

'Also,' went on de Belame, 'our own names, the names of us still living, are written in black, but underneath each is a red line!'

He laughed hoarsely, and his bloodshot eyes glared at the faces beside him. He picked up the arrow, a short, stout bolt, the shaft and feathers being a jet black.

'This is a trick of that saucy knave, Robin Hood,' he said. 'He thinks to frighten us, the braggart fool. He would do justice, as he terms it, upon me – lord of Wrangby, grandson of Roger de Belame, at whose name the lords of forty castles shuddered when he lived. I have been too mild with this pretty outlaw! I will cut his claws! I will cut his claws! Lads, we will lay our snares, and when we have him in the crucet-house below, we will tame him of his sauciness!'

But in spite of de Belame's fierce and violent laughter, supper was eaten but moodily.

Next day, strange tales began to spread about the country-side. The noise of the fight at the church spread far and wide. It was said that when Robin and the priest went to bring out the dead from the church, the body of Sir Ranulf could not be found. Men said that the Evil One himself had carried him off, just as it must have been some fiend at whose call he had shown fear, and by whose black arrow he had been slain.

Then a villein raced home late the same night from a village near Hagthorn Waste and said that in the twilight he had seen, across the marsh, a dead man being borne by things that had no bodies but only legs — demons of the fen, no doubt, who were taking home the body of their evil master.

But strangest thing of all was that late that night, the moon being full, the men-at-arms on Hagthorn Castle, watching for the return of their master and his bride, had suddenly heard shrieks of fiendish joy sound far off in the waste, and looking closely they seemed to see where a flickering light danced to and fro, and small black forms that heaped up a great fire. Whereat, fearing they knew not what, they crossed themselves, but said that something fell and evil stalked abroad through the sedgy pools and stony wilderness that lay about them. Closely did they keep watch throughout the night, but at the darkest hour before the dawn a strange drowsiness fell upon those that watched, so that all within the castle slept heavily.

They woke again with fierce flames beating upon their faces, the thick reek of smoke blinding their eyes and choking them. Dashing to and fro, they sought for ways of escape, but found that every door was locked, every egress barred either by flame or by stout iron-studded doors. Then did these men who had never shown mercy cry for it to the red reaching hands of the flames, but found none. They who had tortured the poor and the weak were tortured and tormented in their turn, and all their prayers were unheard.

When dawn broke, the grey light shone wanly over a red and glowing ruin. Men and women from neighbouring villages came and stood marvelling to see it. Thin and poor, with wolfish, famished faces, they looked, and could scarce believe that at length the evil thing was brought to ruin – that the cruel power which had oppressed them and theirs so long was lifted from their backs, that no longer had it power to cripple their limbs, starve their bodies, and stunt their souls.

Far and near, when just men heard of the strange end of Sir Ranulf, slain by an unseen hand, and his castle brought low in fire lit by some mysterious power, they were glad at heart, and said that justice still lived. When Sir Isenbart de Belame and his evil crew heard of the deed they said naught openly, but their brows blackened with anger, though fear sat in their hearts.

They gave great heed to the watch which they set at night in the castle, and looked this way and that when they rode forth, and most of them avoided the forest ways. Then when King Henry died and his son Richard of the Lion Heart was anointed king and went upon his Crusade, some of them fared to the East with him. But de Belame stayed behind, biding his time.

Meanwhile, there was no happier, cheerier man in all England than Jack, Wilkin's son. For was he not now a freeman, and reaped his own free land? Jack whistled and sang about his work all day, a great thankfulness in his heart, both at his own good fortune and at the thought that he had brought happiness to his own fair lady, in helping to wed her to the man she loved best in all the world.

CHAPTER SIX

How Robin Gave Aid to Sir Herbrand

Robin Hood sat in his bower in Barnisdale Forest, and his men were waiting for their dinner. In the glade where they lay the crackle of fires under the pots and the bubbling of the stews in the cauldrons made pleasant sounds, and the smell of cooked venison and crusty pies when the cooks opened the earth-ovens put a keen edge on every man's appetite.

But Robin would not give the signal to dine, for they had had no adventure that morning. The men who had been lying in wait along the roads for travellers had reported that there seemed to be no one moving, and that day Robin had felt that he had no desire to dine until he had a stranger to sit and make cheer with him.

'John,' said he at length to his lieutenant, who was lying on the grass near him honing the point of an arrow, 'go you, lad, with Will and Much, the Miller's son, and wend ye to the Sayles by Ermin Street. From that place, since it lies high, ye may chance to see some wayfarer. If it be so, bring him to me, be he earl or baron, abbot or knight, or the king's justice himself.'

Cheerfully Little John rose from his place, and taking his bow and arrows, called Will Stuteley and Much, and together they went through the forest-ways until they came to where the land lay high. Here, in clearings of the forest, were two little stone houses, ruined now and deserted. Ten years ago they had been dwelt in by freemen, who had farmed their few acres of land and fed their swine in the forest. But the evil lord of Wrangby had passed that way, had demanded of Woolgar and Thurstan, the freeholding dwellers, to own that they held their lands from the Wrangby lord. The farmers had been men of Danish blood, who could not brook such tyranny, and had defied the evil Sir Isenbart, with result that by force they had been dragged from their holdings, their crops destroyed, and their houses fired and broken down. Woolgar had been slain defending his home, and his wife and children had become serfs at Wrangby. Thurstan had taken to the woods with his two boys, and had fled away, as men said, vowing that someday he would come back and help to burn down the Evil Hold and slay its lords.

'Remember Woolgar and Thurstan,' said Little John, as they passed the broken houses, with tall weeds nodding from the windows.

'Aye, aye,' said Much and Will, 'they are two of the poor broken men for whom we will strike a big blow someday.'

Passing through leafy paths the three outlaws at length reached the highway, where their feet beat on the high-crowned road that had been built by Roman hands eight hundred years before.

They came at last to where five roads met. The ground was high here, and there was a wide space where the forest-ways ran into each other. On all sides the ground sloped down, and they could see far over the tossing heads of the great forest which stretched away on all sides. They looked east and they looked west, but no man could they see. Then they looked north into the deep hollow of Barnisdale, and they were aware of a rider coming slowly along a narrow track between the trees to the left, which led from the town of Pontefract some seven miles away.

The horseman was a knight in mail, with a lance in his right hand, and he rode with bent head as if in deep thought. As he came nearer they could see that his face was grave, almost sad; and so dispirited was he that while one foot stood in the stirrup the other swung free, with the stirrup beating against it.

Little John hastened forward to meet the knight, and bending on one knee before him, said:

'Welcome, Sir Knight, to the greenwood. For these three hours hath my master been expecting you, and hath fasted until you came.'

'Thy master hath expected me?' said the knight, looking with surprise at the kneeling outlaw. 'Who is thy master, good woodman?'

'He is Robin Hood,' replied Little John, 'and he craves that you should dine with him this day.'

'I have heard of him,' said the knight, 'for a good fellow and a brave and just man. I will willingly take meat with him, though I had thought to have pushed on to Blythe or Doncaster before I dined. But how mean ye that thy master hath been awaiting me, since I know him not?'

'Our master will not dine today unless he have some wayfarer to keep him company,' replied Little John. ' 'Tis a habit which our master hath at times.'

'I fear me,' said the knight, 'I shall be but poor cheer for thy good leader.'

In a little while the knight and the three outlaws stood before the bower of branches and leaves in which Robin Hood was seated. The outlaw rose and looked keenly in the face of the knight, and said:

'Welcome be ye, Sir Knight. I would have thee dine with me this day.'

'I thank thee, good Robin,' replied the knight. 'God save thee and all thy men!'

Then bowls of water and a napkin were brought, and after Robin and the knight had washed their hands, they sat down to dinner. There was bread and wine, venison pies, fish, roast duck and partridges, besides stewed kale or cabbage, and the knight appeared to relish the rich repast laid before him. Robin did not ask the knight who he was, for it was not his custom to ask this of his guests until they had eaten. When at length the repast was finished and they had washed their hands again. Robin said laughingly:

'Now, Sir Knight, I hope you have dined well?'

'That I have, good Robin,' was the reply. 'Such a dinner, in faith, have I not had these three weeks.'

'Well, now,' went on Robin, smiling; ' 'tis unheard of that a yeoman should pay for a knight. I must ask toll of thee ere thou wendest farther through these woods.'

'My good Robin,' said the knight with a sad smile, 'I have naught in my purse that is worth thy accepting.'

'Come, come,' replied Robin, 'thou art a knight with a knight's lands. Tell me truth now. What hast thou ill thy saddle-bag?'

'I have no more than ten shillings,' said the knight, and sighed heavily.

'Ho, there!' cried Robin. 'Little John, go to this knight's horse and search his saddle-bag and see what he hath therein.' Little John went off at once to do his master's command.

Robin turned to the knight, and said: 'If indeed thou speakest truth I will not touch one penny thereof, and if thou hast need of more I will lend it to thee.'

In a few moments Little John came back, and said: 'Master, I find but this half a pound in the saddle-bag,' and he held out the silver coin in one broad brown palm.

'Fill up thy beaker to the brim,' said Robin to the knight; 'thou'rt a true man of thy word.' Robin and the knight drank to their mutual health and safekeeping.

' 'Tis a marvel,' said Robin, 'to see how thin is thy clothing. Never have I seen a knight so poor-seeming as thou art. Tell me truly, and I will not tell it to any man. Art thou a knight by birth, or wert thou made a knight by force for some brave deed, while thy means could not keep thee in dignity; or hast thou muddled thy wealth away, or been a brawler and a waster? How dost thou come to such a sorry pass?'

'None of those things which thou speakest of is the cause of my poverty and lowness,' said the knight gravely. 'For a hundred winters have my ancestors lived upon our land at home, and ever have they kept up the dignity of our name. But often it befalls, Robin, as thou must know, that a man falls into misfortune not by his own act, and only God who sitteth in the heavens may amend his state. Within the last two years, as my friends and neighbours know, I had four hundred pounds of money which I could spend, but now I have naught in all the world but my wife, and my lands that soon I must lose.'

'How is it thou hast fallen into such dire need?' asked Robin.

'Because of my son, who slew a man,' replied the knight. ' 'Twas done in fair fight, but the kin of the slain man did oppress me, and it was their evil purpose to ruin me because of my son's deed. I have paid them much money, but they demanded more, and therefore I have had to pledge my lands to the abbot of St Mary's. And in my heart I believe mine enemies will do all they may to gain my land, and would fain see me beg my living along the wayside, for they are most bitter against me, and have so worked by fear and threats on all my neighbours that no one will lend me the money wherewith to pay the abbot.'

'Now by my troth,' said Robin, and beat his knee with his clenched hand, 'shall we never be done with hearing of the evil deeds and crafty ways of the fat abbot of St Mary's? Tell me, now,' he said to the knight, 'what is the sum that thou owest?'

'Four hundred pounds,' replied the knight sadly. 'Four hundred have I already paid mine enemies, and they did demand four hundred more, which I was compelled to borrow from the abbot. And as I cannot pay it to the abbot tomorrow, I shall lose all I possess.'

'Now, if you lose your land,' asked Robin, 'what have ye in mind to do?'

'I will busk me and go to the Crusade,' said the knight, 'but first I go to the abbey of St Mary's to tell the abbot that I have not the money.' He rose from his seat as if there was no more to be said.

'But, Sir Knight,' urged Robin, 'have ye no friends who will aid thee?'

'Friends!' said the knight bitterly. 'While I was rich, friends boasted how they loved me, but as soon as they knew I was in need, and that powerful were mine enemies, they fled this way and that for fear that I should beg help of them.'

Pity was in the eyes of Little John and Will the Bowman, and little Much the Miller's son, turned away to hide a tear. The knight looked so noble and was so sad that the little man felt he would have done anything to help him.

'Go not away yet,' said Robin to the knight, who reached for his sword to buckle it to his side; 'fill thy beaker once more. Now, say, Sir Knight, if one should lend thee this money to save thy land, hast thou no one who will be a surety for the repayment?'

'Nay, by my faith,' said the knight reverently, 'I have no friend but Him that created me.'

'Jape me no japes!' replied Robin. 'I ask thee if thou hast not thine own friend – not one of the saints, who are friends to all of us, but who cannot pay thy debts.'

'Good outlaw,' said the knight, 'I tell thee truly, I have no friend who would answer for such a debt except Jesus and His Mother, the sweet Virgin!'

'By the rood!' cried Robin, and beat his knee again; 'now thou speakest to the point. If thou didst seek all England through, thou couldst not find a surety better to my mind than the blessed Virgin, who hath never failed me since I first called upon her. Come now, John,' he went on, turning to Little John, 'go thou to my treasury and pay out four hundred pounds, and let each coin ring true and sound and be unclipped and uncut. The tale of money must be truly the amount which the evil abbot will take, so that he may not be able to throw back a single bad coin and thus seize the land of our friend.'

Little John, with Much the Miller's son and Will Stuteley, went together to the secret place where Robin kept his chest of gold, and together they told out four hundred golden pounds, and wrapping them in a cloth which they tied up, Little John brought the money to Robin.

'Now here, Sir Knight,' said Robin, untying the cloth and showing the gold to the knight, 'are four hundred gold pounds. I lend it to thee on the surety of our dear Lady the Virgin, and by her blessing thou shalt pay me this money within a year and a day from now.'

The tears ran down the knight's thin cheeks as he took the money from Robin's hand.

'Sir outlaw,' said he, 'never did I think that any man was so noble of mind as to lend me on such a security. Good Robin, I thank thee, and I will see to it that thou shalt not suffer the loss of a single penny of this money, but in a year and a day will I return with the full sum. And now I will tell thee, that though I had heard thee well and nobly spoken of by my son who loves thee, little did I think I should find that his words spoke less than all the truth.'

'Who is thy son, Sir Knight?' asked Robin, 'and where hath he met me?'

'My son is Alan-a-Dale, ' replied the knight, 'whom thou hast aided more than once, and chief of all, for whom thou didst gain him the lady he loves best.'

'Now this is a goodly meeting,' said Robin, 'as he and the knight clasped each other's hands. 'Alan hath spoken to me of his grief concerning thee, and how he had not the wherewithal to save thee and thy land from the clutches of the crafty monk. But little did I guess that thou wert Sir Herbrand de Tranmire himself. Glad am I indeed, Sir Herbrand, to be able to aid thee, for I love thy son Alan, and would do all I could to bring joy to him and to the father whom he loves. Now thou art another whom those evil lords of Wrangby have oppressed and wronged. Tell me, wilt thou in good time aid me to pull down that Evil Hold of theirs, and scatter the vipers in that nest?'

'That will I most gladly,' said Sir Herbrand, and his voice was stern and hard. 'Not only for my own sake will I do this, but for the many tyrannies and evils which they have done to poor folks, as I know, in the lands which run from their castle in the Peak to the marches of Lancaster. Much would it gladden me to aid thee, and I promise to give thee all help in this matter when and as thou wilt.'

Then Robin Hood, from among his store of rich garments, took a knightly dress of fine array and donned it upon the knight, and it became him well. Also he gave him new spurs and boots, and afterwards, when the knight had to continue upon his journey, he gave him a stronger and better horse than his own.

When he was about to set out, after the knight had thanked Robin with tears in his eyes for all the kindness he had shown him, Robin said:

'It is a great shame for a knight to ride alone, without page or squire. I will lend thee a little page of mine own to attend thee to the abbey of St Mary's, so that he may wait on thee, and afterwards bring me word how things befall. John,' he called to his big lieutenant, 'do thou take horse and ride with Sir Herbrand, and do all that is squire-like, and bring me back word of how the abbot and his crafty crew do receive him.'

'I thank thee, good Robin,' said Sir Herbrand with a smile, 'for the little page thou sendest with me. And here I promise, by the sweet Virgin who hath never failed me, to bring to thee within a year and a day the money thou hast so nobly lent me, together with gifts to repay thee for those thou hast given me.'

'Fare thee well, Sir Herbrand,' said Robin as he shook hands with the knight, 'and send me back my little page when thou hast no longer need of him.'

As Little John rode off behind the knight there was much laughter and many jokes about the little page, and the knight was advised not to spare the rod, 'for,' many said, 'he was a saucy lad and needed frequent whipping'.

For some time the knight and Little John rode on along the lonely forest roads, and the talk between them was of Robin Hood and the many deeds of goodness which he had done.

'I fear me,' said the knight at length, 'though I will bring all the men I may to aid him, that he will find when the time comes that to pull down that evil nest of Wrangby will be beyond our strength. Isenbart de Belame is a crafty and skilful fighter, and I fear your master hath little knowledge of warfare and of how to take a strong castle such as Wrangby.'

'I have no fear of it,' said Little John with a laugh. 'My master is as wise a man as that limb of Satan. Besides, he hath right on his side, and is under the special care of Our Sweet Lady, and he that hath her blessing, who may avail against him?'

' 'Tis true,' replied the knight, 'the Blessed Virgin is worth a strong company of men-at-arms. But so far and wide do the evil plots of Belame and the Wrangby robbers spread, and so fearful are men to incur their displeasure, that from here to Doncaster on the east and to the marches of Lancaster on the west, I doubt if justice and right are ever allowed to be done if it comes to the ears of those evil men.'

'Ay,' said Little John sadly, 'they have laid the fear of death or torture on all who wish to live in peace, but, as I hope to be saved, I believe their wicked days are numbered. In every village lives some maimed wretch who bears the marks of their torture, in every manor-house or castle dwells some lord or lady, knight or dame, who hath been put to shame, or suffered ill by their ruffian deeds. And it is in my mind that, were my master once to rise against the evil crew, every peaceful man from here to Lancaster would rise also, and never lay aside his weapons until the cruel band were utterly wiped out.'

'May the Virgin grant that it be so!' said the knight. 'But what are those that follow after that man? It would seem that they have it in mind to rob or injure him.'

A little way before them was a group of some five or six men, walking in the middle of the road, and as the knight and Little

John approached them they could see that each of the five men behind bore a naked sword in his hand, while the man in front held a cross before him and was almost naked.

' 'Tis some felon who hath sworn to leave the country for some murder or other villainy,' said Little John, 'and those armed men are those whose kin he hath wronged, and who see that he go not out of the king's highway. And by the rood, he that holds the cross hath a right evil look.'

When they reached the group the knight asked courteously what crime the felon had committed. The man with the cross was ungirt, unshod, bareheaded and barefooted, and was clothed merely in a shirt, as if he were about to be hanged on a gallows. His look was black and evil, and across one cheek was the weal of an old wound. The five men who followed with swords drawn were well-to-do townsmen, or burgesses as they were called. One, by his dress, and by a certain authoritative look about him, was a man of power and influence, and he it was who replied.

'This evil wretch here whom we follow is a murderous knave, by name Richard Malbête,' he said. 'Our father was an old and doting man who, because he had ever dwelled in peace and quiet in his shop in Mercers Row, in our town of Pontefract, loved to hear tales of travel, and to speak to men who had fought and done warlike deeds. He fell in with this wretch here, who told many tales of his great adventures. Our father, John le Marchant, took this loose rascal into his house, much against the will and advice of us his sons. This Malbête, or Illbeast, as he rightly names himself, did slay our father, in a right subtle and wicked manner, and then fled with much gold upon him. We raised the hue and cry after him, and he took sanctuary in St Michael's church, and afterwards he did swear before the coroner to abjure and leave this realm, and to go to the port of Grimsby and there take ship. And we follow to see that he escape not.'

By the looks the five brothers gave the murderer it was evident that they would almost welcome any attempt he might make to escape, for then they would be justified, if he went but a step off the highway, in slaying him out of hand. There was nothing, really, to prevent them doing that now, for he was unarmed and there was no one by to protect him, but being law-abiding citizens they reverenced the oath which the murderer had taken.

Little John had not seen the robber when he had been disguised as a beggar and had fallen in with Robin, so that he did not recognise him. He looked at the brutal face of the man keenly, and noted the cruel and crafty glances which Malbête cast at the five brothers.

'I would counsel thee to take close heed of this rascal,' said Little John to the sons of John le Marchant. 'That evil face of his, I doubt not, hideth a brain that is full of guile and wile. Take heed lest by a trick he escape ye even now.'

The eldest brother, who had previously spoken, was a man unused to take advice, and resented the counsel of a man who looked to he no better than a woodman.

'I need no counsel to know what to do with a rogue,' he said stiffly. 'This felon shall have his life let from him ere he can hoodwink us.'

Little John laughed and said no more. When he and the knight had gone a little farther the latter said:

'I have seen that robber and murderer once before. He was taken up at Gisors for robbing in the very house where King Henry was sleeping. The camp provost condemned him to be hung forthwith, but I heard that by a trick he had escaped the hands of the camp marshals and got clean away. He is a man of a most evil life, and his mind is full of plots and crafty contrivings.'

'I knew it by his sly face,' said John, 'and I doubt not that one or more of the stiff-necked merchants behind him will pay with their lives for his escape.'

Nothing further happened to the two wayfarers until they reached the town of York just as daylight was dying from the skies. They were among the last to enter the city as the guard was shutting the huge gates. They went to a decent inn which the knight knew, where they supped and slept that night.

Next morning, in the chapter-house of St Mary's Abbey, were gathered the chief officers of the house. There was Abbot Robert, with proud curved lips, double chin, and fierce red face, and beside him on the bench was the prior, who was second in authority. He was a mild, good man, and did as much by kindness as the abbot did by his ways of harshness and tyranny.

Before them on a table were many parchments, for this was the day when tenants came to pay their rents or dues, and others came to appear in answer to some charge or demand made by the abbot. At the table were two monks who acted as clerks. On the right of the abbot sat one of the king's justices, who was travelling in that part of the kingdom, trying cases in the king's name. There were one or two knights also sitting there, together with the sheriff of York.

Many came in and paid their rents either in money or in goods; others came and complained of the way in which the abbot's bailiffs or stewards had oppressed them, and it was a wonder to hear how many manors held by the abbey seemed to have harsh bailiffs to rule them in the name of the abbot. To all such complaining the abbot gave little heed, though the good prior tried to make inquiry into the worse wrongs of which the poor freemen or villeins complained.

'They are all a pack of grumbling rascals,' said the abbot angrily at length. 'Save thy breath, prior, to say thy prayers, for I would rather leave my bailiffs to do as they think needful than meddle in matters of which I know little.'

'Nevertheless, when such great wrongs are charged against the stewards of the abbey,' said the prior, 'methinks that for the honour of the abbey and for the grace of the Holy Virgin after whom our house is named, strict inquiry should be made, and if our servants be shown to have acted without mercy they should be punished.'

'If things were left to thee, prior,' said the abbot mockingly, 'we should all go bare to give the rascally villeins all that they craved. Have done, and say no more. I am abbot, and while I am chief of this house I will do as it seems to me fit.'

Just then into the chapter-house strode a tall and fierce-looking man. He was dressed in half armour, having a hauberk on his body, with a sword slung by a belt about his middle. On his head of rough black hair was a hat of velvet, which he doffed as he entered. Behind him came his squire, bearing his helmet and a heavy mace. The abbot rose in his seat.

'Ha, Sir Niger,' he said with a laugh, 'so thou hast come as thou didst promise. Dost thou think the knight of Werrisdale will baulk us on this his last day of grace?'

'I think we may see him beg his bread of us today,' replied Sir Niger le Grym with a cruel laugh. 'We will see to it that he pays heavily for harbouring his rascal son, Alan-a-Dale, and if we cannot get at that wretched squire himself, we will make the father suffer in his stead.'

'I hear that his son hath joined that villainous robber and murderer, Robin Hood,' said the justice. 'Sheriff,' he went on, turning to that officer, 'you must take strong measures to root out that band of vipers who haunt Barnisdale. He hath not only, as I hear, slain Sir Ranulf of the Waste, but he hath burnt down his castle also.'

'Far be it from me, Sir Justice,' said the prior boldly, 'to take the part of so great a robber, but what he hath done hath been done by barons and lords of our county within this last year, and none of them ever received punishment from thee or from any of the king's justices.'

Sir Niger glared fiercely at the prior and muttered something under his red beard. The king's justice looked angrily at the speaker and could find nothing to say, for he knew it was true that when powerful knights such as de Belame and Sir Niger did evil, their wealth and their influence shielded them from punishment.

'This I know,' said the abbot hastily, 'that if Sir Herbrand of Werrisdale doth not come with four hundred pounds ere this day be done, he loses his land and is utterly disinherited.'

'It is still very early,' said the prior, 'for the day hath but half gone. It is a great pity that he should lose his land. His son slew the knight, Sir Ivo, in fair fight, and ye do Sir Herbrand much wrong so to oppress him. He is but a poor man, with no powerful friends to aid him.'

'Thou art ever against me, thou quarrelsome man,' said the abbot, and his heavy face went red with anger. 'I never say aught but thou dost contradict me.'

'I would have no more than justice done against high and low, knight or villein,' said the prior sturdily.

Just then there came in the high cellarer, the officer who looked to the provisions which had to be supplied to the abbey. He was so corpulent in body and red in face that it almost seemed that he partook more than was good of the food and drink over which he had control.

Ha! ha!' he said, and laughed in a fat wheezy way; 'this is the day when Sir Herbrand de Tranmire must lose his land if he pay

us not four hundred pounds. I'll dare swear that he is dead or
hanged, and will not come hither, and so we'll have his land.'

'I dare well undertake with thee,' said the justice, 'that the
knight will not come today. And as I did lend thee some of the
four hundred pounds, I count that I gain more than I sent thee,
seeing that the knight's lands are worth much more than what
they are pledged for.'

'Ye say right,' said the abbot. 'We be all sharers in the land of
the knight except Sir Niger, and he seeks revenge alone.'

'Come you now to meat,' said the cellarer, and he led the way
to the wide hall, where all the company sat down to a rich meal,
served on silver platters by pages in fine attire. They laughed
and jested as they ate, for they felt sure that the knight could not
pay the money he owed, and therefore they would all make a
great profit out of his land.

In the middle of their feasting there came the knight himself
into the hall. He looked sad and sorrowful, and was dressed not
in the rich clothes which Robin had given him, but in his old and
worn garments. Behind him came Little John, clothed like a
poor squire, in patched and sailed jerkin and ragged hose.

'God save you all!' said the knight, kneeling with one knee on
the floor.

The abbot looked at him, and gladdened to see how mean and
poor he looked. 'I have come on the day thou didst fix for me,
father,' went on the knight.

'Hast thou brought my money?' asked the abbot in a harsh
voice.

'Not one penny,' said the knight, and shook his head sadly.

The abbot laughed. 'Thou art an unlucky fellow!' he said,
mocking him. Then raising his flagon of wine, he said to the
justice:

'Sir Justice, drink to me, for I think we shall have all we hoped
to get.'

Then, having drained the flagon, the abbot turned and said to
the knight:

'What dost thou do here, then, if thou hast not brought my
money?'

'To pray you, father, for a little further time,' said the knight
in a sad voice. 'I have striven hard to find the money, and if thou

wouldst give me but four more months, I shall be able to make up the sum due to thee.'

'The time is over, my man,' said the justice in a scornful voice. 'As thou hast not the money, thou wilt no longer have thy land.'

'Oh, for sweet charity's sake,' prayed the knight, 'do thou be my friend, Sir Justice, and shield me from these that would strip me to see me starve.'

'I am a friend of the abbot's,' said the justice coldly, 'and I will see naught but justice done between thee. If thou hast not the money, thou must lose thy land. 'Tis the law, and I will see it fulfilled, hark ye!'

Then the knight turned to the sheriff. 'Good Sir Sheriff,' he said, 'do ye plead with the abbot on my behalf to grant me a little longer time.'

'Nay,' said the sheriff, 'I will not – I may not.'

At length the knight, still kneeling, turned to the abbot.

'I pray thee, good Sir Abbot,' he pleaded, 'be my friend and grant me grace. Hold ye my land until I make up the amount which is due to thee. I will be true man to thee in all things, and serve thee rightfully.'

'Now by the rood,' said the abbot, and he was furiously angry, 'thou art wasting thy breath to ask such foolish prayers. I tell thee thou mayest get other land where thou wilt, but thy land is mine now, and never more shalt thou possess it.'

'By my faith,' replied the knight, 'and he laughed bitterly; 'thus is tested indeed the friendship which thou didst once profess to me!' The abbot looked evilly upon the knight, for he did not like to be reminded of such things in the presence of the enemies of Sir Herbrand.

'Out upon thee, traitorous and cozening man!' he cried. 'Thou didst make the bond to pay me on this day, and thou hast not the money. Out! thou false Knight! Speed thou out of my hall!'

'Thou liest, abbot!' cried the good knight, and got up from his knees. 'I was never a false knight, but ever a man of honour. In many lands have I fought, and in jousts and tournaments have I borne a lance before King Henry and the kings of France and Germany. And ever in all places did I get praise until I came hither in thy hall, Sir Abbot!'

The justice was moved at the noble knight's words, and he

thought the abbot had been harsh and oppressive. Therefore he turned to Abbot Robert and said:

'What wilt thou give him beyond the four hundred pounds so that he release all claim on his land to thee?'

Sir Niger looked black, and growled at the justice in his beard. 'Give him naught!' he said in a low tone to the abbot.

'I'll give him a hundred pounds!' said the abbot.

'Nay, 'tis worth two hundred – six hundred pounds in all,' urged the justice.

'Nay, by the rood!' cried the knight, and came to the foot of the table, and with flashing eyes he looked forward from one to other of his enemies. 'I know thy plots against me,' he went on. 'Ye foul-living monks desire my land, for thou art ever yearning to add acre to acre, and to grind down the souls and bodies of thy poor villeins to get more wealth from them. Thou, Sir Niger, wouldst revenge thyself of the death of thy kinsman, whom my brave son slew in fair and open combat. But chiefly thou desirest to have vengeance upon me because thou art not bold enough to seek for Robin Hood, who aided my son against thee. Therefore thou wouldst ruin and oppress me who cannot fight against the evil power of your Wrangby lords. But I tell thee, have a care how far thou goest. As for thee, Sir Abbot, here are thy four hundred pounds!'

With that he drew a bag from his breast, untied the mouth, and emptied the golden coins upon the table.

'Have thy gold, abbot,' he said mockingly, 'and much good may it do thy immortal soul.'

The prior came forward with two monks, and having counted the gold and found it was the proper amount, the prior made out a quittance and handed it to the knight. Meanwhile the abbot sat still, dumbfounded and full of shame, and would eat no more. The faces of the others also showed how bitterly they felt the way in which the knight had turned the tables upon them. Sir Niger le Grym, with a red and angry face, chewed his nether lip and darted fierce glances at the knight, who stood boldly meeting his gaze.

'Sir Abbot,' said the knight, waving the receipt in their faces, 'now have I kept my word, and I have paid ye to the full. Now shall I have my land again for aught that ye can say or do.'

'I pray thee, good Sir Abbot, be my friend'

With that he turned and strode out of the door, followed by Little John. Getting on their horses, they went back to their inn, where they changed their clothes, and having dined, rode out of the town and took the road toward the west, for the knight desired much to reach home swiftly, to tell his dear wife how well he had sped, thanks to the noble kindness of Robin Hood.

'Sir Knight,' said Little John, as they rode together through the forest-ways a few miles from York, 'I liked not the evil look upon that knight's face who sat at table with the abbot. 'Twere well to take heed against a sudden onfall or an ambush in a secret place.'

'I fear not Sir Niger le Grym,' replied the knight, 'nor any other knight so he come against me singly. But the Wrangby knights are full of treachery, and seldom fight except in twos or threes. Therefore thy words are wise and I will take heed. Do thou leave me now, good woodman, for I would not take thee so far out of thy way.'

'Nay,' said Little John, 'I may not leave thee in the forest. My master said I was to be thy squire, and I would stay with thee in case thou needest me until thou hast reached thy own lands.'

'Thou art a faithful fellow,' said Sir Herbrand, 'and I would that I could reward thee. But as thou knowest, I am bare of money and jewels.'

'I need no such rewards, I thank thee, Sir Knight,' replied Little John. 'I was ever ready to go out of my way for the chance of a good fight, and I think we shall have a few knocks ere we have gone far, or I know not a murderous look in a man's eyes.'

Little John felt sure that Sir Niger le Grym had meditated treachery when Sir Herbrand had put down the money, and he did not doubt that at some likely spot the knight would be set upon and perhaps killed in revenge.

As they rode along both kept a sharp look-out when the road narrowed and ran through thick woods, but they cleared the forest, and towards the end of the afternoon they found themselves upon the desolate moors, and there had as yet been no sign of their enemy. But now they were in the wild country, where the power of Sir Isenbart, Sir Niger, and their evil companions was strongest, and the two riders pushed on swiftly, hoping to reach the town of Stanmore before nightfall.

In this solitary country they met few people except a shepherd or two, or a couple of villeins now and then passing homewards from some errand. Once they saw a hawking-party in the distance, and another time they met a band of merchants with their baggage ponies. At length they began to mount a long and steep ascent towards a high ridge called Cold Kitchen Rigg, at the top of which was a clump of fir trees, their heads all bent one way by the strong wind which seemed always to blow up there.

As they pushed their jaded horses up the last few yards, suddenly from between the bushes beside the trees came the sound of a whizzing arrow, and next moment a bolt rattled harmlessly against Little John's buckler, which hung beside his knee, and then fell to the ground. Glancing down at it, he saw it had a short black shaft, and knew at once who it was that thus warned him. He called to the knight, who rode a few paces before him, ' 'Ware the trees, Sir Knight!' But even as he spoke, out from the firs came a horseman in mail armour, with lance set, and rushed at Sir Herbrand. At the same time, from the other side of the narrow road, another horsed knight dashed out with a huge mace in his hand and came towards Little John. The road was steep, and they thought that the speed with which they came down the track would without doubt dash the two riders to the ground. But both the knight and John were prepared in a measure for the attack. Sir Herbrand had drawn his sword as he heard the arrow whiz from the bush, and now dressed his shield, so that when the first knight sped against him he parried the lance with his buckler, and as his opponent, foiled of his blow, swept helplessly by him, he brought his sword down upon the other's neck with such force that the man rolled from the saddle. The horse careered madly down the hill, and the knight's spur catching in the stirrup, he was dragged along the road, his body leaping and bumping over the rough places.

Next moment, however, a third knight had come swiftly from among the trees, and had attacked Sir Herbrand with his sword so fiercely that, on the steep road, it required all the good knight's strength to keep his horse from falling, and at the same time to ward off his enemy's shrewd blows.

As for Little John, he was in hard case. So fiercely had the second knight dashed at him that John scarcely had time to dress his buckler, and half the blow from the descending mace was received upon his arm, numbing it so that it seemed almost powerless. With drawn sword, however, John did his best to defend himself; but the stranger being mounted on a stronger horse, as well as being protected by full armour, John could but just hold his own, while he could do little hurt to his opponent. Fiercely the blows from the heavy mace came down upon the yeoman's buckler, and the stranger pressed his horse so violently against the weaker animal which John bestrode, that John knew that it would be but a matter of a few moments before he would be overthrown upon the sloping road.

Suddenly the knight checked in his assault and seemed to shiver; a hollow groan came from the headpiece, the mace fell from the lifted hand, and the mailed figure swayed in the saddle. John looked and saw the end of a short black arrow jutting from the armpit of his enemy. At such close range had it been shot that it stood deep in the flesh. Little John looked around and saw a hazel bush beside the way, and from among its leaves the round, tanned face of Ket the Trow looked out, its usual good-nature now masked by a terribly savage look of triumph.

With a clatter the knight pitched to the ground, and his horse stood shaking beside the corpse of its master. Seeing the fall of his comrade, the third knight, who was fighting with Sir Herbrand, suddenly put spurs to his horse and dashed away through the trees. Rushing down the slope beyond, he could be seen riding swiftly over the moor in the direction of Wrangby Castle. Sir Herbrand, who was wounded, forbore to pursue his enemy.

Not so Ket the Trow. With a stealthy movement he ran across the road and was swallowed up in the tall bracken fronds.

'Who is that?' cried Sir Herbrand. 'Is it one of the men of these felon knights who have attacked us?'

'Nay,' said Little John; 'it is one to whom I owe my life today, for if his arrow had not ended this rogue's life here, I think I should have been overborne.'

'Who is this knight?' said Sir Herbrand, and getting off his horse he went and lifted the dead man's visor. 'By Holy Mary!' said the knight, 'it is Sir Niger himself!'

'Then there is one less of that evil crew,' said John, 'or perhaps two, for I doubt not that he on whose neck thou didst beat is dead by now, for if he was alive when he fell, his horse hath killed him by now.'

'Do you ride back, John,' said Sir Herbrand, 'and if the knight and his horse are to be found, bring them back, for I would give him proper burial. Moreover, by all the laws of combat, his harness and his horse are mine.'

John did as the knight bade him, and having retraced his steps about half a mile he found the horse quietly cropping the grass by the wayside, the body of its rider being a few yards away, the spur having become loosened when the horse had ceased its wild running. He lifted the dead man on the horse, and went back to Sir Herbrand, and leading the two captured horses, each with its dead master on its back, the knight and Little John pursued their way, and in an hour came to a wayside chapel. There they entered in, but the hermit who was its guardian was absent. Having stripped the armour from the two dead knights, Sir Herbrand laid the bodies decently before the altar, and then with Little John kneeled down and said a prayer.

Afterwards, taking the two horses with the armour piled upon them, they pursued their way to their night's lodging-place, and the next day Sir Herbrand reached his home, and was fondly welcomed by his wife and by all his people. When he had told them how he had been befriended by Robin Hood, his dame and her household made much of Little John, and wished him to stay with them for many days. But on the second day John said he must return to his master, and finding that he would not longer stay, Dame Judith made him up a good bag of meat and gave him a gold ring, and the knight made him a present of a strong horse, and gave him in gold the value of Sir Niger's horse and armour, which he said belonged by right to Little John. Thereafter the good outlaw bade farewell, and Sir Herbrand, at parting, shook his hand and said:

'Little John, thou and thy master have been good friends to me and my son, and may evil betide me if ever I forget thy good fellowship and aid. Tell thy master that within a year and a day, God willing, I will seek him and bring the money he hath so nobly lent me on the surety of Our Lady, and with that money will I bring a present. And tell him, also, from me, that if, as I think is likely, evil days come upon our dear land through the wrong and despite which Duke John beareth to his brother King Richard of the Lion Heart, there will be need for a few good and valiant men like thy master. And if he should at any time require my aid, tell him I can arm a hundred brave fellows to follow me.'

John promised to give the message faithfully, and so departed and reached Barnisdale without mishap.

Now, on the evening of the day on which the knights had set upon Sir Herbrand and Little John, the third knight, sorely faint and wounded, rode up to the gate of Wrangby Castle, which poor men called Evil Hold, and in a weak voice shouted to the gate-guard to lower the bridge across the moat. When this had been done he rode into the courtyard. Without dismounting he rode forward into the very hall where Sir Isenbart and his fellows were at their wine.

' 'Tis Sir Bernard of the Brake!' said the knights, looking up amazed at the swaying figure on horseback which came up to the very verge of the high seat.

'Where are Sir Niger and Sir Peter?' thundered Sir Isenbart, his fear of the truth making him rage.

'Dead!' said the knight, and they could see the white face within the helm. Give me wine – I – I am spent.'

A goblet of wine was handed to him, while men unloosed his helm and took it from off his head. Then they could see how he had been sorely wounded, but his great strength had kept him up. He drank off the wine and held out the vessel for more.

'The knight slew Sir Peter,' went on Bernard of the Brake, 'and the knave, I suppose, slew Sir Niger, for I saw him fall to the ground.'

All the knights looked gloomily at each other, and said no word.

Just then a man-at-arms from the gate-guard came running into the hall. In his hand he bore an arrow, which he laid on the table before Sir Isenbart.

'This, lord, hath just been shot through the bars of the portcullis, and narrowly missed my head. We could not see who shot it in.'

Sir Isenbart glanced at the short black arrow and his face went dark with rage. Along its shaft were notches, seven in number, which were stained red.

'Quick!' shouted Sir Isenbart, 'the wretch that shot it cannot have gone far. Out with you and search for him and bring him to me.'

There was bustle and noise for a few moments as some score of men-at-arms seized their weapons, and knights donned their armour and rode out, thundering over the drawbridge. There was a cleared space of a great extent before the gate, so that it was a marvel that anyone could have crept up unobserved by the men on watch at the slits over the drawbridge. The horsemen and footmen scoured the country for half a mile round, but not a sight or sound could they see of any lurking bowmen.

Darkness soon put an end to their search, and by ones and twos they returned to report their non-success. When the last had straggled across the drawbridge, the latter, with many creakings and shrieks as the rusty chains came over the beam, was hauled up for the night, and the portcullis ran down with a clang that shook the tower. Then, from beneath a little bush that overhung the outer edge of the ditch near the gate crept a small, lithe form. Slowly and with great care it drew itself out of the water, so that no splash could be heard by the men in the room of the gate-guard. It was Ket the Trow, who had been set by Robin Hood to keep watch on the Evil Hold. His bow and arrows he had kept dry by holding them in the bush above him.

He looked up at the black mass of the castle rising high and wide on the other side of the ditch. Light from cressets or torches shone out from the arrow slits here and there, and the gleam of a headpiece flashed up as a man-at-arms passed or repassed, walking on his watch. For some time Ket gazed, an arrow notched to his taut string, hoping that some face would come to look out from some near aperture, at which he might get another shot; But time passed, and no opportunity offered. He loosened his string, and turned reluctantly away.

'Seven have gone,' he muttered, 'but many are left. As they slew, so shall they be slain – without ruth, without pity.'

He trotted slowly away, looking back now and then at the dark bulk with little points of light here and there. For a mile he thus half ran until he came to where the forest began. Then in the darkness he passed through the deep gloom between the great trees until he came to one which was a giant among giants. With the stealth of a wild animal he looked about him and listened for a long time; then with an almost incredible swiftness he climbed up the trunk by means of tiny projections of knot and bark here and there until he disappeared in the massy leaves overhead. Higher and higher he mounted into a world where there was nothing but dark masses of leaves which murmured in the night wind, which was purer and stronger the higher he mounted. At length he reached a place where three great limbs jutted from the trunk, and in their midst was a space heaped with sweet-smelling fern fronds. Ket turned and looked forth to the way by which he had come. He was over the tops of all the other trees below him, which swayed and whispered like softly moving waves as the wind stirred them. Looking forth from among the leaves of the giant oak from where he sat in his lair, Ket could see far away the dark mass of the Evil Hold rising against the black sky behind it. A few lights still gleamed here and there, but every moment these were becoming fewer.

Casting off his wet clothes, Ket hung them securely on a limb to dry; then he wriggled deep into the great heap of fern, and having drawn food and drink from a hiding-place in the tree he munched and drank, his eyes never leaving the castle. When all the lights but those over the gate were darkened, he curled himself up in the scented fronds and fell to sleep instantly, and the murmur with which the wind strained through the leaves all about him was a lullaby that softly sang through the short summer night.

CHAPTER SEVEN

How Robin Hood Rescued Will Stuteley
and Did Justice on Richard Illbeast,
the Beggar-Spy

It was daybreak. A bitter wind blew down the forest ways, tearing the few remaining leaves from the wintry trees, and driving those upon the ground in great wreaths and eddies into nooks and corners. The dawn came with dull, low light over the forest, and seemed never to penetrate some of the deeper places, where the thickets of holly grew closer, or the bearded grey moss on giant oaks grew long.

Will of Stuteley, as he walked along a path, looked keenly this way and that into the gloomy tunnels on either side, for during the last three days he had seen a man, dressed as a palmer, lurking and glancing in a very unpalmer-like manner, just about this place, which the outlaws called Black Wood. Will was warmly dressed in a long brown capote, or cloak, which reached almost to his feet, with a hood which covered his head.

The first snows of the winter had already fallen, and most of Robin Hood's band had gone into their winter quarters. While frost and snow lay over the land, there was little travelling done in those days, and therefore a great part of the outlaws had gone to live with kinsmen or poor cottars in out-of-the-way places either in the forest or in villages not far distant. For a time they would dress as peasants, help in the little work that was done, and with this and what animals they trapped or caught, pay for their warmth and shelter until the spring came again.

Robin, with about a dozen of his principal men, lodged either in the secret caves which were to be found in many places through the wide forests, or, sometimes, one or other of the well-to-do forest yeomen, such as Piers the Lucky, Alan-a-Dale's foster brother, would invite Robin and his twelve to stay the winter in his hall. This year Sir Walter de Beauforest had invited him to pass the winter at a grange, or fortified barn, which lay in the forest not far from Sir Walter's manor-house at Cromwell, where Alan-a-Dale and his wife, the fair Alice, now lived in great happiness.

Robin had accepted Sir Walter's invitation, but if the weather was open he never stayed long in one place, and now he was living in a secret bower which he and his men had made at Barrow Down, which lay a few miles east of Mansfield, in a desolate piece of country where were many standing stones, old earthworks and barrows, or graves of the ancient dead. It was in one of these latter that Robin and his men now lived, for they had scooped out the interior of it and made it snug and habitable.

Every morning Will Stuteley and others of the band, having broken their fast in the Barrow, would walk out over a certain distance round their place of hiding, to find whether there were any traces of their enemies having approached during the last few hours. The ground was scanned for strange footmarks, the bushes and trees for broken twigs, and the outlaws were as keen-sighted as Indians, and as experienced in all the sights and sounds which should show them whether strangers had been in the neighbourhood during the hours of the night.

Suddenly Will stopped in the path down which he walked, and looked at the ground. Then, after a keen glance round among the hazels and young oaks which grew near, he knelt and examined a little hollow where in the springtime storm water would run. There was the distinct mark of a slender foot in the yielding earth. He looked further, and found two others of the same marks. They were quite freshly made, for the edges were keenly shown. Indeed, he felt sure that the person who had passed that way could not be far off. But who was it? The marks were those of a young lad or even of a girl. Whoever it was, the person was poor, for he could see marks which showed that the sole of one shoe was broken badly.

Stealthily he crept along picking up the trail here and there. He had proceeded thus some fifty yards, finding that the footsteps led deep among some brambles, when all at once he stopped and listened. He heard a low sobbing somewhere in among the thickest part of the bushes. Very carefully he stole in the direction of the sound, making no noise, until as he turned about a tall hazel tree he saw the figure of a girl a little way before him. She was picking berries from the bramble before her, and placing them in an old worn straw poke or basket which she carried.

As she plucked the berries she wept. Will could see the tears falling down her cheeks, yet it was with restraint that she sobbed, as if she feared to be heard. He saw how her hands were torn and bleeding from the brambles, and that her feet, pushed into her shoes, were uncovered and were blue with the frost.

He made a movement. She turned at the noise, her eyes wide with terror, her face white. Crushing the basket to her breast, she came and threw herself at the feet of Will.

'Oh,' she said in a weak, pitiable voice, 'slay me now, and do not seek my father! Slay me, and look no further! He is nigh to death, and cannot speak!'

Her tears were stayed now, her hands were clasped and raised in appeal, and in the childish face, so thin and wan, was a look that seemed to say that the child had known a terrible sorrow and now looked for nothing but death. She was a Jewess, as Will was quick to note.

The honest woodman smiled, as being the quickest way to cheer the girl. It went to the old outlaw's heart to see such sorrow in the child's eyes and voice.

'My little lass,' he said in his kindly voice, 'I mean thee no harm. Why should I harm thee, clemmed with the cold as thou art? And why art thou culling those berries? Thy poor starved body craves better food than that.'

He took her hands and lifted her up, and the child looked at him bewildered and dazed, as if she did not realise that kind words had been spoken where she had looked for brutal speech and action. She peered into Will's face, and her looks softened.

'You – you are not – you do not know the man – the man Malbête?' she stammered.

'Malbête?' said Will, and frowned. He remembered what Robin had told them of this man, and had heard from wandering men of other crimes and cruelties which this robber and murderer had committed. 'Poor lass,' he said; 'is that wretch thy enemy, too?'

'Yes, sir, of my poor father!' said the girl, and her voice trembled. 'My father fled from the massacre of our people at York – thou knowest of it?'

'Ay,' said Will, and his brow became black and his eyes flashed in anger at the memory of the dreadful deed, when many innocent Jews had been baited by evil knights and the rabble, and having shut themselves up in the castle, had killed their wives and children and afterwards themselves rather than fall into the hands of the 'Christians'.

'What happened to thee and thy father?' asked Will.

'We hid in the castle until all the slaying was over,' replied the girl, 'and then a kindly man did get us forth, and we fled secretly. My father wished to go to Nottingham, where there are some of our race who would aid us if they knew we were in need, but we have starved through these forests, and oh, sir, if you are a good man as you appear, save my father! He lies near here, and I fear – I fear whether – help may not be too late. But, oh, betray us not!'

'Take me to him, poor lass,' said Will, and his kindly tone and look dissipated whatever suspicion still lingered in the heart of the poor little Jewess.

She led the way through the almost impenetrable bushes until they reached a chalky cliff, and here in a large cave, the opening of which was screened by hazel thickets, she showed him her father, an old and white-haired man, dressed in a poor gaberdine torn by brambles and soiled by mire, lying on some bracken. The girl stood trembling as she looked from Will to her father and back again, as if, even now, she dreaded that she may have betrayed her dearest possession into the hands of a cruel enemy.

The old man awakened at their entry, opened his eyes, and in an instant the girl was on her knees beside him, her hands stroking his, and her eyes looking fondly into his face.

'Ah, little Ruth,' said the old man, gazing fondly into her eyes, 'I fear, dear, I cannot rise just yet. I am stiff, but it will pass soon, it will pass. And then we will go on. We shall reach the town in a few hours, and then my little Ruth will have food and fitting raiment. Your cheeks are pale and thin, dear, for you have hungered and suffered. But soon – ah, but whom have we here?

Who is this? O Ruth, Ruth, are we betrayed?'

In the gloom of the cave he had not at first noticed the outlaw, and the despair with which he uttered the last few words showed with what terror his mind was filled for his daughter's sake. Will felt that this was a brave old man who would not reveal the suffering he felt to his daughter, but though he was himself very sick, yet buoyed up her courage.

'Have no fear, master,' said Will, bending down on one knee, so that his eyes looked into the old Jew's face. 'If I can aid thee and thy daughter I will gladly do so.'

'I thank thee, woodman,' said the Jew, and his voice trembled; 'it is not for myself I fear, but for this my little maid, my one ewe lamb. She hath suffered sights and woes such as no child should see or know, and if she were safe I would be content.'

Tears fell down the poor old Jew's face. In his present state of starvation and weakness he felt that he had not long to live; but the greatest anguish was to think that if he died his little daughter would be left desolate and friendless.

'What ye both need,' said Will, his homely mind grasping the situation at once, 'is food and warmth. I can give ye a little food now, but for warmth I must ask the counsel of my master.'

Saying which, Will drew forth from his food-pouch some slices of bread and venison, which he gave to the girl, bidding her eat sparingly. But the girl instantly began to cut up the bread and meat into tiny pieces, and with these she fed her father before she touched the food herself. Though both she and her father had had little food for two days, they ate now with great restraint, and very slowly.

Afterwards Will offered them his pilgrim's leather flask, and when they had drunk some of the good wine which it contained, it was a joy to see how their eyes brightened, and their cheeks began to redden.

'Little Ruth,' said the old man, when they had returned the flask to Will, 'help me to get upon my knees.'

When this had been done, with the aid of the outlaw, the girl also knelt, and to Will's great discomfiture the Jew began to pray very fervently, giving thanks to God for having brought to them him that had delivered them out of death and misery. He called down such blessings on the head of Will the Bowman that the worthy fellow, for all that the light in the cave was but meagre, did not know where to look. When they had finished, Ruth seized the outlaw's hand and kissed it again and again, while the tears poured down her cheeks, but her heart was too full to say a word of all the gratitude she felt.

'Now,' said Will gruffly, 'enough of these thanks and tears. Ye must bide here while I go to take counsel of my master what is best to be done.'

'Who is thy master, brave woodman?' asked the Jew.

'He is Robin Hood,' replied Will.

'I have heard of him as a good man,' said the old man. 'Though an outlaw, he hath more pity and justice, as I hear tell, than many of those who are within the law. Do ye go to him, good outlaw,' he went on, 'with the greeting of Reuben of Stamford, and say that if he will aid me to get to my kinsmen of Nottingham, he shall have the gratitude of me and my people for ever, and our aid wherever he shall desire it.'

The old Jew spoke with dignity, as if used to giving commands, and Will answered:

'I will tell him; but if he aids thee, 'twill be for no hope of thy gratitude or thy gold, but because it is always in his heart to help those in wretchedness.'

'Bravely and proudly spoken, Sir Outlaw,' said Reuben; 'and if thy master is as kindly as thou art, I know he will not leave us to starve and perish miserably.'

Will thereupon set off back to Barrow Down, and arriving at the big mound wherein the outlaws dwelled, he found Robin there and told him of the Jew.

'Thou hast done rightly, Will,' said the outlaw. 'Go thou with two horses, and bring the Jew and his daughter to the Lynchet Lodge hereby, and I will question them concerning this ruffian, Richard Illbeast. I have heard of his evil deeds at York, and I think he is not far from Nottingham.'

It was done as Robin had commanded, and Reuben and Ruth were lodged in a secret hut on the slope of Wearyall Hill, not far from where the outlaws were staying. Both father and daughter were very weak, and the old Jew was much wasted as the result of his sufferings, but with generous food, and the warmth of good clothes and a huge fire, a few days saw them stronger in health

The girl was on her knees beside him

and better in spirits. Their gratitude to Robin was unbounded, but it was expressed more by their shining eyes than by words.

When the old man felt stronger Robin asked him to tell how he had fallen into the wretched state in which Will Stuteley had found him, and Reuben willingly complied.

'Thou hast heard, doubtless, good outlaw,' said the Jew, 'that when the great and brave King Richard was crowned at Westminster last autumn, the rabble of that great city did turn upon the Jews and sack their houses and slay some of my poor people. And your king did punish the ringleaders of the mob who slew and robbed our people, by hanging some and branding others with hot irons. But when, a short month ago, he left the country with his knights and a great army, to go to Palestine upon the Crusade, thou knowest that in many towns the rioting against us began again. Many knights and lords were gathering to depart for the Crusade, and a great mob collected with them. And because many of my kinsmen had lent the knights money, some of the more evil of them excited the mob to burn our homes and to rob us. Such evil deeds took place, as doubtless thou hast heard, in Stamford, Lynn, and Lincoln. I was dwelling at Lincoln, but I travelled to York and so escaped the pillage for a time. Now it chanced that a kinsman of mine, Rabbi Eliezer, a chief man among us, had lent much money to a baron named Alberic de Wisgar, a wasteful and a tyrannous lord. He laid a plot with others against the Jews of York, to plunder them and to destroy the records of the debts which they owed to my kinsmen. They plundered the house of a Rabbi whom they had slain in London, and fearing that the same fate would befall us, for safety we fled with our wives and children into the castle of York. We were there beset by a great mob of Crusaders, apprentices, and country folk, and he that was their leader was an evil man in the company of the Lord of Wisgar. He was named Richard Malbête, or Illbeast, and with much fury he egged on the people to besiege the castle and to endeavour to drag us out. We had no weapons, but with our naked hands we tore the stones from the walls inside and kept back the rabble with these. For three days, without food and without weapons, we beat them away, but when they brought a high engine against us and made it ready for the next morning, then we knew that we could hold out no longer. Never, while mine eyes can weep, nor my mind recall the past, shall I forget the grief, the terror, and the sorrow of that night. Long time we talked, counselling what should be done, though in our hearts most knew that there was but one way for us to take. At length Rabbi Eliezer arose amongst us, and said, "O men of Israel, God – of whom no man asketh, Why dost Thou permit this? – God hath commanded us to lay down our lives for His law, and behold death standeth at the door. Now, therefore, let us freely offer up our lives to God who gave them, as many of our people have done in times past, worthily delivering themselves out of great tribulations." '

For a little while the memory of that night of sadness over-powered the old man; tears rolled down his cheek, and he could not proceed. The little girl Ruth was also weeping softly, but at the same time she strove to comfort her father.

'Do not weep for them, my father,' she said, while she wept bitterly herself. 'God took them, and though they suffered death at the hands of those they loved, they are now in the bosom of Abraham for evermore.'

'Sir,' said the old Jew, 'she says truly. When Rabbi Eliezer had finished speaking we went apart and said no more. I cannot speak of all that then took place. All of us burned or destroyed such goods as we had with us, and those who had no hope slew their dear ones and then slew themselves. But I could not bring myself to do the same. I wished not life for myself, for rather would I have died; but for the sake of this my little daughter I found a place of hiding in the castle, in the hope that when, as would surely happen, the rabble broke in, I might be able at least to find a way for her to escape, though I had no hope of being spared myself. Next morning those who had not been willing to die opened the gates and went forth begging to be baptised, thinking thus to escape the fury of the multitude. From where we lay hidden I saw all that took place. The evil man, Richard Illbeast, came to the first Jew, Ephraim ben Abel, who kneeled before him, pleading for his life. "Where are the treasures of the Jews?" he asked. "Burned and destroyed," said Ephraim. "Where is Rabbi Eliezer?" he then demanded. "He and all but those who are here with me have slain themselves and their families," replied Ephraim. "Then die thou likewise!" said Illbeast, and at

the words the rabble slew the kneeling Jews and spared not one.
Then the mob poured into the castle, and we lay expecting every
moment to be found and dragged forth. After some time they
left the castle and rushed away to the cathedral, where, as thou
knowest, the king keeps the records of the loans made by my
people to the Christians in those parts, and those parchments
they burned utterly, so that now Alberic of Wisgar and the other
evil knights are free of all their debts.'

'How got you free?' asked Little John, who, with Will the
Bowman, Scarlet, and Arthur-a-Bland, were listening with Robin
Hood.

'God, in answer to our prayers, softened the heart of a
man-at-arms, who discovered us, but would not betray us for
pity of our sufferings. He got food for us and soldiers' cloaks to
disguise us, and on the second night he took us and let us out of
the town by a privy gate, and directed us on our road to
Nottingham.'

'Know you what befell those ruffian knights and robbers?'
asked Robin.

'The soldier, whom God reward for his noble heart,' said the
old man, 'told us that all had fled the town fearing the anger of
the king's officers. The knights had quickly gone forward to the
Crusade, while of the rabble and the robbers some had fled to
Scotland or taken to the forests, and others lay hid in the town.
And he said further that the king's justices would visit the ill-
doing heavily upon the town, and that already the sheriff and
principal merchants were quaking for fear. And now, Sir Outlaw,' continued Reuben, 'I have a boon to ask of thee. I have a
daughter and a son in Nottingham, to whom we were hastening.
They grieve for us as dead, and I would crave that you let one of
your men go to their house and tell them that we are safe, and
that we will be with them when it shall please you to let us go,
and I am strong enough to set forth.'

'Surely,' said Robin, 'that shall be done. Who will go of you
and take the message to the Jew's people? What do you say,
Will, as 'twas you who found them?'

'I will go with a good will,' said Will Stuteley. 'Give me thy
message and tell me where I may find thy kinsfolk, and I will set
out forthwith.'

Both Reuben and Ruth were warm in their thanks, and having given Will the necessary directions and messages, Will departed to dress himself in a disguise which would prevent his being recognised by any of the citizens who may have seen him when they had been required to pay toll to outlaws when passing through the forest.

That afternoon, therefore, a pilgrim in his long dark robe, his feet in ragged shoes, a scallop shell on his bonnet and a stout staff in his hand, might have been seen passing through Bridlesmith postern gate an hour before sunset, when the gates would close for the night. He took his way through the streets with a slow stride as befitted a pilgrim who had travelled far and was weary.

Will the Bowman did not think that there was any likelihood of his being recognised in his disguise, but though he seemed to keep his eyes bent humbly to the ground, he looked about keenly now and then to pick up landmarks, so as to know that he was going the right way to the house of Silas ben Reuben, one of the chief men in the Jewry of Nottingham, to whom he was to take the message from the old Jew.

At length Will entered the street of the Jewry, and began counting the number of doors from the corner, as he had been told to do by Reuben, since he was not to excite attention by asking anyone for the house. The outlaw noticed that while several of the house doors were open, through which he could see women at work and children playing, others were fast locked and their shutters closed, as if the dwellers feared that what had happened to the Jews in other towns might happen to them also.

When at length he came to the ninth house, he knocked at the door, which was barred, and waited.

A wicket in the door was opened and a man's dark eyes peered out.

'What is it thou wantest?' he asked.

'I wish to see Silas ben Reuben,' replied Will; 'I have a message for him.'

'What secret words or sign hast thou that thou art not a traitor, who would do to me and mine as has been done to others of our people?' came the stern reply through the wicket.

'I say to thee these words,' went on the outlaw, and said certain

Hebrew words which he had been told by Reuben.

Instantly the face disappeared from the wicket, bolts were drawn, and the door swung open. 'Enter, friend,' said the Jew, a short, sturdily built man. The outlaw entered, and the door was barred behind him. Then the Jew led him into an inner room, and turning said:

'I am he whom thou seekest. Say on.'

'I come to tell thee,' said the outlaw, 'that thy father, Reuben of Stamford, and thy sister Ruth, are safe and well.'

'Now, thanks be to God,' said the man, and clasping his hands, he bowed his head and murmured words of prayer in some foreign tongue.

'Tell me how thou didst learn this,' he said when he had finished his prayer; 'and where they are, and how soon I may see them?'

Thereupon the outlaw told Silas the Jew the whole story of his discovery of little Ruth and her father, and of their sufferings as related by the old man. When he had finished the Jew thanked him for his kindness to Reuben and Ruth, and then went into another room. When he returned he bore in his hand a rich baldrick or belt, of green leather, with a pattern worked upon it of pearls and other precious stones.

'Thy kindness is beyond recompense,' he said; 'but I would have thee accept this from me as a proof of my thanks to thee.'

'I thank thee, Jew,' said Will, 'but 'tis too rich a gift for me. It befits my master more. But if thou wouldst make a gift to me, give me a Spanish knife if thou hast one, for they are accounted of the best temper and make throughout Christendom.'

'I will willingly give thy master this baldrick if he will take it of me,' said the Jew, 'and thou shalt have the best Spanish knife in my store.'

He thereupon fetched such a knife and presented it to the outlaw, who tried the keen blade, and found that it was of the finest make.

It was becoming dark now, and the outlaw wished if possible to leave the town before the gates were shut. Arrangements, however, had to be settled with the Jew as to how and when he would send horses and men to meet Reuben and Ruth at a spot where Robin Hood and his men would take them from their present hiding-place. It was quite dark by the time all things were settled, and the Jew wished Will to stay the night with him, saying there was no one else in the house with him, as he had sent his wife, his sister, and his children into a place of greater safety for fear of the rabble.

'I thank thee, Jew,' said the outlaw, 'but I would liefer sleep at a place I wot of, which is near the gate, so that I may slip out o' the town at the break of day when they first open.'

As the outlaw went along the narrow street of the Jewry after leaving the house of Silas, two men walking together passed him silently, looking at him furtively. They did not seem to have the dress of Jews, and he wondered at the silence of their footsteps. He slowed his own steps to allow them to get farther ahead of him, but they also went more slowly, and kept at the distance of six paces before him. One of them looked swiftly behind from time to time. He knew then that they watched him, and that either because they knew he was of Robin's band, or because he had visited the Jew's house, they meant harm to him.

As he thought thus, he gripped the haft of his Spanish knife and stopped, determined to sell his life dearly if they also stopped and turned round upon him. At the same moment he felt a hand upon his arm, and a voice whispered in his ear:

'Friend of Silas ben Reuben, the spies dog thee. Come with me.'

The outlaw saw a dark form beside him. A door opened noiselessly, and Will was pulled into what seemed to be a narrow winding passage. Along this the hand upon his arm led him for several yards until suddenly he felt the night air blowing upon his face, and he looked up and saw the stars.

'Go to the left,' said the same voice in his ears; ' 'twill lead thee to the Fletcher Gate.'

'I thank thee, friend,' said Will; and strode to the left. A few steps took him into the narrow street which led to the gate named, and Will Stuteley hurried forward, thankful that by the aid of the unknown Jew he had been saved from capture. Without further delay the outlaw went to an inn which overlooked the town wall, and whose landlord asked no questions of his custom-ers. There in the common room Will partook of a frugal supper, and then, ascending to the sleeping-chamber, a large room on the first floor where all the lodgers of the house would sleep when they sought repose, he threw himself in a corner on the straw which covered the floor, and was soon sound asleep.

As time went on, others came up from the room below, found suitable places along the wall, and composed themselves to sleep. Stuteley awoke as each came up, but having glanced at the new-comer by the light of the rushlight which, stuck in a rough tin holder on one wall, gave a dim light about the apartment, he turned and slept again. Very soon the room became almost full, and the later comers had to step over the prostrate forms of snoring men to find places where they could sleep.

After a time, however, the house became quiet; no more men came up into the sleeping-room, and the house seemed sunk in slumber. The wind moaned a little outside the house, and crooned in the slits of the shutter at a window hole, and sometimes a sleeper would murmur or talk in his sleep with thick almost unintelligible words, or fling his arm about as if in a struggle, or groan as if in pain. The street without was dark and silent, cats slunk in the gutter which ran down the middle of the street, or a stray dog, padding through the streets, would come to a corner, sniff the wind and howl.

Before the first glint of dawn had showed itself in the cold street, Stuteley was awake. He loved not houses; their roofs seemed to press upon him, and when in the forest he was wont to issue from the bower or the hut in which he slept, and to walk out from time to time to look at the sky, to smell the odour of the forest, and to listen to the murmur of the wind in the sleeping trees. As he lay there in the dark he longed to be up and away in the cool air of the forest. He cautiously rose, therefore, and feeling his way over the sleeping men, he made his way to the door, where a ladder of rough wooden steps led to the room below.

As he strove to open the door he found that a man's body lay before it. He stirred him gently with his foot, thinking that the man would understand that he wished to open the door and would seek another place.

'A murrain on thee, fellow,' came a voice beside the outlaw. 'Why so early astir? The town gate will not open till I am there. Are ye some thief that seek to flee the city before men are about?'

'No thief am I,' said Stuteley; 'I am but a poor pilgrim who must fare to the holy shrine at Walsingham. And as I have far to go I must needs be early astir.'

By this time the man before the door had risen, and had himself opened the door and stood at the head of the stairs. Stuteley followed him and waited for him to descend, for the stairs were not wide enough for two men to pass. The man who had spoken also came forth, and in the faint dawn they glanced keenly at the outlaw. They were sturdy fellows, and were dressed in sober tunic and hose, as if they were the servants of a well-to-do burgher.

'A pilgrim art thou?' said the one who had spoken already. He laughed in a scornful manner as he looked at Stuteley up and down. 'A pilgrim's robe often covers a rogue's body.'

Saying this, he gestured to the stairs, and Stuteley hastened to descend, feeling that he would better serve his purpose by appearing to be harmless than to answer with a bold speech. The other men followed closely upon his heels, and all three entered the living-room together. Two men sat at a table, and at sight of the two others behind Stuteley they rose and advanced. The foremost, a big man with a villainous cruel look, and the scar of an old wound across his cheek, came forward and said:

'Who have you there?'

'A pilgrim, captain, as he doth declare himself.'

Stuteley saw that he had been caught. His hand leaped to his belt, but at the first movement the two men behind him had gripped his arms.

'Show his left hand,' cried the captain; 'that will show whether this pilgrim knows not another trade! Ah, I thought so!' he went on, as one of them thrust forth Stuteley's left hand, the forefinger of which showed where a corn or hardening had grown by reason of the arrow shot from the bow rubbing against the flesh. 'This is our man – one of that ruffian Robin's band!'

Quick as thought the outlaw wrenched himself free and darted towards the door. He hoped that he might be swift enough to lift up the bar and dash out; but they were too quick for him. Even as he raised the heavy beam which rested in a socket on each side of the door, the four men were upon him. Still holding the bar, he swept round upon them and sent one man crashing to the floor, where he lay senseless. Then, using the beam as a weapon, he beat the others back for a moment. Suddenly, however, the big captain got behind one of his own men, and catching him by the shoulder, he thrust him against Stuteley. Down came the beam on the man's head, stretching him senseless; but before the outlaw could recover himself, the captain and the other man had rushed upon him and overpowered him, holding him down on the floor.

The landlord, roused by the noise, came rushing in, and the captain commanded him to bring ropes. Now the landlord knew Will Stuteley, who had often stayed in his house disguised as a beggar or a palmer, and felt very grieved that one of bold Robin Hood's band should be taken by the sheriff's men. He therefore affected to be very distraught, and ran about from place to place, pretending to look for a rope, hoping that somehow Will might be able to get up if he were given time, and break away from his captors.

But it was all in vain. 'A murrain on thy thick wits!' yelled the captain from where he kneeled holding one of Will's arms. 'If thou findest not ropes in a twinkling, thou rogue, the sheriff shall hear of it.'

'Oh, good captain!' cried the landlord, 'I am all mazed, and know not where anything is. I be not used to these deeds of man-taking, for my house was ever a quiet one.'

Seeing that it was no use to delay longer, the landlord found some rope, and soon Will's arms were strongly bound. While this was being done, the landlord managed to give a big meaning wink to the outlaw, by which he gave Will to know that he would be his friend and would send tidings of his capture to Robin. Then Will was jerked to his feet, and with mocking words was led off to prison.

The landlord sent a man to the forest as soon as the town gates were open. It was late in the day ere he fell in with one of Robin's band, and he told the outlaw, who happened to be Kit the Smith, how Will had been taken, but had slain two men with a door beam before he was overpowered. When Kit the Smith had brought the man to where Robin was seated, deep in the forest, they found that a good burgher, who had been befriended by Robin some time before, had already sent a man who told the

Using the beam as a weapon, he beat the others back

outlaw that Stuteley had been tried before the sheriff that day, and that he would be hanged outside the town gate next morning at dawn.

'Already, as I set out,' said the man, 'I saw the timber being brought and the old gallows being repaired. 'Twas in honour, they said, of the first of Robin's men whom they had taken, but they thought now 'twould not be long ere many others of your band should hang from the gallows-beam.'

'What meant they by that?' asked Robin.

'Well, maister,' replied the burgher's man, an honest, forth-right-looking fellow, 'they say that the sheriff hath took a crafty thief-catcher into his service, a man who hath been in many wars in France and Palestine, and who is wise in stratagems and ambuscades; and they say it will not be long ere he lays some trap which will take all your band.'

'What manner of man is this thief-catcher?' asked Robin. 'How is he named?'

' 'Tis a tall big man, a swashbuckling boaster, with a loud hectoring voice and a great red face. Some name him Captain Bush or Beat the Bush, but others call him the Butcher.'

'Whence comes he?' asked Robin, who did not recognise this boastful captain.

'That no one knows,' replied the man. 'Some do say he is but a rogue himself, and that the king's justice would love to have him in irons. But he is in great favour with the sheriff just now, who takes his counsel in all he does.'

Robin was greatly grieved to hear of poor Will being captured, and his voice had a stern tone in it as he turned to those of his band about him, and said:

'Lads, you hear the evil news. Poor Will the Bowman, good honest old Will, is taken and is like to die. What say you?'

'He must be rescued!' came the fierce cry. 'If we have to pull down Nottingham town we will save him!'

The hard looks on the faces of the outlaws showed how resolute they were.

'Ye say truly, lads,' said Robin. 'Will shall be rescued and brought safely back amongst us, or else many a mother's son of Nottingham shall be slain.'

Robin gave orders for the two townsmen to be entertained and kept in the camp until the morning, and the men willingly gave their word not to return to Nottingham. This Robin did so that no word should leak out of his attempted rescue; for he guessed that it would be a difficult task in any event to get Will Stuteley out of the hands of the sheriff and his new 'ancient' or lieutenant, Captain Beat the Bush.

Meanwhile, in the sheriff's house in Nottingham, the sheriff was deep in counsel with his thief-taker. They had tried to question Will, but had naught but defiant answers from the brave outlaw, who had told them to do their worst with him, but that they should get no secrets from him.

'Take him away!' the sheriff had cried at last in a rage. 'Prepare the gallows for him, and he shall swing at dawn tomorrow's morn.'

Without a word Will heard his doom, and walked with proud look to his dungeon.

'Sir Sheriff,' said Captain Beat the Bush when they were alone, 'I have that to propose which of a surety would enable us to learn the secret lair of the robber band of Robin Hood.'

'Say on,' replied the sheriff. 'I would give a hundred pounds to have that rogue and his meinie scotched or slain.'

'It is this,' went on the captain, and his villainous face had a crafty look upon it. 'Let this man go; he will fly like a bolt from a bow to his chief in the greenwood. Let two or three sly fellows follow him and keep him in sight until they know where the rogues lie hid. Then, when we learn where is their lair, swiftly thou canst gather thy men, and, led by me, we will surround them when they look not for attack, and we will take them every one.'

The sheriff frowned gloomily and shook his head.

'Nay,' he said, 'I'll not lose this one that I have. He shall swing! Once let him go, and the rogue Robin is so full of wiles and stratagems that, Master Bush, thou mightest find thyself ambushed and put to scorn.'

'Then,' replied Captain Bush, 'I have another plan, which will please your worship better. I have told thee how my spies have kept a watch upon the house of Silas ben Reuben, and how they saw this rogue enter there and converse some long time with the Jew. Now I doubt not that there is some evil plot between the Jew and this rogue Robin o' the Hood. Thou knowest thyself that the outlaw deals in necromancy and black magic, and I doubt not that he and that evil brood of Jews do plot to work some evil against us Christians.'

'What will ye?' demanded the sheriff in a sudden burst of rage. 'Would you stir up the people to bait and spoil the Jews? Do you plot to have me thrown out of my office, fined to the half of my estate, and every burgher of this town required to pay a third of his goods? That hath been done at York and at Lincoln by the king's justice. Thou rogue!' he ended, fury in his narrow eyes, 'what evil plot hast thou against me? What knowest thou of Silas ben Reuben? Art thou, belike, one of those rogues whom the sheriff and merchants of York would gladly find so as to make thy skin pay for the penalties which the king's justice hath put upon them?'

Captain Bush was not expecting so fierce an outburst, and he looked crestfallen. Indeed, seeing the startled look in his eyes, one would have thought that the sheriff's last question had reached a surer mark than he suspected. The sheriff stalked up and down the room in his rage, and did not see the sudden fear in the other's eyes.

'I tell thee, my brave thief-taker,' he cried in a raging scorn, 'I'll have none of thy plots against the Jews. 'Tis easy enough for a nameless rogue such as thee to stir up a cry to spoil the Jews, and to lead a cut-throat mob of rascals to slay and loot and plunder. But when the king's justice comes to demand penalties it is not thy hide that smarts, nor thy cobwebby pocket that pays. Go, then, get thee from my sight, and see that the gallows is ready by dawn tomorrow, and name no more of thy rascally plots to me.'

'As your worship and lordship pleases,' said the captain in a soft tone. Then with ironical respect he bowed and swept his hat almost to the floor as he retired from the chamber, leaving the sheriff to fume and fret his anger away

'The dolt! the sheep's head!' said Captain Bush to himself as he stood outside and thought for a while. 'When he is not so hot I will make the fool take back his words – for he is an ass that I can fool to the top of his bent. Yet, willy-nilly, I will keep watch on the house of Silas ben Reuben. I doubt not that old Reuben lives, and that Robin is hiding him. Old Reuben knows where his kinsman, Rabbi Eliezer, hath buried his vast treasure, and I will not let that doltish sheriff keep me from trying what a little torture will do to make old Reuben give up his secret. Silas the Jew, I doubt not, will send or go to meet his father and the girl, to take them to some safe place; my men shall follow, and at a fitting spot I will fall upon them, and hale them to some secret place and work my will upon them.'

Thereupon the captain went forth into the market-place and called to him a man who stood chewing a straw, and who looked even more villainous than himself, and said to him:

'Go, tell Cogg the Earless to keep strict watch upon the house of Silas the Jew. Today or tomorrow I think Silas will go forth; let him be followed whithersoever he may go. If, as I think, he will go to some inn to join others of his race with horses, send word to me by one of our fellows. Silas will go to the forest, I doubt not, to meet an old man and a girl. I will come with others, and we must take the old man alive to some secret place.'

The man slunk off across the broad market square and disappeared in one of the narrow crooked lanes that led to the Jewry. Then Captain Bush went to the Northgate, and going forth found that the sheriff's men were busy putting up new beams on the little hill called Gallows Hill, which lay just beyond the town wall.

'Make it strong, lads,' he cried, with a laugh, 'for 'tis to hang the first of that evil band of robbers. And I doubt not that 'twill not be long ere others of his friends will swing from the same beam.'

The sheriff's men said naught, but one or two winked at each other in mock of him. They liked not this upstart braggart who had suddenly been put over them, and they obeyed him unwillingly.

Next morning the dawn broke gloomy and chill. Thick clouds rolled slowly up across the sky, the wind blew bitterly from the east and the smell of snow was in the air. Beside the gate of the town that looked upon the gaunt gallows-tree a poor old palmer sat as if waiting till the gate was opened, so that he could enter the town. He looked towards the gate and then at the gallows, and presently tears came into his eyes.

'Alas,' he said, 'that I should find my poor brother again after all these years, and only to hear that he is to be hanged within this hour.'

This was the elder brother of good Will the Bowman, who, years before, had fled from the village of Birkencar because of having slain a man who cruelly oppressed him. He had made the long and dangerous journey to Rome, there to expiate his crime by prayer and fasting and penance; and then had gone farther still upon the rough and perilous road to Jerusalem, where for two years he had stayed among the pagan Mussulmans. Then he had slowly made his way back to England, craving to see his younger brother again, whom he had greatly loved. Three days before, he had gone to Birkencar, and had heard how Will had fled to the greenwood with Robin Hood. He had come through the forest, and by asking villeins and poor men, he had learned that Robin Hood's band was wintering not far from Nottingham. Pushing on, he had reached Ollerton, and there, at a little inn, a woodman had told him, not knowing who he was, that Will Stuteley was to be hanged at dawn before the north gate of Nottingham. He had come on at once, walking through the forest by night, and had sat and dozed in the bitter wind before the door, so that he could get a sight of his brother, and perhaps a word with him before he died.

As he thus sat, a short, slim, dark man came out of a little clump of bushes at the foot of the hill, and approached the old palmer.

'Tell me, good palmer,' said he, 'dost thou know whether Will the Bowman is to be hanged this morn?'

'Alas and alack!' said the old palmer, and his tears ran forth afresh, 'it is true as ye say, and for ever woe is me. He is my younger brother whom I have longed to see these ten years, and I come but to see him hanged.'

The little man looked keenly at the old man, as if for the moment he doubled his tale; but his grief was too real and his words rang too true to allow of doubt.

'I have heard,' went on the old palmer, 'that he ran to the greenwood with young Robert of Locksley – a brave lad, bold of speech and noble of heart when I knew him. And poor man and villeins have told me as I came through the forest that he hath not changed, but that he fled because he could not brook the oppression of proud priests and evil knights. He was ever a bold lad, and it gladdened my heart to hear their rough mouths say how he had ever befriended the poor and the oppressed. Oh, if he were here now! If he but knew the death poor Will must die, he would quickly send succour. With a few of his bold yeomen he would soon take him from those who have seized him.'

'Ay, that is true,' the dark man said, 'that is true. If they were near unto this place they soon would set him free. But fare thee well, thou good old man, farewell, and thanks to thee.'

So saying, the stranger, who was dressed in the rough and rusty garments of a woodman, strolled away and disappeared into the bushes again.

No sooner had he gone than voices were heard behind the stout wooden gates, iron-plated and rivet-studded, and soon with creaking and jarring the great double doors swung open, and twelve sheriff's men with drawn swords came forth. In their midst was Will Stuteley, bound with stout cords; but his look was bold and his head was held high as he walked, fettered though he was. Behind walked the sheriff in his robe of office, and beside him was Captain Bush, a smile of triumph on his face. At a little distance behind them came a man with a ladder, accompanied by a small group of townspeople, who followed the sheriff's men towards the gallows-tree.

Arrived there, they placed Will Stuteley beneath the arm of the high gallows, and at the word of command the ladder was reared against the post, and a man ran up it holding a rope in his hand.

Will Stuteley, while these preparations were being made, looked around over the bleak country. He had hoped to see the forms of the outlaws issuing from the dark wood which began on the top of the down beyond the hollow at the foot of the gallows hill; but there was no sign of life anywhere, except the figure of a poor old palmer who was running towards them. Will turned to where the sheriff stood, with Captain Bush beside him.

'Now, seeing that I needs must die, grant me one boon,' said Will; 'for my noble master never yet had a man that was hanged on the gallows-tree. Give me a sword all in my hand and let me be unbound, and with thee and thy men I'll fight till I lie dead on the ground.'

The sheriff scornfully turned his back, and would not even condescend to reply to him.

'Thou mayest be the first, thou thieving varlet,' sneered

Captain Bush, stepping up and flicking his glove in the face of the bound outlaw; 'but I caused this gallows to be made fresh and strong, because I think thy death will bring us luck, and that now it will not be long ere most of thy cut-throat comrades shall follow each other up that rope. When I put my wits to work, thy noble master shall smart, look you; for I owe him much for that which nothing shall wipe out between us!'

'I know not of what you charge my good chief,' said Will proudly, 'but if he hath harmed you, 'twas because thou wert a rascal, of that I am sure.'

'Prate not with the robber,' cried the sheriff, who was on tenterhooks until Will should be hanged, so greatly did he go in fear of the wiles and stratagems of Robin Hood. 'Adjust the rope and end him!'

'Sir Sheriff,' cried Will, 'let me not be hanged. Do but unbind my hands and I will die fighting with them alone. I crave no weapon, but let thy men's swords slay me!'

'I tell thee, rogue, thou shalt die by the rope,' cried the sheriff in a rage; 'ay, and thy master too, if it ever lie in my power.'

At that moment, into the circle of sheriff's men pressed the poor old palmer, tears streaming down his cheeks. He came to Will and put both hands upon his shoulders.

'Dear Will,' he said, 'thou rememberest me? Heavy is my heart to find thee in this plight. Far have I wandered, but ever have I longed for the day when I should see thy face again, and now – '

The rough hand of Captain Bush was thrust between them, and next moment the palmer lay on the ground, half senseless. The captain kicked him as he lay.

'Here,' he said, 'take this rubbish away and cast it in the ditch there!'

But the old palmer got up slowly, and with a last look at Will turned away and limped towards the sheriff.

'He is my younger brother, Sir Sheriff,' said the old man. 'I have come from the Holy City, and my heart yearned to see him.'

'Put the rope about the rascal's neck, and up with him!' shouted the sheriff, ignoring the trembling palmer before him.

'Farewell, dear brother,' said Will. 'Sorry I am that thou hast returned only to see me hung from the shameful tree. But my noble master will avenge me!'

Captain Bush turned and smote his fist heavily upon Will's mouth.

'Take that, thou thieving rascal and cut-throat,' he cried, 'for thy vain boasting. 'Twill not be long ere thy worthy master himself will need avenging.'

The coiling rope descended from above upon the ground beside Will, and Captain Bush picked it up and placed the noose over Will's head. The outlaw looked with terrible eyes into the face of the other and said:

'I said thou wert a rascal, and if thou canst beat me thus when I am bound, I know thou art less than the lowest thief.'

For answer the captain tightened the noose savagely about Will's neck, and, turning, he shouted to the sheriff's men to haul on the rope which was passed over the gallows-beam, so that Will should be dragged off his feet and pulled up until he slowly strangled.

'To the rope, fellows,' he cried hoarsely; 'altogether! . . . one . . . two . . .'

The word that would have jerked Will into the air was never uttered. A stone came flying straight and swiftly, and hit the captain full on the left temple. With a low groan he fell like a log at the feet of the outlaw. At the same time Little John leaped from a bush below the hill, and accompanied by Ket the Trow, from whose hand had come the stone that had laid Captain Bush low, he ran towards Will. Swiftly he cut the bonds about Will's hands, and then, dashing at a sheriff's man who was running towards him with uplifted sword, he caught the fellow full in the breast with one fist, while with the other hand he tore the sword from his grasp.

'Here, Will,' he said with a joyful laugh, 'take thou this sword, and let us defend ourselves as best we may, for aid will come quickly if all goes well.'

Back to back stood Will and Little John, while the sheriff, recovered from the stupefaction caused by the sudden events of the last few moments, found his voice and furiously bade his men seize the villain who had cut the prisoner loose.

The men advanced in a body against the two outlaws, urged by the angry cries of the sheriff, and their swords clanged against those of the two outlaws. For a few moments the attack was furious; then suddenly, like the boom of angry bees, three great arrows dashed among them. One quivered in the body of a man next to the sheriff, and the latter turned and saw fast coming over the down a troop of men in green with taut bows. At their head was a man dressed all in red, with a bow taller than himself, and as he ran he fitted a great arrow to it, that looked as long as a lance.

'Haste, haste,' cried the sheriff. 'Away! away!'

So fearful was he lest next moment he should feel that long arrow pierce his side that, without more ado, he picked up his robe and ran towards the city gate for dear life, followed swiftly by his men, except two. One lay still, having been slain by the first arrow; and over the body of the other Ket the Trow was kneeling. With the rope that was to have hung Will Stuteley, he was deftly binding the arms of the still unconscious Captain Bush.

Robin and his men ran up, and there was much shaking of hands with Will Stuteley, and patting on the back and rough jests and cheering words between them all.

'I little thought,' said Will, his honest eyes lit up with thankfulness as he looked from Robin's face to the faces of his fellows, 'that I should get free of that rope. It was tight about my throat, and I was praying, when – whang! – came the stone. Who threw it?'

He looked about him for a reply.

' 'Twas I, master,' came a voice from about their feet, whence they had not expected it to come. Looking down they saw Ket the Trow just finishing his task. 'Master,' he said as he rose from his knees, 'I would not slay this fellow, for I thought thou wouldst sooner have him alive. He hath done thee much evil, and had it in his mind to do much more.'

Robin stepped up and looked at the face of the unconscious man.

' 'Tis Richard Illbeast!' he said. 'Ket, clever lad, I thank thee! Now justice shall be done to him at long last.'

For fear that the sheriff should get aid from the knights in the castle, Robin gave instant orders. A horse was quickly brought up from where it had been left in hiding by Little John, for use in case Will had been in need of it, and the body of the Jew-baiter was thrown across it. Then with quick strides the outlaws left the spot, and the gate-guard, looking from his chamber over the great doors, which he had closed by command of the sheriff as he hurried through, saw the outlaws disappear into the dark leafless forest on the farther down.

When the band had threaded many secret ways until they had reached the depths of the forest, thus making pursuit almost impossible, Will Stuteley left the side of his brother the palmer, with whom he had been having much joyful talk, and went to Robin and told him that he had arranged that Silas should go that day two hours after noon, with men and horses, to meet his father Reuben and his little sister Ruth, and that he had appointed a spot called the Hexgrove or Witchgrove, on the highroad by Papplewick, where they should meet. As time pressed, therefore, Robin called Ket the Trow and told him to push forward quickly to Barrow Down, where he was to prepare the old man and the girl for the journey, and then he was to lead them to the Hexgrove, where Robin and his band would be waiting.

Having arranged this, Robin turned in the direction of the place indicated, and pursued his way with less haste. By this time Richard Illbeast had revived, and his evil eyes, as he realised where he was, told more than words the hatred in his heart against Robin and his men. His sullen looks glanced from face to face of the men walking beside the horse on which he lay bound, and in their stern looks as they met his he knew there was as little mercy for him as there would have been in his own heart if they had fallen into his hands.

Trained woodman as he was, Robin never travelled through the forest without having scouts thrown out on all sides of him, and to this habit of perpetual watching he had owed many a rich capture, and avoided many an ambush. When they were already half a mile from the Hexgrove, a scout came running up to Robin and said:

'Master, Dick the Reid (Red) saith there is a man in rich dress with six archers riding down the road at great speed. He will reach the Witch trees about the time thou reachest them.'

Having given his message, at which Robin merely nodded, the scout disappeared again to take up his place ahead. Robin quickened the pace of the party and gave a quick eye at the figure of Richard Illbeast to see no bonds were loosened.

In a little while the band of outlaws were hiding in the dense leafless thickets on both sides of the grove. Very soon they heard the rapid beat of horses' hooves, and round the turn of the track came a horseman, short and sturdy of build. He wore a rich black cloak, edged with fur, fastened on the right shoulder by a gold buckle in which shone a rich ruby. A white feather jutted from his black beaver hat, also fastened by a jewel. The horse he bestrode was a fine animal, richly caparisoned. If his dress had not bespoken the rider to be a man of authority and power, the masterful look on his heavy red face, with beetling eyebrows, thick jaw, and stern eyes would have said plainly enough that this man was accustomed to wield wide powers of life and death. Yet there was also a dignity in his look and bearing which showed that he had good breeding.

Behind him were six archers, dressed in stiff jerkins, their legs also thrust in long leather boots reaching halfway up their thighs. Stout men and stalwart they were, with quick looks and an air of mastery. Robin's heart warmed to them. Such doughty fellows ever made him long to have them of his company.

At sight of the richly dressed man in front Robin had smiled to himself, for he knew him, and then, seeing how rapid was the pace at which they were riding towards where he and his fellows were hidden, he chuckled. When the horsemen were some six yards away Robin led the horse from out of the thickets into the road right in the path of the pounding horsemen.

Richard Illbeast, turning his face towards them, went a sickly pale. At the same time the leading horseman, reining his steed with a strong hand, came to a halt some few feet from Robin, and having shot one keen glance at the bound man he turned round and cried in a curt voice:

'There is our man! Seize him!' at the same time pointing to Richard Illbeast, who writhed in his bonds at the words.

Three of the archers spurred forward as if to lay hands on the bound man, when Robin drew back his horse and, holding up his hand, said:

'Softly, good fellows, not so fast. What I have I hold, and when I let it go, no man living shall have it.'

'How now, fellow!' cried the man in the rich cloak. 'I am marshal of the king's justice. I know not how thou hast captured this robber and cut-throat. Doubtless he has injured thee, and by good hap thou hast trussed him on thy horse. But now thou must give him up to me, and short shrift shall he have. He hath been adjudged worthy of death a many times, and I will waste no more words over him or you. Want you any more than justice of him?'

Robin laughed as he looked in the face of the justice's marshal. The six archers gaped at such hardihood, nay, recklessness, in a man who looked to be no better than a poor woodman. Men usually doffed the hat to Sir Laurence of Raby, the marshal of the king's justice, and bent the knee humbly, yet this saucy rogue did naught but laugh.

'Justice!' cried Robin scornfully. 'I like thy words and thy ways but little. All the justice I have ever seen hath halted as if it were blind, and I like thy hasty even less than thy slow justice, Sir Marshal. I tell thee thou shalt not touch this man.'

'Seize the prisoner, and beat down the peasant if he resists,' cried the marshal angrily.

The three archers leapt from their horses and came swiftly forward. When they were within the reach of an arm, Robin put his fingers to his mouth and whistled shrilly. There was the noise of snapping twigs, and next moment the three archers recoiled, for twenty stalwart outlaws, with taut bows and gleaming arrow points, stood on both sides of the road.

The marshal went almost purple with rage. 'What!' he cried, 'thou wouldst threaten the king's justice! On thy head be it, thou knave, thou robber!'

'Softly, good marshal,' replied Robin with a laugh. 'Ye know who I am, and ye know that I reckon the king's justice or his marshal at no more than the worth of a roasted pippin. Thy justice!' He laughed scornfully. 'What is it? A thing ye sell to the rich lords and the evil-living prelates, while ye give naught of it to the poor whom they grind in the mire. Think ye if there were equal justice for rich and poor in this fair England of ours that I and my fellows would be here? Justice! by the rood! I tell thee this, Sir Marshal, I know thee for a fair man and an honest one — hasty and hot perhaps, yet straight in deed except your will be crossed. But I tell thee, if thou wert as evil as others of thy fellows, thou shouldst hang now as high as this rogue here shall shortly hang, and on the same stout tree!'

The outlaw's voice rang out with a stern stark ring in it, and his dark eyes looked harshly in the face of the marshal. For a moment the latter's eyes were fierce; then his face cleared suddenly, and he laughed:

'Thou rascal, I know thou wouldst! I know thee, Robin, and pity 'tis so stout a fellow is driven to the woods.'

'Stay thou there, Sir Marshal,' said Robin sternly, 'and thou shalt see justice done as well and more cleanly by men who ye say are outside the law as thou canst do it, who sell the king's justice.' Then, turning to Little John, he bade him release Richard Illbeast from the horse, and set him beneath a bough.

Just as this was done, out of the woods came riding the old Jew Reuben and his daughter, accompanied by Ket the Trow and four outlaws. The little girl, Ruth, cast her keen glance round the strange assembly, and suddenly caught sight of the evil face of Richard Illbeast. With a shriek she leapt from her horse, and running to Robin, fell on her knees before him, crying out in a passion of words:

'That is he who slew our poor people! Oh, save my father! Save my father! Let him not hurt us!'

Then she rushed away and stood by the side of her father, clutching him with both hands, while with flashing eyes and trembling form she turned and defied the scowling looks of Richard Illbeast.

'Reuben of Stamford,' Robin cried, 'is this the man whom ye saw slaying thy people at York?'

'Ay,' replied the old Jew, 'it is indeed he. With his own hand I saw him slay not only the hale and strong, but old men and women, and even – may conscience rack him for the deed – little children.'

'And thou, Sir Marshal, what crimes hath thy justice to charge against this knave?'

'Oh, a many!' said the marshal. 'But one will hang him as high as Haman. He slew Ingelram, the king's messenger, at Seaford, and robbed him of a purse of gold; he filched a pair of spurs from the house where the king slept at Gisors, in France; he slew an old and simple citizen of Pontefract, and when he swore to pass beyond the sea as an outlaw, and was followed by the sons of the citizen, he by a trick escaped them after slaying two and wounding a third. But for the evil deeds done at York he hath been proclaimed far and wide, and my master the king's justice hath been much angered to learn that the miscreant had fled, who led the murdering and robbing of his majesty's loyal Jewish subjects. But enough, Robin! Up with him, and let us begone!'

Not a word spake Richard Illbeast, but he glared about with wild and evil eyes, and knew that the bitterness of death, which he had meted out to others so often, was his at last. And thus he died, with no appeal for mercy or pity, for he knew too well that he had never given either the one or the other to those who had craved it of him ere he slew them.

When all was done, the marshal bade goodbye to Robin with hearty words, saying quietly in his ear as he walked with him:

'Robin, 'tis not only the poor folk that have thought well of many of thy deeds, believe me. Thy justice is a wild justice, but like thy bolts, it hits the mark. I forgive thee much for that.'

'Fare thee well, Sir Marshal,' replied Robin. 'I have had little to do with thy justice, but that little hath driven me into the forest as thou seest. Yet I would have thee remember to deal gently with poor men, for thou must bear this in mind, that many of them are pushed to do violent deeds because they cannot get justice from them whom God hath placed over them.'

'I will not forget thy words, good Robin,' said the marshal; 'and may I live to see thee live in the king's peace ere long.'

When, a little later, Silas and his men came up, the old Jew and Ruth were given into their charge, and Robin sent twelve of his men as a guard to convey them to the town of Godmanchester, where the Jews would take up their abode for the future.

The noise of Robin's deed was carried broadcast through the countryside. Men and women breathed again to think that so evil a man as Richard Illbeast was slain at last, and Robin's fame for brave and just deeds went far and wide.

CHAPTER EIGHT

How Robin Hood Slew the Sheriff

It was a year and a day since Robin had lent the four hundred pounds to Sir Herbrand de Tranmire, and again he sat in his bower, and the rich odours of cooking pasties, broiling and roasting capons and venison cutlets blew to and fro under the trees. Anon Robin called John to him.

'It is already long past dinner-time,' said Robin, 'and the knight hath not come to repay me. I fear Our Lady is wroth with me, for she hath not sent me my pay on the day it is due.'

'Doubt not, master,' replied Little John; 'the day is not yet over, and I dare swear that the knight is faithful and will come ere the sun sinks to rest.'

'Take thy bow in thy hand,' said Robin, 'and let Arthur-a-Bland, Much, Will of Stuteley, with ten others, wend with thee to the Roman way where thou didst meet the knight last year, and see what Our Lady shall send us. I know not why she should be wroth with me.'

So Little John took his bow and sword, and calling up the others, he disappeared with them into the deeps of the forest which lay close about the outlaws' camp. For an hour Robin sat making arrows, while the cooks cast anxious glances in their pots now and then, and shook their heads over the capons and steaks that were getting hard and overdone. At length a scout ran in from the greenwood, and coming up to Robin said that Little John and his party were coming with four monks and seven sumpter or baggage horses, and six archers. In a little while, into the clearing before Robin's bower came marching the tall forms of Little John and his comrades, and in their midst were four monks on horseback, with their disarmed guard behind them.

At the first glance at the face of the foremost monk Robin

laughed grimly. It was Abbot Robert of St Mary's Abbey! And the fat monk beside him was the cellarer.

'Now, by the black rood of York!' said Robin, 'ye be more welcome, my Lord Abbot, than ever I had thought thou wouldst be. Lads,' he said, turning to those of his fellows who had run away from Birkencar, 'here is the very cause of all thy griefs and pains whilst thou wert villeins, swinking in the weather, or getting thy back scored by the scourge; it was he who forced thee to flee and to gain the happy life ye have led these several years in the greenwood. Now we will feast him for that great kindness, and when he hath paid me what the Holy Mother oweth me – for I doubt not she hath sent him to pay me her debt – he shall say mass to us, and we will part the greatest friends.'

But the abbot looked on with black looks, while the cellarer, fat and frightened, looked this way and that with such glances of dread that the foresters laughed with glee, and jokingly threatened him with all manner of ill-usage.

'Come, Little John,' said Robin, 'bring me that fat saddle-bag that hangs beside the cellarer, and count me the gold and silver which it holds.'

Little John did so, and having poured out the money on his mantle before his master, counted it and told out the sum. It was eight hundred pounds!

'Ha!' said Robin, 'I told thee so, Lord Abbot. Our Lady is the truest woman that ever yet I knew, or heard tell of. For she not only pays me that which I lent her, but she doubles it. A full gentle act indeed, and one that merits that her humble messengers shall be gently entreated.'

'What meanest thou, robber and varlet?' cried the abbot, purple in the face and beside himself with rage to see such wealth reft from his keeping. 'Thou outlaw and wolf's-head, thou vermin for any good man to slay – what meanest thou by thy tale of loan to Our Lady? Thou art a runaway rogue from her lands, and hast forfeited all thou ever hadst and thy life also by thy evil deeds!'

'Gently, good abbot,' said Robin; 'not on my own account did Our Lady lend me this money, but she was my pledge for the sum of four hundred pounds which I lent a year ago to a certain poor knight who came this way and told a pitiful tale of how a certain evil abbot and other enemies did oppress him. His name, abbot, was Sir Herbrand de Tranmire.'

The abbot started and went pale. Then he turned his face away, and bit his lip in shame and rage to think that it was Robin Hood who had helped Sir Herbrand, and so robbed him and the lords of Wrangby of their revenge.

'I see in all this, Sir Abbot,' said Robin sternly, 'the workings of a justice such as never was within thy ken before. Thou didst set out to ruin and disgrace Sir Herbrand. He fell in with me – was that by chance, I wonder? – and by my aid he escaped thy plots. On his way home three evil knights set on him from that nest of robber lords at Wrangby. Two were slain, and Sir Herbrand and his squire went on their way unharmed.'

The abbot glared with shame and rage at Robin, but would say no word.

'Hadst thou not better forsake evil and oppressive ways, Lord Abbot,' went on Robin, 'and do acts and deeds more in the spirit of Him who died upon the tree for the sake of the sinfulness of the world? But now, lads,' he went on, turning abruptly to his men, 'we will dine our guests in our generous greenwood way, and send them off lined well with venison and wine, though their mail bags be empty.'

And right royally did the outlaws feast the abbot and the cellarer and their guard. The abbot indeed made sorry cheer and would not be roused, and ate and drank sparingly, almost grudgingly, for he felt the shame of his position. To think that he, the Lord Abbot of St Mary's, one of the richest and proudest prelates in Yorkshire, should have been outwitted, flouted, and thwarted by a runaway yeoman and his band of villeins, who now sat around him casting their jokes at him, urging him to make merry and to be a good trencherman! Shame, oh, shame!

When dinner was ended, Robin said: 'Now, Lord Abbot, thou must do me a priestly office this day. I have not heard mass since yesterday forenoon. Do thou perform mass, and then thou mayest go.'

But the abbot sullenly refused, and all Robin's persuasions were in vain.

'So be it,' said Robin, and ordered ropes to be brought. 'Then tie me this unpriestly priest to that tree,' he commanded. 'He

The abbot stood tied to the tree like a felon

shall stay there till he is willing to do his office, and if it be a week, no food shall pass his lips till he do as I desire.'

Not all the prayers and entreaties of the high cellarer or of the other monks availed to move the stubborn heart of the abbot at first, who stood tied to the tree like a felon, looking with anger on all about him. The high cellarer and the other monks appealed to him to do what the outlaw required, so that he should get quickly out of their hands, but it was only after long persuasion that the abbot consented.

Reverently Robin and his men listened to the sacred words, and just as they had risen from their knees a scout came running in to say that a knight and a party of twenty men-at-arms were approaching. Robin guessed who this might be, and therefore he commanded the abbot to wait awhile. When Sir Herbrand, for he was the knight, rode into the camp, and after dismounting came towards Robin, he was astonished to see the angry face of the abbot beside the smiling outlaw.

'God save thee, good Robin,' said Sir Herbrand, 'and you also, Lord Abbot.'

'Welcome be thou, gentle knight,' replied Robin. 'Thou hast come doubtless to repay me what I lent thee.'

'I have indeed,' answered the knight, 'with a poor present of a hundred good yew-bows and two thousand steel-tipped arrows for your kindness.'

'Thou art too late, Sir Herbrand,' said Robin, with a laugh; 'Our Lady, who was thy warrant for the sum, hath sent her messenger with twice the sum to repay me. The good abbot hath come with eight hundred pounds in his saddle-bags which he hath yielded up to me.'

'Let me go, thou mocker,' cried the abbot, his face red with shame. 'I can bear no more. Thou hast put greater shame upon me than ever I can forget.'

'Go then,' said Robin sternly, 'and remember that if I have put upon thee so grievous a shame, thou and thy evil servants have put burdens upon poor folks that many times have weighed them down in misery and death.'

Without another word the abbot was helped on his horse, and with his monks and guards rode out of the camp back along the road to their abbey.

Then Robin related to Sir Herbrand how the abbot had fallen into his hands, and Sir Herbrand said:

'I doubt that for so proud and arrogant a prelate as Abbot Robert of St Mary's such a shame as thou hast put upon him will eat out his life. But, by Our Lady, for his high-handed deeds he deserves such a shame. He hath been a tyrant all his life, and his underlings have but copied him.'

Robin would not take back the four hundred pounds which the knight had brought with him, but he gladly accepted the hundred good bows and the store of bolts which he had brought for a present. That night Sir Herbrand and his company spent in the greenwood with Robin, and next morning, with many courteous and kindly words, they parted, the knight to go back to his manor, and Robin to go deeper into the greenwood.

Now it befell with the abbot as Sir Herbrand had thought. Such great distress of mind did he suffer from the shame and disgrace, that his proud mind broke down under the thought, and never again was he so full of pride and arrogance. In a month, indeed, he fell sick, and was ill and weak for all the rest of that year until, when the next spring came, he died of grief and vexation, as the brothers of the abbey declared. And they buried him richly and with great pomp.

Then the monks gathered together and elected one of their order to be abbot in his stead, and sent him they had elected to London, so that he might be formally accepted by the High Chancellor of England, William de Longchamp, who ruled the land while King Richard was in Palestine fighting with Saladin for the possession of the Holy Sepulchre. But the Chancellor, urged by his own wishes and the wishes of his cousin, Sir Isenbart de Belame, did reject the man chosen by the monks, and in his stead appointed a nephew, Robert de Longchamp, to be abbot.

This Robert, as might be expected, was of a fierce and wily character, and he determined that in some way he would capture Robin Hood and destroy him and his band. Therefore he entered into plots with his kinsmen at Wrangby, with Sir Guy of Gisborne, and with the sheriff of Nottingham. Many ambuscades, sudden onfalls, and stratagems did they prepare either in the forest of Sherwood or in that of Barnisdale; but so wary was Robin, so many and watchful were his scouts, and so zealously did the villeins in the forest villages aid him by giving timely warning, that never did Robin lose a man in all these attempts. Often, indeed, his enemies, who were lying in ambush for him, fell themselves into an ambush which he had made for them, and escaped only with the loss of many men.

At length there was peace for some months, and some of Robin's men believed that the sheriff and the Wrangby lords were tired of their continual defeats and would not attempt to attack them any more. Then, one day, as Robin and Much were walking disguised as merchants through the town of Doncaster, they saw a man ride into the market-place, and checking his horse he cried out:

'Oyez, oyez, oyez! Hear, all good people, archers, serjeants and men-at-arms, woodmen, foresters, and all good men who bear bows. Know ye that my master, the noble sheriff of Nottingham, doth make a great cry. And doth invite all the best archers of the north to come to the butts at Nottingham on the feast of Saint Peter, to try their shooting one against the other. The prize is a right good arrow, the shaft thereof made of pure silver, and the head and feathers of rich red gold. No arrow is like it in all England, and he that beareth off that prize shall for ever be known as the greatest and best archer in all the northern parts of England beyond Trent. God save King Richard and the Holy Sepulchre!'

Then, turning his horse, the crier rode out of the town to carry his tidings throughout the countries even up to the Roman Wall which ran from Carlisle to Newcastle.

'What think you of that, master?' asked Much. 'Is it not some sly plot of the sheriff's to attract thee into his power, since he knoweth that thou wilt never let this shooting go without thou try thy bow upon it?'

'I doubt not, indeed, that such may be their plot,' said Robin, with a laugh; 'nevertheless, we will go to Nottingham, however it fall out, and we will see if the sheriff can do any more in the open than he hath done in the greenwood.'

When they got back to the camp at the Stane Lea, where the outlaws were then staying, they found that all the talk was of the trial at the butts of which many had heard the cry made by the sheriff's messengers. Robin took counsel of his chief men, and it was decided that the most part of the outlaws should go to Nottingham on the day appointed, entering into the town by various gates as if they came from many different parts. All should bear bows and arrows, but be disguised, some as poor yeomen or villeins, others as woodmen or village hunters.

'As for me,' said Robin, 'I will go with a smudgy face and a tattered jerkin as if I am some wastrel, and six others of ye shall shoot with me. The rest shall mingle with the crowd, and should it be that the sheriff means ill, then there will be bows bent and arrows buzzing when he shows his treachery.'

On the day appointed, which was fair and bright, great was the multitude of people which gathered by the butts. These were pitched on a level piece of green sward outside the northern gate, and not far from where the gallows stood, from which Little John had rescued Will Stuteley. Away to the north, beyond the gently rising downs, lay the green and waving forest, and down the roads from Mansfield and Ollerton the wayfarers still thronged, anxious to see the great feats of archery which should give fame through all the North Country.

A scaffolding of seats was set up near the shooting-place, and in this sat the sheriff, some of the knights of the castle of Nottingham and others of their friends. Near by stood the officers of the sheriff, who were to keep the course and regulate the trials.

First came the shooting at a broad target. It was placed at two hundred and twenty yards, and a hundred archers shot at it.

Each man was allowed three shots, and he that did not hit within a certain ring twice out of thrice was not allowed to shoot again. Then the mark was placed at greater distances, and by the time it was set up at three hundred yards the hundred archers had dwindled down to twenty.

The excitement among the crowd now began to grow, and when the butt was removed and the 'pricke' or wand was set up, the names of favourites amongst the competing archers were being shouted. Of the seven outlaws, one had fallen out, and there remained Robin, Little John, Scadlock, who had become an excellent bowman, Much the Miller's son, an outlaw named Reynold, and Gilbert of the White Hand, who by constant practice had become very skilful.

At the first contest of shooting against the wand, seven of the twenty failed, among them being Scadlock and Reynold. Then the wand was set farther back at every shooting until, when it stood at four hundred yards, there were not more than seven archers remaining. Among these were Robin and Gilbert; three others were bowmen in the service of the sheriff, the sixth was a man of Sir Gosbert de Lambley, and the remaining one was an old grey man of great frame and fierce aspect, who had said he was a yeoman, and called himself Rafe of the Billhook.

Now came the hardest contest of all – 'shooting at roavers' as it was called, where a man was set to shoot at a wand of which he had to guess the distance, so that he had to use his own wit in the choice of his arrow, and as to the strength of the breeze.

'Now, bully boys of Nottingham, show thy mettle!' cried a stout man with a thick neck and a red face, who stood near the sheriff's seat. He was Watkin, the chief officer or bailiff of Sheriff Murdach. He had taken the place of Richard Illbeast, and like him had got the worst in several attempts to capture Robin Hood, whom, however, he had never seen.

'Forward, sheriff's men,' cried a citizen in the crowd, 'show these scurvy strangers that Sherwood men are not to be overborne.'

'Scurvy thyself,' said a voice somewhere in the rear. 'Yorkshire tykes be a breed that mak' Sherwood dogs put their tails atween their legs.'

The horn sounded its note to show that the contest had begun, and all eyes were bent upon the rival archers. The Nottingham men went first, and of these two failed to hit the wand, the arrow of one going wide and the other's falling short. The third man struck the top of the wand with his bolt, and the roar of triumph which went up showed how keenly the defeat of the other two Nottingham men had been felt.

Then Robin stepped up to the shooting-line. He had put aside the huge six-foot bow which he had used for shooting at the butt, and now bore one which was but a yard in length, but so thick that a laugh went up here and there, and a young squire cried out mockingly:

'Does this ragged wastrel think he can shoot with that hedge pole?'

'Stand at twelve score paces and see!' said a quiet voice somewhere near at hand.

'He'll drill a bolt through thy ribs at fifteen score paces,' said another, 'and through thy mail shirt as well.'

Robin, in a ragged and frayed brown tunic and hose, with a hood of similar hue, raised his bow, notched his arrow, and looked for one long moment at the mark. He had let his hair and beard grow longer than usual, and both were unkempt and untidy. With the aid of some red dye he had coloured his face, so that he looked to be but a dissipated haunter of ale-houses and town taverns, and men wondered how he had shot so well as to keep up so far.

'Dry work, toper, is't not?' cried a waggish citizen. A great laughter rose from the crowd at the joke. The archer seemed not to notice it, and shot his bolt. All craned their necks to see how it had sped, and a gasp of wonder came and then a hearty shout. The wand had been split in two!

'Well done, yeoman!' cried a well-dressed citizen, going up and clapping Robin on the back. 'Thy hand and eye must be steadier than it seems by thy face they ought to be.' He looked keenly in Robin's face, and Robin recognised him as a burgher whom he had once befriended in the forest. The man knew him and muttered as he turned away, 'I thought 'twas thee. 'Ware the sheriff! Treachery is about!'

Then he strolled back to his place in the crowd. The other three now shot at the mark. Rafe of the Billhook missed the wand by the width of three fingers' span, and the bolt of Sir Gosbert's man flew wide. Young Gilbert of the White Hand now shot his arrow. Very carefully he measured with his eye the distance of the wand, chose an arrow with a straight-cut feather, and then discharged it. The bolt made a beautiful curve towards the wand, and for a moment it seemed that it must strike the mark. But a wandering breeze caught it and turned it, so that it flew about a hand's space to the left. The crowd cheered, however, for the youth and courteous bearing of the lad made them feel kindly towards him.

The contest now lay between the sheriff's man, by name Luke the Reid or Red, and Robin. In the next shooting there was no difference between them, for the bolt of each fairly struck the wand. Then the sheriff spoke:

'Ye are fairly matched, but you cannot both have the golden arrow. Devise some play that shall show which of you is the keener bowman.'

'By your leave, my Lord Sheriff,' said Robin, 'I would propose that we look not on the wand while it is shifted to some distance you may choose, and that then we turn and shoot while one may count three. He that splits the wand shall then be judged the winner.'

There were murmurs of wonder and some mocking at this proposal. It meant that a man must measure the distance, choose his bolt, and shoot it in a space of time that allowed little judgement, if any.

'Are you content to accept that, Luke the Reid?' asked the sheriff of his man. The latter stroked his grey beard for a moment, and said:

' 'Tis such a shoot I have seen but thrice made, and only once have I seen the wand struck, and that was when I was a boy. Old Bat the Bandy, who was the chief archer to Stephen of Gamwell, was he who split the wand, and men reckoned that no one north of Trent could match him in his day. If thou canst split the wand, yeoman,' he said, turning to Robin, 'then for all thou lookest like a worthless fellow, thou art such an archer as hath not been seen in the North Country for the last fifty years.'

'Oh,' said Robin, with a careless laugh, 'I served a good master who taught me the bow, but such a shoot as I propose is not so hard as thou deemest. Wilt thou try it?'

'Ay, I am willing,' returned Luke, puzzled at Robin's careless air; 'but I tell thee beforehand I cannot hit the wand.'

The two archers were then commanded to turn their backs, while an officer of the sheriff's ran to the wand and moved it ten paces farther off. Then at the word of the sheriff, Luke turned, and while Watkin the chief officer counted slowly 'One – two – three!' he shot his arrow. The great crowd held its breath as the arrow sped, and a groan of disappointment broke from them when they saw it curve to earth and stick in the ground, some six paces short of the wand.

'Now, boaster!' cried the bull-necked officer angrily to Robin. Then, speaking quickly, he shouted, 'Turn! one – two – three!'

Robin's arrow sped forth as the word 'three' was uttered, and men craned their necks to mark the flight. Swiftly and true it sped, and sliced the wand in two. Men gasped, and then a great shout rose, for though Robin, being a stranger and looking to be but a mean fellow, had turned most of the crowd against him, the sense of fair play made them all recognise that he had fairly won the prize.

Luke the Reid came up to Robin and held out his hand to him. 'Thou'rt a worthier man than thou lookest, bowman,' he said, and his honest eyes looked keenly into Robin's. 'So steady a hand and clear an eye go not with such a reckless air as thou wearest, and I think thou must be a better man than thou lookest.'

Robin shook his hand and returned his keen look, but said no word in reply.

The note of the sheriff's horn rose as a signal that the prizes were to be given. There were ten of these for those who had shot the best according to certain rules, and one by one the men were called up to the sheriff's seat and his wife presented the gift to the successful archer. When it was Robin's turn he went boldly to the place and bent his knee courteously to the lady. Then the sheriff began to speak, and said:

'Yeoman, thou hast shown thyself to have the greatest skill of all who have shot this day. If thou wouldst wish to change thy present condition and will get leave of thy lord, I would willingly take thee into my service. Come, archer, and take from my lady the golden arrow which thou hast fairly won.'

Robin approached Dame Margaret, and she held out the golden arrow to him, smiling kindly upon him as she did so. He reached out his hand to take the gift and met the lady's eyes. She went pale, her mouth opened as if she was about to speak; then she bit her lips, returned Robin's final courtesy, and immediately burst out laughing. Robin knew that she had recognised him, but that she would not betray him. The knowledge that the sheriff was inviting the outlaw who had once put him to such shame to become his man tickled her sense of humour, so that she could not keep from bursting into a long fit of laughter.

The sheriff looked keenly at his wife and then suspiciously at Robin, as the latter turned away and tried to get among the crowd. Men and women pressed about the outlaw, however, congratulating him with rough good humour, and Robin could not hide himself from the sheriff's eyes. Suddenly, something familiar in the look of Robin struck the sheriff. He rose quickly and whispered in the ear of the bull-necked man, who, turning, saw Robin in the midst of a crowd of men bearing bows, who seemed to be talking to him as they all walked away. Watkin the bailiff plunged forward and thrust this way and that among the archers, bidding them in a thick fierce voice make way in the name of the sheriff.

Suddenly men turned upon him and shouldered him off. 'Let me come, varlets,' he cried. 'I will have thee whipped and branded. I am Watkin the sheriff's bailiff!'

'Let him go, lads,' rang out a clear voice. It was Robin who thus commanded his men who had rallied about him.

'I arrest thee, Robin Hood, outlaw! in the name of the king!' shouted Watkin, though he was still some paces away.

'Enough of thy bellowing, thou town bull!' said Little John, who was beside Watkin, and picking up the sheriff's man, the giant ran with him to the outskirts of the crowd and dumped him heavily on the ground, where he lay dazed for a few moments.

A bugle note rang clear and shrill. It was the call of the greenwood men, and from all parts of the wide grounds the outlaws gathered. Another horn sounded, and the sheriff's men formed in ranks, with bows strung. Men and women in the crowd between the two parties fled this way and that shrieking with fear, and at a word from the sheriff his men shot a flight of arrows against the men of the greenwood. Next moment, however, the great clothyard arrows of the outlaws snored back in reply so thick and strong, that the sheriff's men, or such as could run, darted this way and that into shelter.

Slowly and in good order the outlaws retreated, sending their arrows into the sheriff's men, who now, under the furious leadership of Watkin, were following them closely from cover to cover. Once they saw a man ride swiftly away from where the sheriff stood, and enter the town.

'That means, lads, that they go to beg help from the castle,' said Little John. 'Once we reach the greenwood, however, little avail will that help be.'

The forest, however, was still nearly a mile away, and the

outlaws would not run. From time to time they turned and shot their arrows at their pursuers, while keeping a good distance from them and taking care that none got round their flanks.

Suddenly with a groan Little John fell, an arrow sticking from his knee.

'I can go no farther, lads, I fear,' he cried. Robin came up to him and examined the wound, while the sheriff's men, seeing the outlaws check, came on more swiftly.

'Master,' said Little John, 'for the love thou bearest me, let not the sheriff and his men find and take me alive. Take out thy brown sword instead and smite my head off, I beseech thee.'

'Nay, by the sweet Virgin!' cried Robin, and his eyes were pitiful, 'I would not have thee slain for all the gold in England. We will take thee with us.'

'Ay, that we will,' said Much; 'never shall I and thee part company, thou old rascal,' he went on. Saying this, he lifted John upon his broad back, and the outlaws went on again. Sometimes Much put John down for a moment, and notching an arrow to his string, took a shot at the sheriff's men.

Then they saw a large company of archers on horseback issue from the town gate, and Robin's face went stern and grim at the sight. He could not hope to win the shelter of the forest before this troop came upon him, and fight as they would, they must in the end be overwhelmed. Robin looked around for some means of escape, but saw none. Already the mounted men were gaining upon them, and the sheriff's men were holding to the stirrup leather of their allies and leaping and running beside them over the down. Three knights were at the head of the troop, and the sheriff rode in front of all.

Rapidly the outlaws retreated, and at Robin's command they fled along a hollow or combe in the downs which would lead them to a knoll of trees, where he thought they could make a last desperate stand. Suddenly he remembered with some bitterness that they were near the castle of Sir Richard at Lee. He knew that Sir Richard loved him, and would help him if he begged aid of him, but seeing that by helping an outlaw Sir Richard would lose lands and life, Robin knew that he would have to make his last flight alone, although within an arrow flight of his friend's castle.

They gained the knoll of trees, and Robin arranged his men and gave them short sharp orders. Behind them rose the castle of Sir Richard, but Robin looked not that way, all his attention being given to their enemies, who were now rapidly coming up. Suddenly a small figure ran up the knoll and came to Robin. It was Ket the Trow.

'Master,' he said breathlessly, 'a troop hath been sent round by the Levin Oak to take thee in the rear. Look, where they ride!'

Robin looked, and grim despair entered his heart. He saw that it was impossible to make a stand. At that moment a knight in armour came riding furiously from the direction of the castle of Sir Richard at Lee. It was Sir Richard himself.

'Robin! Robin!' he cried, 'thou canst not hope to save thyself. Withdraw to my castle. Come at once, man, or all is lost'

'But thou losest life and land if thou dost shelter me!' cried Robin.

'So be it!' said the knight. 'I lose them any way, for if ye stay here I stay with thee, Robin, and end with thee.'

'Come then,' replied the outlaw. 'Friend indeed as thou art, I will accept thy aid and requite thee to the full for thy nobility.'

Not a moment too soon did the outlaws reach the drawbridge. In good order they retreated, and barely did they avoid being caught in the rear by the horsemen who had ridden to cut them off; but a strong flight of arrows dealt destruction among them on the very verge of the ditch, and when they had recovered, they saw Robin was the last to step across the drawbridge, which then rattled and groaned its swift way up, putting the yawning water of the ditch between them and their prey. For a moment the troop, headed by Watkin, the sheriff's officer, stood shouting threats at the walls, until a flight of bolts among them caused them quickly to draw off, taking their dead and wounded with them. They rode to join the main body of the sheriff's forces, who now came up and halted at a respectful distance from the castle walls, on whose battlements steel caps now gleamed amid the bonnets of the outlaws.

The sheriff sent a herald under a flag of truce, charging Sir Richard with harbouring and aiding an outlaw against the king's rights and laws, to which Sir Richard made a valiant answer, in legal form, saying that he was willing 'to maintain the deeds

'I can go no farther, lads, I fear'

which he had done upon all the lands which he held from the king, as he was a true knight'. Thereupon the sheriff went his way, since he had no authority to besiege Sir Richard, who would have to be judged by the king or his chancellor.

'Sir Richard,' said Robin, when the knight came from the wall after giving his reply to the sheriff, 'this is a brave deed thou hast done, and here I swear that whatever befall me, I do avow that I and my men shall aid thee to the last, and whatsoever help thou needest at any time, I will eagerly give it thee.'

'Robin,' said Sir Richard, 'I love no man in the world more than I do thee, for a just man and a brave, and rather than see thee fall into the hands of the sheriff, I would lose all. But I have ill news for thee. Walter, the steward of Sir Richard FitzWalter, sent a message to me this morning, saying that his master is dead, and that Fair Marian is in danger of being seized by the strongest lord amongst her neighbours, so that she may be wedded to one of them and her lands meanwhile held and enjoyed by them.'

'Now, by the black rood!' said Robin, 'the time hath come when I said I would take sweet Marian into my keeping. Sir Richard, I will instantly set forth to Malaset and bring Fair Marian back to the greenwood. Father Tuck will wed us, and she shall live in peace with me and my merry men.'

Quickly, therefore, Robin selected twenty of his best men, and as soon as harness, arms, and horses had been obtained for them all from their secret stores in the forest caves, the band set off towards the western marches, where, in the fair valleys of Lancashire, the castle of Malaset stood in the midst of its broad lands.

On the evening of the second day they approached the castle and found it shut up, dark and silent. A clear call on a bugle brought a man to the guardroom over the gate. This was Walter the Steward, and quickly, with the aid of the menservants, the bridge was lowered, the portcullis raised, and Robin and his men were welcomed by the brave steward into the great hall.

'Where is the Lady Marian, Walter?' asked Robin.

'Alas, Master Robin, I know not!' replied Walter, wringing his hands and the tears starting from his eyes. 'If thou dost not know, then I am indeed forlorn, for I had thought she had fled to thee. She slept here last night, but this morning no signs could be found of her anywhere about the castle!'

'This is hard to hear,' said Robin, and his face was full of grief. 'Hath any robber lord or thieving kinsman seized her, think you?'

'Several have been here since when, three days ago, my lord was laid in his tomb in the church,' replied Walter, 'but ever with her wit and ready tongue my lady spoke them fair and sent them all away, each satisfied that he was the kinsman to whom she would come when her grief was past. Yesterday there came the sacrist of St Mary's Abbey, and did bring with him the order of the king's chancellor, William de Longchamp himself, the Lord Bishop of Ely, commanding her to hold herself and all she possessed as the ward of the king, and telling her that tomorrow would come Sir Scrivel of Catsty, to be the king's steward and to guard her from ill.'

'Scrivel of Catsty!' cried Robin angrily, 'Scrivel the catspaw rather, for he's naught but a reiving mountain cat, close kin to Isenbart de Belame! I see it all! The new abbot of St Mary's hath got his uncle the chancellor to do this, and under cover of being but the steward of the king's rights, he will let that evil crew of Wrangby take possession. But, by the black rood, I must find what hath befallen Marian, and that speedily!'

Next day and for several days thereafter Robin and his men scoured the marches of Lancashire for many miles, asking of the poor folk, the villeins, beggars and wandering people of the road, whether they had seen a tall maid, brown of hair, straight and queenly of figure, pass either alone, or in the power of a band of knights or men-at-arms. But all was in vain. No one had seen such a maid, and at the end of a week Robin was in despair.

Meanwhile word was sent to him by Walter that Scrivel of Catsty with a hundred men had taken possession of the castle, and was furious to learn that the Lady Marian had disappeared. He also was sending everywhere to learn where she had fled. So earnest did he seem in this that Walter thought that he and the Wrangby lords had not had any hand in kidnapping Marian, and that either she must have fled herself or been taken by some party of her kinsmen.

Full of sorrow, Robin at length turned his horse's head towards Barnisdale, and he and his band rode with heavy hearts into their camp by the Stane Lea one morning when the sun shone warmly, when the birds sang in the boughs and all seemed bright and fair. Hardly had Robin alighted, when there came the beat of horses' feet rapidly approaching from the south, and through the trees they saw the figure of a lady riding swiftly towards them, followed by another. Robin quickly rose, and for the moment joy ran through his heart to think that this was Marian! But next instant he recognised the lady as the wife of Sir Richard at Lee.

When she rode up to Robin, he knelt courteously on his knee for a moment. She was greatly agitated, and was breathless.

'God save you, Robin Hood,' she said, 'and all thy company. I crave a boon of thee.'

'It shall be granted, lady,' replied Robin, 'for thine own and thy dear lord's sake.'

'It is for his behalf I crave it. He hath been seized by the sheriff – he was hawking but an hour agone by the stream which runs by a hunting-bower of his at Woodsett, when the sheriff and his men rushed from the wood and seized him. They have tied him on a horse and he is now on his way to Nottingham, and if ye go not quickly I doubt not he will soon be slain or in foul prison.'

'Now by the Virgin,' said Robin, and he was wondrous wroth, 'the sheriff shall pay for this. Lady,' he said, 'wait here with thy woman until we return. If we have not Sir Richard with us, I shall not return alive.'

Then he sounded his horn with curious notes which resounded far and wide through the forest, so that scouts and watchers a mile off heard the clear call through the trees. Quickly they ran to the Stane Lea, and when all had assembled, there were seven score men in all. Standing with bows in hand, they waited for their master to speak. He stood by the lady where she sat on her palfrey, and they could see by his flashing eyes that he was greatly moved.

'Lads,' he cried, 'those that were with me when we shot at the butts in Nottingham know how courteously this lady's brave lord befriended us, and saved us from death. Now he hath himself been seized by the sheriff, who, learning that I was far from Barnisdale, hath dared to venture into our forest roads and hath seized Sir Richard at Woodsett, where the knight hath a hunting-seat. Now, lads. I go to rescue the knight and to fight the sheriff. Who comes with me?'

Every outlaw of all that throng held up his bow in sign that he would volunteer, and a great shout went up. Robin smiled proudly at their eagerness.

'I thank thee, but you cannot all go, lads,' he cried. 'As the sheriff hath a stout force with him, eighty of you shall go with me. The others must stay to guard the camp and the knight's lady.'

Soon all was ready, and silently the band, with Robin at their head, sank into the forest, and quickly yet stealthily made their way to the south-east, towards the road which the sheriff must take on his way back to Nottingham. The sheriff's spies had learned that Robin had disappeared from Barnisdale, and that Little John, still unable to move because of the wound in his knee, had been left in command. Therefore, hearing that Sir Richard had left his castle at Linden Lea and had gone to a hunting-lodge on the outskirts of Barnisdale, the sheriff had thought this would be a good opportunity of capturing the knight, and thus gain the commendation of the Bishop of Ely, the king's chancellor, who had been furious when he had heard how the knight had rescued Robin and defied the law.

Now that the sheriff had captured the knight, he was very anxious to leave the dangerous neighbourhood, for he feared that Robin might return at any time. He therefore pushed his men to do their utmost, and while he himself rode beside Sir Richard, who was bound securely on a horse, the company of fifty men-at-arms had to walk, and in the hot noonday sun of the summer they moiled and sweated woefully at the pace set by the sheriff.

When they reached the town of Worksop, which lay upon their route, the sheriff would only stay long enough before the chief inn to allow each man to have a stoup from a black jack, and would allow no one to rest beneath the wide chestnut tree that threw its dark and pleasant shade in the scorching road. Then onward they had to go, their own feet kicking up the dust which in less than a mile caked their throats again.

At length they got among the deep woods and hills of Clumber Forest, and the sheriff felt more at ease in his mind, though he did not abate the pace at which he went. Under the shade of the great oaks and chestnuts, however, the men felt less exhausted and pushed on with a will.

There was a long steep hill upon their road called Hagger Scar, and up this they were toiling manfully, when suddenly a stern voice rang out.

'Halt!' it cried, and at the same moment, as the men-at-arms looked about them, they saw that on each side of the forest-way stood archers with bent bows, the gleaming arrows pointing at each of their breasts. The whole company stood still, and men angrily murmured beneath their breath.

Out of the wood some ten paces from the sheriff stepped Robin, his bow strung and a fierce look on his face.

'So, sheriff,' he cried, 'you learned that I was away, and therefore stole up to seize my friend. By the Virgin but thou hadst better have stayed within thy town walls. I tell thee I will spare thee no more. Not since seven years have I had to go so fast on foot as I have had to do this morn, and it bodes no good to thee. Say thy last prayer, for thy end hath come.'

Now that he knew that his last hour had really come, the sheriff was brave.

'Thou lawless wolf's-head,' he cried, 'the chancellor will harry every thicket in these woods to catch thee for this deed. I – '

He spoke no more. Robin's arrow pierced the chain-mail coat he wore, and he swayed and fell from the saddle to the ground, dead. Then Robin went to the knight and cut his bonds and helped him from the horse.

'Now,' said he to the sheriff's men, 'throw down thy weapons!'

When they had done this he told them to march forward, take up the body of their master, and proceed on their way. They did as he had commanded them, and soon the fifty men-at-arms, weaponless and sore at heart for having been so completely conquered by the bold outlaw, disappeared over the crest of the hill.

Turning to the knight, Robin said: 'Sir Richard, welcome to the greenwood! thou must stay with me and my fellows now, and learn to go on foot through mire, moss, and fen. Sorry I am that a knight should have to leave his castle to his enemies without a blow and to take to the woods, but needs must when naught else can be done!'

'I thank thee, Robin, from my heart,' said the knight, 'for taking me thus from prison and death. As for living with thee and thy fellows in the greenwood, I wish no better life, since I could not live with braver men.'

Thereupon they set off through the leafy wilderness, and before evening had rejoined the lady of the knight, and great was her joy and gratitude to Robin and his men for having restored her husband to her. A feast was prepared, and Sir Richard at Lee and his dame were entertained right royally, and they said that though they had lost castle and lands, they had never been happier than on this the first night of their lives as outlaws in the greenwood.

When the camp was hushed in slumber, and there was no sound but the crackle of the dying embers of the fires and the rustle of the wind in the trees overhead, or the murmur of the little stream beside the camp, Robin took his way into the dark forest. He was very unhappy and much distressed by reason of the disappearance of Fair Marian. He pictured her a captive in some castle, pining for liberty, oppressed by the demands of some tyrant kinsman or other robber knight, who had captured her for the rich dowry which would go to him she wedded.

Filled with these fears, therefore, Robin determined to walk through the forest to the green mounds where Ket the Trow and Hob o' the Hill lived, to hear whether either of those little men had learned any news of Marian. As soon as he had learned of his lady's danger when he had reached Sir Richard's castle, he had sent off Ket the Trow to Malaset to watch over Marian, but had since heard nothing from the troll, and this silence was very disquieting.

Though the woodland paths were sunk in the deepest darkness, Robin found his way unerringly through the forest, and when he had greeted and left the last scout, watchful at his post, be passed through the dark ways as stealthily as a wild animal. Thus for some miles he went, until he knew that he was approaching Twinbarrow Lea, as the glade was called where the green homes of the little men lay. Cautiously he neared the edge of the clearing and looked out between the leaves of the tree beside him.

From where he stood, his eyes being now quite used to the darkness, he could plainly see the two green mounds, for he was on that side of them which was nearer to the forest. Everything seemed to be held in the silence and quiet of the night. Only the wind rustled in the long grass or whispered among the leaves. From far away on the other side of the glade came faint cries of a hunting owl, like a ceaseless question – 'Hoo-hoo-hoo!' Near by, he heard a stealthy footfall, and turning his head he could see the gaunt form of a wolf standing just on the edge of the forest, its head thrown up to sniff the breeze from the mounds. Suddenly there came a scurry away in the thickets to the rear, a quick shriek, and then stillness. A wild cat had struck down a hare. The wolf disappeared in the direction of the sound to see if he could rob the cat of its prey. A long fiendish snarl greeted his approach, and Robin expected to hear the fury of battle rise next moment as the wolf and wild cat closed in mortal combat. But the snarl died down. The wolf had declined the contest.

Looking intently towards the mound, Robin was now aware of a dark space on the flank of the farther one which looked like the outstretched figure of a man. He knew that this mound was the one in which the brothers dwelt, and he wondered whether Ket or Hob was lying out there sleeping. He thought to give the call of the night-jar, which was their signal by night; but suddenly he saw the figure move stealthily. He watched intently. He knew this could not be either of the brothers, for the man's form was too large, and it wriggled with infinite slowness upwards towards the top of the mound.

Robin knew then that this was some enemy trying to spy out the place where the two little men lived. He wandered if it was one of his own outlaws, and he grew angry at the thought. He had always commanded that no one should approach the mounds or seek to force his company on the little people. If it was indeed one of his men, he should smart for it.

By this time the figure had almost reached the top of the mound, and Robin stepped quietly forth with the intention of going to the man to bid him be gone. Suddenly, against the skyline there leaped from the top of the mound the small figure of a man, which precipitated itself upon the form which Robin had first seen. For a moment the latter was taken by surprise; it half rose, but was pushed back, and instantly the two forms were closed in a deadly grapple. Robin rushed up the mound towards them, catching the glint of knives as he approached. He heard the fierce panting of the two fighters as they struggled on the steep, slippery side of the mound. They pressed this way and that, losing their footing one moment, but regaining it the next. Just as Robin reached them and could see that it was Ket the Trow and one of his own outlaws, Ket thrust the other from him, and the man fell, rolling like a log down the side of the mound, and lay at the bottom still and inert.

'What is this, Ket?' asked Robin. 'Hath one of my own men tried to break into thy house?'

'He's not one of the band, master,' said the panting man, stanching a wound on his shoulder with one hand. 'He is a spy who hath followed me these three days, but he'll spy no more.'

Together they descended the mound, and Ket turned over the dead man. Though the body was dressed like one of Robin's men, he knew by the face that it was not one of his outlaws.

'How is it he wears the Lincoln green?' asked Robin.

'He slew a poor lad of thine, Dring by name, by Brambury Burn,' said Ket, 'and took his clothes to cover his spying.'

'Poor lad,' said Robin; 'Dring was ever faithful. But what hast thou been doing by Brambury Burn? 'Tis far north for thee to roam on the quest I gave thee. How ran the search so far?' asked Robin eagerly, wondering if Ket had aught to tell.

'Thereby hangs my tale, master,' said Ket. 'But do thou come into the mound and listen while I bind my wound.'

Robin followed Ket up the flank of the great barrow. He had only once been inside Ket's home, and he knew that the method of entry was not by the door on the side, which indeed was too small for a man of ordinary girth to enter, but by the chimney, which could be made wide enough to admit him. On the top of the mound was a dark hole, down which Ket disappeared, after telling Robin to wait until he showed a light.

Soon Ket's face appeared in the light of the torch at the bottom of a slanting hole, the sides of which were made of stones. Taking out one here and there Ket made the aperture wider, and then Robin, by alternately sliding and stepping, climbed down the slanting chimney. There was still another similar passage to descend, but at length he stood on the floor of the apartment which was the home of Ket and Hob and of their mother and two sisters. By the light of Ket's torch, which he stuck between two stones, Robin saw that the walls of the cave were made of stones, deftly arranged, without mortar, one above the other, so that the whole chamber was arched in the form of a beehive, the height being some eight feet.

When Robin had helped Ket to bind up a deep wound on his left shoulder, and a cut or two on his arm, the little man looked up into his master's face with a bright, merry air, and said:

'If thou'lt promise to make no sound I'll show thee a treasure I ha' found but lately.'

'Ket!' said Robin in eager tones, 'hast thou really found my dear lady? Oh, good little man!'

For answer Ket beckoned Robin to follow him to a part of a chamber which was curtained off by a piece of arras that must at one time have adorned a lord's hall. Peering behind this, Robin saw reclining on a horse-cloth thrown over a couch of sweet-smelling ferns the form of Marian, sleeping as softly as if she was in her own bed of linen at Malaset. Beside her was the small, slight form of one of Ket's sisters, her dark hair and pale skin showing vividly against the auburn locks and brown skin of Marian. A long time he gazed happily on her face, until at length Ket roused him by whispering:

'Look not on her with such intentness, or her eyes will surely open and seek thine!'

Silently Robin and Ket crept away to the farthest corner of the chamber, and Ket then told his tale.

'When you sent me away to watch over the Lady Marian until you came,' said Ket the Trow, 'I reached the castle by Malaset Wood at evening, and I crept into the castle when no one saw me. I found the Lady Marian in her chamber, and already she had resolved to fly to you, leaving no word behind, so that steward Walter and her people should not be judged guilty of aiding her escape. I bade her wait for you, but she yearned for the open moors and would not stay. By a secret way we issued from the castle at dawn, and took to the moors. Master Robin, thy lady is a wood-wise lass, though over quick to act. She feared that there were those of her enemies who watched the castle, and therefore she would not have us walk together lest, as she said, if both were taken or I was slain, there would be no one to tell you. We started out on the way which should lead us to meet you; but not two miles had we wended ere from the thickets on Catrail Ring twenty men sprang out and seized her. I barely 'scaped them by creeping back, for they would not believe she was alone, and they sought for me. They were men of the Thurlstan lord, whom ye know to be close sib to him of Wrangby. Fierce and evil-looking were they, and not over gentle with my lady, so that more than once I had it in mind to loose a bolt in the throat of Grame Gaptooth their leader. They put her on a spare horse which, with others, lay in the covered way to the Ring, where they had lain and watched the castle in the valley below. All through the livelong day I followed them, and grievous was that journey. Fast they travelled, keeping to the moors and the lone lands, so that hard was I put to it to hold to them on my two feet. That night they reached Grame's Black Tower on the Wall, and when I heard the gate clang down, well, my heart dropped with it, for, as thou know'st, that peel tower is a fearsome place, and not to be broken into like a cheese. Next day they sent two riders south, and I knew that they went to tell the evil man Isenbart that they held thy dear lady and could strike at thee through thy tenderest part. Two days I wandered round that evil and black tower, conning how I could win into it and out again with my dear lady unscathed. On the evening of the third day the riders returned with others, and these were from Sir Isenbart, and at their head was Baldwin the Killer, come to take my lady to the dungeons of Wrangby. Thou know'st, master, that we little people have many secrets and strange lore, and some unkent powers, and how we can break and overcome hard things. It was so now, and by the aid of that knowledge I was able to see the weak part of that strong peel. I think, master, there is no castle that I cannot break into, however high and strong it be, so I put my thinking to it. I entered that peel tower in the dark, and I let down my brave lady from the wall, but ere I left I put so heavy a mark on some that slept that never will they rise to do evil more. Far did we go that night, and ever was she bold and brave. She lay hid by day while I fared abroad to get us food; but by Brambury Burn I met young Dring, and he was hot to go and find thee and tell thee the good news. That rogue that lies dead on the mound outside saw me and Dring as we spoke, and knew me for thy friend, and thinking to win the favour of the

Wrangby lords, he slew Dring, and putting on his clothes followed me. I reached here but four hours agone, and ever since my lady hath slept.'

'Let her sleep long, brave lass,' said Robin, 'for she must have sore need of it. I cannot thank thee enough, good Ket,' he went on, 'for having brought her safe and sound out of such peril. What reward shall I make thee that is fitting?'

'Master,' said Ket, 'there is no need to talk of rewards between thee and me. I and mine owe our lives to thee, and whatsoever we do, you or I, is for the love we bear each other. Is it not so?'

'It is so,' replied Robin, and they gripped hands in a silent oath of renewed loyalty to each other.

Robin slept in the trolls' mound that night on a bed of fern with Ket beside him, and in the morning great was the joy of Marian when she awoke to find Robin himself was near by. Much loving talk passed between them, and both said that never more would they part from each other while life should last. That very day, indeed, Robin went to Father Tuck to prepare him for their marriage.

CHAPTER NINE

King Richard Meets Robin

When it became known throughout the countryside that Robin the outlaw had wedded Marian FitzWalter, heiress to the wide lands of Malaset and ward of the king, some men wondered that he could be so daring as to fly thus in the face of the king's rights, while others were glad that Robin had been so bold, and had shown how he set at naught the powers of prelates and proud lords.

For some time there were rumours that William de Longchamp, the king's chancellor, was going to send a great army into the forests of Clipstone, Sherwood, and Barnisdale, to stamp out and utterly destroy this bold and insolent outlaw. It was said that armies were to go from the strong castles of Nottingham in the south, Tickhill and Lincoln in the east, the Peak in the west, and York in the north, and they were to sweep through the forest, leaving the dead bodies of all the outlaws bristling with arrows or swinging from high trees.

But nothing came of this. Very soon, indeed, William de Longchamp had been chased from the kingdom for his pride and oppression, and the castles of Nottingham and Tickhill had fallen into the hands of Earl John, the king's brother; and for nearly three years after that the nobles and prelates were so full of their own bickerings and quarrels, that they had little memory of the saucy deeds of an outlaw.

Then all good men sorrowed to learn that their gallant King Richard had been captured and lay imprisoned in a castle in Germany, and that a vast sum was demanded for his ransom. To raise the money every man was taxed, be he a layman or a monk; citizens and yeomen, knights and squires had to pay the value of a quarter of their year's income, and the abbots were required to give the value of a year's wool from the vast flocks of sheep which they possessed.

Many men paid these taxes very grudgingly, and the money was long being collected. Meantime the king whiled away the long hours in his prison, feeling that, as he wrote in a poem which he composed at that time and which men may still read:

> True is the saying, as I have proved herein,
> Dead men and prisoners have no friends, no kin.

During all this time Robin and Marian had lived very happily in the greenwood. She had lost her wide lands, it was true, and instead of living in a castle with thick walls, and being dressed in rich clothes, she dwelt in a wooden hut, and had the skins of animals or plain homespun Lincoln green wherewith to clothe herself. But never before had she been so happy, for she was with him she loved best, and ever about her was the free life of the fresh woods and the wild wind in the trees.

So much did Robin desire that his king should speedily be freed that, when he learned what taxes were imposed in order to raise the king's ransom, he collected the half of all his store of gold and silver, and having sold many fine garments and rich clothes, he sent the whole of the money under a strong guard to London, and delivered it into the hands of the mayor himself, who, having opened the parcel when his visitors had gone, found therein a piece of doeskin on which was written:

'From Robin Hood and the freemen of Sherwood Forest, for the behoof of their beloved king, whom God save speedily from his evil enemies at home and in foreign parts.'

Thereafter, also, Robin set aside the half of all he took from travellers and placed it in a special secret place, to go towards the king's ransom. When, also, he heard that any rich franklin well-to-do burgess or yeoman or miserly knight, abbot or canon, had not yet paid his due tax, Robin would go with a chosen party of his men and visit the house of the man who begrudged liberty to his king; and if the yeoman or knight did not resist him he would take from the man's house what was due for the tax, but if, as sometimes happened, the man fought and resisted, then Robin would take all he could find, and leave the curmudgeon and his men with their wounds and their empty purses.

For fear, therefore, that they should lose much more, many hastened to pay at once the tax which otherwise they would never have paid; and some from whom Robin had taken what was due were forced to pay again by the king's tax-gatherers. The tales of Robin's dealings spread abroad far and wide, until they got to the ears of Hamelin, the stout Earl of Warenne himself, who was one of the king's treasurers, and he declared heartily that it was a pity the king had not such a tax-gatherer as Robin in every county, for then the king would have been freed in a few weeks. He learned all he could concerning Robin, and said in the hearing of many noble and puissant lords, that he would like to see that stout yeoman, for he seemed to be a man much after his own heart.

When King Richard was at length released from prison, most of his enemies who were holding castles on behalf of his brother John, who had plotted to win the crown for himself, gave them up and fled for fear of the king's vengeance. Others were besieged by the friends of King Richard and surrendered after a little while. There were certain knights who held the castle of Nottingham for Earl John, and they resisted the besiegers very fiercely, and would not give up the castle to them. When King Richard landed at Sandwich after coming from Germany, he heard how the castle of Nottingham still refused to submit to his councillors, and being greatly angry, he marched to that city and sat down before the castle with a vast army. He made an assault upon it, and so fiercely did he fight, that he captured part of the outer works and laid them in ruins, and slew many of the defenders. Then he ordered gibbets to be erected in sight of the besieged, and upon them he hung the men-at-arms whom he had captured, as an example to the rebels within the castle.

Two days afterwards the wardens of the castle, among whom was Ralph Murdach, brother of the sheriff whom Robin had slain, came forth and surrendered the castle, and threw themselves upon the mercy of the king. He received them sternly, and ordered them to be kept under a strict guard.

Now when the king and his lords sat at dinner one day, it was told King Richard how there was a bold and insolent outlaw who harboured with many lawless men in the forests of Clipstone, Sherwood, and Barnisdale, which lay north of Nottingham.

More especially did his chancellor, William de Longchamp, wax wroth at the recital of Robin's crimes.

'Such a man, my lord,' he said, 'thy father King Henry, of blessed memory, would not have suffered to commit his crimes for all these years, but most surely he would have sent an army of archers into the forests where he hideth, and would have hunted out every rogue and hung him forthwith.'

'It was thy office, my Lord Bishop, to do this,' retorted Richard sternly. 'I left thee to rule my land justly, and to keep down robberies and murders and brawls, but thou seemest to have added to the confusion and disorder.'

Many of the nobles who hated the bishop smiled to see the look of chagrin on William de Longchamp's face. They had chased him from England because of his pride and oppression, and the king's reply pleased them mightily.

'Moreover, sir,' said Hamelin, Earl de Warenne, 'had my Lord Bishop been able to hang this stout outlaw, it is likely your highness would have been longer in prison.'

Men looked in surprise at de Warenne as he said this, and saw the smile on his face.

'How is that, de Warenne?' asked King Richard. 'What had this rascal to do with my release?'

'This, sire,' was the reply, 'that though he loves his king's deer overmuch, wherein he sins with many others, both rich and poor, it seems that he loves his king also, and in that he doth exceed the love that many of thy knights and lords bear thee. He lives by taking toll from travellers through thy forests, and, as I have been informed, he had gathered much wealthy gear and a store of money. Half of that wealth he did send to my Lord Mayor of London, and the amount of it was an earl's ransom. With it he sent a message which ran: "From Robin Hood and the freemen of Sherwood, for the behoof of their beloved king, whom God save speedily from his evil enemies at home and in foreign parts." Further, sire,' de Warenne went on, while men looked at each other in wonder, 'he took upon himself the office of tax-gatherer for these parts, and many a fat canon, abbot, or prior who would not have paid the tax which was to set thee free, and many a miserly burgess, knight, or yeoman, hath had a visit by night from this outlaw and been forced to pay the tax. By my head, but as men have told me, they have had to pay their tax twice over – once to Robin Hood, and again to the treasurer's sergeants – and much they grieved thereat!'

The king laughed heartily, and his nobles joined in his merriment.

'And the toll and tax which he thus gathered,' went on de Warenne, 'this outlaw sent again to the Lord Mayor with this message, as I am told: "For to release my lord the king, from unwilling knights, monks, and other surly knaves who love him not a groat's worth, by the hands of Robin Hood and his men of the greenwood." '

'By my faith,' said Richard, and his look and tones were earnest, 'this is a man in whom much sense of right and justice must dwell. 'Tis clear he knoweth and loveth freedom greatly, and hath much pity for those who have to sit in duress and see the sunlight crawl across the floor of their cells. By the soul of my blessed father, if other of my liege subjects had been as loving and as busy in my behalf as this outlaw, I should not have pined in the castle of Hagenau by many a month!'

He looked darkly around the table, and many a face went a little pale, for some knew that they had not been over zealous in raising the great sum which would release their lord. Many, also, had been beguiled a little by the promises of that traitorous brother of the king, Earl John of Mortaigne.

'By my faith, but I will see this outlaw,' said the king, 'and know what sort of man he is. How did he break the law?'

'By the slaying of my brother, sire,' said William de Longchamp. 'He slew Sir Roger on the highway, and afterwards he slew five men-at-arms of the abbot of St Mary's at York. Since then his murders and robberies have been numberless.'

'I think he slew your brother, Lord Bishop, because Sir Roger would have seized FitzWalter's daughter, the Lady Marian,' said de Warenne in a quiet voice. 'Is it not so? Your brother, with a party of varlets, set upon her and her villeins in the forest, and would have borne her off to his castle, which some men call Evil Hold, as I learn, but that this outlaw was in hiding near, and slew Roger with an arrow through his visor.'

'And, by my halidom,' said King Richard, who ever praised brave deeds that had to do with the saving of ladies from

ill-usage or oppression, ' 'twas a righteous deed if, as I remember, 'twas not the first lady thy brother Roger had oppressed, my
Lord Bishop!'

William de Longchamp looked fiercely at Earl de Warenne,
who smiled carelessly at his enemy's wrathful glances.

'I will have you to know, sire,' said William the Chancellor,
turning to the king, 'that if you may not deem the slaying of my
own poor kinsman of much worth, yet this thief and murderer,
Robin Hood, hath done deeds of late that shall surely not gain
him thy favour. He hath slain the sheriff of Nottingham, Robert
Murdach; he hath wed the Lady Marian, one of thy wards; and
moreover hath caused a knight whose lands lie near this castle to
go with him and thieve and rob in thy forests.'

'What is the knight's name?' asked the king, and his look was
stern, for though he might be willing to overlook many things in
a mere yeoman, he would have little mercy for a knight who
forgot his honour and turned outlaw.

'It is Sir Richard at Lee, and his lands lie by Linden Lea, near
by Nottingham,' said William de Longchamp.

'I will seize his lands,' said the king angrily, 'and his head shall
be cut off – the recreant! Make proclamation,' he went on,
turning to one of the clerks of the treasury who stood behind his
seat, 'that whosoever taketh that knight and brings his head to
me shall have his lands.'

'If it please you, sire,' said an old knight, who stepped forth
from a group of richly dressed lords waiting behind the king, 'I
would say that there is no man living who could hold the
knight's lands while his friend Robin and his men can range
through the forest and draw a bow.'

'Who are you?' asked the king, 'and how know you this?'

'I am John de Birkin, sire,' said the old knight, 'and Sir
Richard at Lee was my friend. Since Sir Richard fled, the new
sheriff of Nottingham hath striven to hold his castle and lands in
thy name, but no man will bide there. As they walk to and fro
upon the fields they are pierced by arrows from the woods, their
servants are beaten or have run away, and all the villeins that
dwell upon the land have joined their master in the greenwood.'

'By the soul of my father,' said the king, starting from his seat,
'if ye speak true, then the best men dwell in the forests, and the

caitiffs are law-abiding fools that pretend to rule for me while they let me pine in my prison. I will see this outlaw – look you, de Birkin, send word to this rascal outlaw that he shall have my protection while he cometh and goeth, for I would willingly speak to him who loves me, yet who slays my sheriff and knights.'

When the castle of Nottingham had been surrendered into the hands of the king he went hunting in the forest of Sherwood, which he had never before seen, and he was much pleased with the giant trees he found therein, the beautiful smooth glades, the cliffy hills, and the rolling downlands. On that day the king's party started a hart by Rufford Brakes, which was so fleet and strong that it led horsemen and hounds for many miles north-wards into Barnisdale forest, where, it being late, and the twilight falling, it was lost. That night the king slept at the house of the Black Monks of Gildingcote, and next day he sent his huntsmen through the forests, making proclamation at various villages, castles, and towns that the hart which the king had hunted and lost the day before should henceforth be called a 'hart royal proclaimed', and that no person should kill, hurt, or chase the said hart, which was described by certain distinguishing marks by which any good woodman would instantly recognise it.

King Richard went hunting through the forest every day, and did not stay in one place; but never could he get to learn where Robin Hood was hiding. At last he called to him the chief forester of Sherwood, by name Sir Ralph Fitz-Stephen.

'Knowest thou not, Sir Forester,' asked the king, 'where my messenger may get word with this outlaw? Thou keepest this forest ill, since thou permittest seven score outlaws to live in it unmolested, and to slay my deer at their will. Find me this Robin Hood, or thou shalt lose thy office.'

Ralph Fitz-Stephen was a bold man, and he made reply:

'My lord king, it is not whether I or your Majesty may find Robin Hood, but rather whether Robin Hood will permit himself to be found. I make bold to say, sire, that these several years past have I striven to capture him and his band, and I have aided the sheriffs of every county which march on the forest shaws, but this outlaw is a very fox for hiding, and hath as many holes. Nevertheless, I will do all I may to bring him to thee.'

Fitz-Stephen thereupon gathered together all his foresters, told them what the king·had said, and took counsel with them what had best be done to give the king his desire. Some advised one thing and some another, until the chief forester lost patience with them all.

'Out on ye, ye chuckleheaded loons!' he cried. 'If this rascal outlaw were only half as wary as he is, he would still play with such louts as ye be. Little wonder ye have never been within a mile of catching him. Away with thee to thy "walks", and I will rely upon my own wits.'

Very crestfallen, the foresters went about their duty. Most of them bore the marks of wounds given in many a scuffle with Robin and his men, and they felt that unless their master hit upon some means of finding the outlaw and bringing him to the king, they would soon lose their posts as foresters, which though on occasion brought them wounds or blows, yet gave them opportunities of gaining much pelf and of oppressing poor folks and gaining money or goods from them.

Two days later, Ralph Fitz-Stephen came to where the king was staying at the castle of Drakenhole, and craved audience of him. When he saw the king he bent on one knee, and when King Richard had commanded him to speak, he said:

'Sire, I have learned that since you have kept in these northern parts, the outlaw Robin has been haunting the roads by Ollerton, stopping rich travellers and taking of their wealth. Now I give thee counsel in what way thou mayest get word with this rascal. Take five of thy lords – those who are not hasty or quick of temper, I would advise, lest they betray who ye be before thou hast word with the outlaw – and borrow monks' weeds [garments] from the abbot of Maddersey across the river here. Then I will be your guide, and I will lead you to the road where Robin and his comrades do haunt, and I lay my head on it that ye shall see that rascal ere you reach Nottingham.'

'By my faith,' said Richard with a hearty laugh, 'but I like thy counsel, forester. Do thou get the monkish garb from my Lord Abbot for myself and thee and my five lords, and we will go with thee.'

Though the day was already far gone, Richard would set out at once, and as soon as the monks' garments were brought he put the great black gown over his rich surcoat, which blazed with the leopards of Anjou and the lilies of France, and then upon his head he put a hood and a wide-brimmed hat, such as ecclesiastics wore when they travelled. He was very elated at the prospect of so strange an adventure, and joked and laughed with the five knights whom he had chosen to go with him. These were Hamelin, Earl de Warenne, Ranulf, Earl of Chester, Roger Bigot, William, Earl of Ferrers, and Sir Osbert de Scofton.

In an hour they were on the road, the party having the appearance of five rich monks or chief officers of some great abbey, travelling on the business of their house. Two horses heaped with their baggage followed after, and behind them were three more larger horses, piled with provisions, table ware and other rich gear. The horses were in charge of two foresters, who were disguised as monkish servants.

For an hour they rode until it was dark, Richard joking with his knights or at times carolling in his glee. When night compelled them to call a halt, Ralph Fitz-Stephen suggested that they should turn a little from their way to the house of the canons of Clumber, where they would be sure of a lodging for the night. This was agreed to by the king, and after a short ride through the forest, they were received in the canons' guest chamber. Except for a merchant and his three men who were already eating their meal, and a man who, by his careless air and dress, and his possession of a citole or little harp, seemed to be a minstrel or jongleur, the great hall was empty. The king's party did not tell anyone who they were, or they would have been invited into the private hall to sup with the canons; but King Richard preferred to remain unknown.

Food was therefore brought forth from the store carried on the sumpter horses, and the king and his lords and Ralph Fitz-Stephen ate at one of the tables in the hall, which was dimly lighted by three or four torches which spluttered and flared and smoked in their sockets on the pillars.

'I tell thee thou art a fool!' came suddenly the angry voice of the merchant. He seemed to be in altercation with the jongleur, who laughed and twanged his citole as he made some mocking reply. 'Such a wastrel as thou art knoweth not the value of money, and its loss, therefore, is nothing to thee.'

'What a moil and a coil thy money causes thee, good merchant!' replied the minstrel. 'Thou art condemned from thy own mouth. He that hath money seems ever in fear of losing it. Tell me, canst thou ever sleep soundly at night? Doth thou ever trust wholly one of these thy men? Art thou not ever in fear of some footpad dashing upon thee and cutting thy throat for thy pelf? No, he that hath money taketh unto himself a familiar fiend, which for ever tortures and torments. As for me, why, I have no money, and therefore I care not.'

He twanged his citole, and broke out gaily into the snatch of a gay song.

'Look you, merchant,' he went on, while the other glared sullenly at him, 'I never had more than two rose nobles at a time, and so fearful was I that some wretched fool would say I had stolen them, or would try to steal them from me, that I made haste to spend them, and when the last had gone I felt happy again. Give me a corner away from the wind at night, a little meat and bread and a drink of wine each hour, my citole and the open road before me, and thou, Sir Merchant, may keep thy books of account, thy bales of rich gear, and thy peevish laments over losing a few poor pounds to a bold outlaw.'

'The rogue! He should have his eyes burnt out and his ears cropped!' cried the merchant. 'If I had told him truly all I had, I should not now be robbed of every groat I made at Nottingham Fair!'

'Ha! ha! ha!' laughed the jongleur loud and long. 'There sits the wind, does it? The outlaw played his old trick upon thee, did he? and thou didst fall – thy miserly soul could not tell the truth, and therefore when he found that thou hadst more money than thou didst confess, he took it all! Ha! ha! ha! Sir Merchant, if thou hadst wanted thy money less thou wouldst at least have had some of it now.'

'What sayest thou?' cried the king from where he sat, turning towards the merchant. 'Who hath robbed thee?'

'Who hath robbed me, Sir Priest?' replied the merchant with a jeering voice, for the monks were not beloved by merchants, because of the high tolls and dues they demanded for leave to sell goods in their markets, 'who else but that limb of Satan – that landloping rogue Robin Hood! And if thou travellest that road tomorrow, Sir Priest, I hope he may do as much to thee as he hath done to me.'

'Lord, man, thou art as sore as a bear whose ears the dogs have scored!' said the minstrel, laughing. 'Speak with more reverence to the Church and their servants. Think ye, old sore head, 'twas such as they did baptise thee a Christian – if indeed thou art a Christian and not an unbelieving dog of a Moslem – and with their aid alone thou shalt die and be buried – if ye be not thrown on the roadside at the end as I have seen many a richer man and a finer spoken one!'

The merchant glared and snarled at the minstrel, then turned away and, wrapping himself in his cloak, seemed wishful to forget his loss in sleep.

'Count not his words against him, Lord Abbot,' said the minstrel. ' 'Tis not the man who speaks, but the merchant robbed of his profits. Hallo, here's someone that's as blithe as the merchant is gloomy.'

The door of the hall had opened to the knocking of another wayfarer, and across the straw and rushes on the floor came a poor-looking old man and woman. They were raggedly dressed, and each bore a small bundle, which probably contained all they possessed.

'God bless ye all, gentles,' said the old man, and his face was wreathed in smiles as he doffed his ragged cap, first to the dark-robed monks and then to the minstrel, who grinned in reply, and getting up, swept his own hat with its ragged feather in an elaborate bow before the old man.

'Greeting to thee, old merry heart!' he said. 'Did I not know that the nearest alehouse is twelve long miles away, I would charge thee with having in thee the blessed liquor of the ruddy grape. What cheer, nunks?'

'Sir,' said the old man gleefully, as he put his bag down on the bench, 'I ha' met the finest adventure and the gentlest nobleman that ere I ha' known or heard on. 'Twas but four short miles out of Ollerton, and oh, but I had a dread of the woods! Thick they were with trees, and every moment I was afraid that out of the dark some fearsome robber would dart and cut our throats for the few poor pennies we have.'

'We be only poor folk, sir,' interjected the old woman, who

had a gentle face, though her hands were knotted and lined with a lifetime's toil, 'and we be not used to travelling. We be going to get our poor son from prison at Tickhill.'

'How got thy son in prison, dame?' came a kindly voice from among the black-robed monks. It was the king who spoke.

The old woman was almost overwhelmed at being addressed by one who spoke with an air of nobility, for she was only a poor wife of Nottingham. She curtsied low and replied:

'Oh, Sir Priest, he was tired of the hard toil for Master Peter Greatrex the armourer, and he wandered away to do better, though I begged him to stay with us. And after many months we ha' learned that he ha' been took up for wanderin' and ha' been chained so long in prison at Tickhill till one foot is perished from him. And so we be going to claim him and take him home again.'

'But, good soul,' said the king, 'they will not deliver thy son out of prison to thee.'

'Oh, but we be his parents, Sir Priest,' said the old woman, and tears came to her eyes, 'and we be sure our Dickon hath done no wrong. Surely they will give him to us.'

'Ay, old lass,' said her husband, 'dry thy tears and let be to me. Ha' I not Robin Hood's own words that he will see to it that when we get there they will give Dickon up to us?'

'And is Robin the gentle nobleman ye have met today, old man?' asked the king.

'Ay, Sir Priest, saving your presence, he is that. For 'twas he sent one of his men to us – they spied us through the leaves as we passed along the fearsome road – and when I thought 'twas a thievish rogue come to spoil us, why, 'twas a messenger from Robin himself, who would have us speak with him.'

'I would ha' run e'en then, sirs,' said the old woman, 'so feared was I of this Robin Hood, for he's a great outlaw as I've heard tell. But my old man said – '

'I bade her have no fear, sir,' went on the old man, impatient of his wife's interruption, 'for I told her Robin was too good a man, as I heard tell, to rob poor folks, and belike he would but learn from us whether any rich merchants or priests – saving your presence – were coming behind us. But he asked us naught of that. Nay, sirs, 'twas the gentlest nobleman he was' – the old fellow became quite excited as he went on; his face flushed, his eyes shone, and his hands gestured this way and that. 'He asked us all about ourselves, who we were, whence we came, whither we were wending, and why. Then he ordered them to bring food and wine – he fed us as if we were lord and lady, waiting upon us with his own hands – sirs, 'tis the truth I'm telling ye, as heaven is my witness. Then he crammed bread and meat into my bundle here, and a bottle of wine, and led us to the road again. And he gave me this,' he held up a coin which flashed dully in the torch-light: it was a silver penny; 'and his last words were, "Old lad, I'll see to it that thy son is given to thee when thou gettest to Tickhill. And if any saucy rogue stops thee on the road and would harm or rob thee, say to him that Robin gives thee peace through the forest land, and charge the rogue to let thee go, lest the fate of Richard Illbeast befall him."'

'Saw one ever such a cross-grained rascal as this Robin,' came the shrill voice of the merchant, who had heard all. 'From me he taketh all I possess, and to this old churl, who knoweth not the value of a groat, he giveth a silver penny, and belike it is one the rogue stole from me!'

'Oh, cease thy noise, old huckster!' cried the minstrel sternly. 'I tell thee when the great trump sounds, 'twill be Robin will pass before thee up to St Peter's knee, or I know not what is a good man and a noble doer. I will make a poem of this that thou tellest me, old man, for indeed 'tis a deed worthy of a poet's praise, and of the fame a poet's song can give to it.'

The old man and his wife sat down to their meal; the minstrel became silent and absorbed, his eyes half closed as he murmured broken words over to himself, and began composing his poem; and the merchant and his men again wrapped themselves in their cloaks and turned to slumber on the truckle-beds ranged along the room.

Meanwhile the king had beckoned to de Warenne, and in a low voice asked what Robin had meant by 'the fate of Richard Illbeast', on which the Earl and Ralph Fitz-Stephen told the king all that had happened at York, of the flight of the leader of the mob who massacred the Jews, and of the capture of Richard Illbeast by Robin, who had executed him for his many crimes in the very presence of Sir Laurence de Raby, marshal of the king's justice. When they had finished speaking the king was silent for some time, and was sunk in deep thought. At length he said:

'Methinks this is no common man, this Robin Hood. Almost it seems that he doth right in spite of the laws, and that they be wrong indeed if they have forced him to flee to the greenwood and become outside the law. He robs the rich and the proud who themselves have robbed to glut their greed and their pride; but he giveth aid and comfort to the poor, and that seemeth to be no man's desire to do. I will gladly see this man, and by the favour of heaven I will make him my friend.'

Then the king gave orders that beds should be set up, and all retired to rest.

Next morning the party of the king had not proceeded more than five miles along the leafy highway leading to Ollerton, when suddenly out of the wood came a tall man, dressed in an old green tunic and trunk hose of the same colour. In his hand he bore a great bow taller than himself, at his side was a good sword, and in his belt a dagger of Spanish steel. On his head was a velvet hat, and stuck therein was a long feather from a cock pheasant's tail.

Manly of form and keen of look was he; his face and neck were browned by the summer sun, and his dark curls hung to his shoulders. He lifted his sharp eyes to the foremost rider and said, holding up one big brown hand as he did so:

'Stay, Sir Abbot. By your leave ye must bide awhile with me.'

He placed two fingers in his mouth and whistled shrilly. Almost immediately, out of the shadow of the trees came forth some twenty archers on each side of the road. Each was dressed in green tunic and hose, torn and worn in places; but each was a stout man of his hands, well knit and bold of look, and each bore a bow.

'We be yeomen of this forest, Sir Abbot,' said Robin, for the first man had been the outlaw himself, 'and we live on the king's deer in this forest, and on what rich lords and knights and priests will give us of their wealth. Give us, then, some of thy money ere thou wouldst wend farther, Sir Abbot.'

'Good yeomen,' replied the king, 'I have with me no more than forty pounds, for I have stayed with our king at Blythe, and I have spent much on lordings there. Nevertheless I willingly give thee what I have.'

The king commanded one of the cloaked figures behind him to produce his purse, which being done was handed to Robin, who took it and said:

'Lord Abbot, thou speakest like an honest and a noble man. I will therefore not search thy saddlebags to know whether thou speakest truth. Here,' he said, 'are twenty pounds which I render to thee again, since I would not have thee fare away without money to spend. The other twenty shall be toll for thy safe journey. Fare thee well, Lord Abbot.'

Robin stood away to let the horses pass, taking off his hat in a dignified salute as he did so. But the abbot placed his hand in his breast and produced a piece of parchment, which he opened with much crackling of the stiff skin. There was writing upon it, and below hung a big red ball of wax, bearing a seal upon it.

'Gramercy, good yeomen,' said the king, 'but I bear with me the greetings of our good King Richard. He hath sent thee his seal and his bidding that ye should meet him in Nottingham in three days' time, and this shall be thy safe conduct to and fro.'

Robin looked keenly into the shadowed face within the cowl of the abbot as he approached and took the parchment. He bent on his knee to show his respect for the king's letter, and said:

'Sir Abbot, I love no man in all the world so well as I do my comely king. His letter is welcome, and for thy tidings, Sir Abbot, do thou stay and dine with us in greenwood fashion.'

'Gramercy,' said the king, 'that will I do willingly.'

Forthwith the king and his knights were led on foot into a deeper part of the forest, where, under the trysting tree of the outlaws, dinner was being cooked. Robin placed a horn to his lips and blew a curious blast. Hardly had the last notes died away ere from all parts of the forest which surrounded the glade in which they sat came men in green, with bows in hand and swords at their side. Each had the quick, brave look of men used to the open air and a free life, and each, as he approached where Robin stood, doffed his hat to his leader.

'By the soul of my father,' muttered Richard into the ear of de Warenne, 'this is a seemly sight, yet a sad one. These be fine men, and they be more at this outlaw's bidding than my own knights be at mine.'

The king and his knights did full justice to the good dinner set before them, and when it was over Robin said:

'Now, Lord Abbot, thou shalt see what manner of life we lead, so that when thou dost return to our king thou mayst tell him.'

Thereupon targets were set up at which a chosen number of the outlaws began to shoot, and so distant and small was the mark that the king marvelled that any should hit it. But he marvelled more when Robin ordered a wand to be set up, from the top of which hung a garland of roses.

'He that doth not shoot through the garland,' cried Robin, 'shall lose his bow and arrows, and shall bear a buffet from him that was the better archer.'

' 'Tis most marvellous shooting,' said Richard, as he sat apart with his knights. 'Oh, that I could get five hundred as good archers to come with me across the sea! I would riddle the coat of the King of France, and make him bow to me.'

Twice Robin shot at the mark, and each time he cleft the wand. But others missed, and those who fell before Robin's buffet were many. Even Scarlet and Little John had to bear the weight of his arm, but Gilbert of the White Hand was by now almost as good an archer as Robin. Then Robin shot for the third time, and he was unlucky, for his bolt missed the garland by the space of three fingers. There was a great burst of laughter from the archers, and a cry of, 'A miss! a miss!'

'I avow it,' cried Robin, laughing, and just then he saw through the trees at the other end of the glade a party riding towards them. They were Fair Marian his wife, clad in green, with her bow and arrows beside her, and with her were Sir Richard at Lee and Alan-a-Dale and Dame Alice his wife.

Robin turned to the abbot and said:

'I yield my bow and arrow to thee, Lord Abbot, for thou art my master. Do thou give me such a buffet as thou mayst.'

'It is not fitting to my order,' said the abbot, and drew his cowl closer about his face to hide it from Robin's keen glance and from the eyes of the party riding towards them.

'Smite boldly, Sir Abbot,' urged Robin; 'I give thee full leave.'

The king smiled, bared his arm, and gave so stout a blow full on Robin's breast that the outlaw was hurled some feet away and almost fell to the ground. He kept his feet, however, and coming to the king, from whose face the cowl had dropped away by reason of the violence of his blow, he said:

'By the sweet Virgin, but there is pith in thy arm, Lord Abbot – if abbot thou art or monk – and a stalwart man art thou.'

At this very moment Sir Richard at Lee leaped from his saddle and, doffing his hat, ran forward, crying, ' 'Tis the king! Kneel, Robin!' The knight knelt on his knees before the king, who now thrust the cowl from off his head of brown hair, and revealed the handsome face and blue eyes, in which a proud but genial light shone, of Richard Cœur-de-Lion. Then he tore aside the black robes he wore, showing beneath the rich silk surtout blazoned with the leopards of Anjou and the fleur-de-lys of France.

Robin and his outlaws and Alan-a-Dale kneeled at the sight, and Fair Marian and Dame Alice, getting from their horses, curtsied humbly.

'By the soul of my father,' said Richard with a gay laugh, 'but this is a right fair adventure. Why do ye kneel, good Robin? Art thou not king of the greenwood?'

'My lord, the King of England,' said Robin, 'I love thee and fear thee, and would crave thy mercy for myself and my men for all the deeds which we have done against thy laws. Of thy goodness and grace give us mercy!'

'Rise, Robin, for, by the Trinity, I have never met in the greenwood a man so much after my heart as thou art,' said the king. He caught Robin by the hand and lifted him to his feet. 'But, by the Virgin, thou must leave this life and be my liege servant and rule thyself as a lawful man.'

'This will I do willingly, my lord the king,' said Robin, 'for I would liefer keep thy law and do what good I may openly than live outside the law.'

'So let it be,' replied the king; 'I have heard all that thou hast done. Thou hast wedded a rich ward of mine against all my right and due! Is this fair lady she who hath left wealth and honours and lands for love of thee?'

Fair Marian cast herself upon her knees before the king, who gave her his hand to kiss, after which he raised her to her feet.

'Come,' said the king, 'thou hast given up much to come to thy good archer, fair lady. I can only agree that thou hast chosen a bold man and a brave one. Thou wert ward of mine, and I give thee willingly where thou hast already given thyself.'

So saying, the king joined the hands of Robin and Marian, both of whom felt very happy in having the king himself pardon them for so wilfully acting against his rights.

'But,' went on the king, smiling, 'thou hast committed so many bold deeds, Robin, that I must doom thee to some punishment for them. Go thou and lead a quiet life after these years of strife and hiding. Take thy fair dame and dwell with her on her lands at Malaset, at peace with my deer and all thy fellow-subjects. Uphold the laws which my wise councillors make for the peace and prosperity of this realm. By so doing thou shalt win my pardon.'

'My lord king,' said Robin, deeply moved at the king's generosity, 'for this thy great mercy and favour I will ever be thy faithful and loyal servant.'

'See to it, de Warenne,' said Richard, 'that Robin, by virtue of his dame Marian, be put in possession of all her lands and dues.'

'I will see to it, sire,' said the stout Earl Hamelin, 'the more eagerly because I look forward to having Robin's good help in collecting thy taxes with due promptitude in the manors and boroughs on the Lancashire marches.'

The king laughed and turned to Robin. 'For thy aid in gathering my ransom I give thee thanks,' he said.

Then Robin brought Sir Richard at Lee to the king, who heard Sir Richard's prayer and was pleased to give him his lands again, and to grant him full pardon for having offended against the laws in giving aid to Robin.

Finally, Alan-a-Dale and Dame Alice kneeled before the king, who heard how they, with Sir Walter de Beauforest, the lady's father, had incurred the enmity of Sir Isenbart de Belame, and ever lived in fear of that knight's sudden attack upon their manors and lands. The king inquired narrowly of the deeds of the lords of Wrangby, and his brow went dark with anger when he heard of their manifold and wicked oppressions.

'They are an evil brood!' he said at length sadly. 'But I and my dear father's other undutiful sons did bring them to life, for we plunged the realm in wicked wars and confusion. And my brother John would do the same while I am fighting for the Holy Sepulchre, and these evil lords thrive in his company. De Warenne, I will speak further as to these lords of the Evil Hold! Let me but

Robin receives a buffet from King Richard

settle with that traitor, Philip of France, and thrust him from my lands in Normandy and Aquitaine, and I will come back and sweep these evil castles from the land, and stamp out the nests of vipers and serpents that shelter behind their strong walls.'

Two days later the king's messenger handed a parchment to the gate-guard at the castle of Wrangby, and would not stay for food or lodging, as a sign of the king's displeasure. When Isenbart de Belame read the writing on the parchment his mouth went wry with a bitter sneer.

'So!' he said mockingly, 'the king takes outlaws to his bosom because he wants good archers for his wars in Normandy. And he will have me to know that any harm done upon Sir Walter de Beauforest, Alan de Tranmire or Dame Alice, or any of their lands, manors, villeins, or other estate, will be crimes against the king, to be punished as acts of treason.'

He dashed the parchment to the floor, and his eyes flashed with evil fire.

'I must bide my time a little longer,' he muttered to himself. 'Who knows? The king will play at castle-taking with Philip of France. He may be slain any day, and then when Earl John shall take the throne, I shall have licence to do all I wish with that insolent outlaw and all his friends. I will bide my time.'

As the king had bidden him, Robin went with Fair Marian to the lands of Malaset, and received them back from the guardianship of Scrivel of Catsty, who yielded up the castle, the manor, and the fair broad lands with an evil grace. There Robin dwelled in peace and comfort, tending the estates of his wife with good husbandry and careful rule, guarding the lands from encroachment by neighbouring lords, and knitting all his villeins and freeholders to himself by his kindliness and frankness.

With him went Hob o' the Hill and Ket the Trow, together with their two sisters. Their mother had died in the 'howe', or green mound, a little while before, and they had therefore wished to leave the place. Little John also went with Robin, and Gilbert of the White Hand, who married Sibbie, one of the fairy sisters, and lived in a cottage which Robin gave to them. The other sister, Fenella, wedded Wat Graham of Car Peel, a brave fighter from the borderlands, and their children were long said to have the fairy gifts of second sight, invisibility, and supernatural strength.

The other outlaws all yielded to King Richard's offer of high wages and great loot, and went with him to Normandy, there to fight the French king and the rebellious 'weathercocks' of Poitou. Most of them left their bones there; a score or two came back, after King Richard was slain, some rich with plunder, others as poor as they went forth, and all these gradually drifted to Malaset, where 'Squire Robin,' as he was called, settled them on lands.

With those who came back from France were Will the Bowman, Scarlet, and Much, the Miller's son. Arthur-a-Bland was slain at the taking of the castle of Chaluz, where the king also met his death, and Scadlock was drowned in a storm at sea, just outside Rye. With the old outlaws who remained, Robin formed as fine a body of fighting men as ever marched south under the banners of the barons when, in the year 1215, they at length set their hands to the struggle with their king to wrest from him freedom from tyranny and oppression.

Sixteen years thus passed over the heads of Robin and his fair spouse Marian; and in spite of the trouble and confusion which agitated the minds of men and brought disorder into the kingdom when King John defied the pope, these were happy years at Malaset.

But in his castle of Wrangby Sir Iscnbart de Belame still brooded on the vengeance he would wreak upon Robin Hood, and bided his time in patience. And to him often came Sir Guy of Gisborne, and with them spoke Sir Baldwin the Killer, Sir Roger of Doncaster, and Sir Scrivel of Catsty, and all took secret counsel together how they should best take and slay Robin when the time came.

CHAPTER TEN

The Burning of Evil Hold

It was an early winter day in the year 1215. A band of men were marching across the high moorlands east of the wild waste lands of the Peak. At their head rode Robin Hood, clothed in chain mail, the helm upon his head sparkling in the westering sun. Behind him came sixty of his men, bronzed, honest-faced yeomen, each with his bow and quiver, and a sword strapped to his side. A score of them were his old outlaws, and head and shoulders above them stalked Little John, his brown, keen eyes looking sharply this way and that over the wide moors which stretched away to the purple distance on every side. Immediately behind Robin walked Ket the Trow, sturdy though small, a fighter, yet a man of craft in every look and gesture of him. Not far off were Scarlet, Will Stuteley, and Much, the Miller's son.

The face of Robin wore a thoughtful, even a moody air. He had gone with the barons when they had wrested the charter of liberty from the tyrannous hands of John; and had stayed south with them, believing that the fight for freedom had been gained. Then suddenly they had learned that foreign mercenaries were landing to aid the king against his rebel barons; the foreign hordes, thirsting for blood and plunder, had been seen in such strength that the barons had almost lost heart and had retreated. Many had gone to defend their own castles and lands when they learned that the king's mercenaries had stolen north, harrying, burning, and slaying, and Robin Hood had done likewise, fearing lest evil should befall his gentle wife in the peaceful vale of Malaset upon the marches of Lancaster.

Robin wondered, indeed, whether he had started too late. At every step of the way northwards they saw the marks of rapine and massacre where the king had passed with his foreign hordes. Every house and village they passed was destroyed by fire, corpses lay stiff on the snow, or weltered on the hearthstone which had known the laughter and the joy in life of those who now lay dead. Smoke rose over the wintry horizon, showing where the burning and slaying of the ruffianly army of the shameless king still went on. One castle which they passed was a smoking ruin, and in its blackened and smouldering hall they found two young ladies, one dumb with grief, the other half mad in her sorrow, leaning over the body of their father, an old knight, whom his king had tortured to death in an attempt to wring from him the place where he had hidden his store of money.

Now and then, as he rode, Robin raised his head and glanced quickly before him. He dreaded lest he should see a cloud of smoke which should show that some band of the evil army of the king had come so far westwards to Malaset. But against the violet clouds of the wintry sky where the sun was sinking there was no blur of rolling reek.

At length the road descended from the moors and wound round crags and limestone cliffs down towards the valley of Malaset. Almost unconsciously Robin pushed on faster, so eager was he to reach a point where, at a bend in the road, he could see the castle. At length he reached the place, stopped for a moment, and his men, hurrying behind him, heard him give a dreadful cry. Next moment he had struck spurs into his horse's flanks and thundered down the sloping track.

They reached the bend and looked upon the low keep of the castle. A light grey smoke, as if from smouldering timber, rose from the pile, and a dreadful silence brooded over all. The men groaned, and then began to run, uttering fearful cries of vengeance and despair as they rushed towards ruined homes and slain loved ones.

With a strange, cold calmness on him, Robin leaped from his horse in the courtyard, in which bodies of men lay here and there, still and contorted. He strode into the hall; a thin reek of smoke filled the apartment. The place had been fired, but the fire had not caught. Only some broken benches smouldered in a heap, amidst which the bodies of defenders and their assailants were mingled together in the close fierce embrace in which they had given each other death. Up the winding stair in the wall he strode, to the solar or lady's bower.

The door was shut, and he opened it gently. There in the light of the westering sun lay a figure on the bed, its face very white and set. It was Marian. Her body was draped in black, and was very still, and he knew that she was dead. On her breast her long fair hands were folded, and her dark hair framed her face and breast in a soft beauty. A short black arrow lay beside the corpse.

A sudden movement came from behind the arras, and the slight figure of a woman darted towards him and threw herself on her knees before him. It was Sibbie, wife to Gilbert of the White Hand, the fairy maid who had been tirewoman to Fair Marian. She did not weep, but her face looked up into his with grief in the great brown, faithful eyes.

'Who has done this, Sibbie?' asked Robin in a quiet, low voice.

'Who but that fiend Isenbart de Belame!' said the woman in a fierce restrained voice. 'He slew her while she spoke with him from the gate-guard room. With this arrow – the selfsame arrow which my brother Hob shot in his table at Evil Hold – he let out her dear life. She fell into my arms, smiled at me, but could not speak, and so died. On the second day – 'twas but yesterday they left – they stormed the castle, but bitter and hard was the fighting in the courtyard and the hall, and then, for fear you should return, they plundered far and wide through the manor, and so left, with Hob my brother wounded and a prisoner, and ten others, whom they promised to torture when they reached Evil Hold again.'

Ket the Trow had crept into the room immediately behind Robin and heard all. His sister turned to him and silently they clasped hands. Then, loosing them, they each raised the right forefinger in the air, and swiftly made a strange gesture as if they wrote a letter or marked a device. It was the sign of undying vengeance by which the people of the Underworld vowed to go through flood and fire, pains and pangs, and never to slacken in their quest, never to rest, until they had avenged the death of their lady.

Robin bent and kissed the cold forehead of his wife. Then, uncovering, he knelt beside her and prayed. He spoke no word, but he craved the aid of the Virgin in his vow to stamp out utterly the life and power of the lord of the Evil Hold and all his mates in wickedness.

That night, by the light of torches, the body of Marian was

lowered to the grave beside her father and her kinsfolk in the little church of Malaset, while in the castle those of the villeins and freemen who had fled from their farms and holdings at the approach of de Belame and his evil horde were busily engaged in furbishing up arms and harness. All were filled with a hard resolution, and each had made up his mind to die in the attempt to pull down the Evil Hold and its power.

At dawn, in silence, Robin and his band set forth. They did not look back once, but stubbornly they mounted the moorside road and kept their faces fixed towards the east. At the same time Robin sent a messenger to Sir Herbrand de Tranmire, now an old man, reminding him of his promise to aid him in breaking down the castle of Wrangby, and asking, if he could not come himself, to send all the men he could spare, well armed, to meet Robin at the Mark Oak by Wrangby Mere. Similar messages were sent by Robin to other knights and freemen who had suffered from the oppression of de Belame. Many had promised 'Squire Robin' aid if ever he needed it, for all had recognised in him a brave man and a generous one; and all had known that someday they would have to join their forces with him to end the villainies and wicked customs of the Evil Hold.

On his way to Wrangby, Robin called at the castles and manor-houses of other knights to ask their aid. Some places he found were gutted and in ruins, with their brave defenders lying dead, the prey of their king's malignant cruelty. Many men, however, quickly responded to his appeal, so that when at evening, as the twilight was creeping over the misty moor, Robin rode in sight of Wrangby Castle, he had three hundred men at his back, sufficient at least to prevent the garrison from breaking forth.

He stopped a bowshot from the great gate and sounded his horn. On the tower above the portal appeared two men in complete mail, one wearing a bronze helmet which shone dully in the faint light.

'I would speak to Isenbart de Belame!' cried Robin.

'Wolf's-head!' came the reply, like the snarl of a wolf, 'you are speaking to Sir Isenbart de Belame, lord of Wrangby and the Fells. What do you and your rabble want?'

'I will tell ye,' cried Robin. 'Deliver yourself up to me with the prisoners you have taken! You shall have the judgement of your peers upon your evil deeds, and for the murder of my wife, the Lady Marian. If you do not do this, then we will take your evil castle by storm, and the death of you and your men shall be on your head!'

'If ye do not leave my lands by dawn,' was the fierce reply, 'you and your tail of whipped curs and villeins, I will come out and beat you to death with my dogwhips. Go, wolf's-head and rascal! I will speak no more with thee!'

With a gesture, as if he had no more attention to bestow on creatures so mean, he turned aside and spoke to the other knight who was with him. Both had their visors down, and in the gathering twilight their figures were becoming dimmer every moment. Suddenly a little figure sped forward in the gloom before Robin's horse, then stood still, and the twang of a bowstring was heard. Next moment the knight beside de Belame was seen to put his hands to his visor and then stagger. He recovered himself instantly, however, and drew an arrow from between the bars of his helmet. With a gesture of rage he dashed it over the battlements and yelled something in derision which could not be heard.

It was Ket the Trow who had made this marvellous shot in the twilight, so that men wondered that it could have reached the mark so unerringly. Yet by reason of the fact that the bolt had been shot at so great an angle, the arrow had only torn the flesh on the forehead of the knight.

That night Robin and his men hemmed the castle closely, so that no one could come out or go in unseen. Under the Mark Oak he took counsel with the knights who had brought aid.

'Squire Robin,' said one, Sir Fulk of the Dykewall, 'I cannot see how we can hope to beat down that strong keep. We have no siege engines, we cannot break down the wall in any place, the ditch is full of water, and I doubt not that such a man as de Belame is well provisioned for a long siege.'

'I see no reason why we should not take the castle,' said young Squire Denvil of Toomlands, as eager and brave as a hawk. 'We can get the Wrangby peasants, who hate their lords, to cut down trees and make rafts for us. With these, and under cover of our shields we can pole across the ditch and cut the chains of the drawbridge. Then we can prise up the portcullis, and once within can hack down the gate.'

After long council, this seemed the only way by which they could hope to take the castle. It would mean the loss of many lives, no doubt, but the walls of the castle were thick and high, and there was no other way out or in but by the great gate. Ket the Trow was called and bidden to go to the villeins of Wrangby in the hovels a mile from the castle, and ask them to come to aid Robin in rooting out their evil lords. In an hour he returned.

'I went to Cole the Reeve,' he said, 'and gave him the bidding. He called the homagers [chief men] and told them what you wanted. Their eyes said they would quickly come, but long they thought in silence. Then one said, "Six times hath the Evil Hold been set about by strong lords, and never hath it been taken. Satan loves his own, and 'tis vain to fight against the evil lords. They have ever had power, and will ever keep it." And they were silent to all I urged upon them, and shook their heads and went away.'

Robin thereupon commanded parties of his own men to take it in turn during the night to cut down young trees to make rafts with them, and short scaling-ladders to get at the chains of the drawbridge, and by the light of torches, in amongst the trees, the work went on all night, while Robin went from place to place seeing that strict guard was kept. Just before daybreak he took some sleep, but was awakened by the arrival of a band of peasants from Wrangby, the very men who, the night before, had refused to aid him against their lords. At their head was an old man, grey, of great frame and fierce aspect. In his hands he bore a tall billhook, with a long wide blade as keen and bright as a razor. When Robin saw him he knew him for one of the men who had shot with him at the contest at Nottingham before the sheriff.

'Master,' said the old man, going to Robin, 'I bring you these men. They denied you last night. They were but half men then, but I have spoken with them, and now they will help you to pull down this nest of bandit lords and slayers of women and children and maimers of men.'

'I thank thee, Rafe of the Billhook,' replied Robin, and turned to the peasants. one of them stepped forth and spoke for his fellows.

'We have taken the oath,' he said, 'and we will go with thee to the end. Rather we will be destroyed now than live longer in our misery under our evil oppressors.'

The poor men seemed depressed and subdued, as if all the manliness had been beaten out of them by years of ill-usage at the hands of their lords.

'Ye will not fail, brothers,' said Rafe, and his look was fierce as he shook his huge billhook. 'I swore, when they thrust me from my cot in Barnisdale Wood and slew my wife and my boy, that I would come back and help to root these fiends out of their nest of stone. The time has come, brothers, and God and the Virgin are fighting for us.'

'You are Thurstan of Stone Cot, whom de Belame thrust from your holding thirty winters ago?' asked Robin.

'You speak truly,' replied Thurstan; 'I have returned at my appointed time.'

Under the guidance of this man, and with the eager help of Little John and Gilbert of the White Hand, preparations were soon ready, and after a good meal had been taken and mass had been heard, the rafts were carried down to the ditch before the great gate. Showers of arrows greeted them, but the raft-bearers were supported by archers who were commanded by Scarlet and Will Stuteley, and who scanned with keen eyes every slit in the walls. Their bolts searched out and struck everything that moved behind the arrow slits, and anyone who came to the battlements of the castle was hit by several arrows. Quickly the rafts were launched and poled across the ditch, and ladders were reared on the sills beside the huge drawbridge which blocked up the portcullis and the gates beyond. Soon the blows of iron upon iron told how mightily the smiths were striving to cut the chains on either side which held the drawbridge up. For a time it looked as if they would have an easy task, for Robin's archers made it impossible for anyone to lean from the battlements to shoot them. Suddenly, however, the inside gates were thrown open and a crowd of bowmen began to shoot at the smiths through the bars of the portcullis. One smith fell from his ladder into the ditch, a great arrow sticking in his breast; the other had his hand transfixed.

Others took their places at once, however, and Scarlet, Will the Bowman, and two other archers stood on the ladders with the smiths, and returned the shooting as best they could, though the space was so confined that hardly could they draw their bows. At length a shout went up – one chain was cut through and the drawbridge shook and trembled. A few more blows with the hammer on the other side, and with a mighty crash the draw-bridge fell across the moat, being smashed in half by reason of its weight. Robin and a select band of archers swarmed over the ruined drawbridge, which held together sufficiently to allow of this, and shooting between the bars of the portcullis, poured in such flights of arrows that the garrison, which was indifferently provided with bowmen, was compelled to retreat behind the gates, which finally they had to close.

Then a great tree trunk was run forward by forty willing hands, and the bridge having been covered with rafting to support the weight of extra men, the battering-ram was dashed against the portcullis. Again and again this was done, the archers on the bank picking off those on the castle wall or at the arrow slits who tried to shoot down the besiegers. Many of Robin's men were killed, however, for the defence was as bitter as the attack, and everywhere in the castle could be heard the voices of Sir Isenbart and his fellow-knights, Sir Baldwin, Sir Scrivel, or Sir Roger of Doncaster, angrily urging the archers and stone-throwers to continue their efforts. Several of Robin's archers and those of the ramming-party, though these had shields over their heads, were either killed or disabled by bolts or crushed by huge stones, but still the great tree trunk hammered at the portcullis, making it to shake and crack here and there.

At last the castle gate was thrown open again, and a deadly flight of arrows flew out, dealing death from between the bars of the portcullis. But Robin led up his archers, and again compelled the garrison to retreat, while other men-at-arms took the vacant places beside the ram, the head of which was now so split and torn that it seemed like a mop. Still it thudded and crashed against the bars of the portcullis, two of which were so bent and cracked that soon the great grille would be broken through sufficiently to allow men to enter.

Robin, Sir Fulk, and another knight, Sir Robert of Staithes, were standing beside the ramming-party urging them on, Robin with a watchful eye on the inner gate, lest it should open again to let forth a shower of bolts.

'Three more good blows from master oak, lads,' cried Robin, 'and in we go. The wooden gate will not keep us long!'

Just then there came quick shouts from Will the Bowman, who stood with his archers on the bank.

'Back! back!' he cried; 'they throw fire down!'

'Into the moat!' shouted Robin, hearing the warning cries. Most heard him and jumped at once. But other poor fellows were too late.

Down from the battlements poured a deluge of boiling tar, and quickly after came burning brands and red-hot stones. Some half-dozen men who had not heard the cries were whelmed in the deathly rain and killed. The lighted brands and red-hot stones instantly set fire to the rafting, the drawbridge and the ram, which were covered with tar, and soon a furnace fire raged, cutting off the besiegers from what a few moments before had seemed almost certain victory.

Robin and those who had escaped swam to the bank, while Will and his archers searched the walls with their arrows. But they had not been able to prevent the tar from being heaved over, for the men who had dragged the cauldron to the battlements had been protected by shields held before them by others.

Robin looked at the gulf of fire before him, and at the angry and gloomy faces of his men.

'Never mind, lads,' he cried. 'They can't get out themselves, and when the fire has burned itself out we will cross by fresh rafts. A few more blows and the bars will be broken enough to let us in. Will and you, Scarlet,' he cried, turning to Stuteley and the other old outlaw, 'see that you let no one of the evil crew mend those broken bars.'

'He will have to mend the hole in his own carcass first,' said Scarlet, with a laugh. He cocked his eye quickly over arrow slit and battlement as he held his bow in readiness to shoot.

It was now past noon, and while a party watched the portcullis, and others took a hasty meal, a third party were sent with the peasants to cut fresh rafts.

As Robin was directing the work of the woodcutters, he saw, coming over the moor, a great party of footmen, preceded by two knights on horseback. His keen eyes gazed at the blazons on their shields, and at sight of the three white swallows of the one, and the five green trees of the other, he waved his hand in welcome. They were Sir Walter de Beauforest and young Alan-a-Dale, and in a little while they were shaking hands with Robin.

'We received thy message yesterday,' said Sir Walter, 'and we have come as quickly as we could. I trust we have not arrived too late'

'Nay, the castle hath not yet fallen into my hands,' said Robin, 'and your forces will be welcome.'

He then related what had been done and the plans he had made for taking the place, which they found were good, and promised to aid him all they could. Alan told him that Sir Herbrand was sending a party to help Robin, but being old and feeble he could not come himself, much as he would like to have struck a blow against his enemies of Wrangby.

Now all this while Ket the Trow wandered through the camp with a gloomy look. Sometimes he took his place with the archers by the moat, and his was the keenest eye to see a movement at an arrow slit or on the battlements, and his was the swiftest arrow to fly at the mark. But things were going too slowly for Ket. He yearned for a speedy and complete revenge for the murder of his beloved mistress. Moreover, he knew that inside that castle his loved brother Hob lay in some noisome dungeon wounded, perhaps suffering already some cruel torture.

Round and round the castle Ket went, creeping from cover to cover, his dark eyes searching the smooth stone of the walls for some loophole whereby he could enter. He had been inside once, when he had shot the message on the table before Sir Isenbart de Belame, when Ranulf of the Waste had been slain. That night he had followed some of the knights when they had returned from a foray, bringing rich gear as spoil and captives for ransom. He had been close on their backs, and in the confusion he had marched in through the gate and had secreted himself in the darkness. Then at night he had crept down a drain which opened out some twelve feet above the ditch, and, under cover of a storm of wind and rain, had dropped into the water and so got safely away.

But now, try as he might, the great high walls baffled him, for he could see no way by which he could win into the strong keep. Once in, he doubted not that he could worm his way to his brother, release him, and then slay the guards and open the gates to Robin and his men.

He lay in a thick bush of hazel at the rear of the castle and scanned the walls narrowly. Now and then he cast his eyes warily round the moorland to where the forest and the fells hemmed in the Wrangby lands.

What was that? At one and the same moment two strange things had happened. He had seen a sword flash twice from the battlements of the castle, as if it was a signal, and instantly there had been a momentary glint as of a weapon from between the leafless trees of a wood on the edge of the forest some half a mile away. He looked long and earnestly at the point, but nothing stirred or showed again.

'Strange,' thought Ket; 'was that a signal? If so, who was he to whom the man in the castle was making signs?'

Ket's decision was soon taken, and like a ferret, creeping from bush to bush, he made his way towards the wood. He reached the verge and looked between the trees. There, with the muzzles of their horses tied up to prevent their making a noise, lay some thirty fierce moss-riders. He knew them at once. They were the men of Thurlstan, from whom he had rescued Fair Marian several years before. A man raised his great shock head of white hair and looked over the moor towards the camp of the besiegers. Then his teeth showed in a mocking sneer, and Ket knew that this was old Grame Gaptooth himself, lord of Thurlstan.

' 'Twill be dark in an hour, and then we will make that rabble fly!' said the old raider.

Ket guessed at once, and rightly, that these marauders, kinsmen to Sir Isenbart, had ridden to join him in the plundering foray of King John, lured by the hope of slaughter and booty. They had discovered that the castle was besieged, had made their presence known to their friends in the castle, and now lay waiting for the short winter day to end. Then they would ride down fiercely among Robin's band, and by their cries they would give Sir Isenbart the signal to issue forth. Then, surprised, and taken between two forces, who knows? perhaps Robin Hood and his men would be cut to pieces.

With the stealth of a wild cat, Ket began to back away and to creep deeper into the wood behind where the moss-riders lay. With infinite care he proceeded, since the cracking of a twig might reveal his presence to the fierce raiders. When he had covered some fifty yards he carefully rose to his feet and then, like a shadow, flitted from tree to tree through the forest towards the camp of Robin.

The Thurlstan men heard from where they lay the shouts of men as they yelled defiance at the garrison; and the short, sharp words of command of Robin and the knights as they supervised the placing of the rafts of timber in the ditch before the gate. Then, in a little while, the twilight and the mist deepened over the land, the forest seemed to creep nearer, and darkness descended rapidly.

'Now, lads,' said Grame Gaptooth, getting to his feet and grasping his horse's bridle, 'mount and make ready. Walk your horses till ye are a hundred yards from where thou seest their fires burning, then use the spur and shout my cry, "Gaptooth o' the Wall." Then with spur and sword mow me those dogs down, and when Belame hears us he will come forth, and the killing will be a merry one between us. Now, up and away!'

Quietly over the long coarse grass the raiders passed, and then, with a sudden fierce shout, they dashed upon the groups about the fires. But, strangely enough, the men-at-arms they rode among turned as if they expected them; three knights rode out of the gloom against the raiders, and amidst the shouts of 'Gaptooth o' the Wall, Gaptooth o' the Wall,' the fierce fighting began.

Counselled by Ket the Trow, Robin had ordered his men to retreat a little towards the castle, so that the garrison should hear clearly when the border men attacked them; and this was done. Eagerly the moss-men followed, and their enemies seemed to fly before them. They pressed on more quickly, still shouting their war cry. Suddenly they heard answering cries. 'Belame! Belame!' came like a fierce bellow from the castle gate, which was dashed open, the portcullis slowly mounted, and out from its yawning jaws swept knights and men-at-arms. Robin had placed the rafts over the blackened timbers of the drawbridge, so that the garrison could come out without delay, and over these they came in a mad rush, causing the timbers to heave and rock, and soon the cries of 'Gaptooth' and 'Belame' mingled in fierce delight.

Suddenly, above the din, came the dear call of a bugle from somewhere in the rear. At the same time three short, sharp notes rose from beneath the castle walls. Out of the forest of the Mark Oak swept ten knights and a hundred men-at-arms, the force which Sir Herbrand had sent, and which had arrived as darkness fell, in time to form part of the plan which Robin and the knights, with the counsel of Ket the Trow, had formed for the destruction of their enemy.

The men who had seemed to be caught between those who shouted 'Belame' and those who cried 'Gaptooth' now suddenly came back in greater numbers. The troop of de Belame heard the rush of men behind them where, as they thought, they had left none but their own garrison; and the moss-riders turned, as avenging cries of 'Marian! Marian!' answered by other shouts of 'Tranmire and St George' sounded fiercely all about them.

Then indeed came the fierce crash of battle. Caught between the two wings of Robin's party, which now outnumbered de Belame and his friends, the Wrangby lords fought for dear life. No quarter was asked or given. Peasant with bill or axe fought men-at-arms on foot, or hacked at the knight of coat-armour on horseback; and everywhere Rafe of the Bill fought in fierce delight, his glittering bill in his hand, looking out meanwhile for Sir Isenbart himself. Robin also sought everywhere in the gloom for the slayer of his wife. Distinguishable by the bronze of his helmet, Sir Isenbart raged like a boar to and fro, dealing death or wounds with every blow, chanting the while his own fierce name. Robin saw him and strove to follow him, but the press of battle kept them asunder. Close behind Robin stalked Little John, a huge double-headed axe in his hand, making wider the path cleared by his master through their foes.

'John, for the love of the Virgin, go strike down that bronze helm,' cried Robin at length. 'It is de Belame! Man, for love of me, let him not escape!'

Little chance there seemed of that now, even if the brave, fierce tyrant wished to run. He was checked in his path of slaughter now, for Rafe of the Bill and twenty Wrangby villeins had surrounded him, tearing at his limbs, wrenching at his armour to drag him down among their feet. Long years of hatred and misery thrilled in every nerve, but more skilful with the humble weapons of the soil than with arms, they went down before his keen sword like stalks of wheat before the sickle. Swiftly he struck here and there, shaking off his assailants as a bear tosses off the dogs. Rafe strove to reach him with his great bill, thrusting and hacking at him, but de Belame's stout shield received all the fierce blows, and for the moment it seemed that he would win through.

Robin and John broke through the weakening ranks of their foes at last, and leaping over the dead that lay in heaps they rushed towards Sir Isenbart. But too late they reached him. With a great shearing blow, the bill in the vengeful hands of old Thurstan had lighted upon the right shoulder of the knight, cutting deep into the bone. Another moment and the bill would have swept de Belame's head from his shoulders, but Robin caught the stroke on his shield, crying:

'Kill him not; the rope shall have him!'

Rafe dropped his bill. 'Ay, you are right,' he growled. 'He deserves not to die by honest steel – let the hangman have the felon.'

De Belame, his right arm paralysed, yet kept his seat and cried:

'Kill me, wolf's-head! Kill me with thy sword! I am a gentleman of coat-armour! *I* yield not to such carrion!' He thrust spurs into his horse, and strove to dash away from among them.

But the great arms of Rafe were about him, and they dragged him from his seat.

'Coat-armour,' snarled the fierce man. 'Had I my way I would blazon thy skin with as evil a pattern as thou and thy fiends have cut on poor folks' bodies. Coat-armour and a good hempen rope will go well together this night!'

'John and you, Rafe, bind up his wound, then bring the prisoner to the castle, which I doubt not is ours,' said Robin, and he would not leave them until he saw the wound bound up. Then, securely tied, de Belame, silent now and sullen, was carried towards the castle.

The battle had ceased everywhere by now. Few of the Wrangby men were left alive; so fierce had been the hatred of them that no more than a dozen had staggered away in the darkness, and among these was only one knight, Sir Roger of Doncaster, a sly man who preferred plotting to fighting. Of the moss-riders not one was alive, and Gaptooth himself had ridden his last cruel foray.

As to the castle, following the plan which Ket the Trow had made, this had been quickly seized. With young Squire Denvil and a chosen party of forty men, Ket had silently hidden in the water beside the rafts which lay before the great gate. When de Belame and his men had dashed from the castle in exultant answer to Gaptooth's call, and the gate-guard were standing under the portcullis, certain of victory and grumbling at being left behind and out of the killing, dripping men had risen as if from their very feet, and hardly had they realised what it meant before death had found them. Then, silently, Ket and the Squire of Toomlands, followed closely by their men, had swept into the castle, cutting down all who opposed them. They had gained the place without the loss of a single man, and as all but a dozen of the garrison had sallied out to what all had thought was certain victory, the struggle had been brief.

A little later, into the hall where Sir Isenbart and his fellow-knights had often sat carousing over their cups or torturing some poor captive, came Robin and such of the knights who had aided him as had come unharmed through the battle. Taking his seat in de Belame's chair at the high table, the knights in other seats beside him, Robin bade the prisoners be brought in. Torches gleamed from the pillars of the hall on the scarred, hacked armour of the conquerors, and the face of every man-at-arms, peasant, and knight was hard and stern as he looked at the group which entered.

There were but two prisoners, Sir Isenbart de Belame and Sir Baldwin the Killer, who had received his name for the cruelty and number of the deaths he had inflicted in years of rapine and foray throughout the lands of Wrangby and the Peak. As the door of the hall opened men heard the sound of distant knocking of axes on wood: the gallows were already being reared before the gate of the Evil Hold.

'Isenbart de Belame,' began Robin in a stern voice, 'here in thy castle, in thy hall where often thy miserable captives, men and women, rich and poor, gentle and simple, craved thy mercy and got naught but brutal jests or evil injury – here thou comest at last to find thy judgement. All who have anything to charge against this man de Belame, or his comrade in cruelty and oppression, Baldwin, stand forth, and as God hears and sees all, tell the truth on peril of their souls!'

It seemed as if the whole body of yeomen, peasants, and franklins standing by would come forward to charge upon the two scowling knights deeds of wrong and cruelty. 'He put out my father's eyes!' cried one. 'The harvest failed one year,' cried another, 'and because I could not pay him my yearly load of wheat, he pressed my son to death,' said another. Others stepped quickly up, and each gave in a few harsh words his tale of cruel deeds. When all had ended, Ket the Trow stood forth.

'With his own evil hand that man slew the kindest lady between Barnisdale and the Coombes o' the Moors,' he cried, and pointed his finger at de Belame. 'He slew her while she spoke to him from her castle gate, and he laughed when he saw her fall.'

'He stood by and jested when Ranulf of the Waste tortured by fire our father, Colman Grey!' cried Hob o' the Hill, limping forth with bandaged leg and arm, and shaking his fist at de Belame, whose face was white as he saw the hatred burn on every face about him.

'It is enough – and more than enough!' said Robin at last. 'What say you, Sir Knights? These men are of knightly blood and wear coat-armour, and so should die by the sword. But they have proved themselves no better than tavern knifers and robbers, and I adjudge them a shameful death by the rope!'

A great shout of assent rang through the lofty hall, 'To the rope! to the rope with them!'

'We agree with thee, Squire Robin,' said Sir Fulk of the Dykewall when silence was restored. 'Both these men have lost all claim to their rank. Their spurs should be hacked from their heels, and their bodies swung from the gallows.'

It was done. Amid the shouts of triumph of the fierce men standing about, Little John hacked off the spurs from the heels of the two Wrangby lords, and then with a great roar of rageful glee they were hurried out amid the surging crowd, torches tossing their lurid light upon hard faces and gleaming eyes, whose usual good nature was turned to savagery for the moment.

When the act of wild justice had been done, pitch and tar and oil were poured into every chamber of the castle, and torches were thrust in, and lighted straw heaped up. Then all fled forth and stood before the black walls, through whose slits the black and oily smoke began to curl. Leaping tongues of fire darted through the ropy reek and coiling wreaths, and soon, gathering power, the fire burst up through the floors of the great hall and the chambers above, and roared like a furious torrent to the dark sky. Great noises issued as the thick beams split, and as balk and timber, rafter and buttress fell, the flames and sparks leaped higher until the light shone far and wide over the country. Shepherds minding their sheep far away on the distant fells looked and looked, and would not believe their eyes; then crossed themselves and muttered a prayer of thankfulness that somehow the Evil Hold of Wrangby was at length ruining in fire. Bands of plunderers from the king's evil army, as they streamed across the highlands of the Peak, or on the hills of Yorkshire, saw the distant glare, and did not know then that one of the blackest strongholds of their callous king and his evil lords was going up in fire at the hands of those who, long and cruelly oppressed, had risen at last and gained their freedom.

Next morning a smoking shell of shattered and blackened stones was all that was left of the strong castle that had been the sign of wrong for at least two generations. A white smoke rose from the red-hot furnace within the walls which still stood; but so rent and torn and seamed with fire were the stones, that never again could they be made fit for habitation.

Robin rode forth from the shadow of the Mark Oak, where he and his army had passed the night, and looked at the smoking ruins and the two stiff gallows which stood before, on each of which hung, turning round and round, the bodies of the evil Baldwin and de Belame.

Doffing his steel cap, Robin bent his head and in silence gave up a prayer to the Virgin, thanking her for the help she had so amply granted him. His men gathered round him, and taking off their helms prayed likewise.

From over the plain came a crowd of peasants – some running, some walking slowly, half disbelieving their own eyes. Some among them came up to Robin, and old men and women, their faces and hands worn and lined with toil, seized his hands and kissed them, or touched his feet or the hem of his coat of mail with their lips. A young mother lifted up the baby she held in her arms, and with tears in her eyes told the child to look at Robin Hood, 'the man who had slain the evil lords and burned their den!'

'Master,' said Rafe of the Bill, 'go not far from us, lest someone as evil as those lords that now swing there shall come and possess again these lands, and build another hold of fiends to torture this land and its poor folk.'

'By the sweet Mother of Heaven,' said Robin Hood, and held up his right hand in the oath gesture, 'while I live no one shall possess these lands who ruleth them not in justice and mercy as I would have him rule them!'

'Amen!' came in deep response from all about him.

CHAPTER ELEVEN

Of the Death of Robin Hood

Never again, after the death of his wife Marian, did Robin Hood leave the greenwood. The lands at Malaset were taken by a distant kinsman of the Earl FitzWalter, who ruled them well and treated his villeins and yeomen kindly, with due regard to the customs of the manor.

Many of those who had been outlaws with Robin and had become his tenants at Malaset refused to go back there, but once having tasted again the wild free life of the greenwood, kept with Robin; and the numbers of his band swelling by reason of the cruelties and slaying, sacking, and plundering by the tyrannical king, they eagerly fell in with Robin's proposal to harass the royal army. Therefore, when Wrangby Castle had been levelled with the ground, so that not one stone stood upon another, Robin fared north and, taking to the woods and waste places, hung upon the flanks of the marauding Flemings, Brabanters, Saxons, and Poitevins who composed the king's army. Many a raiding party, engaged in some dreadful deed of plunder and torture of knights or yeomen, did Robin and his brave men fall upon, and with their great war arrows destroy or rout them utterly, thus earning the gratitude of many a knight and dame, villein and franklin, who ever after held the name of Robin Hood in special reverence.

When at last King John died at Newark by poison, and his son Henry was crowned and acknowledged king by all the great barons and lords of the realm, Robin took possession of his old quarters in Barnisdale and Sherwood. The land was still full of oppression and wrongdoing, for the king was but a boy; some of the evil lords refused to give up the castles they had seized during the war between John and his barons, and having long lived by pillaging their neighbours, would not now cease their habits of living by plundering and spoiling those weaker than themselves. Whenever, therefore, Robin had word, by a breathless villein or weeping woman, who came begging for his aid, that some evil deed was on foot, he issued with his chosen band from his forest lairs, and so stealthily he passed through the land, and so suddenly his arrows flew among the wrongdoers, that it was seldom he failed to beat back the rascally lords and their companies of thieves, besides giving them fear of his name and of his clothyard arrows which never missed their mark, and that could pierce the thickest chain-mail.

By good hap the councillors of the young king gave the lands of Wrangby into the keeping of a just lord, a kinsman of Earl de Warenne, who treated his villeins and tenants with mercy, so that soon the memory of the evil days of oppression and cruelty under Sir Isenbart de Belame became so faint that it seemed almost as if they never could have been.

But in other parts of the kingdom oppression and misery still stalked through the land. Insolent barons sent parties of armed men to seize the young king's lands in various places, and either put his tenants to death or chased them away into poverty; weaker neighbours were ever in fear of being attacked and slain, or their lands wrested from them, and under cover of this disorder robbery and extortion were committed daily. Indeed, bands of highway robbers wearing the livery of great lords infested the forest roads and lonely ways in many parts of the country, ready to fall upon merchants travelling with their wares, or even upon poor villeins or franklins carrying their goods to market.

One day Robin was with Little John and Scarlet on the borders of Sherwood and Barnisdale. They were waiting for news of a party of evil men who had begun to haunt that part of the country, and who were in the pay of Sir Roger of Doncaster. This was the knight who, with some ten men-at-arms, had managed to escape from the fight before Evil Hold. Robin knew that Sir Roger's aim was to lie in ambush for him one day and to kill him, but until now the outlaws had not actually come into touch with the marauders.

They sat in a small glade which was screened all round by

thick bushes of holly, but from their place of vantage they could
see through the leaves up and down the two main tracks or roads
through the forest. By-and-by there came the sound of a
scolding squirrel, and Robin responded, for this was a sign
between the scouts. In a few moments Ket the Trow came into
the glade and went up to Robin.

'Master,' he said, 'I and Hob have watched the manor-house,
at Syke, of Roger of Doncaster. He and his men left at dawn this
morning, and have gone towards the Stone Houses by Barnisdale
Four Wents. I think they lie in wait there to fall upon the
bishop's convoy of food and gear which goes today from
Wakefield Abbey to Lincoln.'

'Up, John,' said Robin, 'and thou, Scarlet, and do thou go
quickly to the Stane Lea and take all the men thou canst find and
try thy wits against that robber knight and his hedge-knifers. As
for me, I will follow thee anon.'

With instant obedience Little John and Scarlet started off, and
soon were lost in the winding paths of the forest. Ket stood still
and waited for further instructions.

'Ket,' said Robin at length, 'do thou go to Will the Bowman,
and bid him bring the score of men he hath watching with him,
and scatter them across the road and forest tracks from Doncaster
hitherwards. If thou seest thy brother Hob, send him to me.'

With a gesture of his hand that showed he understood, Ket
turned and vanished into the forest, wondering a little at his
orders. If, thought he, Sir Roger's men were going north-west to
Barnisdale, and Robin had sent his men to waylay them, why did
he wish to have the southern road from Doncaster watched? Ket
was quick of wit, however, and he thought: was it because Robin
believed that Sir Roger's journey towards Barnisdale was a feint,
and that another party would be sent south in the attempt to
seize or slay Robin? He remembered that very often his master's
keen brains knew more than any of his scouts could tell him.

When Ket left him, Robin went out of the glade into the road
and began to walk under the leafy boughs. When he had gone
about half a mile towards the south he came to a small path which
ran through the trees at the side, and looking down this he saw a
low-browed man, with a cruel look, dressed like a yeoman,
standing looking furtively up and down the narrow path. In his

hand he bore a bow, and a quiver of arrows hung beside him.

'Good-morrow, good fellow,' said Robin. 'Whither away?'

'Good-morrow to you, good woodman,' replied the yeoman, who was taken somewhat by surprise at Robin's quiet approach, and his eyes glanced here and there, and did not look straight at Robin. 'I ha' lost my way through the forest. Canst thou tell me my way to Roche Abbey?'

Robin seemed to look at him carelessly as he replied: 'Ay, I can lead thee into thy road. Thou hast come far out of thy way.'

'Ay, 'tis easy in this pesky forest to go astray,' said the yeoman grumblingly.

'When didst thou find thou wast wandering out of thy road?' asked Robin.

'Oh, but an hour or two,' was the reply. 'I was told at Balby that my road lay through the hamlet of Scatby, but hours have I walked as it seemeth, and never a roof do I see in these wild woods.'

Robin laughed. He could have told the man that he must have been wandering since the previous midday, when he had seen him through the leaves skulking like a wild cat through the forest-ways, as if wishful to spy on someone, but desiring not to be seen himself.

' 'Tis but a mile or two more thou must go,' replied Robin, 'and thou wilt strike the right road. But by the bow thou bearest it would seem that thou shouldst be a good archer.'

'Ay,' said the man with a crafty look, 'I am as good a bowman – and better – than many a braggart thief who ranges these woods and shoots the king's deer.'

'Then let us have some pastime,' said Robin, 'and see who is the better archer of us two.'

'I am with thee,' said the man, and drew an arrow from the quiver beside him. His eyes looked narrowly at Robin, and there was an evil glint in them.

Robin went to a hazel bush and cut down two straight hazel wands, which he peeled in their upper parts, so as to show up more plainly. One of these he stuck in the ground where they stood, and from the top he hung a rough garland of dogwood leaves, which were now turning red in the autumn, and therefore stood out against the white of the hazel.

'Now,' said Robin, 'let us measure off fifty paces. I will set this other wand at the place from whence we shoot.'

While doing all this Robin did not turn his face from the other man, who all the time had had his arrow half notched upon his string, as if eager to begin the shooting. He laughed as they walked side by side measuring off the distance.

' 'Tis a plaguy hard shoot thou wouldst have us try,' he said with a growl; 'I am used to bigger marks than these new-fangled rods and wreaths.'

Robin took no notice, but went on counting until he had completed the fifty paces, and the man, almost as if against his will, sullenly walked with him. Robin bade the man shoot first at the mark, but he said he would rather Robin had the first try. Robin took two arrows from his quiver and shot one at the mark. The arrow went through the garland, about two fingers' span from the wand.

'I like not this way of shooting,' growled the low-bred man. ' 'Tis such shooting as thou seest silly squires and village fools use.'

Robin made no reply, and the man shot at the mark. As was to be expected, he missed the garland altogether and his arrow went wide.

'Thou needest more practice, good friend,' said Robin. 'Trust me, 'tis well worth thy while to test thy skill at a fine mark such as this. 'Tis no credit to creep up and shoot on top of thy game from behind a tree – often a long shot is the most honest. I will try again.'

So saying, Robin took careful aim, and this time his arrow went true to the mark, for it struck the thin wand and split it in twain.

' 'Twas not fair shooting!' cried the other in a rage. 'A flaw of wind did carry thy bolt against the wand!'

'Nay, good fellow,' said Robin in a quiet voice, 'thou art a fool to talk so. 'Twas a clean shot, as thou knowest well. Do thou go now and take this wand here and set it up in place of that which I have split. I will cut a new one, and we will set it up at thirty paces, so that thou mayest have a little practice ere I lead thee on thy way.'

With muttered words and dark looks the rascal took the wand which stood where they had been shooting, and went away with slow steps towards the split mark fifty paces away. When he had got some twenty paces he turned his head quickly and saw that Robin was apparently busy at a hazel thicket, searching for a straight stick. Swiftly the rogue put an arrow to his string, and shouted as the bolt left his bow:

'Thou art the mark I seek, thou wolf's-head!'

Robin seemed to fall into the bush as if struck, and with a cruel laugh the man stepped nearer as if to make sure that he had really slain the outlaw for whom he had been spying so long. He could see the legs sticking out stiffly from among the hazels, and he grinned with delight. Then, putting his fingers to his lips, he whistled long and shrill, and came forward at a run to gloat over his victim.

But suddenly with a jerk the dead man arose, and in one hand was the arrow which the would-be murderer had shot. It had missed Robin, who, however, had pretended to be struck; and the bolt had caught in the thicket before him. Already it was notched to the bow which Robin bore in his other hand. The man came to a sudden standstill, a cry on his white lips.

'Thou bungling hedge-knifer!' said Robin with a scornful laugh. 'Even the mark at which thou hast been loosing thy arrow these two days thou canst not strike, and that at twenty paces! Ay, thou canst run, but thy own arrow shall slay thee!'

The man had turned, and with swift steps was running this way and that from side to side of the path, so as to confuse Robin's aim.

Robin drew his bow to its utmost, and paused for one moment; then the string twanged with a great sound, and the arrow sped. The man gave a yell, jumped three feet clear up into the air, then fell flat upon the ground, the arrow sticking from his back.

At the same moment, Robin heard the sound of breaking branches beside him, and hardly had he thrown down his bow when out of the hazel bush beside him leaped a strange figure. For a moment, as Robin took a step back to give him time to draw his sword, he was startled, so weird was the figure. It seemed as if it was a brown horse on its hind legs which dashed towards him. The great white teeth were bared as if to tear him, and the mane rolled behind, tossing in the fury of attack.

Then Robin laughed. The horse's skin contained a man; in

one hand was a naked sword, in the other a buckler. It was Sir
Guy of Gisborne who, with the fire of hatred in his eyes, now
dashed upon the outlaw.

'Ha, ha! Guy of Gisborne, thou false knight!' cried Robin
mockingly. 'Thou hast come thyself at last, hast thou? For years
thou hast sent thy spies, thy ambushers, thy secret murderers to
slay me, and now thou hast come to do the deed thyself – if thou
canst!'

Guy of Gisborne said no word in reply. Fierce hatred glared
from his eyes, and he rushed with the fury of a wolf upon his foe.
Robin had no buckler, but he had that which was almost as great
a guard; for while the other beat full of rage upon Robin's blade,
the outlaw was cool of brain and keen of eye.

For some time naught was heard but the clang of sword upon
sword as stroke met guard. Round and round they trod in this
fierce dance that should end in death for one of them, each with
his eyes bent upon the keen looks of the other. Suddenly Robin's
sword leaped over the guard of the other's sword, and his point
pierced and ripped the horse's hide and cut into the shoulder of
Sir Guy.

'Thy luck hath fled, Guy of Gisborne!' said Robin in triumph.
'Thou didst 'scape with thy life once from thy burning house in
that horse's hide, and thou didst think it would bring thee luck
against my sword point.'

'Thou wolf's-head! Thou hedge-robber!' cried Guy of Gisborne.
' 'Twas but a scratch, but my good sword shall yet let thy life out!'

With a double feint, swift and fierce, Guy thrust under
Robin's sword arm. His point cut through Robin's tunic of
Lincoln green, and a hot spark seemed to burn the outlaw's side.
Guy's point had wounded him slightly. It did not check Robin
for an instant. Swiftly as a lightning stroke the outlaw lunged
forward, and ere Guy could recover Robin's sword had pierced
his breast. The cruel knight dropped his sword, staggered back,
spun round once, and then fell heavily to the ground, where he
lay still as a stone.

Robin, breathless, leaned upon his sword as he looked down
upon his slain enemy.

'Thus,' he said, 'my sword hath avenged, by the aid of the
pitiful sweet Virgin, all the cruelties and oppressions which thy

Robin meets Guy of Gisburne

evil will and cruel mind hath caused – the torture of poor men by hunger, scourging, and forced labours, the aching hearts of women and children, whom thy evil will did not spare from blows and tears. Would that my sword could slay as easily the tyranny and wrongdoing of all those in high places today who make poor men weep and suffer!'

Turning, he saw Hob o' the Hill approaching him, who now ran up and said:

'Master, I saw the good fight and the shrewd stroke thou gavest him. There is only one now of all thy enemies who yet liveth, and he is Sir Roger of Doncaster.'

'Nay, Hob,' replied Robin; 'there are a many of the enemies of poor men who yet live in their strong castles and carved abbeys whom I shall never slay.'

'Ay, ay, master, thou speakest truth,' said Hob. 'While the poor villein hath to sweat at his labours and suffer blows, and is kept for ever at his chores, unfree, possessing naught, not even the wife and child he kisseth when he leaves for his work in the dawn, so long shall we have enemies. But now, master, I come to tell thee that Roger of Doncaster's men have doubled south, and even now are at Hunger Wood. I guess that they do but follow the orders of this slain steward here, and will to ambush thee.'

'Where are Will the Bowman and his men?' asked Robin.

'They are scattered upon the southward road, and do spy upon Roger's rascals.'

'Go thou and hasten to Little John. Bid him turn back if he hath not already learned that Roger's men are coming south. Let him get behind them, but not so that they know he is nigh them. When he is north of Hunger Wood, bid him make two horns through the woods so as to encompass the rogues. Then with Will's men I will drive them back, and John should see to it that not one escapes alive. 'Twill be a lesson to my enemies not to put their heads into the wolf's mouth again.'

Swiftly Hob darted away, while Robin hastened towards the Doncaster road, where he soon found Will the Bowman waiting in a glade.

'How now, master,' said old Will, grizzled and grey, but as hale and sturdy as ever; 'my scouts tell me that these rascals are many and do come through the woods as if they feared naught.

'Tis said that a wily rogue, a Brabanter cut-throat named Fulco the Red, doth lead them, and he has warred through France and Allemain and Palestine, and knoweth all the arts of war. We are but a score here, and Little John and his party are three miles to the north-west.'

'I have sent Hob to tell Little John to return,' replied Robin. 'He will be here in an hour. Till then we must hold these rascals in check. John will smite them in the rear, and I think for all their rascally knowledge of burning and plundering which they have gained under our tyrant king, these Flemings and Brabanters will yet find death at our English hands.'

In a little while a scout came in to say that the enemy was marching towards Beverley Glade, and Robin instantly ordered the score of archers under Will to hide themselves in the thickets on the edge of the glade. Soon, issuing from the trees on the other side of the clearing, could be seen the headpieces of the foreigners. Fierce and cruel were the faces of these men, for they warred for any hand that paid them well, because of the loot and the wealth which they obtained in the lands where they fought. The English peasant hated these foreign marauders bitterly, for they spared neither women nor children, and were most tyrannical and cruel.

There were some fourscore of them, twenty of them with crossbows, and at their head was a man with a red face of fierce aspect, clothed in complete mail from head to foot. They advanced warily, with scouts on their flanks amidst the trees, and they looked to and fro keenly as they advanced. Each of the men-at-arms bore a buckler in his left hand, and his naked sword flashed in the other. Not until they were within twenty paces of the thickets where the outlaws lay hid did Robin give the signal agreed upon. Then, at the shrill whistle, twenty great arrows boomed through the air, and so true was the aim of each that as many of the enemy staggered and fell, each with the great shaft sticking deep in the thick jerkin or in the throat. Among those that fell were fifteen of the crossbowmen.

At another call, and before most of the marauders had recovered, another flight of arrows was launched against them, and twelve more fell dead or wounded.

Then with a fierce yell of command the leader, Fulco the Red, dashed forward into the thickets, followed by his surviving men, who still outnumbered the outlaws. As quick as ferrets and as stealthily, Robin's men retreated, running from tree to tree, but whenever opportunity offered, a great arrow buzzed out from some innocent-looking bush, and another rascal fell writhing in his death-throes. The others ran here and there fiercely searching for their hidden enemies. Three of the outlaws were slain in the first rush, but as the foreigners dashed from bush to bush and looked behind this tree and that, they were marked by the wily woodmen, and again and again the grim song of an arrow suddenly ended in a death-cry as it reached home in some cruel heart.

Nevertheless, the band of mercenaries pressed forward and the outlaws had to retreat, for they could not dare to meet the others in the open. So fiercely did Fulco follow upon the retiring woodmen that several more fell to the sword, and Robin saw with anger and despair that already he had lost eight men. He wondered what he should do to check the enemy, but was at a loss.

Suddenly he saw Fulco dash forward at a bush where he had seen a lurking outlaw. It was Gilbert of the White Hand, who, finding himself discovered, and not having time to draw his bow, sought safety in flight. He rushed close beside the tree behind which Robin stood, Fulco following with uplifted sword. As the Brabanter passed, Robin dashed forth with sword in hand and beat at the foreigner. The latter quickly parried the blow with his buckler, and next moment had swung round and had fiercely engaged Robin. Round and round in a wild fight the two wheeled, their swords clanging, as stroke on stroke was guarded. Suddenly one of the other men crept up, resolved to slay Robin from behind. Will the Bowman saw what he intended and dashed forward, sword in hand, only to be hewed down as another Fleming leaped from behind a tree. The old man cried out with his dying breath, 'Robin, guard thee!'

An arrow flew from a bush, and the man who was creeping upon Robin leaped up, then fell heavily and lay still. A second arrow slew the man who had slain Will Stuteley, and then for the time both parties in their hiding-places seemed to stand and watch the combat between the two leaders.

The Brabanter, famed for his sword play as he was, had found his match. Such strength of wrist, such force of stroke as was in Robin, he had never met before, and it was in vain that he tried his wiles upon the slim man who seemed to be surrounded by a cage of steel, while yet it was only the one sword that leaped so swiftly to guard. Fulco, rageful at the long resistance, was wearing out his strength in vain though fierce attacks. Suddenly he saw Robin's eyes gleam with a strange look which almost fascinated him with its fierce intentness. Then he saw the outlaw make a pass which laid his left breast open. Quickly the Brabanter, parrying the pass, dashed his point at Robin's breast. The outlaw leaped aside, Fulco's sword lunged into the empty air, and next moment, with a great sweep of his arm, Robin's sword had hewed deeply into the neck of the marauder, who fell dead at his feet.

A great cheer rose from the throats of the outlaws, and heartened by the victory, the bowmen pressed into the open and sought their enemies. These, losing courage at the loss of their leader, began to retreat, running backwards from tree to tree. But in vain they sought shelter. The deadly arrows, like great bees, searched their hiding-places narrowly. Sometimes they would gather heart and dash back at the venturesome outlaws, but only for a time. They would be compelled to retire before the hail of arrows which converged upon them, bringing wounds and death from enemies who had instantly disappeared.

Suddenly, from three directions behind them and beside them, came the challenging call of the blackcock. So saucily it sounded, that from hidden outlaws here and there chuckles of laughter rose, while others wondered whether it could indeed be Little John, whose warning cry this was. An answering call from Robin reassured them on that point, and soon through the trees could be seen coats of Lincoln green darting from tree to tree.

At the knowledge that this meant that they were taken in rear and flank, the Brabanters and Flemings, knowing that from the hands of Englishmen they could expect no mercy, rushed together, resolved to sell their lives dearly.

It is needless to dwell upon the last fight. It could but end in one way. The Englishmen hated these foreign invaders with a hatred too deadly for mercy, and as they shot them down they knew that their arrows were loaded with vengeance for

unutterable deeds of murder and cruelty committed upon de-
fenceless women, little children, and unweaponed men, when
these marauding wretches had spread like a plague through the
land under the banner of King John, bringing ruin, fire, death,
and starvation to hundreds of humble homes and peaceful
villages.

Roger of Doncaster, waiting with his half-dozen men-at-arms
on the edge of the forest, wondered why Guy of Gisborne and
Fulco lingered so long. There were no cries of triumph heard
coming through the dim aisles of giant trees, no flash of arms
could be seen, however often he sent twos and threes of his men
into the forest to meet the victors.

Then at last they saw a charcoal-burner coming with his sack
of coal through the trees. Two men-at-arms caught him and
brought him up to where the knight sat on his horse. Sir Roger
asked him whether he had not seen a troop of men-at-arms
coming through the wood.

'Na, na,' said he in his rough speech; 'no living man ha' I seen,
but I ha' seen a pile o' foreign-looking men lying dead in
Beverley Glade, and each had a clothyard stickin' in un. There
mun be threescore of un!'

Sir Roger dragged his horse round, a savage oath on his lips.
'That wolf's-head is the fiend himself!' he said. 'No one can
fight against him in his woods.'

Quickly he and his men hurried off, leaving the charcoal-burner
looking after them. 'Ay, ay,' said he under his breath, 'no one of
thy cruel rascals can hope to get aught but death while Robin is
king o' these forests. Three or four score there were of the
murdering Easterlings, and each had Robin's sign upon him.'

For many years afterwards the place where Robin had wreaked
such vengeance upon the foreign mercenaries was called Slaughter Lea instead of Beverley Glade, and for a long time villeins
and others who passed near the mound which marked the pit
where Robin had buried the slain told the tale to each other.

After this, for many years Robin was left undisturbed in the
forests of Barnisdale and Sherwood, and, outlaw though he was,
most good men came to respect his name, while those that were
oppressors feared him. Never was there a cruel deed done by
some lord on his vassal but Robin exacted some recompense

from the haughty knight; and when a poor man's land was invaded by a stronger, it was Robin's hidden archers who made the place too hot for any but the rightful owner to dwell upon it.

Indeed, I should want a book of the same length as this one to relate all the famous deeds which Robin did while he was in the greenwood at this time. For fifteen years he dwelled there, and every year his fame increased by reason of the deeds he did.

Thus, one great deed was that long fight which he waged on behalf of young Sir Drogo of Dallas Tower in Westmorland. The border men, robbers and reivers all, had thrust Sir Drogo from his lands because he had punished one of their clansmen, and the young knight was in sore straits. With the aid of Robin and his archers he beat back the mossmen, and such terror did the clothyard arrows inspire that never again did a Jordan, Armstrong, Douglas, or Graham venture to injure the man who was a friend of Robin's.

Then there was that deed, one not of warfare but of peace, when Robin compelled the young squire of Thurgoland to do justice and kindness to his mother. She had been a neif, or female villein, on the lands of Sir Jocelyn of Thurgoland, doing the chores and labours of the field. But she was beautiful and modest, and Sir Jocelyn had loved and married her. While her lord and husband was alive she was a freewoman, and she lived happily with Sir Jocelyn. They had a son, named Stephen, who was of so crabbed and harsh a nature that men said he could be no son of the noble Jocelyn and the kindly Avis. When Sir Jocelyn died, Stephen was lord, but the wicked law of that day said that Avis was now again a serf on the land of her son, having lost her freedom with the death of her husband.

For withstanding her son's unjust wrath against a poor villein of the manor, Stephen swore he would be revenged upon his mother. Therefore he had her thrust from the manor-house in ragged attire, and compelled her to house with her villein kin (which of course were also his kin) in a hovel in the village. With spirited words Avis reproached her unnatural son, but in all meekness yet dignity she went about the hard tasks again which for thirty years her hands had not known; while her son took to himself the evil companions which he knew his mother had detested, and which she had ever advised him to avoid.

The story of his thrusting his mother into villeinage spread far and wide, shocking all good men and women. They wondered as the weeks went by that some judgement from heaven did not fall upon so unnatural and harsh a son; but he still rioted in his hall, and nothing seemed to trouble him.

Then, one winter's night, as Squire Stephen held high revel among his boon companions, into the hall strode threescore men in dark robes, and amid the terror of the assembled guests the squire was seized and taken away, in spite of all his furious rage. For a time no one knew whither he had gone. Then the tale went round the country that the squire was working as a villein on the lands of a manor in the forest, and that Robin Hood had willed that thus he should live until he had learned how to act as a man of gentle rank.

For long months Squire Stephen was held a captive, compelled to work like any poor villein of his own kindred, until at length he was shamed and penitent, and confessed that he had been a boor and was not worthy to hold the rank which mere birth had given him. Then, in his villein weeds [garments], he had returned to Thurgoland, and seeking out his mother where she worked in the village he had begged her forgiveness, and when with tears she had kissed him, he had taken her by the hand and made her mistress of the manor-house, and ever afterwards lived nobly as had his father before him.

Men reckoned this was a great deed, and praised the names of Robin Hood and Father Tuck, who by precept and manly counsel had shown Squire Stephen the errors of his life.

There were other deeds which Robin did; such as his fight with the sea-pirate, Damon the Monk, who had harried the coast of Yorkshire so long and cruelly, but whom Robin at length slew, in a great sea-fight off the bay which is now called Robin Hood's Bay, where the pirate ship was brought ashore, after Robin had hanged all her men on their own yard-arm.

One day when Robin had thus passed some ten years in this second period of his outlawry, a lady rode into his camp at the Stane Lea, and getting down from her horse went up to where he stood, and greeted him. For a moment Robin did not recognise her.

'I am thy cousin,' she said at length with a smile, 'Dame Alice of Havelond. Dost thou not remember how thou didst aid me and my husband more than a score years ago when two evil neighbours oppressed us?'

'By my faith,' said Robin, and kissed his cousin on her cheek, ' 'tis so long since I have seen thee that I knew thee not.'

He made Dame Alice very welcome, and she and her two women and three serving-men spent the night in a little bower which Robin caused to be made for them. She and Robin spoke long together about their kinsfolk, and how this one and that one had fared, and what had befallen some through the troubled times. Her own husband, Bennett, had died three years before.

'Now,' said she at length, 'I am an old woman, Robin, and thou art old also. Thy hair is grey, and though thy eyes are keen and I doubt not thy strength is great, dost thou not often long for a place where thou canst live in peace and rest, away from the alarms which thy life here must bring to thee? Couldst thou not disband thy men, steal away, and live in my house with me at Havelond? None would trouble thee there, and thou couldst live out in peace and quiet the rest of thy life.'

Robin did not delay in his answer.

'Nay, dear cousin,' he said, 'I have lived too long in the greenwood ever to crave any other living place. I will die in it, and when my last day comes, I pray I be buried in some glade under the whispering trees, where in life I and my dear fellows have roamed at will.'

'Then,' replied the dame, 'if thou wilt not seek this asylum with me, which I offer to thee in memory of that great kindness which thou didst for my dead husband, then I shall betake myself to Kirklees and live out my last years in the nunnery of which, as thou knowest, our aunt, Dame Ursula, is abbess. I would have thee come to me whenever thou wishest, Robin, for old age makes us fond of our kin, and I would see thee often. And I doubt not that Dame Ursula, though she speaketh harshly of thy violent deeds, would give thee welcome as befitted the son of her sister.'

Robin promised that he would not forget to visit Kirklees to see Dame Alice, and this he did once in every six months, as much for the purpose of seeing his cousin as to have at her hands the medical treatment which his ageing years seemed to demand more and more. In those days women had much lore of medicinal herbs, and instead of going to doctors when they felt sick, people would go to a woman who was famed to have this knowledge, and she would give them medicine. Men also believed that if a vein in the arm was cut and a certain amount of blood was allowed to escape, this was a cure for certain diseases. It was for this purpose, also, that Robin Hood visited Kirklees Nunnery, and he stayed there for two or three days at a time, in order that the wound in his arm might thoroughly heal.

On these visits he often saw his aunt, Dame Ursula, the abbess. She was a dark, lean woman with crafty eyes, but she always spoke fair to him. She often asked him when he was going to buy a pardon and to leave his homeless life, so as to endow some religious house with his wealth for the purpose of getting salvation for his soul.

'Little wealth have I,' Robin would reply, 'nor shall I ever spend it to feed fat monks or lazy nuns. While my forest freres stay with me, and I can still use the limbs God hath given me, I will bide in the greenwood.'

'Nevertheless,' she often said, 'forget not thy aunt and cousin here at Kirklees, and come when thou mayst desire.'

Now it happened one day, late in the summer, that Robin felt giddy and ill, and resolved to go to Kirklees to be tended by his cousin.

'Go with me, Little John,' said Robin, 'for I feel I am an old man this day, and my mind is mazed.'

'Ay, dear Robin, I will go with thee,' said Little John, 'but thy sickness will pass, I doubt not. I would that ye did not go into that nunnery, for ever when ye have gone I ha' wondered as I waited under the trees without whether I should see thy face again, or whether some evil trick would be played on thee.'

'Nay, John,' said Robin, 'they will play me no tricks. The women are my kinsfolk, and what enemies have we now?'

'I know not,' replied John doubtfully, scratching his grizzled head; 'but Hob o' the Hill hath heard that Sir Roger of Doncaster is friend to the nuns of Kirklees.'

'An old man he is, as we are all,' said Robin, 'and I doubt not he thinketh little evil of me after all these years.'

'I know not,' said John; 'but an adder will bite though his poison be dry.'

They prepared to go to Kirklees, Robin and John on horses and the rest of their band on foot. When they arrived at the edge of the forest which overlooked the nunnery, Little John and Robin dismounted, leaving the horses with the men, who were to hide in the woods until Robin returned. Then, supported by John's arm, Robin walked to the gate of Kirklees, where John left him.

'God preserve thee, dear Robin,' he said, 'and let thee come again soon to me. I have a fear upon me this day that something shall befall thee to our sorrow.'

'Nay, nay, John,' said Robin, 'fear not. Sit thou in the shaw, and if I want thee I will blow my horn. I have my bow and my sword with me, and naught can harm me among these women.'

So the two old comrades in arms parted with warm handclasps, and Robin knocked at the great iron ring upon the door. Very soon the door was opened by his aunt, who indeed had been watching his approach from a window.

'Come thou in, Robin,' said she with wheedling tones, while her crafty eyes looked in his face with a sidelong furtive glance. She saw that he was ill, and a smile played over her thin lips. 'Come in and have a jack of ale, for thou must be wearied after thy journey.'

'I thank thee, dame,' said Robin, and wearily he stepped in. 'But I will neither eat nor drink until I have been blooded. Tell my cousin Alice I have come, I pray thee.'

'Ah, Robin,' said his aunt, 'thou hast been long away from us, and thou hast not heard, I ween. Thy cousin died in her sleep in the spring, and now she lies under the churchyard mould.'

'Sorry I am to hear that,' replied Robin, and in the shock of the news he staggered and would have fallen, but that his aunt put her arm about him. 'I – I – repent me,' he went on, 'that I came not oftener. Poor Alice! But I am ill, dame; do thou nick my arm and blood me, and soon I shall be well, and will trouble thee no more.'

'Of a surety, 'tis no trouble, good Robin,' said the abbess, and she guided him into a room remote from the living-rooms of the nunnery. She led him to a truckle bed which stood in one corner, and he lay down with a great sigh of relief. Then he bared his arm slowly, and the abbess took a little knife from a satchel which hung from her girdle. She held the brown arm now much thinner than of yore, and with the point of her knife she cut deep into a thick blue vein. Then, having tied the arm so that he should not move it, she set a jar beneath the cut in the arm as it hung outside the bed.

Then she went from the room and quickly returned with some drink in a cup. 'Drink this, good Robin,' she said. ' 'Twill clear thee of the heaviness which is upon thee.'

She raised Robin's head and he drank the liquor to the lees. With a sigh Robin sank back on his pillow and smiled as he said:

'Thanks, best thanks, good aunt. Thou art kind to a lawless man.'

He spoke drowsily; his head fell back upon the pillow and he began to breathe heavily. The drug which the abbess had placed in the cup was already working. The dame smiled wickedly, and she went to the door of the room and beckoned to someone outside. A man crept into the chamber – an old, thin man, with white hair, sly, shifty eyes, and a weak, hanging lower lip. She pointed with one lean finger to the form of Robin Hood, and the old man's eyes shone at the sight. His gaze followed the drops of blood as they oozed from the cut vein and dripped into the jar beneath.

'If you were even a little like a man,' she said scornfully, 'you would draw your dagger and give him his death yourself – not leave it to my lancet to let his life out drop by drop.'

Robin stirred at the sound of her voice, and the thin old man turned and skipped from the room in terror. The abbess followed him, her beady black eyes bent upon his shifty looks. She drew a long key from her satchel and locked the door of the room where Robin lay.

'When will he be dead?' asked the old man in a whisper.

'If the blood floweth freely, he will be dead by night!' said the abbess.

'But if it do not, and he dieth not?' said the old man.

'Then I and Kirklees Nunnery are richer by thirty acres of good meadow land,' replied the abbess mockingly, 'the gift of the good Sir Roger of Doncaster; and you, Sir Roger, will have to find some other way of killing this fox. Why dost thou not go in thyself and do it now?'

She held out the key to him, but he shrank away, his teeth gnawing at his finger nails, his baleful eyes gleaming angrily at the mocking face of the abbess.

Sir Roger of Doncaster, coward and poltroon, had not the courage to slay a sick man, but turned and slunk away. He left the house and rode away, his chin sunk on his breast, enraged to think how the abbess despised him, and how she might yet outwit him in the wicked conspiracy they had made together for the slaying of Robin Hood.

Little John sat patiently in the shade of the forest trees all the afternoon. When the long shadows began to creep across the wolds he wondered why Robin had not appeared at the door as was his wont. In his anxiety Little John arose and walked impatiently up and down.

What was that? Faintly, from the direction of the nunnery, he heard three bugle blasts – Robin's call!

With a roar like that of an enraged bull, Little John shouted to the men hiding in the thickets:

'Up, lads! Heard ye those weary notes? Treachery is being done our poor master!'

Snatching up weapons, the whole band rushed after Little John, who ran at top speed to the nunnery gate. With blows from a hedge-pole they battered this in, and with the same weapon they beat down the door, and then amid the shrieks and prayers of the affrighted nuns they poured into the place.

Very cold and stern was Little John as he stood before the bevy of white-faced women.

'Ha' done with thy shrieking!' he said. 'Find me the abbess!'

But the abbess was nowhere to be found.

'Quick, then, lead me to where my master, Robin Hood, is lying.'

But none knew of his having come to the nunnery. Full of wrath and sorrow and dread, John was about to order that the whole place be searched, when Hob o' the Hill pushed through the outlaws and said:

'I ha' found where our master lies.'

They stormed up the stairs after Hob, and having reached the door they broke the lock and rushed in. What a sight met their eyes! There was their master, white and haggard, with glazed eyes, half reclining upon the bed, so weak that hardly could he raise his head to them.

Little John threw himself on his knees beside Robin, tears

streaming from his eyes.

'Master, master!' he cried. 'A boon, a boon!'

'What is it, John?' asked Robin, smiling wanly upon him, and raising his hand he placed it fondly on the grizzled head of his old comrade.

'That thou let us burn this house and slay those that have slain thee!'

Robin shook his head wearily.

'Nay, nay,' he said, 'that boon I'll not grant thee. I never hurt woman in all my life, and I'll not do it now at my end. She hath let my blood flow from me, and hath taken my life, but I bid thee hurt her not. Now, John, I have not long to live. Open that casement there and give me my bow and an arrow.'

They opened the casement wide, and Robin looked forth with dim, dying sight upon the quiet evening fields, with the great rolling forest in the distance.

'Hold me while I shoot, John,' said Robin, 'and where my arrow falls there dig me a grave and let me lie.'

Men wept as they stood and watched him hold the great bow in his feeble hand, and saw him draw the string while he held the feather of the arrow. Once he alone of all men could bend that bow, but now so spent was his life that his strength barely sufficed to draw it half-way. With a sigh he let go, the arrow boomed through the casement, and men watched with dim sight its flight over the fields until it came to ground beside a little path that led from the meadows up to the forest trees.

Robin fell back exhausted, and Little John laid him gently down.

'Lay me there, John,' he said, 'with my bow beside me, for that was my sweetest music while I lived, and I would have it lie with me when I am dead. Put a green sod under my head, and another at my feet, for I loved best to sleep on the greensward of the forest whiles I was alive, and I would lie upon them in my last sleep. Ye will do this all for me, John?'

'Ay, ay, master,' said John, choking for sheer sorrow.

'Now kiss me, John – and – and – goodbye!'

The breath fluttered on his lips as John with uncovered head bent and kissed him. All sank to their knees and prayed for the passing soul, and with many tears they pleaded for mercy for

Robin shoots his last shaft

their bold and generous leader.

They would not suffer his body to stay within the nunnery walls that night, but carried it to the greenwood, and watched beside it all through the dark. Then at dawn they prepared his grave, and when Father Tuck, white-haired and bent now, came at noon, all bore the body of their dear master to his last resting-place.

Afterwards, the outlaws learned of Sir Roger of Doncaster's visit to the nunnery while Robin lay dying, and they sought for him far and wide. To escape the close search which Hob o' the Hill and Ket his brother made for him, Sir Roger fled to Grimsby, and barely escaped on board a ship with a whole skin, so close was Hob behind him. The knight sought refuge in France, and there he died shortly afterwards, lonely and uncared for.

When Robin died, the band of outlaws speedily broke up. Some fled overseas, some hid in large towns and gradually became settled and respectable citizens, and others again hired themselves on distant manors and became law-abiding men, if their lords treated them not unkindly.

As for Little John and Scarlet, they were given lands at Cromwell, where Alan-a-Dale now was lord over the lands of the Lady Alice; while Much was made bailiff at Werrisdale, which also belonged to Alan-a-Dale, his father, Sir Herbrand, being now dead.

Gilbert of the White Hand would not settle down. He became a great fighter in Scotland with the bow and the sword, and his deeds were sung for many years by many a fireside in the border lands.

What became of Hob o' the Hill and his brother, Ket the Trow, nobody ever knew for certain. The little men hated the ways of settled life, and though Alan-a-Dale offered them lands to live on, they preferred to wander in the dim forest and over the wild moors. The grave of Robin Hood was ever kept neat and verdant, though for a long time no one knew whose were the hands that did this. Then tales got abroad that at night two little men came out of the forest from time to time and put fresh plants on the grave and cut the edging turf clean. That these were Ket and Hob no one doubted, for they had loved Robin dearly while he lived, and now that he was dead they could never stray far from his grave.